Loans - ALL READERS - return or renew on the date
stamped at latest.

Library books not in immediate use should be on OUR
SHELVES NOT YOURS.

Recordings of use - please initial.

31 MAY 1991 G		
2 2 DEC 1992 A		
1 5 DEC 2000		

THE CARNEGIE TECH MANAGEMENT GAME

An Experiment in Business Education

CARNEGIE INSTITUTE OF TECHNOLOGY

Contributions to Management Education Series

THE CARNEGIE TECH MANAGEMENT GAME

AN EXPERIMENT IN BUSINESS EDUCATION

by

Kalman J. Cohen *Head, Department of Economics and Associate Professor of Economics and Industrial Administration, Carnegie Institute of Technology*

William R. Dill *Associate Dean of the Graduate School of Industrial Administration and Associate Professor of Industrial Administration, Carnegie Institute of Technology*

Alfred A. Kuehn *Associate Professor of Industrial Administration, Carnegie Institute of Technology*

Peter R. Winters *Associate Professor of Business Administration, Stanford University*

1964   RICHARD D. IRWIN, Inc.   Homewood, Illinois

First Printing, October, 1964

Library of Congress Catalog Card No. 64–22215

PRINTED IN THE UNITED STATES OF AMERICA

FOREWORD

Progress in research has, in the past, been more easily accomplished than progress in education. We believe that a major reason for this has been the lack of accepted communication channels. Therefore, any experimentation undertaken is dependent upon word of mouth for its extension to other schools.

With this contributions to Management Educations Series an experiment in communicating the results of educational experiments is launched. It is our belief that continued progress in management education requires more educational experimentation at the individual colleges and improved methods for communicating these results. This series which we are launching with the cooperation of Richard D. Irwin, Inc., is the Graduate School of Industrial Administration's contribution to this process. Our long-run plans are to have at least one educational experiment of significant size under way each year. We hope to present a well-documented history of that experiment including an honest assessment of the results. It will be our aim to show in detail the path that we have followed so that others may take the same path, may save themselves time by rejecting that path, or may be able to modify and improve on the experiment. If we can be true to this objective and if others will undertake similar attempts we are firmly convinced that there will continue to be progress in management education.

Richard M. Cyert

PITTSBURGH, PENNSYLVANIA
September, 1964

PREFACE

In writing about the Carnegie Tech Management Game, we have two objectives. The first is to give prospective users what they need to play it: a detailed description of the Game, a summary of ways in which we and others have used it, instructions for players, instructions for the administrator, and the materials which the administrator needs to put the Game on the computer. From the beginning, we have assumed that our obligation was not only to develop the Game so that it could be used in our own educational programs, but also to make it available for others to use.

The second objective goes beyond simply making it possible for other schools and for business and industrial organizations to use the Game. What we offer here is a description and evaluation of an on-going experiment, not the definitive report on a completed venture. By reviewing the history of the Carnegie Tech Management Game, by discussing our experiences with it in considerable detail, and by naming current problems and suggesting possible directions for future development, we are underlining the preliminary nature of what has been accomplished so far. We invite others to join us in exploiting and developing the Carnegie Game as a new kind of environment for education and research. We believe that what we have to say about the Carnegie Game is relevant in planning more effective use of other kinds of management games. We hope that a full description of what we have done will encourage the development of new and better simulation exercises.

There are four parts to our presentation. The first is a volume which provides an overview of the Carnegie Tech Management Game and its uses in education and research. The second is a *Player's Manual* which contains the instructions that members of Game teams need. The third is an *Administrator's Manual*, available only to Game administrators, which gives instructions for running the Game, discusses problems of interaction between teams and the computer, describes the Game model, and provides flow charts, program listings, and other documentation. The fourth part includes the punch card decks and magnetic tapes for the FORTRAN version of the Game model. Let us discuss each of these in turn.

The main volume is intended to give the prospective user or any reader interested in management games and simulations an understanding of what the Carnegie Game is and ideas about how it can be used. Chapter 1 describes our goals in developing the Game and traces what was involved in designing it and making it work. Chapter 2 describes the present (Mark 1.5) version of the Game and the kinds of decisions that players can make. The second part of the chapter reprints the *Player's Manual* to show the instructions that players are given and to show examples of information and decision forms.

Chapters 3, 4, and 5 of the main volume show how we have used the Game in the Master's degree program at Carnegie. Chapter 3 moves beyond the bare description of the environment which is simulated on the computer to discuss other dimensions of the Game as an educational experience. We describe how we have enriched the basic simulation with role-playing exercises and other assignments and discuss the Game's place as a course in the graduate curriculum. Chapter 4 switches from the faculty to the student point of view—from a discussion of challenges that the Game is meant to provide to a description of how teams of graduate students actually have perceived and met the challenges. Chapter 5 shows how, in a variety of management courses, the Game has been exploited as a substitute for case, laboratory, and field experiences and has been made the focus for class discussions, examinations, and term projects.

Chapters 6 and 7 of the main volume complete our review of how the Game has been used in management education. Chapter 6 reports on the use of the Game in executive and evening programs at Carnegie and in graduate and undergraduate curricula at Tulane University, the University of North Carolina, and the University of Pittsburgh. Chapter 7 summarizes some student reactions to the Game and some data about its educational impact.

Chapters 8 and 9 of the main volume are intended as stimuli to research. Chapter 8 describes how the Carnegie Game and similar games can be used as an environment for research, and reprints examples of studies which have been based on an analysis of the workings of the Game model or on observations of the behavior of Game teams. Chapter 9 suggests ways in which better management games can be built and outlines possibilities for improvement in the design and administration of the Carnegie Game.

As supplements to the main volume, Richard D. Irwin, Inc. is publishing a *Player's Manual* and an *Administrator's Manual*. The *Player's Manual* provides a general description of the environment in which teams operate, describes the decisions that they can make and the constraints which they must observe, tells them what information they have to work with, and provides samples of information and decision forms. The *Administrator's Manual* includes material that is not printed in the main volume. It is a guide for the person who runs the Game;

because it necessarily includes a great deal of information which the administrator may not want to make available to players, its distribution is restricted.

The *Administrator's Manual* contains verbal descriptions of the Game program, flow charts, and program listings. It provides guidelines and instructions to help administrators adapt the FORTRAN program to the computer hardware that they have available, test whether the program is working properly, and meet some of the emergencies which may arise during the Game runs. The *Administrator's Manual* also describes other things which should be done to prepare for using the Game and to help carry the runs through smoothly.

The final part of the package, the punch card decks and magnetic tapes, will not be supplied by Richard D. Irwin, Inc. These will be available, at cost, from the

Management Game Administrator
Graduate School of Industrial Administration
Carnegie Institute of Technology
Pittsburgh, Pennsylvania 15213

The program described in the *Administrator's Manual* was written in FORTRAN for the IBM 7070 computer. The *Manual* also includes a brief description of an adaptation of the 7070 FORTRAN program which has been prepared at the University of Pittsburgh to run more efficiently on the IBM 7090. The version of the Game which is documented in the *Administrator's Manual* will run on the IBM 7070, 7074, 7090, or 7094, and ought to be easily adaptable to other computers which have:

1. A FORTRAN compiler.
2. Core storage of 10,000 or more 10-digit words.
3. Auxiliary magnetic tape or disk memory (equivalent to 5 tapes on the 7070 or 3 tapes on the 7090).

A compatible version, written in GATE for the CDC G–20 or G–21 is also available at Carnegie. With the cooperation of other users, Carnegie will maintain for the future a list of machines to which the program has been adapted and of appropriate sources for information about these adaptations. As this list develops, it should be available from either the Management Game Administrator at Carnegie or from your Irwin representative. As more substantial modifications develop, it may also be possible to summarize through such a list modifications that users have made in the substance and scope of the Game model itself. Purchasers of the *Administrator's Manual* will receive supplementary pages for the *Manual* which will supply corrections to the program and documentation which will describe new adaptations and modifications of the program which we and other users have made.

If real innovations in the use of the Game occur, we can project the need for a subsequent volume in this series which would review not the Carnegie Tech Management Game—but a family of models and applications to which the Carnegie Game has given impetus.

ACKNOWLEDGMENTS

The Carnegie Tech Management Game has been a group effort from its inception, and it continues to be so today. Many faculty members and graduate students at Carnegie Institute of Technology and other universities have made important contributions to the formulation and administration of this Game. Section I of Chapter 1 specifically acknowledges the roles played by some of these people in constructing the Game and in developing its educational and research potential. Here, we shall acknowledge only the contributions that individuals other than the four authors listed on the title page have made to this book.

Separate sections in Chapter 6, discussing the use of the Carnegie Tech Management Game in other educational programs, have been specially written for this book by: Clinton A. Phillips (Tulane University), Edward Sussna and C. Edward Weber (University of Pittsburgh), Richard Levin (University of North Carolina), Melvin Anshen (Columbia University), Neil C. Churchill (Carnegie Institute of Technology), and Richard W. Deckmann and Thomas P. O'Mara (United States Steel Corporation).

To illustrate the types of research projects which can be facilitated by the Carnegie Tech Management Game, slightly modified versions of seven previously published articles by (present or former) faculty members and graduate students at Carnegie Institute of Technology are reprinted in Chapter 8. The authors of these articles are: Ralph L. Day, William R. Dill, George H. Haines, Jr., O. Fred Heider, William Hoffman, Yuji Ijiri, Alfred A. Kuehn, Harold J. Leavitt, Ferdinand K. Levy, Richard C. Lyon, Thomas O'Mara, Daniel Remington, and Doyle L. Weiss.

The contributions of the above-named individuals are indicated by appropriate by-lines and footnotes in Chapters 6 and 8.

Several other people have provided material that we have freely rewritten before incorporating it into this book. Their contributions are acknowledged by footnotes in Chapters 3, 4, 5, and 9. In particular, we wish to thank John Bossons for contributing to the preparation of Section III. C in Chapter 9, William W. Cooper for contributing to the preparation of Section III in Chapter 5, Myron L. Joseph for contributing to the preparation of Section II. C in Chapter 3, Kenneth E. Knight for contributing to the preparation of Section II in Chapter 5, and Allan D. Shocker for contributing to the preparation of Chapter 4.

In writing this book, we found it convenient to adapt some material from several previously written articles which discuss the Carnegie Tech Management Game. Instead of quoting directly from these articles, we have used them as first drafts, into which we have incorporated revised information about various aspects of the Game and its use both at Carnegie and at other universities. Appropriate footnotes indicate where such free adaptations have been made. Most of the material which we have used in this way has been written or coauthored by one or more of us. Here we would like to acknowledge the contributions to this book which have been made by the other authors or coauthors of the original articles: Neil C. Churchill, Richard M. Cyert, Neil Doppelt, Merton H. Miller, Eric Rhenman, Robert M. Trueblood, and Theodore A. Van Wormer.

The Appendixes to Chapter 5 contain excerpts from term papers which were written by the following former graduate students at Carnegie Institute of Technology: Burnham H. Baker, Jr., David R. Bamberger, Lawrence J. Brewer, M. Eugene Carlisle, Jr., John D. Chase, George H. Daggett, C. R. de la Brousse, I. Edward Fraser, Thomas C. Gilmore, Edmund C. Glover, Donald M. Johnson, Richard C. Lyon, and Matthias E. Simon, Jr.

Many of the people whose contributions we have acknowledged above read and made constructive comments on portions of the manuscript. In addition, we would especially like to thank Vincent E. Cangelosi for reading earlier drafts of several chapters and suggesting revisions which have been incorporated in the final version.

Nelson J. Merwitzer made important contributions to the *Administrator's Manual* as well as to the translation of the CDC G–21 GATE program into FORTRAN for the IBM 7070 and 7090 computers. Theodore A. Van Wormer also contributed to the modification of the 7070 program for the IBM 7090 and reviewed sections of the *Administrator's Manual* describing the 7090 system. Thomas C. Gilmore programmed and drafted the description of the finance segment of the program, also contained in the *Administrator's Manual,* and Doyle L. Weiss drafted much of the section describing the marketing functions. Henry J. Gailliot assembled and coordinated the material prepared by the various contributors to the *Administrator's Manual.*

Many other individuals participated in the original development and programming of the Game. Their contributions are acknowledged in Section I of Chapter 1 of this volume as part of the description of the historical development of the Game. We especially wish to acknowledge here, however, the invaluable role played by Neil C. Churchill; as the Game administrator at Carnegie Tech since the summer of 1962, he encouraged the development of a computer program and accompanying documentation to make the Game available to new users, and he supervised some of the people who participated in this task.

Without the innovative intellectual atmosphere and the generous financial support provided by the Graduate School of Industrial Administration, it would have been impossible to undertake the type of experiment in business education represented by the Carnegie Tech Management Game. Both G. Leland Bach, G.S.I.A.'s first Dean, and Richard M. Cyert, its present Dean, have encouraged the Game's development and its widespread use in the curriculum. Many G.S.I.A. faculty members have lent their support by helping administer the Game as members of the Management Game Committee, by serving as members of boards of directors for firms playing the Game, or by integrating the Game with courses they have taught. Student players have often contributed many ideas to make the Game a more effective educational experience. We gratefully acknowledge the splendid cooperation received from our colleagues and students at the Graduate School of Industrial Administration.

We would like to thank the American Marketing Association, *Administrative Science Quarterly, Behavioral Science, California Management Review, Harvard Business Review,* Harvard University, *Journal of Accounting Research, Journal of Advertising Research, Journal of Business, Management International, Management Science,* Richard D. Irwin, Inc., and Tulane University for permitting us to adapt from or reprint in modified form material which has been copyrighted by them.

Finally, we would like to extend our thanks to those members of the secretarial staff at Carnegie Tech's Graduate School of Industrial Administration who typed and retyped this manuscript under a considerable amount of time pressure: Mrs. Rita Carlson, Miss Rosemary Conte, Mrs. Grace Couchman, Miss Thelma Johnson, Mrs. Nadeane Thompson, and Mrs. Norma Ziker.

While we gratefully acknowledge the contributions to this book made by the many individuals mentioned above, we ourselves accept full responsibility for any errors which may remain.

KALMAN J. COHEN, WILLIAM R. DILL,
ALFRED A. KUEHN, AND PETER R. WINTERS

PITTSBURGH, PENNSYLVANIA
September, 1964

TABLE OF CONTENTS

Chapter 1

BACKGROUND OF THE GAME

The Carnegie Tech Management Game began as an experiment in business education in 1957. Although not the earliest business game to be conceived or implemented,[1] it was, however, the first moderately complex and realistic general management game to be developed and successfully used as a major part of a graduate business school curriculum.

From the start, the Carnegie Tech Management Game was a group effort. A team of interested faculty members and students at Carnegie's Graduate School of Industrial Administration has been involved in the design, programming, and administration of this Game. Since the middle of 1959, the Game has been extensively used at Carnegie Tech. In recent years, Tulane University, the University of Pittsburgh, the University of North Carolina, Indiana University, and the University of Oklahoma have also used this Game in their business school programs.

Enough experience in using the Carnegie Tech Management Game has been accumulated for us to conclude that this experiment in business education has been successful. The Game has become a required course in the M.S. curriculum at Carnegie's Graduate School of Industrial Administration. Three of the other universities where this Game has been played plan to continue with it. Numerous other university business schools, both in the United States of America and in Europe, have expressed considerable interest in the Game.

It is in response to the widespread interest and enthusiasm which other potential users of the Carnegie Tech Management Game have shown that this book is written. We hope it will convey an apprecia-

---

[1] The first widely known business game was the AMA Top Management Decision Simulation, whose development was begun by the American Management Association in 1956. An extensive discussion of the history of management games, together with numerous references citing descriptions of these games, is contained in Kalman J. Cohen and Eric Rhenman, "The Role of Management Games in Education and Research," *Management Science*, Vol. 7, No. 2 (January, 1961), pp. 131–66. In this connection, also see: Paul S. Greenlaw, Lowell W. Herron, and Richard H. Rawdon, *Business Simulation in Industrial and University Education* (Englewood Cliffs, N. J.: Prentice-Hall, Inc., 1962), chap. I and appendix II; and Joel M. Kibbee, Clifford J. Craft, and Burt Nanus, *Management Games* (New York: Reinhold Publishing Corp., 1961), chaps. I and II and pp. 315–36.

1

tion of some of the advantages which can be obtained when a complex management game is used for business education and research. We hope it will enable potential adopters to see in detail the set of business problems embodied in the Carnegie Tech Management Game, so that they can judge whether the Game is appropriate for their curriculum needs. We hope it will provide enough information about the computer programs which are currently available for the Carnegie Tech Management Game to enable new adopters to run the Game on their own electronic digital computers.[2]

Most of all, we hope that this book will enable others to join with us in continuing the experiment in business education which the Carnegie Tech Management Game represents. While the experiment has been successful to date, we hope that it will continue to be regarded as an experiment. Other users, as well as ourselves, should continue to regard our Game as tentative and fluid. Where defects are perceived in the present form of the Game, we hope that improvements and modifications will be introduced. We hope that new ways of using the Game and of integrating it with other parts of the curriculum will continue to be discovered. Finally, we hope that our Game will eventually be adapted and reformulated so that it will better suit the educational and research needs of its new users. To all future experimenters with the Carnegie Tech Management Game, we extend the hope that this book will provide a starting point rather than a stopping point.

In the following section, we shall discuss the historical development of the Carnegie Tech Management Game, trying particularly to indicate the extent to which numerous individuals besides ourselves have been responsible for various aspects of the design and implementation of the Game. Finally, to conclude Chapter 1, we shall review some of the specific reasons which motivated the development of this Game.

I. HISTORY OF THE GAME

The development of the Carnegie Tech Management Game began in December, 1957, when Dean Richard M. Cyert, then Head of Carnegie's undergraduate Department of Industrial Management, brought

---

[2]Both for reasons of economy and security, detailed descriptions of the models which form the Carnegie Tech Management Game and the available computer programs are not presented in this volume. They are contained in a separate *Administrator's Manual for the Carnegie Tech Management Game,* by Kalman J. Cohen, William R. Dill, Alfred A. Kuehn, and Peter R. Winters, published by Richard D. Irwin, Inc. This *Administrator's Manual* is intended to provide enough information about the Game and its FORTRAN computer program to facilitate its adoption by new users. University faculty members and industrial training directors who are sincerely interested in exploring the possibilities of running the Carnegie Tech Game themselves may order copies of the *Administrator's Manual* from the publisher.

together a small group of GSIA faculty to consider the construction of a "complex management game" for use in business education.

The concept of business gaming was still quite new at the time. Attention had first been drawn to business gaming in the spring of that year by the American Management Association's use of a game developed in conjunction with IBM.[3] Shortly thereafter, in the fall, Dr. Tibor Fabian addressed a seminar at the University of Pittsburgh, in which he described a management game being constructed by the Management Science Group at UCLA.[4] Both of these games were the essence of simplicity, being designed for the primary purpose of creating awareness among "players" of the importance of interrelationships among the various functions of a business enterprise. The UCLA Game was being tested with introductory management students at the sophomore level. The AMA Game was used with executive personnel attending management seminars. A very desirable attribute reported for both games was motivation—both executives and introductory students enjoyed participating in the operation of a firm from a top-management point of view.

Dean Cyert saw great potential in the use of a business game as a vehicle for integrating various aspects of business training and providing an organizational setting within which students could acquire simulated business experience. To achieve these goals, however, a game would require greater complexity than that found in the AMA and UCLA Games. Depth in content is necessary to provide: (1) the richness of experience required to maintain continued interest on the part of players over an extended period of time; (2) a basis for reference and study in various business courses; and (3) sufficient complexity in decision making to provide experience in, and to demonstrate the desirability of, task-oriented organizational activity. To lay the ground work for the development of such a game, Dean Cyert organized a game development committee consisting of himself and Professors William R. Dill, Merton H. Miller, Alfred A. Kuehn, Frederick M. Tonge, and Peter R. Winters.

The work of the game development committee was divided, with

---

[3]An extensive description of the original AMA Game is contained in Franc M. Ricciardi et al., *Top Management Decision Simulation: The AMA Approach,* ed. Elizabeth Marting (New York: American Management Association, 1957).

[4]The UCLA Game is discussed in James R. Jackson, "UCLA Executive Decision Games," Management Sciences Research Project Research Report No. 58, University of California, Los Angeles, December 9, 1958 (reprinted in *Proceedings of the National Symposium on Management Games,* Center for Research in Business, The University of Kansas, Lawrence, Kansas, May, 1959, pp. VI–9 through VI–15) and also in James R. Jackson, "Learning from Experience in Business Decision Games," *California Management Review,* Vol. 1, No. 2 (Winter, 1959), pp. 92–107.

Professor Dill exploring the administrative and organizational problems and opportunities of a complex game, Professor Miller examining the educational potential in the areas of finance and accounting, Professor Kuehn assuming responsibility for the marketing and product research functions, and Professors Tonge and Winters investigating the alternatives available in the area of production. Professors Melvin L. Anshen and Dewitt C. Dearborn also attended some meetings of the group and contributed to the development of the Game. Dean Cyert prodded the group through evening and Saturday meetings, first until a consensus was reached on the goals of the project, then until the general content of each functional area was delineated and agreed upon, and finally until drafts of the models, related descriptive material, and an operating manual were prepared. Without his guidance, efforts at mediation and arbitration, and participation in drafting the results of the committee's work it is likely that the effort would have stalled at this or some later stage. The magnitude of the effort that would be required was certainly not recognized by the committee members at the outset.

To achieve an operating game in a reasonable amount of time it was found necessary to lower the aspirations of the members of the game development committee, each of whom had pushed for some details which he wanted to see incorporated into the Game. Many of these "necessary" details were, however, likely to delay the development of an operating game. Consequently, the immediate goals of a Mark 1 Game were agreed upon. It was thought that this would be followed by the Mark 2 Game in which all our dreams were to be realized. Later we recognized that several revisions would be required, so we began thinking of the Mark N Game. Neither the Mark 2 nor the Mark N Game has yet been completed, although the current Mark 1.5 version which evolved as a revised and extended Mark 1 contains elements originally planned for those later versions. Perhaps the most important effect of the establishment of the Mark notation at an early date was its role in facilitating the acceptance of an operational goal, the Mark 1 version, which met some, but not all, of our aspirations.

The research activities of the GSIA faculty found expression in the Game. The choice of the detergent industry as a frame of reference for the Game was influenced in large part by an advertising-pricing model that had previously been developed to describe consumer behavior in the purchase of grocery products. The research that had been pursued at GSIA in the area of production-inventory-work force scheduling similarly influenced the design of the production function. Later, research into the determinants of common stock prices was to form the basis for the development of a corresponding model for the Game.

As work progressed, many members of the GSIA faculty and several students played important roles in the development, administration, and (eventually) revision and extension of the Carnegie Game. Dr. Theodore A. Van Wormer played a most important role; he took major responsibility for writing the IBM 650 computer program for the original Mark 1 version of the Game. He was assisted in this task by Dr. Alexander J. Federowicz, Mr. Edward C. Evans, and, in the production area, Professor Winters. Dr. Van Wormer did more than program, however; he played an important role in setting up the accounting function for the Game, and he evaluated many of the features of the models specified for the Game, frequently suggesting modifications to improve their performance characteristics. In addition, he processed the Game decisions through the computer in the first year of play, an operation which included additional debugging, testing, and modifications under severe time pressures.

Professor Kalman J. Cohen became the first administrator of the Mark 1 Game. Its initial trial runs were in July, 1959, with GSIA faculty members managing the Game firms. In August, 1959, participants in the Ford Foundation–sponsored Faculty Seminar in New Developments in Business Administration, meeting in Denver, became the first outside group to play the Game. The first extended Game play, in which GSIA students participated, occurred during the 1959–60 academic year. During this introductory period, Professor Cohen and members of the original game development committee had to deal with the many problems of integrating the Game into the graduate school curriculum. Questions about the role of faculty members as board members and teachers had to be resolved, student teams chosen, operating procedures and schedules developed, and previously undetected flaws in the Game noted and corrected. In the subsequent development of the Mark 1.5 version of the Game, Professor Cohen also modified, extended, and reprogrammed the original product research function.

Professor Dill assumed prime responsibility for the study of player reaction to the Game. By means of questionnaires administered during and after play, students provided their impressions of the work load imposed by the Game, evaluations of the Game as part of the curriculum, and suggestions as to how the Game experience might have been made more useful to the players. Player reaction to the Game has also been solicited periodically after students have graduated and taken jobs in industry. The information compiled in this research has served as a guide in subsequent experimentation with the Game to improve its educational value.

Professor Kuehn's involvement with the Game continued to center about improvements in the marketing functions as a realistic description of consumer behavior. The CIT Marketing Game, developed by Professor Kuehn and Mr. Doyle L. Weiss, has facilitated this research and provided an operational means for testing methods of estimating the market parameters in the Game, establishing market equilibria, and developing "optimal" marketing decisions. Procedural methods have been derived for the solution of some of the problems posed by the Game and are being tested in actual practice in conjunction with manufacturers of packaged grocery products. Thus the Game has given direction to applied research which, in turn, has produced results which could be used to achieve greater realism in the Game.

Professor Winters has taken responsibility for several important tasks since the original development of the Mark 1 game. He continued to play the leading role in the development of the production area of the Game. He also was in charge of programming the Mark 1.5 version of the Game in both 20–GATE and FORTRAN, assisted by Professor Cohen and Messrs. Thomas C. Gilmore, George H. Haines, Jr., Nelson J. Merwitzer, and D. L. Weiss. Finally, Professor Winters assumed the responsibility of guiding the Mark 1.5 version's initial runs at GSIA by serving as Game administrator in 1961–62.

Many other GSIA faculty members and students have contributed to the development and administration of the Carnegie Tech Management Game throughout the years. Mr. Gilmore helped design and program the accounting and finance models in the Mark 1.5 version. Mr. Lowell K. Strohl assisted in drafting the *Player's Manual* and in the administration of the Game.[5] Professors Dearborn, Neil C. Churchill, Miller, and Robert M. Trueblood made major contributions in the areas of finance and accounting, introducing among other things the financial and management audit conducted by introductory accounting students. Professor Miller was also Game administrator in 1960–61. Professor Churchill assumed, in the summer of 1962, the responsibility of being Game administrator and guiding its continued improvement, and he received programming assistance in these efforts from Mr. Joseph F. O'Grady. Other contributions to the development and administration of the Game have been made by Professor Anshen and Mr. Weiss in the area of marketing; Professors John F. Muth and Gerald L. Thomp-

---

[5]Other graduate students who have helped run the Game include Samuel D. Beaird, John L. Gable, Jon Timothy Heames, Arnold H. Kaplan, and Robert S. Silverthorn.

son in the area of production; and Professors John R. Coleman, Myron L. Joseph, Leonard A. Rapping, W. Phillip Saunders, Jr., Kenneth G. Scheid, and John C. Shearer in labor relations. Professor William W. Cooper, by his strong support of the Game at crucial points in both its development and its introduction into the GSIA curriculum, helped insure enthusiastic acceptance of this educational innovation by the GSIA faculty. Professors Cohen, Cooper, Dill, Kuehn, Harold J. Leavitt, James G. March, and Herbert A. Simon (assisted by Mr. Kenneth E. Knight) have integrated the Game with course work by assigning term projects based upon analytical and organizational aspects of the Game. In 1963, Professor John Bossons developed the Carnegie Stock Exchange, providing a market in which Carnegie Tech students and faculty were able to trade shares of the Management Game firms. Professors Anshen and Dearborn introduced the Game into Carnegie's Program for Executives in 1961, and Professor Churchill ran the Game for a Pennsylvania Bell Telephone Company training program in 1963. In addition, during the past five years, virtually all members of the GSIA faculty and many Pittsburgh business executives have participated in the play of the Game as members of boards of directors.

Special mention must be made of the innovative role played by Tulane University in connection with the Carnegie Tech Management Game. As the first outside user of this Game, Tulane helped reprogram the Mark 1 version so that it would run on an IBM 650 computer having magnetic tapes instead of a random access memory. The other business schools where the Mark 1 version of the Game has been run used the Tulane rather than the Carnegie Tech computer program. Tulane University also was host at a conference held in New Orleans during April, 1961, to describe the details of the Carnegie Game and its computer program to other prospective users. Details of some of the educational innovations which Tulane has introduced in its use of the Game are described in Chapter 6.

More recently, we have had a great deal of help from members of the University of Pittsburgh faculty in completing the FORTRAN version. Professor D. L. Weiss assumed major responsibility in preparing the detailed descriptions of the marketing functions, and Professor T. A. Van Wormer worked with Professor Kuehn and N. J. Merwitzer to adapt our original FORTRAN version—written for the IBM 7070 —so that it would run on the IBM 7090. (Notes on the 7090 FORTRAN version are included in the *Administrator's Manual*.)

Our review of its history indicates that the Carnegie Tech Management Game has been the outgrowth of the hopes and hard work of many individuals at Carnegie and elsewhere. However, much valuable experience has also been gained by the faculty members at other business schools where this Game has been played: Tulane University, the University of Pittsburgh, the University of North Carolina, Indiana University, and the University of Oklahoma. Their efforts have shown that many of the advantages which we have sought from our Game at Carnegie Tech can also be obtained when such a complex game is incorporated into the curricula at other business schools. By bringing to a broader group of business schools the Carnegie Tech Management Game and the experiences of those who have used it here at Carnegie and elsewhere, it is our hope that this book will contribute to the progress which is being made on many fronts in improving teaching methods.

II. REASONS FOR DEVELOPMENT OF THE GAME[6]

In the preceding section, we have indicated that our objectives in designing the Carnegie Tech Management Game were considerably more ambitious than the goals of the earlier game developers. For example, it has been stated that the educational purpose of the IBM Game is to teach men "to discard emotional blocks and to use [their] best judgment."[7] In a similar vein, an executive wrote of his experience with the AMA Game: "The complex problems of running a business are presented in a way that seems to facilitate rapid comprehension, active participation, and intense involvement in the process of planning, review, and analysis."[8] Such relatively simple general business games are not intended to teach managers specific skills; their emphasis is limited to reminding experienced specialists that the functions (and people) of a business are interdependent and that many decisions must be made under time pressure by the cooperative judgments of several individuals.

However, an undergraduate or graduate student of business (and probably even a seasoned executive) does not become an effective manager simply by discarding emotional blocks or participating intensely in an absorbing, but grossly oversimplified, substitute for a real management environment. We began work on the Carnegie Tech Game with the hope of doing more, for we wanted to provide an environment

---

[6]The material in this section has been freely drawn (with minor modifications) from K. J. Cohen, R. M. Cyert, W. R. Dill, A. A. Kuehn, M. H. Miller, T. A. Van Wormer, and P. R. Winters, "The Carnegie Tech Management Game," *Journal of Business,* Vol 33, No. 4 (October, 1960), pp. 309–16.

[7]This remark was made by Ben R. Faden of the International Business Machines Corporation. See the *Proceedings of the National Symposium on Management Games, op. cit.,* p. IV-11.

[8]Clifford J. Craft and Lois A. Stewart, "Competitive Management Simulation," *Journal of Industrial Engineering,* Vol. 10, No. 5 (September-October, 1959), p. 363.

in which players could test and develop some of the positive skills which a manager must employ. This concern is reflected both in the design of our Game and in the arrangements we have adopted for its administration.

What must a manager do well to be effective? We do not pretend, of course, to have anything like the whole answer to this, but we believe that the following skills, at least, will be universally recognized as important.

1. *An ability to set goals and to define them operationally.* There are many different goals, such as profits, share of market, public service, etc., which business firms may pursue. These various possible objectives may not be compatible with each other. It is important for the managers in a firm to agree on a set of operationally defined organizational goals which can be used as a basis for planning.

2. *An ability to abstract, organize, and use information from a complex and diffuse environment.* Managers live in a world which lavishes information on them but which affords them little time and little guidance for its use. A key function of management is to discover the pertinence of various data to the organization's objectives, to isolate the problems which deserve immediate attention, and to identfy the constraints which must be observed in seeking a solution.

3. *An ability to forecast and to plan.* The complexity of modern business operations and the time lags that occur before the effects of decisions are realized put a premium on the manager's ability to look ahead. The student of management needs to recognize at an early stage not only the immediate, but the cumulative, effects of his actions (or lack of action). He should predict the consequences of his decisions so that he can measure what he accomplishes against what he planned to achieve.

4. *An ability to combine the role of generalist and specialist.* The image which simple management games present of managers as a team of generalists, all concerned with overall company policy, seems to have a limited basis in real life. Most managers, as individuals, are as much specialists as generalists. Even in the top positions of organizations, men are committed by experience, expertise, loyalties, and job responsibilities to such subareas as production, marketing, and finance. Their commitments as specialists affect their behavior on top policy decisions; and, at the same time, their identification with the enterprise as a whole requires them to cooperate at lower levels in the planning of many detailed operating decisions.

5. *An ability to work effectively with other people.* Managers must effectively maintain three kinds of cooperative working relation-

ships with other people in an organizational setting. In relation to their own superiors—who may be other managers, directors, stockholders, or others who have influence on company goals and on the evaluation of managerial performance—managers are required to negotiate about the objectives toward which they are working and about the impact of these objectives for operating decisions. Second, when goals have been established or inferred, managers must work together to produce good decisions with the resources they have at their disposal. Third, managers must work through a subordinate organization to elaborate and implement their policies and decisions; therefore, control procedures are essential to insure that management's wishes are actually carried out correctly and on time.

Our objective in designing the Carnegie Tech Management Game was to provide an environment in which these abilities might be developed. We did not expect that a game, any more than any other single teaching technique, could take over the whole task of molding men into managers; but we hoped that complex management games could play an important role in such efforts.

We made the Carnegie Tech Game complex so that it would serve as a means for sharpening players' skills as analysts and evaluators of information. Early games gave players only small amounts of information and required only a few decisions. Ours provides players with between 1,000 and 2,000 items of information for each "month" of play and permits them to make over 300 decisions each period.

In addition to providing players with a great deal of information about what they and their competitors have accomplished and about what they will confront in the future, the Carnegie Tech Game presents players with different and not always consistent measures of how well they have done. Players are impressed with the need to define their objectives for themselves and with the complex and inconsistent relationships that sometimes exist between such goals as short-run profit and long-term growth, which they may carelessly assume are always compatible.

Players are expected to develop routines for scanning and evaluating the information that they receive and for deciding what additional information they should get, either by analysis that they do themselves or by purchasing information from "independent research organizations" that are programmed into the computer. When players buy information (about customers or about competitors, for example), they learn some of the relationships between the costs of surveys and the reliability of the information that they obtain. Random errors are introduced into the program where it is appropriate for players to learn to expect—and to deal with—uncertainty and imprecision in data.

Most of the functions in the Game, though, are deterministic. Management is usually believed—except in moments of despair—to be more a "game of skill" than a "game of chance." We wanted to encourage players to seek broad "cause-effect" relationships in the data that were presented to them, and at the same time to have an environment too complex to allow the discovery of the details of the mathematical functions which govern the Game. Truly "optimal strategies" in the Game, as in real life, are hard to find, not so much because the individual functions are difficult in themselves as because their interactions are extremely complex and unpredictable.[9]

Starting with the first extended plays of the Game, we observed teams behaving in ways which suggest that the design of the Game has been effective in getting teams to learn the importance of organizing and formalizing the handling of information. Some have set up their own internal accounting systems to preserve and to highlight the information they need. Some have formalized, in writing, procedures which will insure prompt and complete circulation of essential information. Some have isolated decisions which do not require monthly review and, in effect, resorted to a combination of setting general policies on a quarterly basis and using the monthly intervals merely to check and modify their quarterly policies.

The way in which the Game is administered can increase its utility as an environment for sharpening information-processing skills. Three features of the administrative arrangements are particularly important —team size, the subordination of each team to a board of directors, and the incorporation of a variety of supplementary assignments and role-playing exercises. Since these are discussed in detail in Chapters 3, 4, and 5, in this section we shall merely indicate the ways in which the size of teams and the use of boards of directors were considerations relevant to the type of game we have evolved.

The Carnegie Tech Game is complex enough to permit teams of five to ten men whose members have clearly differentiated functions to perform. Because no one man consistently has time to absorb all of the

---

[9]Those who designed the Game were the first to play it. We can testify to the difficulties of predicting the Game's behavior. We would have been happy to be able to achieve even some modest targets in sales and profits, and we quickly lost any aspirations we might have had to "optimize." The Game was designed, however, in such a way as to permit the use of sophisticated approaches to data analysis and decision making in certain specialized areas. We gave the production manager a central plant and warehouse and four district warehouses, for example, and provided him with information about storage, shipping costs, and shipping times. To establish policies for the shipment and transshipment of finished products, he and his subordinates can try to fit the data of their problem into an appropriate mathematical decision model. In marketing, where players must prepare a sales forecast, there are a variety of ways in which key concepts from statistics, economics, and the psychology of consumer behavior can be applied.

information made available to the firm, players must learn to interpret and summarize incoming results in a way that helps their teammates as well as themselves. The financial officers must be able to talk to the production officers about relevant aspects of the company's financial condition without discussing all the details of cost trends, current cash position, stock prices, or negotiations with outside lenders. The marketing officers must be able to translate their detailed marketing experience into a sales forecast on which the finance officers can base their cash budgets and projected income statements and on which the production officers can base orders for raw materials, production schedules, and schedules for shipment of finished goods to district warehouses.

Starting with the first extended play of the Game, boards of three to four faculty members and outside businessmen have been appointed for each firm. The directors' job is essentially to test the players' understanding of their environment, to force them to communicate information about their positions and plans, and to direct their attention—when appropriate—to particular problems and goals. Regular meetings of the boards of directors with the members of their firms are held at the end of every three or four moves in the Game. At these meetings the officers of the firms review the results of their past operations and present their plans for future operations.

At the end of every (simulated) year of play, each firm may be required to present a written annual report to its directors. This report usually includes financial statements for the current and recent years; a review of developments in production, sales, finance, new products, plant facilities, and organization during the current year; an evaluation of the present competitive position of the firm; and a review of plans for changes in operations and for new investments in products, market development, and new plant or warehouse facilities for the future, with an explanation of the reasons behind these plans.

Considerable stress has been placed on problems of planning. The boards of directors are an ever-present stimulus to planning, because they require officers to submit plans on a quarterly basis and because they expect teams to carry through their plans once they have been approved. Over and above the presence of directors and of time pressure on the officers, though, the Game itself has been intentionally designed to encourage planning and to penalize lack of attention to future needs.

One purpose of the early business games was to dramatize to executives the dangers of narrow concentration on one facet of managing a firm. As a consequence, these games provided little exercise for the specialist. The production manager's task, for example, in most of the simpler games consists of just a few decisions, such as the amount of a single homogeneous product to produce or the amount to invest in undifferentiated new capactiy.

To give more realistic training in the problems of balancing specialized and general considerations in a firm, the Carnegie Game makes the separate areas of finance, production, and marketing challenging and absorbing in themselves. The range of decisions which specialists in these areas must make is described in detail in Chapter 2.

More than the simpler management games, the Carnegie Tech Game may lure the careless player into the trap of excessive specialization. But in real life, too, the manager must learn to be a generalist under conditions where the temptations are strong to remain a specialist. Here we rely primarily on the unsatisfactory income statements and balance sheets of teams which do not plan and coordinate their activities to draw their attention to the needs for considering the firm as a whole. The boards of directors are also expected to draw attention to any lack of integration in the behavior of various groups within the firms. Through these devices we have tried to emphasize interdepartmental cooperation both on short-term actions and on broad policy questions.

We have mentioned three kinds of interactions in which managers should be skilled: interactions with the people who have formal power to set objectives for them and to judge their performance, interactions with one another to agree on objectives and means of achieving them, and interactions with subordinates who bear the main responsibility for elaborating and implementing decisions.

The boards of directors, of course, are our main means of providing experience in the first kind of interaction. Their reactions are regarded as extremely important by the players. The officers are faced with the problem of communicating their ideas clearly and concisely, orally and in writing, to the directors. Some decisions, such as the establishment of a formal organization structure or a change in dividend rate, must be specifically approved by the directors; here, the officers must be able to persuade the directors of the merits of their proposals.

The Game is administered in such a way that neither the directors nor the Game itself puts clear and simple values on the different possible indexes of company performance.[10] Each team must learn to show initiative and leadership in deciding what it wants to achieve and in

---

[10]There is considerable latitude within the structure of the Game to focus the goals toward which players work. By adjusting initial conditions and parameters, the Game can be adapted to emphasize specific problems, such as production scheduling or financial solvency. The administrators can highlight different measures of performance and, through the use of appropriate rewards and sanctions, reinforce the saliency of certain measures to the players.

elaborating its general goals into workable plans for the company's operation.

The complexity of the Game and the possibility of operating with teams ranging in size from five to ten people permit many experiments with the organization of the players themselves. Some of the implications this has for research are discussed in Chapter 8. In designing the Game, we recognized that by using large teams and a fairly tight time schedule for play, we could force the players to think about problems of organization. Large groups proved too unwieldy to function effectively for long as an informal committee of equals, the pattern that most student groups seem at first to prefer. After several simulated months of play, the groups which were given freedom to organize as they chose have all moved steadily in the direction of formalized, hierarchical patterns.[11]

There are many ways in which players must take cognizance of the "men" on whom they depend to achieve their objectives. There are constraints on the speed with which the work force can be expanded or reduced. There are costs associated with hirings and layoffs. Worker productivity is not a known constant; it varies according to a number of factors that in real life affect employee performance.

These are only first steps, however. It is possible to incorporate the possibilities of strikes and slowdowns. Players can also be forced to consider many basic personnel questions in much the same way as they now plan expenditures on product research. By introducing more details of a labor market, we could broaden the task to include questions of wage policy, manpower recruiting, and manpower selection.

It will be as important—but more difficult—to incorporate effects of the players' attitudes, behavior, and communications on subordinates. As we gain more experience in other aspects of the Game and make the kinds of improvements which seem feasible for the short run, more of our attention can be devoted to devising ways of impressing players with the relevance of *all* their behavior as company "managers" to the results that they achieve.[12]

---

[11]Because it is hard to arrange times when all members of the group can be together, definite responsibilities have been assigned to individual team members. Because not all players are equally enthusiastic about the Game and because the boards of directors insist on a degree of unity and organization in the presentations that are made to them, the office of company president has evolved from a titular honor to a responsible position. The president must be sure that decisions are made on time and must act as spokesman in many contacts with the directors. Issues of team motivation, personal status, and organizational politics have arisen.

[12]Two lines of approach suggest themselves. The first would involve expansion of the Game to include as players men who operate as a distinct "second echelon" of management. The players who make the overall policy decisions would not have direct access to the computer in most instances. For the bulk of the information that they want, they

The managerial skills we have mentioned are commonly recognized and discussed. One other skill we hoped that our Game would help teach has received less attention. The exposure of players to games and to the experience of learning from them is one way to introduce them to several of the new tools available to managers that are becoming increasingly important in their lives. Students at Carnegie have not only been involved in playing the Game; they have also been involved in debates about our Game and games in general as means for management education. They have seen some of the ways in which computers can be used to process business data and to simulate business operations and experience. As they gain familiarity with the model of the world that forms the core of the Carnegie Tech Game, they will become aware of the kinds of questions which we have answers for— or still seek answers to—in trying to understand how a firm or an industry functions. In a world which is changing very rapidly, an outlook that includes a willingness to experiment with new ideas and a maturity in evaluating them is very important for effective managers.

---

would have to make inquiries of the second echelon managers. As they make decisions, they would communicate what they want to the second echelon, and the latter group would translate these policies into decisions for the computer.

The second approach would involve using umpires as judges of the teams' competence in matters of communication and supervision. Either by observing the teams' deliberations or by requiring the teams to report the manner in which they elaborate and implement their decisions in the subordinate organization, the umpires would make judgments about ways in which the computer's transformation of decisions into results should be modified.

Chapter 2

GENERAL OVERVIEW OF THE GAME

Management games show great variety in the extent to which they simulate real world firms and industries. However, if they are intended to have educational rather than mere entertainment value, they must embody at least some degree of verisimilitude. The decisions that must be made by members of game teams are modeled on the types of decisions actually made in business firms. The levels of the decisions vary, but most games concentrate on decisions at a high executive level. The development of the computer has stimulated the growth of business games by making it possible to devise environments which are reasonably faithful simulations of segments of the economy. As the simulation of the environment becomes more realistic, so also can the decisions that must be made become more like the decisions of an actual business firm.

As we have already indicated in Chapter 1, our fundamental premise in developing the Carnegie Tech Management Game was that by increasing the realism of business games, more effective educational and research tools than previously existed could be created. After a period of development and experimental trials, we now have a game which we feel has achieved an appropriate degree of complexity and realism. As we indicate in Chapter 9, however, we recognize that many additional improvements still remain to be made.

I. MAIN FEATURES OF THE MODEL[1]

The packaged detergent industry has served as a general framework for the Carnegie Tech Management Game. The selection of this industry was primarily one of convenience. Its advantages included the existence of a national market, a small number of firms, and a set of differentiated products. In addition, some of us had an intimate knowledge of the industry. Our Game is not, however, an exact simulation of the detergent industry. Only those real-world features deemed useful

---

[1]The material in this section has been adapted from K. J. Cohen, R. M. Cyert, W. R. Dill, A. A. Kuehn, M. H. Miller, T. A. Van Wormer, and P. R. Winters, "The Carnegie Tech Management Game," *Journal of Business,* Vol. 33, No. 4 (October, 1960), pp. 303–9.

in terms of our fundamental educational and research purposes have been incorporated in the Game.

Three companies comprise the packaged detergent industry in the Carnegie Game. The players assume the roles of executives in the three competing firms. Each company has a factory which is located in one of the four geographical territories that comprise the total detergent market. At this factory are the following facilities: (1) a raw materials warehouse, (2) production facilities that can be used to produce different mixes of product, (3) a factory warehouse for the storage of finished product, and (4) offices and facilities for new product research and development.

The firm maintains, in addition, a district warehouse for finished products in each of the four marketing regions. These facilities, in contrast to the facilities at the central plant, are leased rather than owned.

Depending on the particular initial conditions which are used, each firm will be marketing one or more products which are usually neither very good nor very bad in terms of their basic characteristics: washing power, sudsing power, and gentleness. By expenditures for new product research teams can generate potential new products. If, on the basis of laboratory reports or market test data, a team wants to put a new product into production, it can do so, as long as the total number of its brands in production does not exceed three.

The factory makes all products with the same equipment, using the same work force. During each month the work force divides its time among products which are scheduled for production. The managers are not concerned, therefore, with detailed scheduling of products among men or machines, and they can regard equipment and work force as homogeneous.

All products in the Game are developed from a basic set of seven available raw materials, which must be ordered from suppliers before they can be used in production. Deliveries of raw materials are usually made on schedule. Lead times vary for different materials, and prices may occasionally change. All suppliers of raw materials offer a discount of 3 percent if the firm pays its bills within one month of delivery of the materials; payment is required within two months of delivery.

Production within each monthly operating period is scheduled by the players, but the actual monthly output does not necessarily meet their schedule. The computer is programmed to impose realistic constraints on the attainment of production goals. Rules in the model determine how output is affected by raw material run-outs, by expenditures for maintenance, by limits to plant capacity and to the utilization of overtime, by limits to the rate at which the work force can be expanded, and by undertime and overtime effects on employee productivity. Production costs, as well as output, will be affected by these factors; costs will also depend on longer-run decisions concerning the expansion of production and storage capacties.

All production for a given month is available at the beginning of the following month in the warehouse to which it has been consigned. Reasonable shipping times and costs are associated with shipments from factory warehouse to district warehouses or from one district warehouse to another. Sales may be lost because of inventory run-outs, and run-outs adversely affect future demand.

The sales of a Game firm consist of shipments from its district warehouses to the wholesalers or retail chains who are its customers. All products which the firm has or can develop are distributed at the retail level through supermarkets and grocery stores for home use. According to rules incorporated in the Carnegie Game model, the computer model simulates the behavior of consumers in purchasing detergents in retail stores, the behavior of retailers in pricing detergents and ordering them from wholesalers (or directly from manufacturers, in the case of large retail chains), and the behavior of wholesalers in pricing detergents and ordering them from manufacturers. The firm sets one wholesale price for each product in each region; retail prices may vary considerably by region as well as by individual store.

To develop new products or to improve existing products, the teams must spend money for product research and development. Firms can choose to pursue as many as three different kinds of research activities. The most general kind is an unconstrained search for new product ideas. It is also possible to try to synthesize a modification of any product currently being marketed by a competitor or by one's own firm. Finally, management can provide specific directions to research effort regarding attributes desired in potential new products. The amount of money spent over time on a research project determines the probability that new product ideas will be generated. The more narrowly a firm defines the goals guiding the expenditure of research funds, the less likely will these funds generate any new product ideas, but the more likely will any new products actually generated satisfy the stipulated goals. As in real life, most new product ideas will not be worth very much; even when a good product is developed, its superiority need not be immediately apparent. Laboratory reports on new products will describe their composition (in terms of the quantities required of up to seven raw materials), the standard labor requirements for them, their characteristics (sudsing power, washing power, and gentleness) as revealed by laboratory tests, and the raw material costs per case at standard raw material prices.

If the players think a product idea is worth further study, they can spend money to draw a sample of consumers and test their preferences for the characteristics of this new product in comparison with the characteristics of any other product. From such test studies, the team will have to decide whether or not to put the product into full-scale production.

Each company is a "going concern" when the players assume its management. The firm will already be in business producing and distributing one or more products. The financial condition in which the firm begins the Game can be made to vary, depending on the educational objective of the particular play. Normally, however, we start with each team in reasonably sound financial condition with a modest liquid reserve and an established dividend policy.

The managers can obtain additional funds during play in most of the ways that would be open to a real firm, but they must anticipate their needs for funds. Except for emergency measures, the quickest means of financing—a three-month bank loan—requires at least one month between the filing of an application and the release of funds to the firm. To qualify for a short-term bank loan, the company must meet the same general standards which commercial bankers in reality impose upon firms. These are not specifically spelled out to the players beyond the statements that the bank will consider the history of the firm's deposit balances, its past performances in meeting financial obligations, its overall credit rating, and the reputation of its management. The maximum size of such a loan is not rigidly specified, but in general it is limited by the firm's current assets and recent income, in accordance with sound banking standards.

The managers can also obtain term loans of two to ten years' duration. They must indicate how much they want, when they want it, and the desired repayment terms. The simulated bankers in the Carnegie Game program may either accept or reject the application completely depending on whether it is prudent or ridiculous when measured against sound banking practices. However, the bank may also respond by making counteroffers, and it may choose to impose a variety of realistic constraints on the firm's future operations. Unless one side chooses to cease negotiations, the offers and counteroffers continue until arrangements satisfactory to both the company and the bank have been made.[2]

The players usually begin the Game with an authorization to issue

---

[2]In some runs of the Carnegie Tech Management Game we have bypassed the portion of the computer program which determines whether or not firms are able to obtain bank loans, and instead introduced direct negotiations between the firms' financial officers and representatives of the "Carnegie Bank and Trust Company." Both our own faculty members and officers of a major Pittsburgh commercial bank have role-played Carnegie bankers in these negotiations.

some additional common stock. If the market value of the stock is adequate, the players may get additional authorization to issue common stock. Funds from new flotations will be available five months after the team applies to market the shares at the price then ruling. Flotation costs will be reflected in the spread between the offering price to the public and the price received by the company. The market price of the stock of each firm is determined every month. The stock price function, based on recent research findings, makes price vary in the long run according to the growth potential of the industry, to other investment opportunities available to the shareholders in the market, and to the demonstrated efficiency of the players in managing the shareholders' investment. In the short run, price may also vary both in response to financial decisions of the firm and in response to random factors.[3]

As an aid in financial planning, players can count on all customers settling their accounts within 30 days following delivery. Their collections are known fairly well one month in advance, and some of them will come in early enough to minimize the problems of synchronizing receipts and payments within the month.

If the firm gets into financial difficulties, there will be provisions for temporary relief. The team can sell any government bonds it may be holding to get immediate access to extra cash. Players can postpone payments to their suppliers for one month at the cost of their discount. If the firm meets minimal requirements, the due dates for short-term bank loans can be extended or temporary demand notes may be issued.

The players may wish to expand their plant at one or more points during the Game, particularly since there are costs associated with overutilization of facilities. They are permitted to expand existing production and storehouse facilities, but not to add new locations.[4] The district warehouses' capacities can be expanded simply by leasing new space, but all other facilities' capacities can be expanded only by capital investment. The players may decide to enlarge the raw materials warehouse, the factory warehouse, or the production plant. After a period of six months, when construction is completed, the costs of production and storage will be adjusted to reflect the additions to capacity.

---

[3]In Game play during the autumn semester of 1963–64, a "Carnegie Stock Exchange" has been organized to permit shares in Game firms to be traded by officers, directors, and other students and faculty members. The stock price function in the computer program was then bypassed, with stock prices for each firm being established each day as a result of actual trading on the Carnegie Stock Exchange. Provision was made for new equity issues by Game firms to be underwritten by a syndicate which would then resell the stock on the Carnegie Stock Exchange. For further details, see Section II.D in Chapter 3.

[4]The University of North Carolina is modifying the Carnegie Game to permit firms to build new factories and warehouses in other regions. See Section III in Chapter 6.

The team can make capital expenditures to expand capacity, but not to modernize its equipment. The rate of technological obsolescence of production equipment in the detergent industry is very low. Rather than modernize, the players will be concerned with spending sufficient sums of money for maintenance. Necessary replacement will be assumed to occur as a result of maintenance expenditures.

Companies in the Carnegie Tech Management Game can be differentiated from each other in many ways. Each firm will eventually market products with different characteristics. The computer is programmed so that it is easy to make the firms differ in cost structure, in initial financial position, in plant capacity, in access to markets, and in a variety of other ways.

The basic actions of the players must be oriented around two activities. They must analyze the output generated by the computer, and, on the basis of this analysis, they must make decisions. The output information is detailed and varied and it is designed to be complete enough to allow modern mathematical techniques to be utilized for planning and decision making. It will be necessary for the firms to develop a system of accounting as well as a system for processing the information received. The magnitude of the problem can be better appreciated by looking at the information received in the areas of production, marketing, and finance.

Production men will receive forms that summarize the following information:

1. The raw materials situation: stocks on hand, quantities on order, deliveries during past month, usage during past month, and current prices.
2. Factory performance: actual quantities produced and shipped (by product and destination), raw material and labor usage by product, employment levels, amounts of overtime and undertime, maintenance expenditures, and equipment downtime.
3. Warehouse transactions: opening and closing inventories, receipts from other warehouses, shipments to other warehouses, sales, and receipts from factory.

The production men will also get, at the beginning of the Game and later at irregular intervals, information about the following:

1. Raw material requirements for each product.
2. Required lead times for raw material orders.
3. Space requirements for raw materials storage.
4. Estimates of "normal" worker productivity for each product.
5. Current hiring and firing costs.
6. Current wage rates (straight time and overtime).
7. Space requirements for storing finished goods.
8. Charges for excess inventory storage.

9. Shipping costs and required shipping times from factory to warehouses.
10. Storage costs at district warehouses.
11. Price changes for various raw materials.

They will get less explicit "reports of past experience" about plant capacity; about the impact of maintenance expenditures, raw material shortages, overtime, and undertime on production; and about the rules for rescheduling shipments to warehouses if actual production differs from scheduled production.

The marketing man will know, after each operating period, the following information about their firms:

1. Expenditures by product and by region for advertising, for retail allowances, and for sales force and promotional efforts.
2. Total expenditures for market research, sales office and administration, and product research and development.
3. Information about the environment, such as current and forecasted annual rates of gross national product, and salesmen's reports on brands introduced and dropped by competitors in each region.
4. Sales by brand and by district warehouse.

As the occasion warrants, they will receive laboratory reports on new products. These reports will scale each product on sudsing, washing power, and gentleness. They will tell raw material requirements and raw material costs. There will also be estimates of expected labor productivity in making the new product.

The company can pay to get additional marketing data on brand preferences of consumers and on market variables, such as share of market or competitors' advertising, distribution, and retail prices. The accuracy of these estimates depends on how much money is spent to obtain them.

Initially, the marketing men will start the Game knowing some specific information about the costs of market studies on various scales and the characteristics of the company's given products (and, to a lesser extent, of competitors' products). They will have less explicit "experiential" data on the potential gains from different kinds of marketing and research expenditures, about the structure of the market, and about the firm's position vis-à-vis competitors.

The finance men will receive at the end of each month the following information:

1. A summary of trial balance accounts, showing the total debits and total credits to each account during the month, as well as the net balance of each account at the end of the month.
2. A balance sheet.
3. Current information on the availability of financing.
4. General information on money and capital markets.

5. An income statement.
6. At the end of every quarter a balance sheet and an income statement for each competitor.

In addition, they will have detailed initial reports on the ways in which accounts are kept and on the ways in which various cash receipts and disbursements occur. The considerations relevant to obtaining various forms of financing will be stated.

As the Carnegie Game is played, the above types of information become the basis for a whole complex of decisions. In the area of production, the players must regularly:

1. Order raw materials.
2. Decide on size of labor force.
3. Decide how much overtime to authorize.
4. Plan how much to spend for maintenance of plant and equipment.
5. Schedule the total quantity of production for the month by product.
6. Decide how to allocate production among warehouses.
7. Decide what transshipments of existing inventories need to be made from factory to district warehouses or among district warehouses.

In the marketing area, the players must regularly:

1. Set wholesale prices and retail allowances by product and by region.
2. Determine advertising expenditures by product and by region.
3. Decide on the total size of sales force, as well as the allocation of salesmen to particular products and regions.

In the financial area, the players must regularly:

1. Authorize certain specific types of disbursements for the coming month.
2. Decide what share of profits should be allocated as dividends to stockholders.
3. Decide (in case there are inadequate cash reserves) what steps should be taken to cut expenditures.

In addition, to survive and grow in the face of competition from other firms, the players must be prepared to consider at frequent intervals:

1. Expenditures for research on new products and for test market studies on consumer acceptance of the products.
2. Expenditures for general market research into the nature of consumer preferences, into the patterns of retail sales, or into the performances of competitors.
3. The desirability of dropping, changing, or adding products or of extending marketing efforts into a new territory.
4. Investments in new facilities for the storage of raw materials or finished goods.
5. Investment in new plant and equipment for production.
6. The advisability of applying for:
   a) Renegotiation of current debt.
   b) Additions to working capital by short-term bank loans.
   c) Long-term additions to capital by issuing stock or by term loans.

Decisions on these matters may not be made very often; when made, they will frequently be long-term commitments. However, the players must be continually alert to their long-run interests, and they must anticipate their requirements while there is still time to act.

The players do not necessarily have to turn in decisions each month pertaining to all aspects of their firm's activity. If no specific decisions are submitted at the start of a month for areas such as marketing and marketing surveys, production, raw material ordering, and product research and development, then the previous decisions will remain in effect. All other decisions are regarded as "one shot" decisions: unless specific authorizations are made at the start of a month, no new actions will be taken in initiating new construction (or cancelling construction already in progress), introducing new products, requesting product comparison tests, ordering transshipments between warehouses, changing accounting statements, nor in undertaking any of the financial transactions for which specific decisions are normally made. Because of this feature, firms in the Carnegie Tech Management Game can be regarded as having a built-in middle management organization which will keep them operating for an indefinite period without continual direction from top management. This provides a great deal of flexibility in the administration of the Game. To increase the ratio of simulated to real time (in order to emphasize some of the long-range aspects of the Game situation), the players might be asked to make complete sets of monthly decisions only in the first month of each quarter. There would then be a choice of either letting the simulated middle-management organization continue these decisions in force (according to the previously stated conventions) or else of allowing the players to spend a brief time examining the results of the first or second month before making a few new decisions for the second or third month of the quarter.[5]

The original Carnegie Tech Management Game is now referred to as the Mark 1 version. It was used at Carnegie from the summer of 1959 through the spring of 1961, and it has also been played at Tulane

---

[5]Despite the large number of decisions which may be made by firms in the Carnegie Tech Management Game, there are of course some areas which may occupy considerable amounts of time for real-world detergent industry managers but which have no direct counterpart in the Game model. In the production sphere, these include process planning and design considerations, product sequencing decisions, and the details of personnel relations. In the marketing area, the details of hiring, training, and supervising salesmen; the details of advertising campaigns; and considerations of coupons, deals, samples, and package design are not incorporated in the Game model. In finance, there are relatively few investment alternatives in the Game, and there are no possibilities for diversification. Through role playing or by modifications of the computer model, however, any of these considerations could be introduced into the Carnegie Game. For example, some suggestions for incorporating personnel problems into the Game are discussed in Section I of Chapter 9.

University, the University of Pittsburgh, the University of North Carolina, Indiana University, and the University of Oklahoma. Mark 1 was programmed for an IBM 650 electronic computer having either one random access memory disk unit or two magnetic tape units as auxiliary storage. It is being reprogrammed at the University of North Carolina for use with a Univac 1105 computer.[6]

In the summer of 1961, we undertook an elaborate revision of the Game model, and we reprogrammed it to run on Carnegie's CDC G–21 electronic computer (with at least two magnetic tape units).[7] For this book the CDC G–21 version, written in GATE, has been translated into compatible FORTRAN versions for the IBM 7070, IBM 7090, and comparable machines. We refer to the new game as the Mark 1.5 version of the Carnegie Tech Management Game.[8] It is the Mark 1.5 game which we have been primarily considering in this section. In the following section, we shall present a detailed description of the Mark 1.5 version of the Carnegie Tech Management Game as it appears to the players, together with blank copies of all decision (input) and information (output) forms which are used. To conclude this chapter, we shall indicate the ways in which the original Mark 1 version of the Carnegie Tech Management Game differed from the present version. This is useful not only for those interested in the evolution of our Game, but it also will enable readers to understand the features of the original Game used for some of the educational and research experiments which are discussed in following chapters.

II. PLAYER'S MANUAL FOR THE CARNEGIE TECH MANAGEMENT GAME[9]

A. Introduction

In this Manual you will find most of what you need to know in order to participate in the Carnegie Tech Management Game. You will be

---

[6]See Section III in Chapter 6.

[7]This computer was called a Bendix G–20 when it was originally installed at Carnegie in 1961. The change in names reflects both the acquisition of the Bendix Computer Division by Control Data Corporation (CDC) and the addition of a second central processor and an enlarged core memory. Throughout this book, we shall simply call this computer a CDC G–21, even though it may be known as a Bendix G–20 or a CDC G–20 at other locations.

[8]It is not called the Mark 2 version because some of us were brash enough to state in print the characteristics we intended to incorporate in Mark 2. Time pressures prevented us from including all these changes in the new Game. Since the current version is about half way between the original version and what we envisioned for Mark 2, we use the name "Mark 1.5" for it. See Kalman J. Cohen and Merton H. Miller, "Some Thoughts on the Management Game of the Future," in (William R. Dill, James R. Jackson, and James W. Sweeney, (eds.), *Proceedings of the Conference on Business Games as Teaching Devices* (New Orleans: Tulane University, 1961) pp. 73–80.

[9]This section is also separately published by Richard D. Irwin, Inc., in a paperback edition under the title, *Player's Manual for the Carnegie Tech Management Game*, by Kalman J. Cohen, William R. Dill, Alfred A. Kuehn, and Peter R. Winters.

given the past history of your firm and you will have an opportunity to raise questions about the details of this exercise at a special briefing session which will be held before your firm is asked to make any decisions. Requests for additional information should be addressed to the Game administrator.

1. Purpose of the Game. The Carnegie Tech Management Game has been developed for both educational and research purposes. As an educational device, it has been designed to give participants an opportunity to apply to complex planning and operating problems the analytical tools and specific skills they have acquired through business experience or study programs. As a research instrument, it has been designed to provide opportunities for studying the decision-making process, small-group behavior, and many related issues.

This Game allows teams of players, functioning as managers in business firms, to compete against other similar firms in a complex economic environment which is simulated by an electronic computer. As managers, the participants make numerous interrelated decisions in marketing, production, finance, accounting, and research. Many of these decisions involve forward planning. Since the participants manage their firms over a sequence of time periods, they should try to develop coordinated policies and programs for the efficient use of the resources under their direction.

As will become clear from your reading of this *Manual,* the word "Game" is used with a specialized meaning in this context. The primary purpose of this exercise is education, not recreation, although you should also find it an interesting and enjoyable experience. This Game was developed as a serious attempt to surmount some of the limitations of the traditional "case study" method of instruction in business by providing a continuing "live" case in which the players must select and identify their own problems, provide the solutions in an organizational rather than a classroom setting, and live with and learn from the results of their decisions and actions. Like most of the ordinary case studies, the content of the Game is based to some extent on an actual business situation, namely the packaged detergent industry. No attempt has been made, however, to provide a completely realistic simulation of that industry. A mountain of specialized detail has been cut away and many additional features not found in the real detergent industry have been deliberately added to provide a Game which was both feasible to play and which captured the essence of a wide variety of the most common business problems.

2. Overview of Industry and Firms. The Carnegie Tech Management Game is a simplified simulation of the packaged detergent industry. The three competing firms in this industry were initially of equal size, but because of differences in their former managements, they will differ slightly when you assume responsibility for their operation. Each firm sells its output in a national market which, for Game purposes, is divided into four geographic areas: East, South, Central, and West.

Each firm has a single factory, located in the Central region. At this factory are the following facilities:

1. A raw materials warehouse.
2. Production facilities having limited total capacity which can be used flexibly to produce different mixes of products.
3. A factory warehouse for the storage of finished products.
4. Facilities for new product research and development.
5. Corporate headquarters and general offices.

In addition, the firm leases warehouse space for storing finished products in each of the four sales regions.

All products are made in the factory on the same equipment with the same work force. In other words, the work force divides its time among products which are scheduled in sequence for production on the same equipment. Therefore, management need not be directly concerned with detailed scheduling of products among workers or machines.

All products are manufactured from one or more of seven basic raw materials. The firm must order raw materials from suppliers in advance of their use in production. Although lead times vary for different materials, deliveries will be made on schedule.

Prices of raw materials are relatively stable. They may occasionally change, but suppliers will normally give at least one month's advance notice of any impending price changes.

The factory production schedule may be modified each month, if management wishes. Actual monthly output may not be the same as scheduled, however. Factory performance (in terms of costs, as well as output) is affected by raw material run-outs, by expenditures for maintenance, by plant capacity and overtime utilization, by limits on the rate at which the work force can be expanded, and by overtime effects on employee productivity.

Management may sometimes find it desirable to expand its facilities. This may be done by increasing capacities of existing facilities; new locations cannot be added. The capacities of district warehouses may be increased simply by leasing new space, but the capacities of the other warehouses and of the factory can be expanded only by capital investments.

All products which the firm has or can develop are distributed through supermarkets and grocery stores for use in the home. Thus the firm's sales consist not of retail sales, but of shipments from their district warehouses to wholesalers and to retail chains. The firm sets only the wholesale prices for their products in each region. Since there is no "fair trading" of detergents, retail prices may vary considerably by region. Retail sales of the firm's products in any month depend on the total retail demand for detergents and on the company's relative effectiveness in influencing consumer behavior by its advertising expenditures, pricing decisions, retail allowances, outlays for sales force and promotion, availability in stock, and by the quality of the product (in terms of three basic product characteristics: washing power, gentleness and sudsing power).

When you take over operation of your firm, it will have one or more products already in production and a backlog of potential new products developed by its laboratories. To develop additional new products, the firm may wish to spend money for product research and development. The greater the expenditures for this purpose over time, the more likely is it that new product ideas will be generated. As many as three independent product research projects can be carried on by the firm's laboratories at any time: undirected research, research directed toward simulation of a product on the market, and/or research directed toward development of a product with specified characteristics.

If management thinks a new product idea is worth further study, it can spend money to draw a sample of consumers to compare it with any other product. These product comparison tests are made without identifying the brands involved, so they are unaffected by such marketing decisions as price, advertising, and distribution. From such test studies, management can decide whether to put the product into actual production.

If at any time management should wish to obtain additional funds, these may be secured in most of the ways normally open to firms. However, the need for outside financing should be anticipated in advance in order to obtain favorable terms.

The quickest means of external financing—a three-month bank note —requires at least a month between the filing of an application and the availability of funds. The size of such a loan is limited by the firm's current assets and recent income.

Term loans of two to ten years' duration are available. In applying for such a loan, the firm is required to state the uses to which these funds will be put. To obtain a term loan, management may have to accept a number of restrictive covenants.

Management may decide to issue additional common stock, provided that it has the necessary authorization. Funds from a stock sale can be available five months after application to an investment banker. The market price of the stock varies according to the growth potential of the industry, other opportunities available to shareholders, and the efficiency of the administration of the shareholders' investment. In the short run, price may vary because of random factors or because of financial decisions of the company.

If the firm gets into financial difficulties, there are provisions for temporary relief. If it is holding any government securities, it can sell some or all of them. Payment on accounts with suppliers can be delayed one month, although discounts for prompt payment will be lost. If the firm meets minimal requirements, three-month bank notes can be renewed for as many as six additional months, or notes may be negotiated into a term loan, or temporary demand notes may be obtained.

Initially, balance sheets and income statements will be given to the management. Within a short time, however, on the basis of the complete trial balance summaries which are provided, the firm's accounting organization is expected to develop statements and reports tailor-made to fit the firm's internal and external needs. An internal control system should also be designed, implemented, and maintained. Each firm is free to adjust the ledger accounts which form the basis for the trial balance summaries which are automatically provided, or to maintain their own accounting systems consonant with accepted accounting and auditing practices.

3. *General Management Functions.* With your board of directors, you must work out your firm's objectives. Yours is a *management* job, requiring development of coordinated policies and proposals for action, interpretation of the results of previous periods to determine what these mean for future policy decisions, and translation of general policy objectives into specific plans and instructions. The job of management can be viewed as progressing along two lines at once—short-run tasks and long-run tasks—as shown in Table 2–1.

Your task as a *management* group is to study performance information, month by month and over longer periods. You must assess what you have done well and what you have done poorly. You must devise ways of summarizing and storing useful information about your performance for future reference. You must prepare summaries of important information for one another. Marketing, for example, should prepare sales forecasts for use in production. Production and marketing should coordinate their information and decisions about inventory levels, raw materials ordering, and introducing new products into production. Research should coordinate its activities to advance innovation

TABLE 2-1

THE JOB OF MANAGEMENT

Function	Short-Run Tasks	Long-Run Tasks
Assimilation of data	Analysis of operating data	Integration of recent data with data from earlier periods and with information received at start of Game
Communication and storage	Pooling of analyses and evaluations of past performance and expected problems	Development of systems to process and record useful data on past performance and future problems
Decision making	Formulation of plans for next operating period and molding these plans into a feasible program for the firm as a whole	Formulation of plans for change: expansion, innovation, financing
Decision implementation	Translation of plans into recorded Game decisions	Translation of plans into specific instructions for members of firm or into recorded Game decisions

efforts while meeting the needs of marketing and production. All managers should also prepare joint forecasts of receipts and expenditures to help in financial planning. Finance in turn should interpret the firm's cash position for the other managers so that they can plan realistic operating and developmental expenditures. Accounting should determine the accounting report needs of the other managers and meet those needs efficiently. The success of a firm in meeting the challenge posed by the market and by the competition is likely to be very much affected by how well and how quickly its management can solve internal problems of communication, coordination, and control.

B. Detailed Description of Industry and Firm Operations

1. Marketing. The detergent industry in the Carnegie Management Game consists of three large manufacturing firms. These firms sell directly to wholesalers or to chain store central warehouses, which in turn distribute the detergents through retail outlets, where they are bought by consumers. The consumers compare products on the basis of three fundamental characteristics—sudsing, washing power, and gentleness—and they buy detergents which suit their needs. Consumers are influenced by retail price, advertising, retail displays and shelf space, competing products, and, of course, whether or not the product is stocked by their favorite grocery. The national detergent market is divided into four geographical regions: East, South, Central, and West; consumer tastes and reactions to advertising, price, and so on, may differ among these regions.

Retailers estimate future demand for each product on the basis of its recent demand, and they place orders with the wholesalers in an attempt to maintain balanced inventories. The wholesalers respond in a similar way, in ordering from the manufacturing firms.

Market demand and sales, and the retail-wholesale structure are simulated on a weekly basis. Orders placed by retailers in one week are received by them at the end of the following week; wholesalers receive their shipments from the firms' warehouses at the end of the week during which orders are placed.

The retail detergent market is seasonal. Summer months may range as high as 25 to 30 percent above the average monthly sales; during the winter, sales tend to fall off, as much as 20 to 30 percent below the average; spring and fall months tend to be grouped around the average.[10]

Firms can purchase market survey estimates, for their own and for competing products, of advertising expenditures, retail selling prices, retail case sales, the percentage of retail stores normally carrying specific brands, and the percentage of retail stores normally carrying a specific brand which temporarily do not have it in stock.

a) Advertising. The firm employs the services of a large national advertising agency, through which it can make advertising expenditures for each product in each geographical region. Presently the advertising agency is allocating these funds to specific media such as television, magazine ads, radio, and direct mailing, and it has been effective in doing so.

At the beginning of each quarter (that is, in months 1, 4, 7, 10), the firm can make three-month advertising contracts for each region. The contract amount stipulates what the firm intends to spend in *each month* of the quarter in that region. Presently, contracts provide for a 10 percent discount on the stipulated amount. If more than the contract amount is spent in a month, the excess will be charged for full value. Should less be spent in a month, no discount is given and all discounts awarded earlier in the quarter will be rescinded and must be paid in the following month.

A contract's advertising expenditure in a region may be divided among products in any way desired. As an example, suppose an adver-

---

[10]Months 1, 13, 25, . . . correspond to January; months 2, 14, 26, . . . correspond to February; etc.

tising contract is made in month 4 for the Eastern region for $100,000, and that in this month $60,000 is spent on product A and $40,000 on product B. These products will receive $100,000 of effective advertising, and the firm will be charged $90,000. Suppose that in month 5, $70,000 is spent on A and $50,000 on B. The products will receive $120,000 of effective advertising and the firm will be charged $110,-000. If in month 6, $60,000 is spent on A and $30,000 on B, these products will get $90,000 effective advertising, but the firm will be charged $90,000; in addition, $20,000 in lost discounts (also charged to month 6 advertising expense) must be paid in month 7.

b) Sales Force. Salesmen employed by the firm devote most of their time to retail outlets, encouraging store managers to stock the firm's products and give them a good location in the store, and helping develop retail promotions, sales displays, and so on. The firm specifies the total number of salesmen it will employ, and how their time and efforts should be divided among products and regions.

There is no direct cost of hiring or laying off salesmen, but new salesmen need to be trained, and erratic hirings and layoffs may affect sales force morale. The combined salary and travel expenses of each salesman cost the firm $1,000 per month. A small sales force may find that it spends a large part of its time traveling, so that it has little time left to sell the product effectively. On the other hand, store managers become annoyed if salesmen call too frequently.

c) Prices and Retail Allowances. The firm sets prices to wholesalers, by product and by region, and its case sales are made at these prices. The average price to the consumer is 35 percent above the price received by the firm. Prices may be set at any level in each region, and they may be changed each month.

Retail allowances set by the firm represent rebates to retailers on the shipments to them from wholesalers. Usually this allowance is passed on to consumers in the form of lower prices at the retail stores. Retail allowances also stimulate the retailers to increase their purchases and inventories. These allowances, to the extent that retailers take advantage of them, are paid by the firm during the month they are given. If allowances are given frequently, they soon represent simply a lower regular price to retailers and consumers.

Both prices to the wholesalers and retail allowances are stated in terms of dollars per case.

d) Market Survey Reports. The firm can obtain information about advertising, retail price, retail sales, percent of retail stores distributing products, and retail stockout levels, both for their own and for competing products, cross-classified by brand and region. Expenditures made for these market surveys determine the quality and extent of their samples, and thus the precision and reliability of the results. Some categories of information are easier and less expensive to obtain than are others.

Advertising expenditures are estimated by media surveys; they thus represent gross expenditures without consideration of any advertising contract arrangements that may have been made. Retail case-sale estimates are based on the physical volume of consumer sales of each marketed product in the region. Distribution percentages are estimates of the percentage of retail outlets that regularly stock each product, adjusted for the sales volume of individual stores or products. Percent stockout similarly represents the percentage of stores currently out of stock that normally carry the product. Estimates are made of average retail prices of each product in a region.

Whenever a firm purchases any type of market survey information, it will automatically and without further charge also obtain a report showing the wholesale prices and retail allowances currently in force for all brands of detergent in each region.

2. Production. Each firm has a single factory located in the Central region. Raw materials that make up the finished product are ordered from suppliers and stored in the raw materials warehouse, to be used as required by the production schedule. These materials are combined in stated proportions by the factory work force to produce the finished product, which may be stored in the finished goods warehouse at the factory or immediately shipped to one of the four regional warehouses.

a) Procurement of Raw Materials. Each manufactured product requires several raw materials. These may be ordered each month at the listed market prices. Different raw materials have different procurement lead times; for example, materials e, f, and g have a one-month lead time, that is, they will be received in the raw materials warehouse at the end of the month in which they are ordered, and will be available for manufacturing in the next month. The other materials have longer lead times. Lead times are given in Table 2–2.

TABLE 2–2

RAW MATERIAL LEAD TIMES

Material	Lead Time
a	3 months
b	3 months
c	2 months
d	2 months
e	1 month
f	1 month
g	1 month

Once a material order has been placed, it is impossible to cancel it. The amounts ordered are always delivered at the time specified. Unwanted raw materials in the warehouse can be dumped by selling them on the open market for 60 percent of their book cost.

b) Factory Operations. The factory, with its equipment and personnel, is capable of producing a variety of products. These are sequenced on the same equipment by the work force.

The initial plant and equipment can effectively utilize up to 300,000 man-hours of work. The actual productivity for any product will depend on the number of workers, machinery downtime, and overtime. Workers on the payroll are paid $3.25 per hour for a minimum of 173 hours per worker per month; the workers receive time-and-a-half for overtime. The number of workers on the payroll may be increased or decreased each month; hiring and firing costs are $1,000 for hiring each worker and $800 for laying off a worker. In one month any reduction is possible, but an increase is limited to the larger of: *(a)* 15 percent of the present work force, and *(b)* 100 workers. Hiring and firing occur at the beginning of the month.

Scheduled production for a month will be automatically reduced if it requires more raw materials than available, if it exceeds the plant capacity, or if it exceeds the overtime limit of the work force. The firm specifies an overtime limit, but regardless of how high this authorization is, there is a natural limit beyond which the work force will not go. Even though overtime is authorized, it will neither be used nor paid for unless scheduled production makes it necessary.

c) Maintenance. Normal maintenance expenditures can be expected to keep machines and equipment at a "normal" operating efficiency. Machinery downtime is deducted from available working hours (both straight time and overtime). Reduced maintenance expenditures will lead to lower operating efficiencies, that is, to more downtime. However, there is a limit to the effectiveness of maintenance spending. Oiling a machine excessively cannot be expected to increase its efficiency significantly.

d) Finished Goods Distribution. The finished goods distribution system consists of a factory warehouse and four regional warehouses. The month's production will be sent, as the firm directs, to any of these five warehouses and will be available for sale (from the regional warehouses) or for transshipment (from any warehouse) at the beginning of the following month. (It is not possible to return goods to the factory warehouse.) Transit time depends on the distance between the warehouses, as shown in Table 2–3. Transshipments are started immediately at the beginning of the month, and as soon as the shipments are received the goods are available for sale. For example, a shipment from the factory warehouse to the Western regional warehouse takes two weeks; the goods would be available in the Western warehouse for sale at the beginning of the third week of the month.

TABLE 2–3

TRANSSHIPMENT TRANSIT TIMES BETWEEN WAREHOUSES

(In Weeks)

	E	S	C	W
FW	1	1	1	2
E		2	2	3
S			1	3
C				2

Shipping and transshipping costs are given in Table 2–4. There is no charge for putting production into the factory warehouse.

TABLE 2–4

SHIPPING AND TRANSSHIPPING COSTS BETWEEN LOCATIONS

($/Case)

	E	S	C	W
Factory	.20	.20	.10	.30
FW	.25	.25	.15	.35
E		.25	.20	.40
S			.20	.35
C				.30

e) Warehouse Storage Costs. No charge is made for materials stored in the raw materials and factory warehouses. These two warehouses have limited capacities, however, and an attempt to store beyond capacity will result in excess storage charges, to cover the costs of handling and storing the excess in nearby, readily accessible locations. The capacities and excess storage costs are shown in Table 2–5.

TABLE 2–5

WAREHOUSE CAPACITIES AND EXCESS STORAGE COSTS

Warehouse	Capacity	Excess Storage Cost
Raw material..............	30,000,000 lbs.	$.01/lb.
Factory finished goods	300,000 cases	$.15/case

Rented regional warehouses offer unlimited storage capacity at a fixed charge per case. These storage charges are shown in Table 2–6.

TABLE 2–6

REGIONAL WAREHOUSE STORAGE COSTS

Warehouse	Cost
E	$.20/case
S	.12
C	.15
W	.18

Storage charges in all warehouses are based on inventories on hand at the beginning of the month.

f) Construction of New Facilities. The firm may increase the capacity of the factory and the raw materials and factory-finished-goods warehouses by constructing new facilities. Investment in new plant and equipment raises the capacity of the factory in terms of effective labor hours. (Note that this investment provides more equipment of the same kind, and does not change the basic productivity of the employees.) Expansion of the warehouses is stated in the same units as are their capacities. After the decision has been made to expand a facility, an engineering company spends one month developing plans, construction begins in the second month, and the enlarged facility is completed at the end of the sixth month, ready for use at the beginning of the following month.

Table 2–7 shows the costs of the various investment possibilities. If the desired increase in capacity is $\triangle$, then the total cost is $m\triangle + b$, which must not be smaller than the minimum investment shown in Table 2–7. For example, a 1,000,000 pound increase in the raw materials warehouse capacity would cost $60,000 [$.04/lb.) $\times$ (1,000,000 lbs.) + $20,000 = $60,000]. Since this is less than the $100,000 minimum investment required for the raw materials warehouse, it would not be permitted. The minimum permissible expansion of raw materials warehouse capacity would be 2,000,000 pounds [($.04/lb.) $\times$ (2,000,000 lbs.) + $20,000 = $100,000].

TABLE 2–7

CONSTRUCTION COSTS FOR NEW FACILITIES

Parameter	Raw Materials Warehouse	Factory	Finished Goods Warehouse
m	$.04/lb.	$110/man-hour	$3.00/case
b	$20,000	$2,000,000	$5,000
Minimum investment	$100,000	$4,000,000	$100,000

Construction costs are to be paid as follows. Suppose the initial construction decision was made at the beginning of month 12. The engineering firm charges 5 percent of the total cost for developing plans and submits this bill at the end of the first month; in the example the bill would be paid at the beginning of month 13. Construction begins at the start of month 13, and a bill for 45 percent of the total cost is presented at the end of this, the second month, and would be paid at the start of month 14. The final bill is presented as the construction is completed in the sixth month (month 17), and in our example would be paid in month 18. The increased capacity is available for use at the start of month 18.

Construction may be cancelled at any time. If this is done, however, partially completed work will be lost, and all construction bills must be paid after they have been presented.

3. *Product Development, Testing, and Introduction.* Product development consists of a range of activities. It begins with product research and development through which the firm attempts to discover new products. Once a product has been developed in the laboratory, product comparison tests of consumer tastes may be made to investigate its potential marketability. Finally, a new product may be introduced first to the factory and then to the market.

a) Product Research and Development. When a new management takes over operations of the firm, it will find that it is marketing either one, two, or three different brands of detergents. The firm may also have a backlog of potential new detergents which have previously been developed by its laboratory. It is possible for the firm to develop additional new detergents, to modify one of its existing brands, or to copy a detergent which a competitor is marketing. This is done by authorizing expenditures for product research and development activities.

Each firm has a laboratory, engaged in detergent research and development. As many as three different types of research projects may be carried on in this laboratory at any time. The "project 1" research goal is to develop new types of detergents, without any restrictions being placed on the properties of these detergents. The "project 2" research goal is to synthesize specific products which are currently being marketed (either by the firm or its competitors). Finally, "project 3" research attempts to develop new detergents possessing a particular set of properties.

To pursue any of these three product research objectives, a firm must spend money for research and development which is directed toward the associated type of research project. The outcomes of any particular research project cannot be accurately predicted, since the development of a new product depends upon a great many chance factors. However, the amount of money spent in pursuing a particular type of research project, when suitably cumulated over a number of months, determines the probability of that project generating a new product idea. Each of the three types of research projects is pursued by a separate staff, so there is no interaction between the amounts of money spent on one research project and the probability of another research project developing a new product idea.

Many of the new product ideas generated by the research laboratories will not be worth very much. Even when a relatively good product is developed, its superiority may not be apparent until product comparison tests are run on it or until it is placed on the market.

Whenever a new product idea is generated by the research laboratories, the firm will receive a New Product Development Report which describes its composition (in terms of the amount of each of seven possible raw materials required to make it), its characteristics (sudsing, washing power, and gentleness) as revealed by laboratory tests, the standard amount of labor required to produce it, and the raw material cost per case at standard raw material prices.

In deciding what directives they wish to give to their research staffs, management should realize that the more narrowly they define the goals guiding their scientists, the less likely it is that these scientists will generate any product ideas. However, when a particular new type of detergent is desired by management, assuming that the desired product is technologically feasible, it is more likely to be obtained from fairly closely directed research than it is from a non-structured research project.

As the general level of technological achievement in the packaged detergent industry increases, a firm's research laboratory is likely to generate better and better new product ideas.

b) *Product Comparison Tests.* The firm may order tests of consumers' "blindfold" reactions to pairs of products, including products on the market and their own unmarketed products, in any combination. These nationwide tests take a month to complete. Any number of paired comparisons may be made in a month; each is independent of the others.

Two types of tests are available, at different costs. The *single comparison* test presents a sample of consumers with the two products in unmarked packages. Information is obtained about the proportions of the sample preferring product 1, preferring product 2, and having no preference between them with respect to sudsing, washing power, gentleness, and overall desirability. Similar to the single comparison test, the second type of test is a *repeat comparison* test, in which the consumers are given samples of the unmarked packages two different times. Information is obtained about the proportion of the sample preferring product 1 on both the first and the second comparisons, the proportion preferring product 1 on the first comparison but product 2 on the second comparison, and so on, for each of the same categories used on the single comparison test. The repeat comparison test is a forced choice, so the no-preference response does not appear.

The testing company charges a fixed fee of $2,000 plus $7.50 per consumer sampled for the single comparison test, and a fixed fee of $3,000 plus $12.50 per consumer sampled for the repeat comparison test.

 c) *New Brand Introduction and Product Replacement.* Any marketed or unmarketed product that a firm has may be introduced under any of the three brand names (A, B, C) at any time.[11] This introduction will be either a product replacement or else a new product introduction (if no product under the same brand name was marketed during the previous month).

In the month a decision is recorded to introduce a product under a hitherto unused brand name, this new product may be produced in the factory. In the following month wholesalers' inventories will automatically be filled from the firm's regional warehouses if a non-zero but reasonable price is charged, and the product will become available at retail outlets during the month. During the first month when wholesalers and retailers are buying a new product to "fill up the pipelines," the firm's sales of this new product may be higher than those it will experience during the next few months. Once the pipelines are filled, then the usual reordering behavior of retailers and wholesalers becomes effective. Any time before this market introduction the firm can spend money on advertising and salesmen for the new product. Advertising and promoting a new product before it is placed on the market usually causes the initial demand to be higher than it otherwise would be.

In the month a decision is made to replace a product, the new product may be produced in the factory. During that month the old product continues to be sold by the firm, but all of the old product left in the firm's finished goods inventory at the end of that month will be dumped at 50 percent of its cost of goods made. The following month the new product will be offered to the wholesalers and retailers in the same way existing products are. The new product is gradually intermixed with the stocks of the old product already in the hands of the wholesalers and retailers, so that the pipeline inventory levels are

---

[11]The only exception is that an introduction or replacement cannot be made for the same brand in two successive months. Thus, for example, if in month 17 a firm introduces a new brand C (either as a product replacement or a new brand introduction), then it cannot introduce an even newer brand C until month 19 at the earliest.

not drastically affected by a product replacement. Some of the old product's advertising and distribution effectiveness will be retained for the brand name, and consumers will be loyal to the brand name to the extent that the new product is as good as or superior to the old product.

4. *Finance.* In the finance area, the firm currently performs five basic functions: disbursing cash, investing in government securities, managing accounts receivable, obtaining debt and equity funds, and controlling the firm's cash level. The first three activities are already organized under capable department heads and require a minimum of direction from top management.

Each firm maintains its principal checking accounts with a large commercial bank in the Central region. In the past no particular bank has seemed markedly different from the others in terms of costs, credit availability, and other services. All debt financing in the past has been arranged by the bank handling the firm's principal checking accounts. Equity funds have generally been obtained through the services of investment bankers.

a) Disbursing and Accounts Payable. The disbursing department carries out much of the work that lies primarily in the realm of middle management. The organization follows the orders and policies laid down by the chief financial officer.

Routine disbursement on accounts such as factory payroll, research, salesmen compensation, retail allowance expenditures, advertising, construction, and others, are made automatically by the financial organization without further directions.

Specific management authorization is needed before any funds will be disbursed for the payment of: (1) raw materials accounts payable, (2) estimated federal income taxes, (3) special types of loan repayments, and (4) dividends to stockholders.

Raw material suppliers' terms are 3 percent/30 net/60. All bills past the discount date must be paid immediately. Other payments to take advantage of the discounts offered should be added to this figure. Advance payments will not be accepted.

A federal income tax payment is required in the third month of every quarter. In the first quarter, one half of the remainder of last year's tax must be paid. In the second quarter, all of the remaining tax liability from last year must be paid. The disbursing department will see that these two payments are made automatically.

In the third and fourth quarters, the firm should make payment on one fourth of the estimated tax for the current year. The disbursing department will act only as directed on these two payments. The Internal Revenue Service usually checks the reasonableness of these estimated payments and may notify the firm if an estimate seems far out of line.

Any tax credit at the end of the year can be carried over and applied in the following year. Such credits cannot be used to obtain cash refunds from tax payments in previous years.

The disbursing department will make *advance* purchases of short-term notes if so directed. Due notes are automatically paid if not renewed.

The disbursing department, acting only on orders from top management, will make both regular and accelerated payments on the principal of term loans. However, it will automatically make the appropriate interest payments and maintain close liaison with the bank in this regard.

Dividends may be declared in the third month of each quarter. If there is a payment deficit outstanding on a term loan after the first of the month, *no* dividends should be declared. The declaration should not exceed the dividend declared (per share) in the corresponding quarter the year before, if the firm has a term loan that contains such a covenant.

The disbursing department will compute the dividends payable using the declared amount per share, make the accounting entries, and prepare and submit the necessary information and statements to the firm's bank. The firm's bank will check for violation of term-loan covenants. Dividend payments will not be altered, but the bank may make the entire loan immediately payable if violations occur. The following month, the bank will automatically distribute the dividend checks as part of its regular service on the firm's account.

b) Government Securities. The firm is assumed to be carrying out government security transactions frequently during every month, dealing with 91-day bills, 182-day bills, and longer-term debt instruments. The government securities department follows the general policies set by the finance manager.

The level of average government security investment can be reduced in any month. The level can be increased in any month in which the firm is free from bank overdrafts. If neither an increase nor decrease is directed, the average investment level will be maintained.

The firm will receive interest on the average amount of securities held during each month at the average market interest rate for such securities.

If the firm holds any government securities, it is assumed that the government securities department is in operation, requiring a fixed expense of $10,000 per month. This expense is avoided when the firm does not have any position in government securities. When the average investment level is changed, additional activity is required and additional transaction expense is incurred, resulting in a variable expense of 0.5 percent of the amount of change.

c) *Accounts Receivable.* Throughout every region, the firm sells on terms of net 30 days. In the past the accounts receivable department has been successful in getting all customers to pay promptly. There are no bad debts. Receipts lag sales by approximately a month, but they are 100 percent of sales.

d) *Sources of Outside Financing.* Each firm has three outside sources of funds: seasonal financing through bank notes, intermediate and long-term debt financing through bank term loans, and long-term equity financing through the sale of common stock.

Ninety-day bank notes and two- to ten-year loans are presently available from the firm's regular bank at interest rates comparable to money market rates, but modified on the basis of the firm's application and position. In the past, more favorable credit terms have been made available to firms which are able to anticipate their needs and communicate them in advance to the bank. A two month's notice is the generally preferred minimum time on such applications.

Bank notes may be renewed to get up to nine consecutive months of short-term funds. At the end of the third and sixth month the firm may maintain, raise, or lower the face amount on the renewal application. Different interest rates can result. While all interest rates are nominally quoted on a per annum basis, they are actually used to discount each note when it is issued.

In its application for a term loan, a firm must clearly state the purpose for which the proceeds of the loan will be used. Covenants which depend on the strength of a firm's application and position and on the proposed maturity are attached to all term loans. In the past, banks have made the most favorable offers on the shorter-term loans of two or three years. A term loan may be obtained to replace an existing loan. Term loans accrue interest on the unpaid balance. Payments on the principal and interest must be made either quarterly or semiannually.

Sale of common stock can be made through a fully underwritten public issue by making arrangements with an investment banker. In the past it has taken five months from the date of application until funds are obtained. This is expected to continue. Investment bankers customarily give quotations of price and cost without any obligation to the firms until authorization to proceed has been given.

Neither the firm's commercial nor investment bankers have many explicit restrictions or requirements which must be met before a firm's application is received. In fact, the bankers may well make exceptions to their usual "rules of thumb" when considering applications from promising firms.

Details of application procedures, considerations, offers, and terms for each type of outside financing are given in the following three sections. General interest rates may fluctuate from time to time, and this will affect bank loan offers. However, changes in interest rates and stock prices will be noted in the *Tech Street Journal* each month.

i) Ninety-Day Bank Notes. To apply for an initial ninety-day loan, the firm should be free from existing notes, or else it should be requesting a note to start two or more months after the present note is due, or else, if it is in good standing, it should be requesting a note to start one month after the present note is due.[12]

The bank will compare the amount of the application with the firm's cash generating ability demonstrated in the last three months and with the size of the firm's current assets. The bank will further consider the firm's relations with its suppliers, relations with the bank on regular account, relations with the bank on previous notes, the timing of the application, and the firm's overall financial status. This will include a check on the firm's current ratio, which should be 1.33 or higher if no ending cash balances have been below the minimum specified in any note within the last six months. If there have been minimum cash balance violations, either a current ratio of 2.0 or better in each of the last six months or an average current ratio of 2.2 or better over the last six months will be required.

The bank will either: (1) accept the application for the amount desired and at the time desired, stating the interest rate for the loan and the minimum cash balance that must be maintained while the note is held; or (2) make a counteroffer on a reduced amount and/or at a later availability; or (3) reject the application, stating some of the reasons for its action.

If the bank has made an offer by accepting the application or making a counteroffer, the firm can:

1. Accept the offer. This course of action is automatically assumed, unless (2) or (3) below is explicitly chosen. The bank will issue the note at the beginning of the month specified if (2) or (3) below is not otherwise indicated, and if failure of the firm does not become apparent after application.
2. Make a new application (which will automatically cancel any current offer up to and including the month before issue).
3. Reject the current offer (up to and including the month of issue).

The bank will remember failures to give any advance notice on cancellations when considering future applications. If the bank has rejected

---

[12]Warning: the bank will only maintain *one* outstanding offer on a note at any one time. If a firm has an acceptable offer, it should wait until it receives the loan before making application for any other notes.

an application, the firm can make another application or let the situation stand. If a note is issued, it is discounted at the interest rate offered at the time of issue. The entire amount of interest is charged in the firm's accounting records to interest expense of the month issued.

A note can be repaid in three ways:

1. Advance purchase of entire note (at face value) *before* it is due.
2. Payment when due. (In this case, no action is required; the disbursing department will pay it automatically.)
3. Renew the note as of the due date. If the application for renewal is accepted, the bank will automatically adjust the firm's checking account balance to take care of the note becoming due.

If a firm wishes to renew a note, the following are necessary conditions:

1. The bank presently holds a note which is either a new loan or a note which has been renewed once.
2. *a)* One month's notice is given, in the event an equal or lesser amount is being requested on the new note.
    b) Two months' notice is given, in the event a greater amount is being requested on the new note.
    c) If in very good standing, one month's notice is given on an increased amount.

The bank will follow the same procedure on renewal applications as for initial loan applications. It will also make a comparison between net working capital at the time the present note was issued and at the time of the renewal application. The bank's action on the renewal application and the firm's alternatives are the same as for an initial note. However, if a new loan has been renewed twice, it cannot be further renewed.

ii) Term Loans.   If portions of an existing term loan are still outstanding at the time application is made for a new term loan, it will be assumed that through a combination of regular and accelerated payments, the present term loan will be repaid at least by the month the loan applied for becomes available. (A part of the new term loan can be used for this purpose.) Any term loan must be outstanding at least six months before an application for another will be considered.

In considering the amount of a term loan application, the bank will appraise the firm's cash generating ability in the last twelve months and the projected debt/equity ratio. It will also consider the timing of application, the firm's relations with its suppliers, relations with the bank on notes, relations with the bank on previous term loans, the firm's overall financial status, the size of the desired regular installment payment, the term of the loan, and the purposes for which the proceeds will be used.

The bank will do one of the following:

1. Accept the firm's application, granting the requested amount of loan for the desired term with the regular installment payment and availability date that were asked for. In this case, the bank will specify the interest rate, repayment interval, the range within which the firm must maintain its working capital (expressed as current ratios), and other covenants which must be maintained until the loan plus interest is repaid.
2. Make a counteroffer on a reduced amount or on a larger regular payment and/or at a later availability.
3. Reject the application, stating some of the reasons for its action.

The firm then has the same alternatives as stated in Section *i* above for ninety-day bank notes.

If a term loan is made, the firm will receive the total amount of the loan. Interest is accrued monthly on the unpaid balance. At the time that each regular payment on the principal is due, the disbursing department will automatically pay to the bank all interest accrued and payable. Payment on the regular principal must be explicitly ordered by management. If the payment on the principal is not made in full, the bank will record the payment deficit, which will remain payable and continue to accrue interest at the rate stated in the loan.

Payment on term loan deficits must also be explicitly directed by management; this should be added to any *regular* payment on principal. While any term loan payment deficit is outstanding, no new construction may be started and no dividends may be paid. If the bank considers that the firm has failed too often to make term loan payments, either too many months in a row or throughout the life of the loan, it will make the entire amount of the unpaid principal and interest immediately payable, at a penalty interest rate twice that at which the loan was made.

Accelerated payments on all or a part of the unpaid principal may be made in any month in which payment deficits and regular payments, if any, are also taken care of, if at least one month's notice of the firm's exact intentions has been given. The disbursing department will notify the bank if so directed and will make accelerated payments as directed. (If the minimum notice is not given or if payment does not reasonably coincide with the statement of intentions, the accelerated payment will not be accepted.) Notice of advance payment may be cancelled at any time, but any cancellations or failures to follow stated intentions will be noted by the bank in the firm's record.

At the time each accelerated payment is made and accepted, the bank will charge the firm for any accrued interest on the principal paid, plus a service charge for the transaction. The latter is based on the interest rate, and considers the number of months the loan has (or had) to run and the number of months' notice given on the accelerated payment of principal.

The bank may make the loan balance immediately payable for violation of covenants. This is not automatically done, however, when any particular loan covenant is violated. Rather, the bank considers its entire banking relationship with the firm before deciding whether to call a loan for this reason.

The bank prefers to make term loans of two, three, or four years' duration, but will consider applications for up through ten years. Terms of whole years are customary. The bank in the past has specified repayment intervals of three months on two-, three-, or four-year term loans, and repayment intervals of six months on term loans lasting more than four years.

The purposes for which the proceeds of a term loan will be used must be specified in the firm's application. If the firm is contemplating use of other funds for expansion of their physical plant, that amount must also be specified at the time of application. If the firm is planning to use all or part of the proceeds to pay off a current term loan, the entire unpaid portion should be considered as "Fixed Liability" for purposes of this application. An acceptable offer should be obtained before giving notice of accelerated payment, if necessary, on the present term loan.

The bank will only maintain one outstanding offer on a term loan at a time. If a firm has an acceptable offer, it should wait until it receives the proceeds before making application for any other term loans.

iii) Equity Funding. In any month when other acceptable stock sale transactions are not proceeding, application will be taken by an investment banker for a fully underwritten public issue four months from the month of application. The investment banker will consider the firm's stock price history and the size of the issue. He will quote probable prices to the public and to the company with an offering date four months after the month of application.

In the month following application, the firm can either:

1. Authorize the investment banker to proceed with the details of the issue (to enlist other underwriters, undertake stabilizing activities, complete an investigation and analysis of the firm, draft a prospectus and SEC registration statement, and arrange for printing, distribution, and other matters). The offering date is set for the first business day of the third month after authorization is given, with all proceeds available by the close of that month. The firm directly incurs a $15,000 financial transaction

expense every month that an issue is in process (for legal fees, prospectus printing, extra clerical help, etc.).

2. Ask for another quotation.
3. Take no action. If authorization on the most recent quotation is not given, the investment banker will withdraw that quotation the month following application.

In the following months, before the date that the SEC registration statement becomes effective (the middle of the month before issue), the firm can either:

1. Postpone the sale *once* for one month at a financial transaction expense of $20,000 to compensate for extension of the effective date of the SEC registration statement and other negotiation expense.
2. Cancel the sale, at a cost of $20,000 per month since authorization was given, to compensate the investment banker for his services to date.

The final sale price to the public will be one dollar less than the stock price at the close of the last business day of the month preceding issue. The final price to the company will be the final sale price to the public less the "investment banker's spread" (difference between the quoted prices upon which authorization was given). The investment banker will obtain proceeds on all shares offered, subtract his discount (charged in the firm's accounting records to financial transaction expense in the month of issue), and turn over the proceeds to the firm by the end of the month. (Common stock will be credited in the firm's accounting records at the gross, or public, price.)

e) Maintaining Cash Level. Most of its cash is kept in a checking account with the same commercial bank from which the firm generally obtains its notes and term loans. The firm should plan cash flows so that the following two requirements are met:

1. There should always be at least enough cash during the month to meet one week's disbursements (that is, the operating cash balance must not be less than one-fourth of the operating disbursements of the month).
2. There is a positive cash balance at the end of each month.

If either condition is not met, the bank will take appropriate action, as follows:

1. A service charge of $1,000, normally waived if the firm maintains the minimum balance required, may be made.
2. A demand note will probably be issued at 12 percent annual interest (minimum charge: one month), which is payable immediately on the first business day of the next month.
3. If the amount of the shortage can conveniently be reduced, the bank may require the firm during the month to liquidate its holdings of government securities and/or to let supplier bills go past the discount date in

order to help meet the shortage. Normally, the bank will avoid issuing demand notes greater than $200,000.
4. The necessity of issuing a demand note and/or correcting cash flows during the month will influence the bank in its consideration of future financial applications.

If the firm receives a bank note, a required minimum cash balance, which may be higher or lower than normal requirements, will be explicitly stated. Any failure to maintain this minimum will be noted as a violation of the note agreement and may adversely affect the availability of future notes or loans.

f) Stock Prices. The market price of the stock over the long run will depend on the market's perception of the efficiency of the management as attested by its ability to generate earnings on the capital currently invested in the enterprise and its ability to achieve a rate of growth in earnings and assets commensurate with the growth potential of the industry. In the short run the stock price is subject to other influences, stemming primarily from the market's interpretation (or misinterpretation) of abrupt changes in dividend rates.

g) Dividend Policy. The firm has an established dividend rate, and it is regarded by the stock market as a company with a dividend stabilization policy. Hence, the market does not expect the firm to raise its rate in the face of rising profits until it is satisfied that the higher rate can safely be maintained without undue strain and with little danger that it might have to be cut back again in the immediate future. By the same token, the market does not expect the firm to cut its dividend rate until it feels that the rate is completely out of line with future earnings prospects for the company. The stock is widely held, predominantly by investors seeking substantial current income and reasonable growth.

5. Accounting. A summary of trial balance accounts will be provided by the accounting department at the close of every month. This summary gives the sum of debits and credits to the accounts during the month, and the new balances at the close of the month.

The firm is responsible for setting up and controlling accounting, cost accounting, and internal auditing policies, as well as for issuing periodic statements and reports to management, the board of directors, and the stockholders.

Certain of the accounts represent the firm's liabilities; these accounts are set up so that liabilities due in the coming month are kept separate from other current liabilities which extend over the rest of the next twelve months.

Accepted accounting conventions have been followed in handling the accounts. In particular, finished goods and raw materials inventories are valued on an average cost basis, in which the units and dollar value of receipts are added to the units and dollar values remaining in the accounts, and withdrawals are credited by the average value per unit at the time of withdrawal times the number of units withdrawn. Credits to the reserve for depreciation are made using the declining balance method, with appropriate rates for different kinds of property.

A special cost-of-goods-manufactured report is prepared monthly. Labor costs represent the actual labor hours spent on each product in the factory. Materials are charged as they are used. Depreciation of the raw materials warehouse and the factory, maintenance, supervisory and factory overhead, and hiring and personnel expense are distributed among products on the basis of cases produced. Idle labor hours are charged to factory overhead. All of these costs are debited to the work-in-process accounts, and credited from these to the finished goods accounts at the end of the month. Costs of shipping and transshipping, regional warehouse storage, and excess storage at the factory warehouse are debited directly to expense accounts, as is the depreciation of the factory-finished-goods warehouse.

If a firm wants to change the accounting procedures currently being followed, it can make offsetting adjustments to any accounts in the next month. These adjustments must be signed by the firm's president and controller, and will be available for the auditors' inspection. Changing the depreciation calculations, for example, will affect current expenses, profits, and taxes, and will eventually affect the firm's cash position. Once a firm adopts a different accounting convention, it must continue to follow this convention consistently.

End-of-year adjustments are automatically made early in January (months 1, 13, etc.) as follows:

a) "Income Tax This Year" is shifted to "Other Income Tax—Last Year."
b) The difference between "Profit—Year to Date" and "Dividends Declared —Year to Date" is added to "Retained Earnings—Beginning of Year," zeroing out "Profit—Year to Date" and "Dividends Declared—Year to Date."

C. Decision Records and Information Reports

1. *Recording Decisions.* In any month a firm may record all, part, or none of the possible decisions summarized in the next section. The only stipulation is that if any decision records are submitted, *each* record submitted must be *completely* filled out. Otherwise, a firm may

select *any number or combination of records it wishes to turn in.* The two basic assumptions made in the Carnegie Tech Management Game plus four supplementary notes are given below.

Assumptions. (1) If no decisions are recorded and submitted in the following areas, no action will be taken (that is, generally, all decisions are "zeroed out"):

Accounting
Construction (see Note 1 below)
Finance (see Note 2 below)
New Product Introduction
Product Comparison Tests
Transshipments
Raw Material Dumping

(2) If no decisions are recorded and submitted in the following areas, the decisions in effect at the end of the previous month will be repeated in the current month:

Marketing Decisions (see Note 3 below)
Market Survey Decisions
Production and Raw Material Ordering (see Note 4 below)
Product Research and Development

Supplementary Notes. (1) Work in progress *will* continue. This assumption applies only to initiation or cancellation of construction. (2) If there are no financial (disbursing) authorizations recorded, all raw materials will be paid for as net 60. All disbursements not requiring special decisions will be made. (3) Advertising contracts will be renewed the first month of each quarter in accordance with the last recorded marketing decisions, even though the contracts may have been broken. (4) Production reports show the "decisions in effect at the end of the previous month." Hence, if scheduled production was reduced in the previous month, because of raw material shortages, capacity restrictions, or other reasons, it will remain reduced.

2. Summary of Records and Reports. Listed below are the names of all the decision records and information reports. Figures 2–1 to 2–25[13] contain a complete set of blank copies of these records and reports; these indicate explicitly the specific decisions which firms may make and the specific information which firms will receive. The exact format and arrangement of the decision records and information forms actually used in the Carnegie Tech Management Game may differ slightly from those shown below because of variations in data processing systems among users of the Game.

---

[13]These figures are placed at the end of the chapter, on pages 55–73.

Decision Records

1. Financial Authorization (Figure 2–1)
2. Short-Term Financial Application and Stock Sale Application (Figure 2–2)
3. Long-Term Financial Application (Figure 2–3)
4. Account Adjustments (Figure 2–4)
5. Production and Raw Material Ordering Decisions (Figure 2–5)
6. Transshipments and Construction Decisions (Figure 2–6)
7. Marketing Decisions (Figure 2–7)
8. Market Research Decisions (Figure 2–8)
9. Product Research and Development Decisions (Figure 2–9)
10. New Product Introduction (Figure 2–10)
11. Product Comparison Test Order (Figure 2–11)
12. Raw Material Dumping (Figure 2–12)

Information Reports

1. Product Comparison Test Report (Figure 2–13)
2. Market Survey Report (Figure 2–14)
3. Raw Material Inventory Report (Figure 2–15)
4. Factory Operations Report (Figure 2–16)
5. Sales and Finished Goods Inventory Report (Figure 2–17)
6. Construction Report (Figure 2–18)
7. Cost of Goods Made and Transshipments Report (Figure 2–19)
8. New Product Development Report (Figure 2–20)
9. Firm Trial Balance (Figure 2–21)
10. Financing Available (Figure 2–22)
11. Firm Balance Sheet (Figure 2–23)
12. Firm Income Statement (Figure 2–24)
13. Money Market and Stock Market Data (Figure 2–25)

III. COMPARISONS OF MARK 1 AND MARK 1.5

The original Mark 1 and the current Mark 1.5 versions of the Carnegie Tech Management Game have a great deal in common. Both versions are simulations of the packaged detergent industry, with three firms in the industry. Each firm makes its detergent in its own plant, and sells from one to three brands in four geographical regions. After two years of experience using the original version of the Carnegie Game, it became apparent to us that several modifications should be made both to improve its educational and research values and to make it more realistic. These were implemented at the same time we reprogrammed the Game for use with our new electronic computer during the summer of 1961. Since both versions of the Carnegie Tech Management Game are so similar to each other, the easiest way to convey to the readers of this book an understanding of the Mark 1 version is to mention only those aspects in which it differed from the Mark 1.5 version.

The marketing function was much more aggregative and considerably less realistic in the Mark 1 version. Expenditures on "distribution" for each brand in each region were treated as decision variables. The players generally regarded the effects of distribution expenditures as being qualitatively the same as the effects of advertising expenditures, although they recognized that different parameter values in the demand functions might make the quantitative effects somewhat different. In the Mark 1.5 version, distribution is interpreted not as a decision variable, but—more realistically—as the retail availability of a brand, which in turn depends upon the interactions of market share and three decision variables which did not appear in Mark 1: discount to retailers, size of sales force, and allocation of sales force.

In the Mark 1 version, all consumers in a region were regarded as being homogeneous with regard to preferences for product characteristics. In the Mark 1.5 version, each regional market is segmented into submarkets based upon three different end uses for detergents. This means that the set of product characteristics which it might be optimal to have in a product is not invariant with respect to the mix of products currently on the market.

In the Mark 1 version, the firms supposedly made their sales to wholesalers and to central warehouses of large retail chains. However, in fact the firms' sales directly reflected consumer demand at retail. In effect, therefore, the Mark 1 firms were selling directly at retail. In the Mark 1.5 version, wholesalers, retailers, and consumers are clearly differentiated in the marketplace. Although the Mark 1.5 firms sell directly only to wholesalers and to central warehouses of large retail chains, various actions that the firms can take will have differing effects on wholesalers, retailers, and consumers. The behavior of these latter sectors are individually and differently simulated by the Mark 1.5 computer model. Since they do not always act in perfect concert with one another, the Mark 1.5 market is much livelier and less predictable than the single-level Mark 1 market.

Finally, with respect to the marketing area, the sales demand function in the Mark 1 version was much less realistic than the corresponding function in the Mark 1.5 version in the way in which price changes (rather than merely price levels) affect demand for the various products.

The product research and development area was much simpler and less satisfactory in the Mark 1 version than at present. Only one type of research project was permitted; this was identical to what is now referred to as "project 1" research in Mark 1.5. Purely random effects had too great an importance in the Mark 1 product research, since it was not possible to attempt to copy a successful new product which a competitor may have introduced, nor was it possible to give any directions to product development efforts. Thus, in Mark 1 a firm which spent enough money doing research and development and which was also lucky enough to develop a markedly superior product had a large and frequently long-lived marketing advantage over its competitors. In Mark 1.5 product research and development, random elements still are important, but less so in comparison with management decisions than they were in Mark 1.

The finance area had many more specific rules set down for the players in Mark 1 than it does in Mark 1.5. No elements of negotiation between the Mark 1 firms and the commercial or investment bankers with respect to the terms and availability of financing existed. Instead, there was a rigid set of rules spelled out in explicit detail in the Mark 1 *Player's Manual.* If a firm was able to meet these specific requirements in Mark 1, then it could count on the availability of new debt or equity financing, up to amounts which themselves were routinely calculable by rules known to the players. We feel that Mark 1.5 is both more instructive to the players as well as being more realistic in not stating specifically the terms and requirements for new financing, but instead allowing the players to negotiate on these with simulated commercial and investment bankers.

All disbursements of funds had to be authorized as specific decisions in Mark 1. This led to many clerical errors, as well as many delays in running the Game, since the Mark 1 computer program would stop if a firm did not have enough cash or had not authorized expenditures for meeting all of its commitments. This has been considerably simplified in Mark 1.5, with a simulated middle management organization handling the routine disbursements of funds. The Mark 1.5 computer program will not stop if a firm is financially unable to meet its commitments; instead prescribed methods will be automatically taken either to obtain additional funds or to reduce expenditures or both.

The accounting area was not regarded as a major management function in Mark 1. Firms automatically obtained considerably more data in Mark 1 than they do in Mark 1.5. Mark 1 did not provide a summary of trial balances, and it did not allow firms to alter the accounting conventions built into the computer program. The accounting was unfortunately handled on a treacherous single-entry basis in the Mark 1 computer program; double-entry bookkeeping is used in Mark 1.5.

The only ways in which the production area differed between Mark 1 and Mark 1.5 is that there were more opportunities to make clerical errors in recording production decisions in Mark 1, and the effects of maintenance expenditures on downtime were less realistically handled in Mark 1.

Mark 1 did not provide any automatic means for continuing operations of its firms in the absence of complete sets of monthly decisions. This made it considerably more difficult to accelerate the ratio of simulated to real time in Mark 1 than it is in Mark 1.5.

Finally, the *Player's Manual* for the Mark 1 version was written for players who were learning the rules of an artificial game. A considerable amount of it was devoted to explanations of how decision forms should be completed. The Mark 1.5 *Player's Manual,* as we have seen in Section II, tries instead to give the player a picture of himself as the manager of a going concern in a realistic business situation. Since the decision records and information reports are considerably simplified and much better designed in Mark 1.5 than they were in Mark 1, there is now less need for the *Player's Manual* to discuss the mechanics of completing and interpreting these forms.

FIGURE 2–1

D–1

INDUSTRY_____ FIRM_____ MONTH_____

FINANCIAL AUTHORIZATION

Accounts Payable:
    Pay raw material suppliers $_____
    Pay estimated income tax of $_____
90-Day Bank Note:
    Make advance purchase of note (check)   [_____]
Term Loan:
    Pay on term loan payable $_____
    Make accelerated payment on principal $_____
Government Securities:
    Increase investment level $_____
    Decrease investment level $_____
Dividends to Stockholders:
    Declare dividends ($/share) $_____

Signature_____
Treasurer

FIGURE 2–2

D–2

INDUSTRY_____ FIRM_____ MONTH_____

SHORT-TERM FINANCIAL APPLICATION AND STOCK SALE APPLICATION

90-Day Bank Note
    Application for initial bank note:
        Amount $_____
        Month desired to start   _____
        Cancel all previous note applications
or
    Application for renewal:
        Amount $_____
and/or
    Rejection of bank offer: (check)   [_____]

Stock Sale
    Initial application:
        No. of shares desired to sell   _____

    Action on quotation:
        Authorization of investment   [_____]
        Banker to proceed (check)

    Decisions on issue underway   [_____]
        Cancel (check)
    Postpone one month (check)   [_____]

Signature_____
Treasurer

FIGURE 2–3

D–3

INDUSTRY_____ FIRM_____ MONTH_____

LONG-TERM FINANCIAL APPLICATION

Term Loan

    Application for term loan:
        Amount $_____
        Month desired to start   _____
        Term desired (in years)   _____
        Preferred regular installment payment $_____
    Proportion of loan for purpose of:
        Plant and equipment investment   _____%
        Inventory investment   _____%
        Reducing current liabilities   _____%
        Reducing fixed liabilities   _____%
        Product research investment   _____%
        Other   _____%
    Other funds earmarked for construction $_____
    Cancel all previous term loan applications.
and/or
    Rejection of term loan offer (check)
and/or
    Notice of accelerated payment:
        Month payment will be made   _____

        and full repayment (check)
        or partial repayment (amount) $_____
and/or
    Cancellation of notice (check)

Signature_____
                                Treasurer

FIGURE 2–4

D–4

INDUSTRY_____ FIRM_____ MONTH_____

ACCOUNT ADJUSTMENTS

Number of Adjustments   [   ]

Adjustment Number	Debit Account Number	Credit Account Number	Amount
1	_____	_____	$_____
2	_____	_____	$_____
3	_____	_____	$_____
4	_____	_____	$_____
5	_____	_____	$_____
6	_____	_____	$_____
7	_____	_____	$_____

Signature_____
                        Comptroller

Signature_____
                        President

FIGURE 2–5

INDUSTRY_____FIRM_____MONTH_____

PRODUCTION AND RAW MATERIAL ORDERING DECISIONS

Production   (Cases of product)

		A	B	C
Destination of production	Factory warehouse___			
	East___			
	South___			
	Central___			
	West___			
	Total___			

Number of workers   _____
Maintenance expenditure $_____
Fraction overtime authorized   _____%

Raw Material Ordering

Material	Quantity ordered (lbs.)	To arrive:
a	_____	End of 3rd month hence
b	_____	End of 3rd month hence
c	_____	End of 2nd month hence
d	_____	End of 2nd month hence
e	_____	End of coming month
f	_____	End of coming month
g	_____	End of coming month

FIGURE 2-6

D-6

INDUSTRY_____ FIRM_____ MONTH_____

TRANSSHIPMENTS AND CONSTRUCTION DECISIONS

Transshipments

[ ]

If no transshipments are to be made, mark "x" in box; if they are to be made, leave box empty and fill in desired shipments.

Number of Cases		Shipped to			
		East	South	Central	West
Factory Warehouse	A				
	B				
	C				
East	A				
	B				
	C				
South	A				
	B				
	C				
Central	A				
	B				
	C				
West	A				
	B				
	C				

(Shipped from)

Construction

Facility being expanded	To initiate construction	To cancel construction*
Raw materials warehouse Pounds of capacity expansion	_____	[ ]
Factory Man-hours of capacity expansion	_____	[ ]
Finished goods warehouse Cases of capacity expansion	_____	[ ]

*If you wish to cancel construction that has been begun, mark an "x" in the appropriate box; otherwise leave box blank.

FIGURE 2–7

D–7

INDUSTRY_____FIRM_____MONTH_____

MARKETING DECISIONS

Region	Decision	Product		
		A	*B*	*C*
East	Advertising ($)			
	Percent of salesmen (%)			
	Price to wholesaler ($/case)			
	Retail allowance ($/case)			
South	Advertising ($)			
	Percent of salesmen (%)			
	Price to wholesaler ($/case)			
	Retail allowance ($/case)			
Central	Advertising ($)			
	Percent of salesmen (%)			
	Price to wholesaler ($/case)			
	Retail allowance ($/case)			
West	Advertising ($)			
	Percent of salesmen (%)			
	Price to wholesaler ($/case)			
	Retail allowance ($/case)			

Total number of salesmen_____

Region	Quarterly advertising contract ($/month)*
East	$_____
South	$_____
Central	$_____
West	$_____

*Leave blank except at the start of a quarter.

FIGURE 2-8

D-8

INDUSTRY_____ FIRM_____ MONTH_____

MARKET RESEARCH DECISIONS

Dollar expenditures for classes of information on a regional basis:

Marketing Information*	Region			
	East	South	Central	West
Advertising	$	$	$	$
Retail price	$	$	$	$
Retail case sales	$	$	$	$
Percent distribution and percent stockout	$	$	$	$

*As long as any marketing information is purchased, a report showing the wholesale prices and retail allowances currently in force for all brands of detergent in each region will be obtained without further charge.

FIGURE 2-9

D-9

INDUSTRY_____ FIRM_____ MONTH_____

PRODUCT RESEARCH AND DEVELOPMENT DECISIONS

Project 1: The goal of this project is *unrestricted new product development research.*

      Current monthly expenditure............ $_____

Project 2: The goal of this project is *to synthesize a currently marketed product.*

      Current monthly expenditure............ $_____

      Product to be synthesized

                Firm_____Product_____

Project 3: The goal of this project is *to develop products possessing a particular set of characteristics.*

      Current monthly expenditure............ $_____

Characteristic	Desired minimum value	Desired maximum value
Sudsing.................	_____	_____
Washing power...........	_____	_____
Gentleness..............	_____	_____
Standard raw materials cost ($/case)................	_____	_____
Labor productivity........	_____	_____

FIGURE 2–10

D–10

INDUSTRY_____ FIRM_____ MONTH_____

NEW PRODUCT INTRODUCTION

For new brand introduction or product replacement

Month during which developed. . . . . _____
Project developing product . . . . _____
Product number. . . . . _____
Brand name for new product (A, B, or C). . . _____

FIGURE 2–11

D–11

INDUSTRY_____ FIRM_____ MONTH_____

PRODUCT COMPARISON TEST ORDER

Products to be compared

Product	Firm	Marketed Product Product Number*	*Or* Your Unmarketed Product Month	Number
1	_____	_____	_____	_____
2	_____	_____	_____	_____

*If a product to be tested is unmarketed, the product number should be 0 and the rest of this row must be completed.

Type of test   Check one

Single comparison   [   ]

Repeat comparison   [   ]

Expenditure $_____

FIGURE 2–12

D–12

INDUSTRY_____ FIRM_____ MONTH_____

RAW MATERIAL DUMPING

Raw Material Being Dumped: *Pounds*

a   _____
b   _____
c   _____
d   _____
e   _____
f   _____
g   _____

This form need be used only when raw materials are to be dumped.

If more material is specified to be dumped than is in fact in inventory at the beginning of the month, only the total inventory of that material will be dumped. Thus to dump all the inventory of a particular material, you may request more than could possibly exist. Materials in shipment may not be dumped.

FIGURE 2–13

I–1

INDUSTRY_____FIRM_____MONTH_____

PRODUCT COMPARISON TEST REPORT

		Firm	Marketed Product	Unmarketed Product Month Developed	Product Number
Products	1	_____	_____	_____	_____
Compared	2	_____	_____	_____	_____

Type of test:

Single comparison

Repeat comparison

Number of Observations _____

Single Comparison

Preferences

	Product 1	Product 2	No Preference
Sudsing	_____%	_____%	_____%
Washing power. ...	_____%	_____%	_____%
Gentleness.........	_____%	_____%	_____%
Overall............	_____%	_____%	_____%

Repeat Comparison

Preferences

Test:	1st	2nd	1st	2nd	1st	2nd	1st	2nd
Product:	1	1	1	2	2	1	2	2
Sudsing..........	_____%		_____%		_____%		_____%	
Washing power....	_____%		_____%		_____%		_____%	
Gentleness........	_____%		_____%		_____%		_____%	
Overall...........	_____%		_____%		_____%		_____%	

FIGURE 2-14

I-2

INDUSTRY_____FIRM_____MONTH_____

MARKET SURVEY REPORT

Region	Firm⟍Attribute ⟍Product	1			2			3		
		A	B	C	A	B	C	A	B	C
E A S T	Advertising									
	% distribution									
	% stockouts									
	Retail price									
	Retail case sales									
	Wholesale price									
	Retail allowance									
S O U T H	Advertising									
	% distribution									
	% stockouts									
	Retail price									
	Retail case sales									
	Wholesale price									
	Retail allowance									
C E N T R A L	Advertising									
	% distribution									
	% stockouts									
	Retail price									
	Retail case sales									
	Wholesale price									
	Retail allowance									
W E S T	Advertising									
	% distribution									
	% stockouts									
	Retail price									
	Retail case sales									
	Wholesale price									
	Retail allowance									

FIGURE 2-15

RAW MATERIAL INVENTORY REPORT

Raw Material	Opening Inventory (lbs.)	Usage during month (lbs)	Received end of month		Closing Inventory	
			(lbs.)	($/lbs.)	(lbs.)	($/lbs.)
a						
b						
c						
d						
e						
f						
g						

Material	To arrive end of next month (lbs.)	To arrive end of two months (lbs.)	Price for orders placed during coming month ($/lbs.)
a			
b			
c			
d			
e			
f			
g			

FIGURE 2–16

I–4

INDUSTRY_____ FIRM_____ MONTH_____

FACTORY OPERATIONS REPORT

		Cases of Product		
		A	B	C
Shipments during month to	Factory warehouse..			
	East..............			
	South............			
	Central...........			
	West			
	Total production......			

		A	B	C	Total
Labor man-hrs. used	Regular time..				
	Overtime.....				

Number of workers...................... _____
Man-hours lost due to machinery downtime. _____
Unassigned man-hours .... _____
Raw materials warehouse capacity (lbs.).... _____
Factory capacity (man-hours)............ _____
Finished goods warehouse capacity (cases) . _____

FIGURE 2-17

I-5

INDUSTRY_____ FIRM_____ MONTH_____

SALES AND FINISHED GOODS INVENTORY REPORT

Sales (in Cases) of Product

	A	B	C
East.............			
South...........			
Central..........			
West............			
Total...........			

Ending Inventory (in Cases) of Product

	A	B	C
Factory warehouse..			
East.............			
South...........			
Central..........			
West............			
Total...........			

FIGURE 2-18

I-6

INDUSTRY_____FIRM_____MONTH_____

CONSTRUCTION REPORT

	Raw Material Warehouse	Factory	Finished Goods Warehouse
Month of decision......	_____	_____	_____
Increase in capacity....	_____lbs.	_____man-hours	_____cases
Expansion will be available beginning of month	_____	_____	_____
Cost of increase........	$_____	$_____	$_____
Partial payments due at beginning of month { 5%	_____	_____	_____
45%	_____	_____	_____
50%	_____	_____	_____

FIGURE 2-19

I-7

INDUSTRY_____FIRM_____MONTH_____

COST OF GOODS MADE AND TRANSSHIPMENTS REPORT

Cost of Goods Made

	Product		
	A	B	C
Materials	$	$	$
Direct labor	$	$	$
Depreciation (RM whse and factory)	$	$	$
Maintenance	$	$	$
Supervisory and factory OH	$	$	$
Hiring and personnel expense	$	$	$
Total cost of goods made	$	$	$

Transshipments

		Number of cases	Shipped to			
			East	South	Central	West
Shipped from	Factory Warehouse	A				
		B				
		C				
	East	A				
		B				
		C				
	South	A				
		B				
		C				
	Central	A				
		B				
		C				
	West	A				
		B				
		C				

.

FIGURE 2–20

I–8

INDUSTRY_____FIRM_____MONTH_____ ____

NEW PRODUCT DEVELOPMENT REPORT

Month during which developed........... _____
Number of firm developing product....... _____
Number of product..................... _____
Number of project developing product..... _____

Product characteristics (scale 0–10)

Sudsing............. _____
Washing power....... _____
Gentleness.......... _____

Raw material composition (lbs./case)

a..................... _____
b..................... _____
c..................... _____
d..................... _____
e..................... _____
f..................... _____
g..................... _____

Productivity (man-hours/case)........ _____
Raw material cost at standard raw
material prices ($/case)............. _____

FIGURE 2–21

INDUSTRY_____FIRM_____MONTH_____

FIRM TRIAL BALANCE

Acct. No.	Account Title	Debit	Credit	Balance
1	Cash.............................			
2	Government securities.............			
3	Accounts receivable...............			
4	Raw materials inventory a..........			
5	Raw materials inventory b..........			
6	Raw materials inventory c..........			
7	Raw materials inventory d.........			
8	Raw materials inventory e..........			
9	Raw materials inventory f..........			
10	Raw materials inventory g..........			
11	Goods in process inventory A.......			
12	Goods in process inventory B.......			
13	Goods in process inventory C......			
14	Finished goods inventory A.........			
15	Finished goods inventory B.........			
16	Finished goods inventory C........			
17	Other current assets..............			
19	Raw materials warehouse at cost....			
20	Allowance for depreciation.........			
21	Factory and equipment at cost......			
22	Allowance for depreciation.........			
23	Finished goods warehouse at cost....			
24	Allowance for depreciation.........			
25	Construction in progress............			
26	Other assets.....................			
28	Demand note....................			
29	Bank note due next month.........			
30	Bank note due later...............			
31	Term loan due next month.........			
32	Term loan due 2–12 months hence...			
33	Term loan due later..............			
34	Accrued interest due next month....			
35	Other accrued interest.............			
36	Income tax due next month.........			
37	Other income tax—last year........			
38	Income tax this year..............			
39	Dividends payable, due next month..			
40	Other liabilities due next month.....			
41	A/P—materials, current...........			
42	A/P—materials past discount date...			
43	A/P—advertising, due next month...			
44	A/P—advertising contract penalty due next month................			
45	A/P—construction, due next month..			
46	Other current liabilities...........			
48	Other long-term liabilities.........			

FIGURE 2–21—*Concluded*

I–9 (2)

FIRM TRIAL BALANCE

Acct. No.	Account Title	Debit	Credit	Balance
50	Common stock outstanding.........			
51	Retained earnings—beginning of year			
52	Profit—year to date..............			
53	Dividends declared—year to date....			
56	Sales of A.........................			
57	Sales of B.........................			
58	Sales of C.........................			
59	Interest income....................			
60	Discounts offered..................			
61	Other income......................			
63	Cost of goods sold A..............			
64	Cost of goods sold B..............			
65	Cost of goods sold C..............			
66	Direct labor used..................			
67	Depreciation......................			
68	Maintenance......................			
69	Excess raw material storage cost.....			
70	Supervision and factory overhead....			
71	Factory personnel department......			
72	Excess finished goods storage cost....			
73	Regional whse. storage cost—E.....			
74	Regional whse. storage cost—S......			
75	Regional whse. storage cost—C.....			
76	Regional whse. storage cost—W.....			
77	Transportation cost................			
78	Advertising.......................			
79	Sales office expense................			
80	Retail allowance expense...........			
81	Government securities department...			
82	Market surveys and product comparison tests...................			
83	Product research and development...			
84	Officers' salaries..................			
85	General administrative expense......			
86	Other operating expense...........			
87	Statistical discrepancy.............			
88	Interest expense...................			
89	Discounts lost.....................			
90	Loss on cancelled construction......			
91	Financial transactions expense......			
92	Other nonoperating expense.........			
93	Provision for federal income tax.....			
94	Net profit after taxes..............			
	TOTALS.......................			

FIGURE 2–22

INDUSTRY_____FIRM_____ MONTH_____

FINANCING AVAILABLE

90-Day Bank Note

Amount available................................. $_____
Month available...................................   _____
Interest rate (%/year)............................   _____
Minimum cash balance requirement................. $_____

Term Loan

Amount available................................. $_____
Term (in years)...................................   _____
Month available...................................   _____
Interest rate (%/year)............................   _____
Repayment interval (in months)....................   _____
Regular payment on principal...................... $_____
Limit on working capital (high)...................   _____
Limit on working capital (low)....................   _____

Other covenants: [number applicable: from covenant 1 through covenant_____]
  1. Submit quarterly and audited yearly financial statements.
  2. Maintain current ratio as specified above.
  3. Make no pledge of assets to any other parties.
  4. New construction limited to.................... $_____
     plus depreciation for the term of the loan.
  5. No increase in officers' salaries.
  6. No increase in dividends.
  7. Submit monthly projected cash flow statements.
  8. Bank officer to have a seat on board of directors for the term of the loan.
  9. One quarter of annual profits after taxes must be applied for the unpaid principal.

Accelerated payment on principal will be accepted in month_____

in full   [_____]   *or*   for the amount of $_____

Stock Sale

Number of shares.................................   _____
Offering date: first business day of month...........   _____
Probable price to public ($/share).................   _____
Probable price to company ($/share)...............   _____

FIGURE 2–23

I–11

INDUSTRY_____ FIRM_____ MONTH_____

FIRM BALANCE SHEET

ASSETS

Cash........................... $_____
Government securities............ $_____
Accounts receivable.............. $_____
Inventory....................... $_____
Other current assets............. $_____
     Total Current Assets........ $_____
Plant and equipment (at cost)...... $_____
Allowance for depreciation........ $_____
Construction in process........... $_____
     Net Plant and Equipment.... $_____
     Other Assets.............. $_____
     Total Assets.......... $_____

LIABILITIES

Bank note..................... $_____
Term loan—current.............. $_____
Accounts payable................ $_____
Accrued interest................. $_____
Accrued taxes................... $_____
Dividends payable............... $_____
Other current liabilities........... $_____
     Total Current Liabilities..... $_____
     Long-Term Debt........... $_____
     Other Liabilities........... $_____
     Total Liabilities...... $_____

STOCKHOLDER'S EQUITY

Common stock (1) (2)............ $_____
Retained earnings................ $_____
     Total Stockholder's Equity... $_____
     Total Liabilities and Equity.. $_____

Footnotes

(1) Shares authorized............. _____
(2) Shares outstanding............ _____

FIGURE 2–24

I–12

INDUSTRY_____FIRM_____ MONTH_____

FIRM INCOME STATEMENT

Sales............................... $_____
   Less cost of goods sold............... $_____
Gross profit.......................... $_____
   Less operating expenses.............. $_____
Net operating profit................... $_____
   Plus interest and other income........ $_____
   Less interest and other expense....... $_____
Net profit before income taxes.......... $_____
   Less federal income taxes............ $_____
Net profit............................ $_____
   Less dividends...................... $_____
Addition to retained earnings........... $_____

Footnote—Depreciation charges totaled.... $_____

FIGURE 2–25

I–13

INDUSTRY_____FIRM_____ MONTH_____

MONEY MARKET AND STOCK MARKET DATA
(From the *Tech Street Journal*)

Interest Rates:
91-day Treasury bills...................................... _____%
Long-term government bonds........................... _____%
90-day bank notes...................................... _____%
Term loans (2–4 years).............................. _____%
Term loans (5–10 years)............................. _____%

Stock Market:
Firm 1 stock price—at close of last business day.......... _____
Firm 2 stock price—at close of last business day.......... _____
Firm 3 stock price—at close of last business day.......... _____
Index of all industrial stocks (1947 = 100).............. _____

Other Information:
Gross national product (seasonally adjusted annual rate)... _____
Percent unemployment................................ _____%

Chapter 3

THE GAME AS A COURSE IN CARNEGIE'S M.S. CURRICULUM

In Chapter 2, we concentrated on the most fundamental aspects of Game play. We described the general characteristics of the simulated detergent industry and presented the manual of instructions which is provided to players. Yet as important as the basic structure of the Game is, a thorough understanding of the Game's potential as an educational and research tool requires an examination of the context in which it is played. In this chapter, we describe the devices beyond the basic computer model which we have used to elaborate and enrich the Game as a course for graduate students at Carnegie. We also discuss the efforts that have been made to find the right place for the Game in the total M.S. curriculum. Although the pattern of enrichment that we describe here may not be the best pattern for other users to follow, we are convinced that the general kinds of elaboration that we have attempted help greatly to improve the Game as an environment for learning.

In Chapter 4, we change from a faculty to a student point of view—from discussion of the challenges that the Game is meant to provide to a description of how teams actually try to meet the challenges. In Chapter 5, we describe how in a variety of regular courses the Game has been exploited as a substitute for case, laboratory, and field experiences and made the focus for class sessions, examinations, and term projects. In Chapter 6, we broaden the discussion to show how the Game has been used in executive and evening programs at Carnegie and to summarize experiences with the Game at other universities. In Chapter 7, we shall present and evaluate some student reactions to the Game and some data about its educational impact.

The experiments and reactions to them are reported in some detail so that readers can evaluate how they might apply to the educational goals and resources of their own institutions. We shall be flattered by imitation and further testing of some of the things which are reported in the chapters which follow, but we shall be more pleased if our experiences serve to stimulate even more imaginative and purposeful uses of the Game by both administrators and players.

I. KINDS OF EXPERIENCE THAT THE GAME PROVIDES

The primary experience that the Game provides is the *competitive* experience of playing against the computer model and other teams. In addition to this experience, students have at least four other avenues for learning from the Game. These (as summarized in Figure 3–1) include the opportunities to handle problems and relationships with groups such as boards of directors that are external to the computer model, the challenge of setting up and maintaining team organization, the challenge of managing Game tasks among many regular academic duties, and the opportunities to work on assignments in other, regular courses which draw on experience in the Game. Briefly, these can be labeled as *negotiating, organizational, personal,* and *anticipatory* or *reflective* tasks.

FIGURE 3–1

Opportunities for Learning That Are Provided by the Carnegie Game

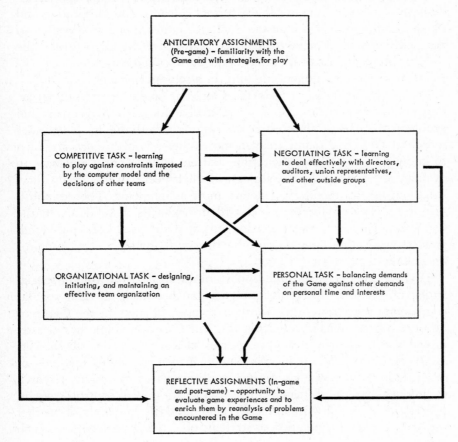

While students work to surpass their competition, the negotiating problems are essentially assignments for them to maintain realistic parallel relationships with some of the other groups that managers in industry must deal with: boards of directors, stockholders, union representatives, bankers, auditors, management consultants, and so on. These interactions can be conducted via letters and memoranda, or they can be conducted "in person" with faculty members, other students, or businessmen playing the external roles. A team's success in establishing and maintaining effective relations with such groups can be included with its success against its competitors as measures of its performance in the Game.

The organizational problems arise from the total demands which the analytic and diplomatic tasks make on a team's time, motivations, and skills. Out of the loose, peer-oriented relations that characterize most student groups, teams must develop working relationships that have many of the hierarchial characteristics, much of the specialized division of labor, and many of the formal rules for communication and control that one finds in industry. Each team must find a *modus vivendi* that will let them achieve their goals, that will prove adaptable to the sudden shocks and crises that may occur during the Game, and that will let them survive as an operating unit for a semester or more.

Out of the tasks that a team faces and out of the organizational arrangements which they adopt, there evolve for each player personal problems of making an effective contribution to the team. It becomes more critical in the Game than in most other school projects for men to know how to allocate their time and energy efficiently and how to evaluate and control their relations with their peers. In the usual course situation, faculty members generate most assignments. They establish priorities. They set limits or standards for what is to be done. In the Game, students have more freedom to set their own goals and standards, to determine how much time they will invest, and to monitor one another's behavior.

Finally, students can find opportunities to learn through special anticipatory and reflective assignments that are made in their regular courses and that draw on either their own experiences in the Game or on their observations of other players. The Carnegie Game has already provided a laboratory for other courses to teach such diverse subjects as the purposes and procedures of a management audit, methods of organizational analysis and design, applications of operations research techniques, design of management information and control systems, operations of the stock market, bargaining skills, methods of market research, and the formulation of strategic objectives and programs. Such assignments have been made to students before, during, and after their involvement on Game teams. The early ones are intended, in part, to help prospective players become familiar with the Game. The later assignments are intended both to get students to look at some of the problems that the Game poses more closely than they would in the regular course of play and, by making them review their experiences, to help them organize and generalize the things that they have learned from the Game.

II. ENRICHING THE GAME WITH EXTERNAL INTERACTIONS

Perhaps the most frequently deplored "weakness" of management games is the limitation that computer models or formal umpiring systems put on teams' abilities to consider problems which cannot be expressed by numbers or by restrictive sets of qualitative statements. The manager, it is clear, must be able to react to people as well as to statistical reports or even letters and memoranda submitted in an impersonal fashion. One of the problems with a game as rich in "numbers" and "structure" as the Carnegie Game is to keep the analytic, essentially quantitative tasks from dominating the Game.

Two of the approaches that can be used are "in-basket" materials and role-playing exercises. "In-basket" materials are letters, memoranda, telephone messages, and other pieces of paper which may announce anything from a machine breakdown to the details of a complicated and troublesome grievance situation.[1] Team actions in response to these problems can be evaluated by the game administrators, and the evaluations can be fed back in two ways. Sometimes the problems and the "scores" that teams get for their solution are kept entirely separate from the operations of the basic computer model. Alternatively, ways can be devised to use judgments about the nature and quality of teams' solutions to modify key factors (like worker productivity, salesman morale, or machine efficiency) in the computer model.

The strength of the "in-basket" approach is that a great variety of problems can be presented on pieces of paper that would be hard now

---

[1]The "in-basket" technique has been developed as a major feature of games like MATRIX (a Procter & Gamble game to acquaint new employees with the job of a plant manager), the HARBETS Simulation Exercise (developed by Harvard Business School and the Educational Testing Service), and the AMA General Management Simulation. For further information on MATRIX, see John W. Plattner and Lowell W. Herron, *Simulation and Its Use in Employee Selection and Training* (Management Bulletin No. 20, Personnel Division, American Management Association, 1962). The work on the HARBETS Simulation Exercise is under the direction of Lewis B. Ward and Stanley I. Buchin of the Harvard Business School and John K. Hemphill of the Educational Testing Service. Its operations are described briefly in "It's Almost Like Working," *Business Week*, August 4, 1962, pp. 94–95.

to present through a computer model or hard to develop as "live" role-playing situations. Problems can be sequenced and scored in such a way that students move from simpler to more complex tasks and have a chance to rework especially difficult ones. The weakness of the approach is that even though the problems concern qualitative relationships with other people, the process that students go through to solve them is essentially as impersonal as the process by which they deal with quantitative data and decisions in the Game. The players read a problem, write out what they propose to do, and wait for a referee to predict what the outcome of their action will be. The players have no one to talk to or to bargain with on a face-to-face (or toe-to-toe) basis.

To present students with opportunities for "live" interaction with other people, we have stressed more the development of role-playing tasks than the development of "in-basket" materials. We find role-playing more exciting for both faculty and students, and we think that the best of these experiments have tremendously enhanced the educational value of the Game. The roles we have set up have been selected (1) to give students experience with groups who are important to the existence and survival of real managers in business and (2) to capitalize on the particular interests and talents of our faculty. Carnegie's faculty and students have taken the part of directors, stockholders, auditors, union negotiators, judges, and bankers *vis-à-vis* the student teams. They might take the part of raw material suppliers, wholesalers or retailers, representatives of the U.S. Department of Justice, or marketing and management consultants. With some minor modifications in the Game, there are also good opportunities, which we are just beginning to exploit, for direct negotiations among the teams themselves—over such issues as sale of raw materials, transfer of warehouse facilities, possible mergers of production and marketing facilities, movement of salesmen from one company to another, or movement of team members from one company to another.

Role-playing in connection with the Game has one very important advantage over role-playing with case materials or other problems from outside the students' daily experiences. The roles which the students play, as managers of a company in the Game, are roles which they have defined for themselves. The roles are ones which they care about and which they do not have to stretch their imaginations and personalities to play. Hence, if the external groups assume their roles with anything like the same degree of naturalness and sincerity, the interactions develop in a very real manner. The level of commitment and emotional involvement on both sides is high.

The best way to show what can be done with supplementary role-playing exercises is to describe the ones which have been most effective in greater detail. In the sections which follow, we shall describe experiments with boards of directors, auditors, union representatives, and stockholders.

A. Boards of Directors

Our first role-playing experiment was to assign to each team a four- or five-man board of directors. Directors have been members of the faculty, and recently, in the case of one or two directors for each team, executives from business and industry who have served on boards or dealt with them in real life. The boards were established to provide faculty members with a meaningful context in which to observe and work with the Game teams and to provide the teams with the kind of realistic external questioning and supervision that company managers face.

1. The Role of the Board. The role of directors has been defined specifically enough to give faculty members information about how it should be played, but generally enough to allow and encourage a natural development of the relationships between each board and its management during the Game. These are the instructions which directors received during the 1963–64 run:

Directors should behave as outside directors in real life would, as *auditors* of management, *not* as teachers or as members of operating management participating actively in making company decisions. Even in "crisis" situations, the board's role is to question and to approve or disapprove policies, rather than to formulate or execute them in management's place. Directors should take as their prime target successful company performance, measured by such "real-world" criteria as current profits and the development of a sound base for future profits, market position, application of sound management techniques, imaginative forward planning, and effective control of operations. While the current management has a tenure of only a few "years" in control of their firm, they are expected to leave their firms in operating condition for their successors. Short-run performance is important; but in guiding management in the selection of its goals and basic decision strategies, directors should insist that short-range plans be formulated so that they are consistent with the long-run health of the enterprise. Directors are also responsible for assessing the management performance and for promoting the development of first- and second-rank officer personnel.

Consistent with their role, directors should demand and support strong management performance. They should insist on thorough analysis of problems and solid documentation of proposed decisions. They should outline to management the kinds of information they would like to have about company operations, a schedule for presentation of this information so that they can come prepared to board meetings, and any details on the format of presentation that they think it necessary to specify. They may request any kinds of reports—oral and written

—that they think appropriate and useful. Providing information to directors about their own company and about estimates of competitors' accomplishments and plans is the responsibility of each management group, not of the Management Game committee. Since the directors are ultimately responsible to the stockholders who own the business, they should require student managers to maintain financial integrity and strength in a manner consistent with that responsibility. They are interested in steps by which management can maintain and increase the value of the company's stock and can maintain and increase the dividends paid to stockholders. They should insist on the maintenance of adequate records and other control devices, and may test these from time to time in any manner they see fit to employ.

Since directors are responsible for evaluating their management's performance and for assigning grades in the Game course, they should also act in any way they find useful to enlarge their acquaintance with the abilities of management personnel and to insure that each member of management has equitable opportunities to demonstrate what he can contribute. This should include requesting special reports from individual managers in areas of their assigned responsibility and extensive participation in board meetings by managers other than the company president. It may also include assigning to members of the board the responsibility of conferring occasionally between board meetings with one or two members of management about more specific aspects of the work of their department or function within the company.

Students may expect to receive assignments from their directors to supplement the basic tasks of the Game. It should be a responsibility of each board chairman, though, to coordinate such assignments in order to spread the work equitably and to prevent unreasonable work loads.

We have not insisted on a great deal of coordination among the boards about their treatment of the management groups subordinate to them. The team's job is to learn to satisfy their board, not boards in general. Periodic meetings of board chairmen before and during the Game run, or between runs, are desirable, though, to clarify the guidelines for board activities. They are essential if the boards are eventually to grade team performance.

2. Staffing the Boards. Because the director is specifically *not* to be a teacher, the role is not an easy one for some faculty members to fill. Care in staffing the boards is an essential ingredient of their success. The most critical position is that of the chairman. If he has an understanding of what boards of directors do, he can keep the faculty from slipping into an advisory or teaching role and can establish conditions which will make the students take the board seriously.

Ideally, the chairman might be a faculty member who has actually served on a board of directors in business or industry, but we have also found some very effective board chairmen among younger faculty members whose intuitive understanding of the role and whose seriousness about the Game compensate for their lack of real board experience. A serious interest in the Game is important. The chairman runs four to seven meetings each semester between the board and management, and he is the board's primary liaison with management between meetings. He should know the Game and should be willing to analyze the way his team is playing it.

We have experimented since 1961–62 with the addition of top-level business executives to each board. This is easier to propose than to put into practice. The first job is to find top-level men who can spare two or three hours to come to the campus four to seven times a semester and who are willing to take time to learn something about the Game before they take the assignment. In addition to having had executive experience, the best men have appeared before boards or have served on them. At the same time, they must be flexible enough to adapt their real-world wisdom and habits to the compressed time scale and limited realism of the Game situation. They must be willing to treat incompetent or careless management decisions as they would in real life. Most executives whom we have approached are enthusiastic about the idea, but many have not had the time. Sources of candidates include retired executives; local management groups such as the Young Presidents' Organization; and contacts accessible through the faculty and through the university alumni, placement, development, and extension offices. Each year the recruiting job has become easier. Most of the executives we have hired have been enthusiastic about serving again the following year, and several have volunteered out of their enthusiasm to help us expand our list of candidates.

The results are clearly worth the search and the cost. As directors in the Game, businessmen can play a role very similar to roles they play in real life. They can interact with students as they might with younger subordinates in their own organizations, and they face none of the adjustment problems that businessmen face when they return to campus as lecturers or classroom teachers. Students at Carnegie are so enthusiastic about the inclusion of businessmen on the boards of directors that we now seek at least two outside men for each board.

New board members—whether they are from the faculty or from business—can profit from an intensive pre-Game briefing about what is involved in playing the Game. At a minimum, they should have a chance to read and discuss the *Player's Manual,* the initial company history for their team, and the directors' instructions that have been prepared for them. It is even better, however, if they have a chance to make one or two moves in the Game. This will serve better than many hours of reading or lecturing to illustrate the opportunities which players have and the constraints under which they must operate.

3. Scheduling of Meetings. We have normally asked boards to meet with their teams for periods of two or three hours at least five times during a semester. They meet once or twice early in the Game to issue general instructions to the teams, to approve their plans for organization, and to review with the team the goals and decision strategies it is recommending. Subsequent meetings occur at three- to four-week intervals. If the team is playing at the rate of one move a week, the appropriate time for a meeting is after the quarterly results are available. If the team is playing at the rate of three moves a week, the meetings might be timed to coincide with the issuance of year-end financial and operating statements. Some meetings may be scheduled to correspond with special activities of the Game team—to review a decision about expanding production or warehouse facilities, to discuss the stand that management will take in negotiating a new wage contract, or to hear a report from outside auditors or consultants.

The details of the schedule and the agenda for particular meetings will vary from team to team. The best situation is one where the board can manipulate the frequency, length, and purposes of meetings in order to maintain student interest in the Game, to control the total demands that the Game makes on student time, and to increase the opportunities which students have for useful learning.

The final meeting of the semester, we have found, may usefully be ended by students and faculty stepping out of their roles and talking informally about the Game experience. This gives the faculty a chance to make observations and comments that they could not easily make as directors, and equally important, it gives students a chance to offer suggestions for improving the Game as an educational experience.

4. Influence of Boards on the Teams. The boards add substantially to the tasks that teams face. The team president's main duty, in fact, may be to manage relationships with the board. He deals informally with the chairman, he is the main source of ideas and instructions about getting ready for board meetings, and he makes many of the basic presentations to the board. In choosing their presidents, some teams pay more attention to his skills as an external representative than to his qualifications as an internal leader.

The board's main effect is to increase the pressures for explicit goal setting, forecasting, planning, and decision making by the team. This insures that the teams will devote some time to systematic discussion of what they are trying to accomplish, rather than muddle through on a move-by-move basis. They learn to set agendas and prepare justification for proposed actions. They get practice in presenting their ideas orally and in writing, much in the style of management presentations in industry. They learn to defend and elaborate the things which they propose under questioning from the board, and their ability to carry through their plans is subject to review by the directors.

Although many of the board's comments and questions can seem unnecessary to a team, at their best they help the team greatly to improve its performance. A board which looks behind job titles on an organization chart to find out in detail what each member of management will do can help the team anticipate troublesome ambiguities in their organizational plan. A board can require useful, regular reports about performance and potential. A board can point out inconsistencies between what a team says it is trying to do and what it actually is doing, and they can insist on higher levels of analysis on such key decisions as the decision to build a new plant.

The boards of directors can help impart a sense of urgency to various tasks in the Game. One thing which many teams need to learn is the cost of long delays in decision making under conditions where there are advantages to acting early. The boards need not interfere, but they may prod teams who are postponing action on important capital investments. They can urge comfortably profitable teams to set higher aspirations for performance and innovation. They can exaggerate or diminish the evaluation which teams put on the various errors that they make. Directors can meet informally with individual team members on special problems that come up between meetings.

The job of the board of directors, though, is not solely to goad the teams toward higher performance. In contacts with other outside groups —like auditors, labor negotiators, the game administrators, or even insurgent stockholders—the directors can play a supportive role. They can help a team which is doing well by encouraging them and by rewarding them for the best parts of their performance. The board chairman for at least one team has drafted and sent angry letters to the Game administrators protesting what he regards as inequities in the treatment of his team by the computer.

If the pace of the Game lags, the board shares responsibility for trying to maintain students' interest and enthusiasm. It can make special assignments that will have educational value to the team. It can be available for student consultations. It can insist on reorganization of personnel and jobs within the team. It can begin to modify its measures of team performances—putting more stress, for example, on innovation and growth than on profits and stability once the team has good control of its position in the market.

5. *Student Reactions to the Boards.* By their freedom to intervene in the Game, the directors become influential not only in determin-

ing the tasks with which students must deal but also in determining students' basic attitudes and motivation in the Game. Through the board, students may have access to faculty members or outside business-men whom they would not otherwise know. The students value a chance to gain experience in playing roles that they expect to face later in business. They are likely to respond positively to boards—whatever the general prestige and seniority of their members—who assign problems that dovetail with the main tasks of the Game, who take an active interest in student progress, and who respect the special conditions that the Game imposes.

The relation between students and directors almost inevitably involves some stress. Basically, the directors are supervisors and critics, rather than advisors. As in the real world, their demands will not always square with what management wants to do or thinks it has time to do. Or because the board evaluates and assigns grades, students may probe timidly for cues to what the board wants as a substitute for independently planned actions. Different boards cannot all behave in a consistent fashion unless many artificial restrictions are put on their freedom of action. Demands from the board for plans, for documentation of decisions, and for explanations of performance (especially bad performance) are onerous and sometimes embarrassing. Honesty with the board is important if the teams hope to deserve their trust, but there are often strong temptations to withhold from the board plans and results that reflect unfavorably on a team.

Despite a certain degree of student resentment and frustration, our impression is that the boards do help the students in a way that mere playing of the Game could not. There are marked improvements by most teams in their ability to make intelligent, cogent presentations; in their ability to stand up to board questions and criticisms; and in their ability to control the agenda of board meetings. A major accomplishment for some teams is the ability to control relationships with the board so that they increase their own freedom of action and freedom from unwanted board assignments.

6. Advantages of Board Experience for the Faculty. In evaluating the usefulness of boards of directors for the Game, it is important to note their potential for educating the faculty. For a relatively small time commitment, 10–40 hours per semester, a faculty member gets a chance to try his hand at one of the important jobs in management—perhaps in the company of experienced business executives. More important, he gets a chance to learn about the Game. Service on the board is the easiest way to learn the basic structure of the Game, to observe how students play it, and to collect impressionistic evidence about what the Game is worth.

7. *Ways of Economizing Board Time.* Since the total time investment is small and since we have not asked faculty members to serve as board members for more than one team, we have not offered teaching credit for participating on boards. If there is a shortage of faculty members to do the job or a restricted number who are interested, the following methods might be tried to minimize costs of faculty time:

(a) *Reduction in Size of the Boards.* To be effective, boards of as few as three members are probably adequate if regular attendance can be assured. As an alternative, one man might represent a larger board for most meetings with the team, with sessions of the full board only convened two or three times a semester.

(b) *More Intensive Use of a Few Faculty on the Boards.* Some or all members of a board might monitor several teams and receive teaching credit for their efforts. To preserve competitive conditions, it is not advisable to have boards supervise more than one team in the same industry, but there is no reason why boards could not serve effectively across industries.

(c) *Reduction in the Duties of the Boards to a Few Specific Functions Which You Want to Emphasize in Play of the Game.* Too much emphasis on economy may be profitless, though. Much of the interest and value of the board sessions stems from the fact that it brings together as directors men with a variety of interests and areas of special knowledge, that it assigns them to work with teams to help them do their best in the Game, and that the dimensions of the relationship are what the team and the board make of them. It is a case where infrequent or carefully constrained board activity may be no better than none at all.

B.   The Management Audit[2]

A second role-playing experiment developed from a desire to let students become familiar with the Game before they began play in the second year of the graduate program, and from some ideas for improving the treatment of certain topics in the first-year accounting course. The specific opportunity arose when the instructors in the accounting course decided that students ought to learn something about the philosophy and techniques of auditing.

Since we wished to use auditing primarily as a vehicle to deepen the student's understanding of accounting systems and of the control

---

[2]Much of this account of the management audit is taken from Neil C. Churchill, Merton H. Miller, and Robert M. Trueblood, *Auditing, Management Games, and Accounting Education* (Monograph #2 in the Carnegie Institute of Technology Series on Management Education; Homewood, Ill.: Richard D. Irwin, Inc., 1964). Readers are referred to the longer monograph for a detailed discussion and analysis of the audit experiment from the point of view of its contribution to the teaching of accounting.

process, we felt that field work of some kind was essential to supplement the normal readings and class discussions. We chose to use a real-life project consisting of auditing the teams of second-year students then engaged in playing the Game. With the required complexity of planning, control, and coordination problems, a considerable documentary record of the play over and above the financial statements is inevitably built up by each of the teams.

The Game appeared to offer several positive advantages as a basis for an audit project when compared with either of the other alternatives—a field study in a real business, or an armchair set of practice problems.

In contrast to a practice set, the Game provided a living environment where the student evaluates both the need for control and actual performance. Rather than work from secondary sources, the student must himself discern the actual people-against-people and people-against-record checks that exist. Or, if such checks do not exist, he must design, recommend, and sell them to management.

Compared with sending beginning students into actual business concerns, whether to observe the operation of auditors or to conduct some audit tests themselves, the use of the Game had a number of advantages over and above the very real advantage of not requiring the time of busy corporate officers nor of raising questions about confidential material. The Game kept the students from being overwhelmed by the complexity and detail of real-world systems and allowed the students to see the whole structure of a small audit—rather than a small piece or two of the control system that could be surveyed in a real concern in the limited time available. In addition, the Game permitted the students to play the role of senior auditors rather than junior technicians, which resulted in the emphasis being placed on the philosophy and the principles of auditing. The students' attention in the context of the Game could be directed to the attesting of the general adequacy of management's controls, its stewardship of the firm's assets, and the appropriateness of management's financial statements. This direction contrasts strongly with encouraging a preoccupation with the specialized and detailed procedures which would be appropriate in evaluating a small part of a large organization's control procedures or account balances. An audit of other students would also be more likely to sustain interest and motivation of the beginning students. They would not be confronting experienced professionals, and hence would feel free to question the system with an expectation of finding ample material on which to base letters of recommendation. Finally, from a purely pedagogical point of view, the Game provided a set of independent tasks that were not identical (since each firm was different), but were

still sufficiently similar to make relative evaluation of audit performance fairly easy.

Despite these potential advantages in the Game as a basis for a
field audit, we were aware that there were also certain possible difficulties. We were concerned, for example, that the auditors might not
obtain the necessary cooperation from the Game firms.

A second possible difficulty stemmed from the fact that simulated
Game firms are necessarily highly abstract. The entire human organization of the firm, below the vice-presidential level at which the players operate, is built into the computer—as are most of the accounting
transactions and records underlying the monthly financial statements
the players receive (balance sheet, income statement, and cash receipts
and disbursements). Much of the normal raw material of the standard
audit (bank statements, purchase orders, voucher files, payroll registers,
and the like) has no counterpart in the Game.

At the same time, and much more important in terms of overall
objectives, we emphasized throughout the assignment that the primary
task of the audit teams was to audit the procedures and controls actually
utilized by the student managers in developing general policies for the
team, and in making the separate decisions implementing these policies.
The auditing students were encouraged to evaluate the effective communication of these decisions and policies within the Game team, to the
computer, to the board of directors, and to the public via the published
financial statements. By continual emphasis in class and by providing
many specific examples, we hoped the auditors would come to see that
the Game team's records constituted not only a legitimate file of
auditable materials, but also a viable example of control processes.

First-year students were prepared for the audit by approximately two
weeks of classroom work and by outside readings and problems. These
dealt with the history and philosophy of auditing, with the techniques
that auditors use, with the professional relations between auditors and
clients, and with the specifics of the auditing problem which the Game
poses.

There was one first-year audit team for each Game team, and each
audit team was under the supervision of a managing partner. At the
request of the boards of directors, the audit teams were asked to meet
with the Game teams to arrange for an audit proposal. Then the managing partner and one or two of his associates met with the board and
management to get approval for the scope of the audit and to agree on
an audit fee, which was to be charged to management.

The fee submitted by the auditors was intended to provide the basis
for a discussion of the scope of the audit engagement and of the extent
of the cooperation of the members of the management with the audit

team. The device of the fee gave the audit firms a modest sanction to obtain the necessary cooperation from the management teams. As it turned out, the boards were, if anything, overly conscientious about the matter of fees. They were inclined at first to have a very narrow view of the auditor's function, and many regarded the proposed audit of their company's decision-making performance as constituting management services (for which they were unwilling to pay), rather than as a proper part of an audit engagement looking to the certification of financial statements. A few of the audit teams crumpled under this surprise attack from the boards. Most of the managing partners, however, were able to make a sufficiently convincing case for the broader, modern view of the audit process and successfully justified their estimated fee.

In completing the audit, the audit teams had to work closely with the Game teams to get the information that they needed. The end result was a detailed report, first to management alone, and then jointly to management and the board of directors, of the findings of the audit. In the prior meeting with management, it was not intended that the auditors and management should bargain over the report, but rather that questions of fact and interpretation could be brought out into the open, that misunderstandings could be cleared up, and that both management and the auditors would be placed on notice as to the areas where disagreement existed. It turned out that in some cases, the auditors were indeed hasty in their judgment and rephrased their report. In other cases, the management readily acknowledged the deficiencies that the auditors found. However, in still other instances, mutual agreement was not attained, and both groups retired from the meeting to marshal facts for the defense of their position before the boards. Much potential controversy over items of lesser importance was eliminated by the preparatory meeting with management. Although the reports to the boards contained all the observations that the auditors thought should be disclosed, the preliminary meeting left both sides free to concentrate on the more serious issues when both groups later met with the board.

Prior to the board meeting, representatives from each board met and agreed to schedule their board meetings for a two-hour period. During the first hour and a half, the board, the management, and the auditors discussed the audit report. The management was then asked to leave, and the next fifteen minutes were devoted to private discussion of the audit report between the board and the auditors.[3] Finally, in the last

---

[3]One reason for having the auditors discuss the report with the management absent was to see whether they would bring up items that they hesitated to discuss when management was present and ready to defend itself. As it turned out, some audit teams did just this—mostly to their sorrow.

fifteen minutes, the faculty stepped out of their role as board members and discussed critically with the audit team their performance in the audit, both in its written and its oral phases.

The results of this experiment for the students in the auditing course are treated in a detail in a monograph by Churchill, Miller, and True-blood,[4] but our concern here is to estimate its impact on the men playing the Game.

For the team as a whole, but especially for those who have responsibility for the kinds of records and procedures the auditors are interested in, the anticipation of an audit affects the care with which they set up records and procedures and the care with which they work to make sure that these systems are maintained. The auditor reinforces the board's stress on systematic analysis, careful work, and attention to detail.

The audit also challenges the team to work effectively with a group whose primary mission is evaluative and who can report negative as well as favorable findings to the directors. While the auditors lack strong sanctions to get information from the teams, they could report lack of cooperation from management either directly to the board or indirectly by submitting a larger bill for their services. The team's dilemma in striking a balance in this network of relationships is realistically delicate.

On the whole, though, two qualifications should be made. First, the audit has more impact on how teams play *if* teams know they are going to be audited and have time and motivation to anticipate the audit in their behavior and *if* the team is going to continue play for some reasonable period after the auditors report their findings. One weakness of our use of the audit is that the final reports have come from the auditors at or after the end of Game play. Thus, except for their influence on board evaluations, they are reports which the team can disregard.

Second, even under the broad definition of the audit which was used in this case (a definition whose breadth is apparently not universally acceptable yet among accountants), the audit has impact chiefly on those members of the team who are concerned with accounting and financial matters. They had to spend most time with the auditors, and it was their work that was under closest scrutiny. Unless the notion of an audit is broadly defined, the project is probably not a very valuable addition to the Game from the players' point of view (though it may still be valuable to the accounting course). One way around the issue

---

[4] *Op. cit.*

may be to combine the audit with a more general evaluation of the team's organization. The project is being expanded at Carnegie to become a joint assignment between the accounting course and a first-year course in organizational behavior.

Experience as auditors does influence the way that students subsequently play the Game. In 1961–62, there were 34 students playing the Game who had participated in the initial audit experiment the year before. Of these, ten indicated that the audit experience had had little or no effect on their behavior in the Game, again in many cases because their job in the Game was far removed from the things that they were concerned with. Of the remaining 24 students, Table 3–1 shows the kinds of effects they listed.

TABLE 3–1

EFFECTS OF PARTICIPATION IN THE AUDIT ON SUBSEQUENT PARTICIPATION IN THE GAME*

Effect Reported	Percent of Students Reporting (n = 34)
Little or no effect...	29%
Some effect or effects...	71
Specific effects	
Helped us develop better or more accurate records of team activity.	32%
Helped us keep better control of internal operations.............	29
Helped us develop decision rules..............................	24
Introduced us to the mechanics of the game....................	24
Provided team experience useful in organizing game team........	18
Prepared us better for this year's audit.......................	15
Gave us insight into possible personnel problems...............	9
Helped us get involved in the game more rapidly...............	9

*Based on responses to a questionnaire distributed to all members of management game teams at the end of the 1961–62 run at Carnegie. Only responses from men who also participated in the management audit in 1960–61 have been tallied here. The statistics have been coded from open-ended replies.

The students reported mainly that the audit helped them manage data and decisions more systematically. The audit also made the Game easier to learn, despite substantial changes from one year to the next in the Game model. The problems of organizing and controlling the audit teams gave students useful insight into the problems they would face in organizing the Game teams. And although Table 3–1 does not show this, it was obvious to faculty observers that the men who had been auditors as first-year students were much tougher, as managers, for the new group of auditors to deal with. They established better records and systems, thus cutting their susceptibility to criticism. They were also more adept in negotiating with the board and with the auditors initially to limit the scope of the audit and in controlling what they revealed to the auditors about their procedures and performance while the audit was in progress.

C.   Grievances and Contract Negotiations[5]

To give students realistic experience with labor problems, we have established a collective bargaining agent for the firms' employees as part of the Game environment. The employees were represented by the United Detergent Workers of America, and the firms were given copies of the collective bargaining agreement between the United Detergent Workers of America, representing the employees, and the company. It set forth the conditions of employment that had been agreed to for the current contract period. The contract included a termination or reopening date, and described the procedures that the parties to the agreement would use to initiate negotiations for a new contract. Faculty members with special interest in the field of labor economics and industrial relations played the roles of the union representatives.

1. Description of the Interactions with the Union. To provide a background for the bargaining behavior, news releases were issued periodically, reporting union elections, comments on related collective bargaining developments, and union statements of attitude and intent as the contract termination date approached. Some time prior to the negotiation period, the union representatives initiated and held meetings with management to discuss certain "pressing problems." At these meetings, the union expressed serious concern for its unemployed members, and attempted to obtain an agreement from the companies to limit the amount of scheduled overtime. As a pressure device, the union suggested that failure to limit overtime might lead to reductions in productivity and refusal of overtime assignments. Since these discussions took place during the period of the contract, the companies were formally protected by a broadly worded "no-strike" clause in the agreement. In each case, the union representatives met with management negotiators from individual firms. In some instances, firms agreed to limit their overtime. The others were penalized by having the Game committee provide only a fraction of the scheduled overtime. The impact of this penalty depended on the circumstances of the individual firms, and on the scheduling strategies they used in response to the union-imposed penalty.

At the appropriate time, the union representatives served notice on the firms of their desire to reopen the contract. The notice gave the

---

[5]This section has been adapted from materials prepared by Myron L. Joseph.

firms some indication of the types of demands that were probable. The union was limited by the wording of the reopening clause in the original agreement. The earlier grievance meeting served 'to communicate to the companies the fact that the union was anxious to do something about the unemployment situation. At the initial bargaining session, the union made demands in several areas. The first year, the union asked for a wage increase, a three-level wage schedule in place of a uniform rate, and severance pay. The second year, the demands were for a wage increase, an increase in severance pay, and a limit on the company's right to lay off workers. In all cases, the union obtained substantial wage increases and improvements on one or more of the other issues. The bargaining experience varied considerably. In some cases, the three firms in an industry succeeded in maintaining a solid front in negotiations, even to the point of an industry strike. In one case, a single firm attempted to obtain a temporary advantage in the industry by giving in quickly to most of the union's demand, assuming that the other companies would have to give the union at least as much as they had, and that there might be some gain from the quick settlement. One company became so emotionally involved in the negotiation process that it refused to give in to the union's "outrageous demands" even after the other two companies had granted them. They found themselves in a very serious situation when their plant was struck and the other two companies continued to operate.

The amount and type of management preparation for negotiations varied considerably. In some cases, the companies attempted to document their alleged inability to pay the union demands with comparative data and estimates of income and costs. In most instances, however, the management representatives did not present or prepare substantial evidence to support their positions. Their perceptions of the situation were affected both by the profit situation and the relative importance to the firms of the marginal costs of changes in working conditions. In the first set of negotiations some firms with reasonably high profit positions maintained firm bargaining positions because their boards insisted on detailed explanations of proposed bargaining strategies and reports on the status of negotiations.

In order to approximate a realistic situation, it was necessary to design appropriate penalties for a breakdown in negotiations, and to place artificial constraints on the union representatives. The management teams were constrained by their boards and by the impact on their profits of the wage increases and changes in the labor agreement. The union representatives were pictured as being under pressure from their members to obtain wage increases and improvements in the job security area. Through the publication of coercive comparisons and statements of intent made at union meetings, we tried to communicate the strength of certain demands. The union negotiators, however, were not under a real constraint. There was no real cost to their maintaining a hard and fast bargaining position. To remedy this, the union representatives agreed to follow an established bargaining strategy. They secretly formulated an initial demand and three lower positions. If any firm gave in to the second position, which was very close to the initial demand, the third was to be the minimum acceptable. The fourth position was the ultimate reservation demand, which had to be obtained to avoid a strike. The reasoning behind this strategy was that in general the union should insist on the same pattern from all the firms in the industry. However, if one firm was foolish enough to make an unreasonable concession, the union should not force the others to follow suit. The union position was that unless a firm could demonstrate a clear possibility of going out of business, it should pay the industry wage.

Pressure on the companies included the effective threat of slowdowns if a settlement was not reached as the deadline approached. By scheduling the strike or the start of the new labor contract one week after the decisions were made, companies that settled early and without difficulty could be given a cost advantage for a week on the basis that their employees cooperated with management more effectively than in the plants that negotiated down to the deadline. A predetermined limit was secretly placed on the length of any strike, after which the contract would be signed on the basis of the company's last offer. We scheduled play so that more than one month's decision could be made between the contract deadline and the time limit on strikes. This permitted strikes of varying length.

2. *Value of the Experience.* The bargaining sessions provided the participants with a dramatic example of the attitudes and values of labor union representatives. There was some surprise and resentment when the union representatives would not accept the company-oriented arguments of the management representatives. The union's emphasis on the short run, the introduction of institutional variables, and the apparent unwillingness to be concerned about the employment effect of wage increases were sources of conflict in the negotiations. The least profitable firms were particularly enraged at the union's insistence on a uniform pattern. The participants were forced to come to grips with a pattern of behavior they considered irrational. They discovered that the union representatives were unwilling to accept the assumption that management really knows the employees, and they met violent reac-

tions to seemingly innocuous statements which implied that the union did not accurately represent the employees.

In some cases, the negotiations led to an inquiry into the related labor law. Through reading and consultation with law students on another campus, teams studied their bargaining obligations and the legal limits on the union's striking power. One team discovered that the union could not legally prevent shipments from the rented storage facilities by outside truckers, and made use of this knowledge to strengthen its bargaining position. Another group of teams explored the terms under which they could establish an industry-wide bargaining unit. The role playing gave the participants some understanding of unions as institutions and of the legal environment within which collective bargaining takes place. Only a few points were made for each team, but if they became actively involved in the situation, the impact was strong.

The negotiations made the participants realize that they were involved in a power-bargaining situation. The difference between a problem-solving approach to a situation in which the goals and values are given and the bargaining problem was forcefully illustrated. It made the students very uncomfortable to compare the costs the union could inflict through a strike to the costs of concession. They had difficulty determining the extent to which equity and industry loyalty considerations should enter into the determination of bargaining strategy.

The interdependence of working conditions, wages, and other management decisions was clearly illustrated in the analysis required to evaluate bargaining alternatives. The union was seen as a force constraining or affecting management production and marketing behavior. Wage cost and labor force management were significant elements in management decisions.

The bargaining situation provided another context for demonstrating the strength of competitive behavior and some of the problems of cooperative action. The firms had varying success in their attempts to coordinate bargaining strategies, but in several cases there was a thorough review of the advantages and shortcomings of the cooperative action. This was most successful when the boards forced managers to defend their bargaining behavior.

The experience gave a small number of students the opportunity to participate in a radically different interpersonal communication problem. It is not easy to relate to and communicate with individuals who have a completely different frame of reference.

3. **Problems.** The major problem is establishing a situation in which the marginal costs of changes in the labor contract will be sig-

nificant for the teams. This implies a significant relationship of labor costs to total costs and a substantial price elasticity of demand. It also implies that students will have to live with the results of their bargaining behavior for some substantial period of Game play. The students must see the labor negotiations as an important factor in their overall evaluation as managers. The boards can accomplish this emphasis by pressing the managers to explain their bargaining strategies and by holding them to account for the results. It is helpful to the boards of directors, when they sit down to grade the teams, to have an advisory report from the union negotiators about their experiences with each of the teams.

D. The Stock Market

The most recent addition to the environment which confronts graduate students at Carnegie when they play the Game is a stock market and a large group of stockholders who each have from $10 to $50 of their own money invested in shares of the six Game teams and in simulated government bonds. The market is intended to generate for the Game teams stock prices which provide realistic external appraisals of their performance and potential.[6] It is also intended to help investors understand the institutional workings of a stock exchange and to give them valuable practice in making investment decisions.

The idea of a stock market as part of the environment of the Carnegie Game was conceived by John Bossons in the summer of 1963, and experimentation with the market was approved for the 1963–64 Game runs. Only a brief account will be given here because the effort was experimental and because the full value of the stock market as an aid to teaching finance and as an addition to the Game cannot yet be assessed.[7]

Even in its initial form the stock market exercise was detailed and realistic. In a departure from most previous efforts to incorporate a stock market with Game play, investors put in substantial amounts of their own money[8] rather than investing imaginary funds. Each $10

[6]For descriptions of earlier experiments coupling a stock market to a management game, see Martin Shubik, "Comments upon Games as a Teaching Device," in William R. Dill, James R. Jackson, and James W. Sweeney (eds.) *Proceedings of the Conference on Business Games as Teaching Devices* (New Orleans: Tulane University, 1961), pp. 134–35; and Section I.C of Chapter 6.

[7]A description of the stock market is available in John Bossons, "Player's Manual for the Carnegie Stock Exchange Pool" (dittoed paper, Graduate School of Industrial Administration, Carnegie Institute of Technology, September 1963). Professor Bossons was assisted in elaborating, programming, and administering his design by three graduate assistants: Charles F. Dickinson, Seymour I. Gilman, and Thomas J. Gross.

[8]For students but not for faculty, the School added 50 percent to the first $20 that an investor put in. Thus his initial stake could be as high as $60, and students had some cushion against the cash losses resulting from bad investment decisions.

invested up to the $50 maximum bought a unit portfolio of stocks in the six firms and of government bonds. The investors included members of the Game teams, directors, other faculty members, other graduate students, and students in certain undergraduate finance and economics courses—a large and diverse enough group so that many kinds of investment strategies would come into play. Investors could buy and sell on a daily basis, and they could institute most of the kinds of orders that would be possible on the New York Stock Exchange. Three times a week the *Tech Street Journal* published stock and bond prices, news and rumors about the companies, dividend announcements, reports of "insider" transactions, general information about the economy, and explanations of stock exchange rules and traditions. At the end of the semester the payout to investors was determined by market values of the stocks and bonds as of the close of trading. Each investor's portfolio was evaluated on the basis of these prices, and the original pool of funds paid in (both by participants and by the School's subsidy) was then divided among participants in proportion to the ratio of the value of each investor's portfolio to the total value of all participants portfolios.

In most respects, the stock market exercise did not directly affect the tasks of teams in the Game. In fact, we explicitly tried to rule out such seemingly natural kinds of interactions as stockholders' control over boards of directors and possibilities for proxy battles until, with a year's experience, we might better assess their potential impact on the educational objectives of both the market exercise and the Game.

Still, the existence of the stock market did affect the behavior of teams. Because both directors and student managers had their own money invested, there was sharper interest in profits, dividends, and the other factors that influence external evaluation of the firm. Efforts to sustain and improve management performance continued at a high level through the semester rather than decreasing, as they sometimes had, during the final weeks of play. Teams were encouraged to think about their "image" and to make sure their competitive accomplishments were good in quality and well publicized to investors.

Prompt communication of news that investors had a right to know became important. Teams were warned to learn and observe the laws and traditions governing such things as "insider" trading. Early in the semester, members of one team which was tardy in publishing a dividend decision continued to make heavy purchases of their own stock. Legal charges were brought against the team by a faculty member under a New York State law intended to penalize concealment of information by "insiders." With the help of a lawyer whom they had hired for the occasion, the team members won acquittal. The point was made, though, that prompt disclosure of such decisions was important and that in cases of doubt or delay, team members should either check their obligations with a representative of the Carnegie Stock Exchange or they should refrain from purchase or sales of stock that might be seen as suspect.[9]

Finally, the stock market exercise was exciting enough for some students to divert their attention from their main duties as managers in the Game. The most conspicuous case occurred when a small group from one team combined with several student investors who were not playing the Game in an attempt to buy control of a firm in another industry. The Carnegie Foundation (controlled by the committee in charge of the market and of the Game) held a large portion of stock in each firm so that they could thwart challenges of this sort. Faculty decisions at the beginning of the semester to decouple the market from the Game also made successful completion of the venture unlikely. Nevertheless, encouraged by a ruling that cumulative voting for directors was mandatory under the corporate laws of Pennsylvania and seeing an opportunity to outflank the Game committee, the insurgents continued to buy. When they called a stockholders' meeting and appeared able under cumulative voting to elect at least one and perhaps two of the four directors, the Game committee stopped the action under their earlier commitment to keep the market and the Game separate. Perhaps in another year when the legal system in which the firms operate has been more clearly defined and when the conditions under which students can control the faculty members and executives who serve as directors have been worked out, such a "raid" might be allowed to go to completion. For this year, though, the insurgent students were credited with a strategic victory over the faculty and were given a reason-

---

[9]As protection against future charges, the president of the team involved issued these instructions for others in his organization:

Since the reporting of insider transactions on the Carnegie Stock Exchange makes it impossible for the members of Firm 5-3 to function as private investors when trading in the stock of Firm 5-3, the members of the Company have agreed upon several rules to guarantee that the transactions of individual managers and directors do not reflect unfavorably upon the Firm.

1. The total volume of transactions in the stock of Firm 5-3 in any week by any one manager shall not exceed $\frac{1}{12}$ of the total volume in the stock during the previous week.

2. All transactions shall be for the long term. Short-term speculating (9 months or less) shall be prohibited except in exceptional circumstances.

3. All information which should be released to the investing public will be released as soon as possible according to established procedures. Should there be any gap between a decision and the public release of the decision all members of Firm 5-3 shall refrain from trading in the stock of Firm 5-3 during the interim.

able interval in which to sell excess stock in the firm they had planned to acquire to the Carnegie Foundation at a guaranteed price.

We plan to continue the experiment with a stock market exercise as an adjunct to the Game. The directions of future development are not yet clear, though. One requirement may be to seek a still larger pool of student investors, to broaden the market. A second and clearer requirement is that we prepare for both the stock market and the Game teams a more explicit description of the laws and regulations that constrain their behavior. These laws and regulations will undoubtedly be a mix of excerpts from real-world statutes and rules with provisions that fit the artificial conditions of the stock market and Game environment as educational ventures. A third desire, but not a requirement in the strict sense, is to find reasonable ways of linking the market and the Game so that directors will be somewhat responsible to stockholders and so that at least one stockholders' meeting each semester can become an important and meaningful feature of the Game.

III. STRUCTURING THE ORGANIZATIONAL PROBLEMS THAT TEAMS FACE

The organizational problems which teams must solve are functions of many things—the backgrounds, abilities, and personalities of team members; the schedule for Game play and its relation to the rest of the curriculum; the Game model and the behavior of competitors; and the demands which stem from role-playing assignments built around the Game. Many of the variables which influence the definition of organizational problems are subject to faculty and administrative control. Some of these are discussed in the pages which follow.

A. Setting Up Teams

The organizational challenge depends greatly on the size and the makeup of the teams. We have tried teams of as few as three and as many as ten men. In general, the smaller the team, the more likely it is that it will try to operate as a committee and that it will be able to avoid defining formal jobs and rules for interaction among team members. A team of five or more members, without any direct instructions to do so, is likely to elect a president or chairman and over the course of the Game to give him power to lead and to control. The larger team is likely to establish clearly defined roles and to develop charts or manuals of procedures to make sure that work gets done on time and in the proper sequence. Teams of more than five or six people also face problems of providing prestigeful work or compensating inducements to peripheral members and of instituting controls to protect themselves against the mistakes, delays, and omissions which some-times plague bureaucratic organizations.

The policies used to assign students to teams may be as important as size. So far, at Carnegie, we have tried to use academic performance as the major criterion for assignment to insure that no team has a monopoly of "good" or "poor" students. We have sometimes taken the advice of our graduate assistants or data from sociometric ratings to avoid serious mismatches of people who do not work well together. In competitive educational runs of the Game it seems important to establish teams in ways that no team will feel greatly disadvantaged in personnel relative to the other teams.

For the 1962–63 academic year, mainly because we intended to ask the team president's advice in assigning grades in the Management Game course, we asked the first-year men who would be playing the Game to list men under whom they would like to serve as president (including themselves, if they wanted) and men whom they would like to have on their team. These sociometric preferences for leaders and coworkers were used as the basis for setting up the teams. This approach eased the process of winning acceptance for the presidents' participation in the grading process, and in addition, seems to have reduced the number of instances of serious personal incompatibility which developed on teams in other years.[10]

Another suggestion for assigning men to teams would establish groups of men with homogeneous rather than heterogeneous academic records.[11] By putting men with comparable course records together, one might expect to increase the competition among the best students for influential places in the team organization, to give the poorer students greater motivation to try to excel in the Game, and to make it easier within teams to rotate men from job to job. We are trying this for the 1963–64 runs of the Game. For these runs, we have not only permitted the class to elect the presidents, but—within restrictions to keep the groups homogeneous—we have also let the presidents choose their own teams. Leaving the choices to the students seems to work out well.

For the school which offers majors in various areas of management or for advanced management programs, prior specialization of training or experience may also provide an interesting basis for setting up teams. Such assignments could be made to capitalize on the special training

---

[10]The reasons for grading performance in the Game and the approaches we are trying at Carnegie are discussed in Section V.C.

[11]This is the one of a number of proposals made by William Fox of the University of Florida to make administration of the Game more effective.

that each man has, to give each man the challenge of working outside his previous specialty, or to enhance the competition among teams by pitting men from one department or specialty against another.

B.   External Suggestions about How to Organize

There are a variety of ways, once teams have been assigned, to set constraints on how they organize to do their job. We have tried to set formal constraints on organization in some teams by asking directors to specify the jobs which were to exist and in other teams by asking directors to specify both the jobs and the men who were to fill them. We find, though, that students adamantly prefer to define jobs and to decide who will fill them with a minimum of faculty control. Apart from the dissatisfaction that faculty interference tends to create, there are indications from our Game experience, from Bass's experience with another game, and from many studies in the real world that external assignments of this sort do not have the effects intended.[12] If the team does not like the structure that is imposed on them, they readily develop an informal, partially hidden structure which conforms more closely to their own interests, motivations, and capabilities.

Even if directors do not give direct instructions about how to organize, their influence and the influence of other outside groups are considerable. By asking questions, by altering the operating goals that teams set, and by making other additions to the game task, the directors can impose intentional or unintentional limits on the kinds of organization that teams will consider feasible. A systematic set of internal records and controls is not necessary to satisfy the computer, but it is necessary if the auditors are to certify a team's financial statements.

A two-year forecast of sales, plant capacity, and cash flows may be of little help in making decisions for the computer; but if the board asks for it, someone has to prepare it. Thus, each team must make provision in its organization for men to handle the assignments which outside groups add to their task load. In addition, the team must also make provision for men who can present things effectively to these outside groups. The president may be chosen more for his skills in dealing with the faculty than for his skills in administering the team. The production manager might be chosen for his negotiating ability with the union more than for his skill in doing linear programming analysis of product shipments.

---

[12]Bernard M. Bass, "Production Organization Exercises: An Application of Experimental Techniques to Business Games," in W. W. Cooper, H. J. Leavitt, and Maynard Shelly (eds.), *New Perspectives in Organization Research* (New York: John Wiley & Sons, 1964); Melville Dalton, *Men Who Manage* (New York: John Wiley & Sons, 1959).

C. Changes in Parameters of the Game

Variations in the parameters for the Game model can also mean large variations in the kinds of tasks that teams must organize for. Especially recommended are settings which will induce teams to reconsider their organizational system after the Game is underway, because most of the "organizing" takes place in early moves. If the Game goes smoothly, students are not likely to volunteer time to work at improving what seems to be a successful system. Occasional crises in profits, competitive position, or other aspects of performance are desirable. We have accomplished this, for example, by setting parameters so that after four or five moves teams will need new plant or warehouse capacity. This usually leads to an awkward situation for teams which do not provide time for forecasting and planning activities. By failing to anticipate the need for expansion, the team may have to forego some sales and profits. Furthermore the belated recognition of the need for increased capacity may lead to acceptance under time pressure of superficial suggestions for remedial action.

D. Time Constraints

Especially with large teams and with arrangements for playing the Game as one of five demanding graduate courses, it becomes a major organizational task to schedule time for making decisions. Under certain conditions—such as playing the Game with part-time students who commute to campus from distant homes—it may be nearly impossible for players to schedule meetings without faculty help. To lessen the scheduling problem at Carnegie, we have protected a block of three to five hours in the formal weekly class schedule when teams can meet. We have assigned a certain number of "credits" to the Game so that students can judge roughly what their time is worth. We have imposed regular time limits, ranging from a few hours to several days, between the receipt of information and the deadline for filing decisions for a Game month.

E. Rotation of Personnel

Rather than take steps to change the jobs which men in various positions on a team perform, another way of refreshing interest and of reviving organizational problems is to move players from job to job or from team to team during the Game. If men exchange jobs, they at least get experience in handling another of the specialized positions which their team has established. The new combinations of personality and position should force reconsideration and restatement of some of the "organizational truths" which derived from experience with practices that did and did not work before rotation. After rotation, many old generalizations will seem trivial and new propositions will be needed.

Rotation is hard to accomplish, though. In the first three runs of our Game, we found that most teams intended initially to shift assignments around among team members during the play. Yet these intentions have never been carried through. In order to keep up competitively with other teams, to keep peace with the directors, and to save time for other courses, teams are reluctant to lose the expertise of men who have been doing particular jobs and to disrupt arrangements which are both stable and familiar. If rotation is to occur, the faculty probably has to promote or force it and needs to insure that the team does not simply maintain its old division of labor under new labels.

F. Feedback

Direct observations about the quality of organizational decisions do not come to the teams as often and as clearly as do assessments of the quality of their marketing or production decisions. One of the important jobs of the boards of directors is, by question and comment, to give the students judgments on their organizational prowess and to set reasonable benchmarks for students to use in assessing themselves.

Our experience has indicated that periodic efforts to review and question a team's performance as an organization (or to get them to evaluate themselves) produce beneficial effects of two kinds. Such assessment sessions help players to realize more clearly the problems they have had and the relation of these problems to situations they have found in case studies or readings in their other courses. They also seem to encourage teams to experiment more in the direction of discarding standard stereotypes about how to organize and of devising arrangements that are especially suited to their team and to the Game.

Because the board of directors has a formal supervisory relationship over the team, it cannot be in the best position to play a less formal counseling role on organizational problems. This is especially true when the most troublesome problems are ones which center around relationships with the board. In 1961–62, we tried to increase the rate and quality of organizational learning and organizational experimentation in two ways. The first was by assigning to each team a "coach"— a faculty member who attended all meetings between the team and its board, who attended as many working sessions of the team as he could, who could serve as a consultant to the team, and who was specifically dissociated from the board and from major responsibilities for grading so that team members could talk frankly with him about their problems. Each coach received teaching credit for a course for servicing two teams, one in each of the industries that were run that year. Unlike faculty directors, the coaches could participate very actively in helping the students if their instincts as teachers told them this was appropriate.

The venture with coaches was not a success. In principle, the idea still seems like a good one, but the coach's role is easier to define in words than in practice. In reality, the teams came to depend on the coaches, not for frequent help on a broad spectrum of problems, but for answers to specific questions about a few things that the coaches were expert in and for aid in pleading their case with the Game committee when they objected to the way the computer model dealt with their companies. Because the teams did not do much of their work in plenary session, and because the meetings that were held were often scheduled on an impromptu basis late in the evening in the dormitory, coaches were not able to monitor the teams' private work sessions very effectively. On most matters, because the teams were spending many more man-hours than the faculty in trying to analyze the Game results, the teams were ahead of the coaches in their analysis. Except for advice on how to approach the board of directors, the coach seemed to have little to contribute.

In some ways faculty members may be too remote from the teams to serve effectively as coaches. An alternative which we have not tried —but which might work well—would be to use advanced doctoral students for the coaching role (or in the case of undergraduate players, to use masters' degree candidates).

Our second experiment was more successful. Herbert A. Simon, James G. March, and Kenneth E. Knight used the game as a "laboratory" for a course in organization theory which most of the players were taking at the same time. The details of how they managed this are discussed in Chapter 5 but the basic approach was to challenge the players as individuals and teams to reflect upon and interpret their own behavior.

An eventual development in our use of the Game, we hope, will be a series of informal review sessions with teams and individuals in which they can talk fairly freely about their organizational goals and experiences and in which they can be encouraged to practice skills of self assessment and to become bolder and more imaginative in questions of organizational design.

IV. PROVIDING FOR LEARNING ABOUT PERSONAL CAPABILITIES AND LIMITATIONS

Out of the problems of handling the operating tasks of managing a company and of surviving as a team, there are opportunities of a direct and incidental nature for individuals to learn more about themselves and about their capacities as potential executives. These opportunities were not given much consideration when we designed the Game, but they have become apparent as we have used it.

Because there are no formally scheduled class sessions in the Game and because it is up to the students to define the magnitude of the job that they have and decide how to get it done, each participant faces basic problems of deciding what he will contribute to the team and learning to manage his time so that he can make the contribution. He must weigh other demands on his time, assess the tasks and pressures from his teammates, and make judgments about how much he will do. The duties he has and the deadlines he must meet come to a much larger extent from his fellow students than they do from the faculty.

The Game also provides vivid experience with some distinctions that students often previously did not become aware of until they began working in industry. These are the distinction between analysis and commitment and the distinction between commitment and commitment with carry-through. The most expensive errors that Game teams make, in terms of paper profits and relations with the boards, are usually errors that stem from assuming that an idea or procedure will work automatically, without controls on its accuracy or its completion. The importance of attention to detail and to "follow-through" does not help make the Game popular with bright and ambitious students, but we think it does teach some useful lessons about the standards by which performance is judged in management.

The Game is a challenge to the viability of normal student peer-group relations as a basis for managing a firm. It is tempting, under a tight schedule of work and in a closely knit student community, for players to take division of responsibility too seriously and to acquiesce in proposals or actions that may be cause for regret later on. Especially in those areas where the Game provides move-by-move data on the outcomes of action or inaction, and under conditions where the team's record is under scrutiny by the directors and by outside auditors, it is incumbent on each participant to speak up on things about which he has doubts and to question the easy acceptance of suggestions within the team.

Finally, the Game as a prolonged and intensive group experience provides many players with useful information about how their class-mates view them. Not all of this is pleasant feedback, but some of it is beneficial nonetheless. One man with considerable supervisory ability and experience had a tendency to be dictatorial in his relations with others on the team. His teammates made him president, but their re-sistance to his supervision led him to considerable reflection about how he could improve his behavior. A second man was told bluntly in mid-game that his own problems and his own biases kept getting in the way of his understanding what others wanted. He sought special oppor-tunities from other students and from the faculty to learn how to do a better, more objective job of assessing how others felt. A third man who wanted badly to become president of a team found that his team-mates never considered him for the job because they thought he was not "interested." It is unlikely that he would have been chosen in any case, but since he had a fair degree of leadership potential, the ex-perience taught him something about the necessity of making his am-bitions evident.

We have not really begun to capitalize on the use of the Game as an instrument of specific training for individuals, and we do not really have good evidence of how effective it will be for such purposes.[13] More evidence is needed about the personal effects of game experience on in-dividual players; about ways of using reflective self-assessment assign-ments or student and faculty feedback sessions to challenge and assist individual players; and about ways of modifying the Game tasks, job assignments, and organizational arrangements to suit the needs of particular groups of players.

V.   THE PLACE OF THE GAME IN THE M.S. CURRICULUM AT CARNEGIE[14]

Any educational innovation, if it is to be more than a fad, must eventually be embedded into the relevant curriculum. This does not mean that the whole curriculum must be constructed in the image of the innovation as has sometimes been done with the case method. Rather, it seems to us, an eclectic approach must be taken to the cur-riculum problem. There is a variety of material to be taught and ac-

[13]One experiment toward this end was initiated during the spring semester, 1963, by Professors Harold J. Leavitt and James G. March. In a course in Administrative Action which followed play of the Game, they devoted a great deal of time to having small groups of students discuss, analyze, and evaluate one another's behavior over the two years they had spent together at Carnegie. Behavior in the Management Game, as remem-bered by the students, was important and useful raw material for these discussions.

[14]This section is based on a paper by Richard M. Cyert, "Integration of the Game into the Curriculum," in *Proceedings of the Conference on Business Games as Teaching De-vices, op. cit.,* pp. 44–47.

cordingly a variety of methods are appropriate. There may be—as we have already suggested—an advantage to varying methods from year to year.

For the first two years in which we used the Game at Carnegie Tech with our second-year graduate students, we did not use it as a course. The play of the Game was placed on top of an already crowded curriculum as an overload for both graduate students and faculty. This approach, while obviously far from an optimal one, was deliberately taken as part of an experiment to test the utility of the Game as an educational instrument. At the same time, the approach gave those faculty members not involved in the construction of the Game a chance to acquaint themselves with the details. After two experimental runs, the faculty agreed that we must either build the Game into the curriculum as a regular course or eliminate it. Impressed with its potential effectiveness, we decided to build it into the curriculum.

A. Features of the Game

In trying to determine where in the total curriculum the Game fits best, we tried to evaluate the Game's characteristics. For example, it gives the student an opportunity to apply a number of the quantitative "tools for decision making" that are taught in the first year of our curriculum. In addition, opportunities are presented to utilize knowledge learned from the study of human relations and of organization theory.

The Game, however, must be examined in a more general way as well. Essentially, the Game is a living case. The student is put in a situation with a variety of problems to be identified and solved. More important, the student must be prepared to live with his decisions. In this respect, the Game is unique. No other educational tool presents this opportunity and challenge.

As a living case, the Game has another feature of significance. It presents a natural setting for what might be called "role-playing" situations. Such situations might range from disciplining personnel to auditing or negotiation. A variety of such "real-life" situations arise. The primary advantage of the Game for such exercises is that, if they are properly constructed, the student will not have to act out a role. Since the performance of his firm depends on the solutions he generates, he has real and not artificial motivation for his behavior.

A third, more general feature of the Game must be borne in mind when building it into the curriculum. This feature is its potential for giving a quick feedback on the behavior, intellectual and judgmental, that we are trying to achieve by our educational program. This means, among other things, that with a little imagination we can quickly test the efficiency of our teaching in a way that class problems or exams can never do. By viewing the Game in this fashion and using it accordingly, we may be able to detect, and attempt to remedy, the defects of our program, or encourage the student to do so, before the student has left school.

B.   Implementation

Given, then, that we want to incorporate the Game into the curriculum, the questions of "where" and "how" remain. The question of "where" is, perhaps, slightly easier to answer.

Two points which have been made earlier help to determine the time boundaries. First, since the students should apply in the Game certain techniques which they have learned, the Game obviously cannot come before these tools have been learned. If we are thinking of a four-semester graduate program, this means that the Game should come after the first semester and possibly after the second. On the other hand, if the Game is to give us feedback on the defects of the training of the students, we want it to be played, in part at least, before the fourth semester. Thus, if the Game is to be played for only one semester, the third semester is probably best. This is what we tried in 1961–62. If it is to be played two semesters, then it might be played either in the second and third or the third and fourth semesters.[15]

Although our experience at Carnegie has been solely with a two-year graduate program, we recognize that many prospective users may want to use the Game in one-year programs. If the students entering a one-year program have prior training or experience in busines, it may not matter when the Game is introduced. But if they do not enter with such training or experience, we would recommend—because of the Game's complexity—that play be scheduled for the second rather than for the first semester. Using a game as complex as ours as a first experience to introduce students to business institutions and problems requires much more careful arrangements for supervision and feedback on play than does using such a game to let students test what they think they have learned from prior course work.

The question of whether the Game should be a one- or two-semester

---

[15]There has been some adverse reaction to the notion of playing the Game in the second and third semesters since the summer vacation intervenes. An interesting suggestion has been made by Professor Melvin Anshen which would make a virtue of this hiatus. He proposes to have each firm set out a detailed policy to cover a series of twelve decisions which would then be made by the computer sometime during the summer. In the fall, the firms would then face, most likely, a situation which would be quite different from the one they left.

course or whether it should be a one-semester course played over two semesters cannot be answered categorically. There are two constraints, however, which must be considered in using the Carnegie Game as a course. First, enough moves must be made to allow problems of long-run strategy to emerge. Second, enough time must be given for each decision so that the students will approach the decision-making problem in a reasoned and analytical manner.

The problem of how to use the Game as a course presents some real challenges. We have speculated on the problem and have done only preliminary experimentation. We are not entirely satisfied, though, with the results we have obtained so far.

It has been difficult in one semester to achieve a balance between giving students enough time on each decision and letting problems of long-run strategy develop. We have experimented with ways of increasing what can be done within one semester rather than extend play over two terms. In particular, by using multiperiod moves in conjunction with some form of a computer-based management information and control system, we have been able greatly to increase the speed of play. In this mode of Game play (which is initiated only after the students have learned the basic structure of moves), firms simultaneously make decisions for two or three future months. They also are permitted to write programs which will modify their future decisions on the basis of some of the intervening months' results. It is then possible for these multiperiod decisions to be processed by the computer at a rapid rate, providing feedback on several months' decisions in practically the same amount of elapsed real time as would be required for a single month's decision.[16]

Another solution is to select teams at the end of the spring term so that they have the summer to become familiar with the rules of play and to develop tentative goals, strategies, and an organization. This works best if there are not additions or deletions to the list of players over the summer, if students live close enough together over the summer to be able to meet occasionally, and if the required background materials (such as histories of the firms) can be made available early.

If we do extend the Game into the fourth semester, it will most likely be as part of our course in business policy. The task, rather than to continue play of the Game in the usual manner, may well be to present the students with "case problems" representing their own or other people's experience with the Game. Then, when they propose

---

[16]For further discussion of what has been done and what might be done, see Chapter 4, Section V.C; Chapter 5, Section V and Appendix 5B; Chapter 8, Sections II.B and III.A; and Chapter 9, Sections II.B and III.D.

different strategies for action, the effects of these strategies can be tested by the computer and the results can yield a more meaningful discussion of the consequences of particular kinds of actions.

C. Grading

In making the Game part of the curriculum, we were asked by the students to grade it as a guide to the total emphasis we want put on the Game as opposed to other courses. The problems of grading are somewhat unique. There is a problem of assigning individual marks for what is essentially a group task, under conditions where faculty members have little direct evidence about the contribution each player is making to his team. There is a problem of deciding the basis for grades since we ourselves are not sure what factors in team performance account for differences in profits, sales, and so on, among the firms and since the most direct performance that faculty sees—presentations to the board of directors—may not give good impressions of what a team or an individual is worth.

In 1961–62, grades were assigned by the boards, in consultation with the coaches. If the coach had not kept a close watch on team activities, his help to the board was marginal. In 1962–63 and in 1963–64, the directors consulted directly with the team presidents on grading, and in another year, we may base grades at least partially on some kind of end-of-semester peer rating within the teams. The memorandum about grading for the 1963–64 run reads as follows:

The board of directors is responsible at the end of the semester for recommending course grades for members of their team to the Management Game committee. These grades should reflect the differential contributions that individual student managers may make to the teams; and they should reflect the performance of the team as a whole relative to their competitors, to the comparable team in the other industry, and to the potential level of performance that the team might have achieved.

The board is responsible, in its contacts with the team, for establishing a reasonable basis for assigning grades. This means that the board must monitor the progress of the Game and the work of the team closely enough that they can make some judgments not just about what the team did achieve, but also about what they might have achieved had they played the Game differently. Much of the information on which grades are based comes from the formal meetings of the board with the team and from informal meetings of the directors with members of management.

During the semester, at least as frequently as each board meeting, directors are asked to set down briefly, using letter grades or any other rating categories which seem appropriate, their evaluation of the team and of the individuals on it *at that time*. This will give a better basis than we have had sometimes in past years for making summary judgments at the end of the term.

At the end of play, on a date to be arranged later in the semester, the boards will meet with the Management Game committee to hear and discuss a briefing which the committee will prepare on the relative performance of the six teams, viewed against what their competitors achieved, against what earlier teams in the Game have done, and against what the future for the teams look like. It is hoped that this report will make it easier for the boards to agree on an equitable basis for representing in their grades the relative performance of their teams. At this time, the boards will also receive ratings of students from faculty who have participated in special exercises (labor negotiations, the management audit, bank negotiations, etc.).

The board chairman should also consult with his team president on the relative contributions of individual members to team performance. The board chairman is not constrained to reveal to the president any preliminary thoughts that the board has about grades, and he is not constrained to accept the president's advice. However, it is hoped that the consultation will lead to more adequate consideration by the board of contributions to team performance that have not shown up in their contacts with the team.

Then, working from their observations and ratings over the semester, the data that the Game committee will provide, and the advice of the team president, each board should meet to decide on a recommended set of grades for their team. These grades should be transmitted by the chairman to Professor Churchill, the Game administrator; and after each board has submitted its recommendations, the Game committee will review the grades. It is the committee's intent simply to confirm what the boards recommend; but if there are major questions of equity across teams, the committee reserves the right to convene a meeting of the board chairmen to discuss and resolve the inequities. *Under no circumstances are directors to reveal grades to students until they have been approved by the Game committee.*

This memorandum tries to respond to a problem encountered in previous years: preventing board members from overrating the performance of their own teams relative to other teams and also encouraging the boards to set up some reasonably consistent grading standards. To improve the grading the boards are asked to record written evaluations of the managers after each meeting with them. The Game administrator or the Game committee meets the directors at end of play to make an overall report on the teams. This report contains comparative data on various aspects of team performance and neutral estimates of where present patterns of decision making will lead the firms. In addition, the board chairmen meet together with the Game administrator to compare their tentative allocation of grades before any announcements of grades are made to students.

D. Preserving the Freshness of the Game Experience

Other questions about integrating the Game into the curriculum persist. How do we keep the Game fresh from year to year, as knowledge of it accumulates among the students, and as the routines of running it become familiar and tiresome to the faculty? The solution we propose is to keep innovating—so that the kind of game we run will vary at least in parameter settings from year to year, and occasionally will vary in major ways in the structure of the model. Innovation should also occur in the relation of the Game to other courses. The usefulness and excitement of things like the audit project develop partly from their intrinsic nature as assignments. They also result from the fact that the faculty is working hard to make them interesting and successful as experiments and to the fact that the students see the project as an interesting and novel one in which to get involved.

We have found that the complexity of the Game helps to keep it from "going stale." Even in cases where team members have known a great deal about past years' play and about the structure of the model, a few changes in parameters and the newness of strategies which competitors will choose to follow make much of such expertise irrelevant.

VI.   SUMMARY

As a course, the Game includes much more than the basic competitive task of playing against the computer and two other teams. We have tried to enrich it by posing for students a number of realistic role-playing challenges, in which they deal directly with boards of directors, union representatives, auditors, and bankers on problems that grow out of the operations of their firm. The demands of the competitive tasks and the role-playing situations force the teams into complex, formalized, hierarchical patterns of organization and make the characteristics of the organization that is established a crucial factor for success in the Game. In fulfilling his part in the organization and in balancing the demands of the Game against the demands of other courses, each team member has personal challenges to allocate his time effectively and to work harmoniously with others in his group.

In this chapter, we have reviewed a number of ways of building role-playing opportunities into the Game, of setting up team organizations and giving students opportunities to learn from their experience, and of fitting the Game into the curriculum. We have described some experiments that seem to have worked well, as well as some that we were not satisfied with. Our experiments are meant only as suggestions, since in another curriculum with different kinds of students, quite different ways of enriching the Game might be called for.

Chapter 4

TEAM RESPONSES TO THE CHALLENGE OF THE GAME[1]

In the two preceding chapters, we have described the tasks that confront teams in the Carnegie Tech Management Game. In this chapter, we outline some of the ways in which teams have responded to the basic challenges posed by competitors, by the computer model, by boards of directors, by auditors, by union representatives, by constraints on team organization and development, and by demands on team members' time external to the Game.

From this discussion, we hope to provide an understanding of what is involved in the total experience of playing the Carnegie Game and, furthermore, some examples of the ingenuity with which teams have approached the problems which the Game poses. The material in this chapter is drawn almost entirely from our experiences in using the Game with graduate students at Carnegie. It is supplemented in Chapter 6 with reports of how teams have approached the Game in quite different educational settings.

I. BASIC ARRANGEMENTS FOR PLAY

To understand fully the team behavior that is described below, the reader should be acquainted with some of the administrative arrangements for play that have been followed at Carnegie. As we explained in Chapters 2 and 3, the Game is played with three teams to an industry. There are five to eight students per team, and to accommodate all who are enrolled in the Game course, two industries have been run in parallel. Each industry starts from the same set of initial conditions, but afterwards, there has been no interaction between industries during the course of play. The two industries represent, in effect, two separate Games.[2]

---

[1]Allen D. Shocker has contributed to the preparation of this chapter.

[2]During the 1963–64 run of the Game, interactions across industries were allowed on a limited basis. Firms in one industry were permitted to cross-license products and (with costs and delays appropriate to their being widely separated geographically) were permitted to transship raw materials and some finished products to firms in the other industry. Such interactions greatly enlivened play of the Game. However, to make them an effective part of the Game we need to make changes in the computer model; we need to establish a more elaborate legal system and rules for "international trade";

Before the beginning of play, the Game administrator distributes the *Player's Manual* and histories of the firms' previous operations, describes the rules and traditions concerning relations to boards of directors and other role-playing groups, provides a schedule of moves, and outlines the procedures for submitting decisions to the computer and for picking up the results of the computer runs. To provide team members with some of the continuity and background knowledge that a real management group would have, we have prepared a history for each firm. The history outlines management's decisions and the results of their decisions for the preceding Game year or two of play. Originally, the history was generated by sets of decisions which the Game administrator made, but recently the histories used each year have been largely based on actual decisions and outcomes for an industry from some previous semester of play. The decisions in the history need not be good ones because their main purpose is to give a team some basis for estimating what the outcomes of various decisions will be. The histories for the three firms need not be identical, and if based on actual play, they cannot be. We have found it desirable, though, to choose or to adjust the histories so that teams in an industry will start from situations of similar overall potential in terms of market share, products, costs, productive capacity, and financial strength.[3]

Play begins a week or two after the semester begins. The schedule of moves is built around several considerations. In order to allow the teams to plan adequately for their decisions and in order to permit the punching and checking of input cards, the computer runs, and the preparation and distribution of output, we have usually run one Game move a week over a 15—week semester. It is impossible to play the Carnegie Tech Management Game at the rapid pace often used for simpler games, where play is condensed into a period of a few days, with moves scheduled every 20 minutes or half an hour during that time.

The specific schedule of moves depends on how the Game fits other demands on the students' time and on when it is possible to obtain rapid access to the computer. At Carnegie's Graduate School of Industrial Administration, students have no formal class commitments on Thursdays. On a one-week move cycle, the decisions are due by Friday

---

and for the kinds of interactions which are to be permitted across industries, we need to develop constraints which are both realistic by real-world standards and meaningful within the educational context of the Game.

[3]Sample histories of various kinds and lengths can be obtained from schools like Carnegie which have used the Game. However, it is usually best for each Game user to work from the *Administrator's Manual* to generate their own. In the process of generating histories for the firms, the administrators have their best opportunity to find out whether the Game program is running properly on their computer facilities and whether proposed input and output procedures and schedules of moves will be workable.

noon, cards are punched for a computer run Friday night, and teams get the results back either on Saturday or on Monday. The most important consideration in establishing the move cycle has been to minimize the time between the submission of decisions and the availability of the resulting outcomes, so that the teams have adequate time for analysis and planning before they prepare their next decisions.

The basic single move in the Carnegie Game encompasses decisions and outcomes of decisions for one month in the history of the firms. We have found it advisable at the start of play to require teams to manage their firms through from three to six single moves. Then, if the administrator desires to speed the pace of play and increase the challenge of the Game, he can ask teams to submit decisions for two or three months at a time. With such multiple moves, a team may be allowed to request that its decisions for the second or third month be conditional on the outcomes of the first month's operations; but the decisions and conditional decision rules that are turned in to govern play cannot be revised by the team in any direct manner until after the two- or three-month move has been run. Multiple moves permit teams to play two or three game-years in a one-semester course. Multiple moves provide a long enough time horizon to encourage the development of long-run strategies and formal efforts to plan and budget for the future.

Especially when the Game was new and when significant changes were being made in the Game model or in the university's computer system, we found it desirable to allow slack in the schedule for unanticipated machine breakdowns or difficulties with the program. Dislocations in the schedule that result from such interruptions are not popular either with faculty or with students.

To discourage "end play" in the final few moves of the Game run, we have usually tried to hedge about defining the Game month at which play will cease. We stress that we want teams to leave their firms in solid condition for the next generation of management.

Before play begins, each team has a great deal to read, discuss, and plan. We have tried to issue the *Player's Manual,* other instructions, and the firm's history over the summer so that, at the first orientation meeting in the autumn semester when the Game is played, the administrator can spend more time answering questions that he does presenting a general description of the Game. Early distribution of these materials also improves the quality of the first moves and of the first meetings with boards of directors. It generally advances the date when teams can begin making multiperiod moves.

In the sections which follow, we shall look at several phases of the operations of Game teams: at what they do during the initial learning period; at how they approach their first sets of decisions; at how they work to stabilize their policies and organization and to gain minimal control over their environment; at how they work, once some degree of stability has been achieved, to refine and routinize their decision procedures and their relations with outside groups; and at what they do, if their enthusiasm for the Game remains high, to experiment and to innovate as managers of their firms.

II. THE INITIAL PROCESS OF ORGANIZATION

In deciding how to organize, teams have generally been free to propose almost any form of organization that they want. Nevertheless, their thinking is colored by a variety of real and imagined constraints. First, there is the weight of experience and tradition about what an organization should look like. Tradition calls for job differentiation, for some sort of hierarchy to assure coordination and control, and, of course, for a chart. Second, there are expectations about what the board of directors will require. Usually this means that the main features of organization must be spelled out in writing. Job descriptions are prepared, and questions of ultimate authority and responsibility within the team are discussed.

In deciding how to define the jobs of different team members, players usually take cognizance both of the problems they will face in making decisions and of the problems they will face in explaining and defending these decisions before the board of directors. Success in relations with the board can mean as much as success in competition with other teams. In choosing the president and senior officers in the functional areas, a great deal of emphasis is placed on finding men who have skills for presenting, as well as for generating, decisions.

In setting boundaries between jobs, players are influenced greatly by the differentiation in the *Player's Manual* among activities in marketing, production, and finance. Only infrequently have teams abandoned a primary division of tasks along functional lines for a primary division along product lines, for a primary division between planning and operating personnel, or for a primary division between analysts, decision generators, and specialists in external relations.

The form of organization proposed depends, finally, on the personal characteristics of team members. What have been their previous experiences together on group assignments? Where do they live? What other courses are they taking? What other outside demands do they have on their time? Out of all these factors, a variety of kinds of organizations might develop; but over the years, some basic similarities in organization can be discerned.

A.   General Forms of Organization

As team size increases, it is possible to predict the rough order in which new positions will be added to an organization. The approximate order is as follows:

1. Marketing manager or vice president.
2. Production manager or vice president.
3. Financial manager or vice president.
4. President or chairman.
5. Controller and secretary to the board.
6. Research and development manager *or* assistant in marketing.
7. Planning manager *or* assistant to the president *or* executive vice president.
8. Assistants in the other functional areas (production, finance).
9. Secretary to the board of directors (separate from the controller).

In the initial statements of what the organization is and how it will function, the kinds of things that can be reported on a chart or in a set of job descriptions predominate. Examples of how the charts have frequently appeared are given for teams of six, seven, and eight men in Figure 4–1.

As might be expected with students for whom most relationships are on a peer-group basis and among whom the competition for leadership and status is keen, the initial statements of organization often de-emphasize the formal powers of the president. They are also often optimistic about the degree to which the firm's activities can be routinized and decentralized. Many teams discover after play begins that the president must be given expanded grants of power, particularly to insure coordination, decision accuracy, and active participation by all members of the team. Teams also discover that meetings of the whole management group to discuss issues ranging from basic long-run policy matters to immediate choices among decision alternatives must be held more often than they had originally planned.

The initial statements of organization also tend to concentrate on the description of recurrent operating responsibilities rather than on the responsibilities for handling such tasks as dealing with auditors or union representatives or developing formal decision-making techniques. Teams sometimes plan for rotation of job assignments midway through the term; but when the time for rotation arrives, they usually decide that each member has acquired too much expertise in his present job to make the idea of rotation feasible. They fear that rotation will mean

FIGURE 4-1

SAMPLE CHARTS OF TEAM ORGANIZATION

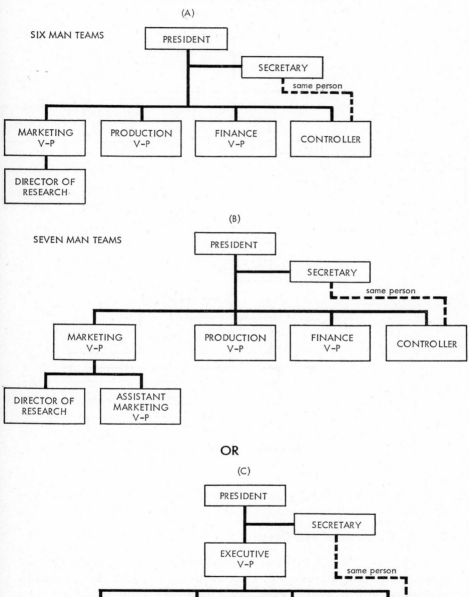

FIGURE 4-1— *Continued*

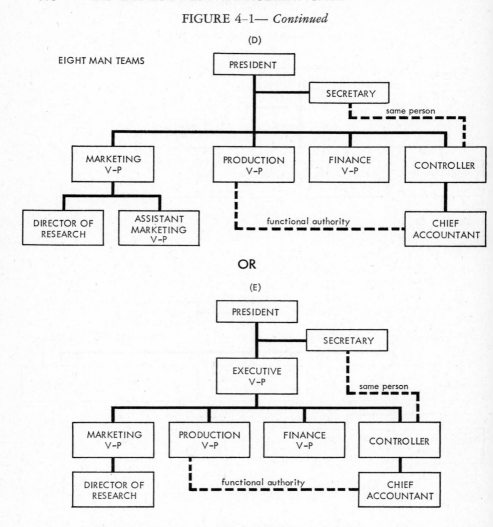

that much time will have to be invested in the Game and that it is likely to hurt the team's position *vis-à-vis* competitors.

B.   The Contents of Job Descriptions

Within the main functional areas, teams have tried in a variety of ways to describe the essential dimensions of the jobs that are to be performed. Briefly in this section, we shall review the major activities in marketing, production, finance, and controllership, and shall describe the president's role as supervisor and coordinator of these functions.

1. Marketing. Of all the functional areas, marketing is generally thought to be most crucial to success in the Game. Within marketing lie decisions relating to the products manufactured and distributed, the prices charged, the sales promotion and advertising used to gain retail distribution, the product and market research activities of the firm, and the marketing support for projected factory and warehouse capacity increases. The principal marketing activity that influences planning in other parts of the firm is the preparation of the sales forecast. The forecast is then reviewed and perhaps modified by discussions with men from production and finance. The sales forecast and the recommended policies for pricing, advertising, and sales force that are designed to achieve the forecasted results form the basis for most other major decisions of the firm.

In attempting to maximize the firm's profits, the marketing manager designs and conducts "experiments" to learn more about the environment in which the firm operates and to learn how to operate in that environment to the best interests of the firm. What kinds of products should the firm seek to develop? What kinds and how many should they market? What will be the effect of a new product introduction or a price increase? How effective is an incremental expenditure for advertising in a region versus the same dollar increment spent for additional salesman? What is the effect of a price decrease on sales and profits? What is the optimum allocation of research funds among different types of research to maximize the probability of obtaining products that can be marketed profitably? These questions and many others that are asked by other members of management and the board of directors provide the challenge for the marketing manager.

2. Production. The production function represents another area of prime importance to the firm's profitability. Production is responsible for supporting the marketing effort of the firm. It is imperative that production and marketing work together to the benefit of the firm as a whole rather than of either function alone. Production controls the manufacture and storage of the finished product, the purchase and storage of raw materials, and the shipment and transshipments of the finished product. The production manager usually prepares the recommendations for facility construction (factory or warehouses). He controls not only the scheduling of production (subject to the capacity limitations of the factory and the raw materials supply), but also the budgeting of maintenance expenditures, the hiring and firing of work force, and the integration of new products into the manufacturing schedule. Thus, the importance of coordination between the production and marketing functions in preparing the sales forecast cannot be over-emphasized. Production imposes constraints on what marketing can sell, and consequently marketing must provide some guide to production as to what and how much to produce and where to ship it.

3. *Finance.* The major function of finance is to prepare financial plans for the company. These indicate to management the financial implications of their marketing and production plans. They usually take the form of *pro forma* income statements and balance sheets. The financial manager is responsible for assuring that necessary funds are available and for having primary jurisdiction in deciding the means to obtain them from among the many alternatives that the Game offers. He may be the primary negotiator with the banker to secure attractive terms. Major policy decisions concerning capital structure of the firm, including short- versus long-run debt and debt versus equity must be made within this realm. Also, the finance manager acts as a brake to marketing and production planning when it becomes advisable to curtail proposed expenditures rather than borrow.

4. *Controllership.* The controllership function becomes particularly important when the firm is being audited because the controller must serve as liaison between the team and the auditors. The controller is responsible for initiating and supervising a system of internal control for the team. This may include the design and maintenance of a full system of accounts to supplement and restate the regular Game output information in ways that will be most meaningful to management. Such a system encompasses checks to assure that all necessary decision forms are filled out completely and that the numbers recorded are reasonable. The controller acts as custodian of team records and maintains management's file of decisions and decision rationales. He often is the team's secretary at board meetings and then is responsible for publishing minutes of the discussions. In addition to the regular accounting and record-keeping functions of the team, the controller will perform special cost studies or analyses for management. Frequently, the controller also assumes the added responsibility of constructing mathematical models designed to help the team in its operations. The controller is in a position to play a most important role in the overall management of the firm and in major policy decisions.

5. *The President.* For each firm, a leader is needed. The president is generally responsible for everything the team does or fails to do. He must have current, accurate knowledge of all phases of the firm's operations, and he must be prepared to get involved in any phase of the firm's decision making. He may be called upon to resolve disputes between team members over courses of action, and it is his job to keep the team's efforts focused toward long-term goals. This requires that

he sometimes placates, sometimes arbitrates, and sometimes overrides the majority will of his teammates. He must insure that work is done completely, done well, done accurately, and done on time. He must maintain the motivation of team members to work together and to carry their share of the load.

It is also inevitable that the president becomes the firm's primary representative in contacts with outside groups. He clearly has the most significant position in relations with the board of directors, and on occasion at Carnegie, he has even been elected to the board of directors by the faculty and the businessmen who are members. He is usually encouraged to have other team members participate actively in the presentations and discussions at board meetings, but the board will hold him responsible for making sure that these presentations are well planned and well executed. Contacts with bankers, auditors, and union representatives may be delegated to other members of the team by the president. Nevertheless, where unanticipated problems arise in these interactions, the president usually becomes involved.

Although a firm may divide responsibilities in a specific effort to equalize the time demands on team members, the presidents of Game teams—like the presidents of real organizations—have almost without exception devoted more time to the Game than other members of management have.

III. MAKING THE FIRST FEW DECISIONS

The approach of teams to their first few decisions in the Game is highly variable. For some students at the freshman and sophomore level who were hired to play a few moves of the Game in a summer seminar at Carnegie, there seemed to be no apparent rationale to their actions. They had a very limited briefing about what the Game involved, they understood almost nothing about the dynamic character of a businss enterprise, and in some instances they did not even know elementary things like the probable response of demand to changes in price. The decisions were randomly made, the results were poor, and the students' rate of learning was slow.

A. Factors Which Influence Early Decisions

Our graduate students, though, start with a better basis for making sensible initial decisions. They have the benefit of one or two lectures describing the Game. They have had time to read and analyze the *Player's Manual* and a history of past performance for their firm. They have had the first year of our Master's program in Industrial Administration, which includes courses in business, economics, quantitative methods, and the behavioral sciences. Some of them have worked in business before returning to graduate school. Increasingly, from their formal role of auditors and from their informal opportunities to talk with men who played the Game a year earlier, they have picked up a great deal of "hearsay" advice about how the Game should be approached.

To guide their approach to the Game, in any introductory lectures or discussion we have stressed the importance of long-range planning (at least over a 6- to 18-month time horizon). We have alerted players in a general way to the problems that are posed by the seasonality of market demand. We have urged them to take advantage of the opportunity to increase their knowledge of the environment by purchasing survey information and by designing some decisions as actions to test the environment rather than as long-term operating commitments.

Teams tend to supplement what they are told and what they can verify from the documents that are given to them with a variety of assumptions that derive from observations of the world outside the Games. Teams have often assumed considerably more complexity and variety in consumer behavior than is actually built into the Game model. They have assumed, sometimes to their sorrow, that no one would put them in charge of a firm for which plant and warehouse capacity were not in roughly equal balance. They have assumed that production might be interrupted frequently by such random factors as wildcat strikes or major equipment breakdowns. They have assumed that it is always good policy to market as many products as the Game permits. (It was not until the fourth year of play at Carnegie that any team committed itself through most of the semester to the production and sale of fewer than the maximum of three products, and it is interesting that the first team to try this strategy was the most successful team in either industry for that semester.) They have sometimes tried to anticipate ways in which Game parameters have been changed since the previous semester's play. As an example, after a semester in which demand was extremely sensitive to changes in price, some teams began with the assumption that the faculty would correct this and, if anything, would overcompensate in the direction of making price less important than it really should be.

At the start of the Game teams cannot attend to all decision issues at once. Since their first set of decisions is due within the first two weeks of the semester, they are initially likely to give either too much or too little attention to long-range strategy questions. If a team really tries to spend time on basic questions of what their long-run market opportunities are, of what their strategic objectives will be, and of what these strategic objectives mean in general for short-term operations, they are not likely to have time to do a good job of familiarizing themselves with short-run prospects and problems. Their first sets of decisions may bear little effective relation either to the long-term strategies they have chosen or to the immediate opportunities and demands in the environment. On the other hand, if a team tried to do nothing more than exploit its immediate opportunities and if it is not pressed for long-term plans by the board of directors, it may drift through the semester on a move-by-move basis with no real purpose or mission. Quite different approaches to decision making may be called for if a team is to focus on profits only during the period of Game play than if it is to focus on leaving the firm in a potentially profitable position for the next generation of management. Some teams and boards tend to stress profits; some, growth; some, share of market; some, a variety of other measures of performance.

The problem of balancing short-term operating obligations against needs for more basic planning decisions is one which players will have to face in the outside world of business. It may be desirable, though, to give teams a longer orientation period than we have usually given so that they can develop a clear statement of their objectives and plans for the semester.[4]

B. Examples of What Players Pay Attention to

To show the kinds of things which may be emphasized early in the Game, some observations of one team's decision activities may be of interest. In Marketing, the whole team discussed the outlook for sales for the next year or two. Attempts were made to anticipate trends in gross national product, changes and improvements in products, and seasonal variations in demand; to estimate the effects of such factors on the detergent market; and finally to set a level of aspiration with respect to the share of the market that the firm might achieve. This particular firm had only one product on the market, with another in production. On the basis of data they had about the characteristics of the second product and on the assumption that there were advantages to being first in the industry to introduce another product, the managers decided to promote and sell their product "B."

Questions about policies on price, advertising, and sales promotion were raised. The managers agreed to follow the same policies in all regions on the assumption that if their policies were stable, they could

---

[4]This may have advantages when the time comes to evaluate or grade team performance. In many ways, a team's ability to accomplish the things it has set out to accomplish is the best measure of its managerial competence.

learn more from watching their competitors' experiments. The president and other team members overruled the marketing manager's desire to be a high-price, low-volume enterprise in favor of a low-price, high-volume policy. Decisions on advertising and sales promotion were based on analysis of the relative importance of each factor in the recent history of the industry and were limited by the firm's cash position. The cash position was tightened by the board of directors' insistence that management either maintain its record of continuous dividend payments or show clearly how suspension of dividend payments would benefit the stockholders. Since management could not present a convincing case for suspending dividends, cash had to be allocated to pay them.

The marketing manager's advice on how much to spend for various market survey information was accepted without question even though he made the common error of budgeting for surveys and tests in proportion to how badly he wanted the information rather than in proportion to the likely costs of executing a reliable and valid survey or test.

In production, the team was faced with obviously excessive inventory and work force commitments. Much attention was given to exploring what inventory and work force levels should be and to deciding how rapidly cutbacks should be made. The president and production manager explored the costs of 15 to 20 alternatives for reducing work force. In doing so, they were relatively unsystematic, and their concern for costs was tempered by a fear of unanticipated events like a strike and by uncertainty about what the directors would approve. The team chose three alternatives, more on the basis of variety than of quality, to discuss with the board.

By assuming that factory and warehouse capacity must be in balance, and by mistrusting their own sales forecasts, the team ignored an immediate need to construct new warehouse facilities. In fact, the finance manager assured the board in a memorandum (which he did not clear with his associates) that no expansion of facilities would be necessary.

The president had time to apply a formula which he had learned in industry to the problem of determining an optimal level of maintenance expenditures. When the formula called for reducing maintenance expenditures to 25 percent of current levels, he did not have the courage to adopt the results. He compromised on a step-wise reduction of 50 percent and expressed confidence that this would be "about right."

In finance, the main issues concerned dividend policy and provisions for continuing a bank loan. The team presented the board with several alternatives on dividend policy, but they were not prepared to discuss the advantages and disadvantages of each in terms that would make sense to representatives of the stockholders. In devising alternatives, they were influenced by real-world dividend rates for the detergent industry.

On the basis of its low cash position and its desire to increase promotional activities, the team felt obliged to continue a large bank loan for several more months. They did not take time, though, to make a detailed projection of cash requirements under alternative directions of development for the firm. They postponed such projections either until they had more time or until the board began to press for them.

The controller and the financial officer began to consult with their associates about the kinds of work sheets, accounting records, and forecasts that would be useful for the team. In the first board meeting, the directors laid down further specifications about the information they wanted to receive on a regular basis to evaluate team performance.

A good many long-term questions were raised for board consideration in the initial meetings, but they tended to be raised for specific functional areas rather than for the firm as a whole. Furthermore, the answers that were adopted were often superficial ones, too often based on what the most vocal members of the team preferred and too often made conditional on hopes that the board would help make the choice. Where the managers did undertake longer-range analysis, as with the sales forecast and the study of maintenance needs, they did not often use the results as an effective constraint on other actions.

The team was forced in early decisions to face problems of compromise—to resolve the incompatibility of proposed marketing programs with current financial resources, and to adjust their desire to keep funds in the firm with the board's desire to satisfy the stockholders' expectations of regular dividends. Other issues, such as the inconsistency of their pricing policy with the nature of the market in which they were selling, did not come to light until several moves had been played.

The men on the team who had clear move-by-move operating responsibilities had no problem of finding work to do. The controller and a man who was made responsible for something vaguely called "planning" had a more difficult time explaining and justifying their functions to the board. The controller was beginning to set up records and systems of accounts, but the marketing and production men were also undertaking to do this for themselves. The planner, unfortunately, was one of the less aggressive members of the team. Although the team uncovered many questions which he might have tried to answer, he did not recognize in the team's discussions an agenda of problems which he might try to solve.

IV. STABILIZING THE FIRM

Assuming that a team can avoid major disasters in its first few decisions, the next task is to weld the organization together and to work toward understanding and controlling the factors which influence the progress of the firm. In addition, they are preparing for the time when they will begin multiple moves, covering two or three months at a time.

A. Organizational Problems

Several things are likely to happen. There are likely to be problems with the initial plan of organization. At an early stage, functional lines may be blurred as all members of the team participate in determining and in evaluating the early sets of decisions. Some members of the team may show particular skills, interests, or persistence in areas that formally have been assigned to someone else. In other cases, it will become apparent that important jobs—such as checking the decision forms for accuracy and consistency before they are turned in to the Game administrator—have not been included as anyone's responsibility. There is usually some discussion about the extent to which decisions should be made in plenary session and the extent that meetings of the group as a whole can be dispensed with. For obvious reasons, there are pressures to minimize the amount of time devoted to meetings. Still, frequent meetings are promoted by the natural tendencies toward free participation in team activities and by the many occasions on which uncertainty about a decision or needs for coordination require group consensus.

Under a reasonably participative management, the marketing manager's job becomes one of studying market data, of proposing basic policies and competitive strategies, and of presenting his recommendations for short-run action. The first-hand exposure of the marketing manager to market data and his role in analyzing such data place him in a position to play the central role in all marketing decisions. His actual influence will depend in large part upon the overall success of the firm, his ability in posing alternative decisions for consideration by other members of management, and his success in presenting a sound rationale in support of his recommended course of action to management and the board of directors. Usually the marketing function is entrusted to one of the ablest members of the team. But by reason of the very importance and complexity of the marketing problems, the man in charge of solving them may have to fend off a great deal of unsolicited help and advice from his teammates.

Other members of the team management face similar problems in gaining acceptance for their recommendations and decisions. In general, however, less judgment is required in the early production and financial decisions. Alternatives can be evaluated with greater precision, resulting in less involvement by all team members in policy decisions. Nevertheless, the managers of production and finance must convince their associates that they are doing a good job if they wish to have substantial control over their designated area.

The president usually learns that to be effective, he should actively seek to maintain a differentiation of status between himself and the remaining team members during the group discussions. It will sometimes be necessary to mediate opposing points of views concerning strategy or even to accept a minority viewpoint in the face of majority opposition when he firmly believes that the majority is wrong. He must see that the group avoids arguments which are basically personality clashes. For the successful accomplishment of these and other roles, it is necessary that the president try to place himself in a position of respect above the personal conflicts of other members of the group, so that when he intervenes, he will be obeyed. In order to maintain this respect, he must try to be impartial when dealing with team members. He should base his decisions on facts rather than personalities. He should seek to guide the team to appropriate decisions, using his ultimate power as infrequently as possible so that the individual team members will be motivated to perform effectively and to assume responsibility for recommendations and decisions in their individual areas.

B. Problems of Decision Strategy

As the Game progresses, teams become more formalized in the treatment of issues such as planning long- and short-run marketing strategies, perfecting a routine for coping efficiently with repetitive decisions and analyses of data, and preparing for its meetings with the board of directors. The initial stage is generally a period of experimentation as the managers make decisions from an intuitive base in a manner designed to learn as much as possible about the environment and the effects of their decisions upon it. In the second stage the firm tends to ask sharper questions about current and past history and to formulate longer-range strategies for pricing, advertising, product research, new product introduction, overtime authorization, maintenance expenditures, inventory control, financial policies, and the like.

Market strategies tend to be developed from the firm's assessment of the relative influence of price, advertising, and size of sales force on the success of the firm's products in the market place. Product strategies stem from decisions of the firm to improve the quality of its products through continued research, to develop new products which have superior characteristics and which appeal to different segments of the market, or to rely upon copying and duplicating new developments introduced to the market by competitors. Anticipations of competitive action and reaction play an important part in these strategic decisions.

The marketing strategies of the firm generally provide the framework within which production and financial decisions are made. If the firm is in financial trouble, however, marketing may be subject to severe constraints. Similarly, production capacity limitations may be the controlling factor. For example, a strategic decision to market three products covering as wide a range of the market as possible will tend to have important consequences for product research, for production, and for finance in planning the firm's capital requirements. A multiproduct line may have implications for constructing new production and warehousing facilities, for controlling raw material and finished goods inventories, and for scheduling production. These are problems which can reach critical proportions during the introduction of a new product (or replacement of an old brand) if team members have not established effective procedures for coordinating their activities.

Through its development of strategies the firm tends to systematize its decision making. This is an important development in the operation of the firm since the Game is sufficiently complex that a systematic approach to decision making is essential for adequate internal control. Playing the Game involves a great deal of paperwork. Numerous calculations which form the basis for later recommendations or decisions must be made. The decisions themselves must be transferred from working papers to preprinted decision forms for input to the computer. The collection and transfer of data that occurs can easily result in errors that would prove costly if not uncovered by control procedures. Some firms institute procedures for a review of all decision forms by persons familiar with the proper magnitudes of the entries made. Some firms establish procedures to compare records of decisions used for key punching with information contained on source documents. In some firms the functional area managers have other members of the firm check their mathematical calculations. Errors can have important, if not crucial, consequences. Omission of a zero may cause the purchase of only one tenth the necessary amount of a raw material. Other figures entered in the wrong space of the decision form may result in errors in the placement of advertising, the shipment of merchandise, or the hiring or firing of employees. Only after experience with errors such as these do some players come to recognize the need for internal control procedures designed to systematize its managerial task.

The Game provides the learning experience of forcing each firm's managers to live with the consequences of their past decisions. The output from the computer each period provides evidence of the success or failure of the firm's past decisions. Each period offers a different environment in which new problems must be considered and some new decisions must be made. Learning occurs as members of the firm are motivated to analyze decisions made in their functional areas, evaluate the actions taken, and seek to discover what might have been done to obtain effects closer to those desired. By this analysis on a period-by-period basis, individual managers acquire knowledge that enables them to perform their tasks better and to guide the evolution of improved firm strategies and policies.

C. Problems of Relationships with the Board of Directors

Throughout the early period of play as management tries to succeed against competitors, it also tries to influence its board of directors. To the extent that an evaluation of the team members is made by the board, the management team may focus too much on things which it believes will please the board. The firm members may provide written reports to inform the board of every major phase of their activities. They may accept some course of action which appears easier to "sell" to the board than another. They may interpret certain remarks of board members in such a way that they feel constrained to avoid certain competitive actions for fear of board reproach. Although there are many benefits to be gained from proper integration of management with the board, the players' perceptions of this relationship may act as a hindrance to effective management. To overcome the tendency to anticipate and fulfill every wish and thought of the board, as a means of obtaining approval of team actions, management must acquire confidence in its abilities and must have maturity to accept the consequences of its decisions. The means by which the board judges the competence of management are often the same as those by which management judges itself. The payoff is in long-run profits. It is important—and sometimes difficult—for the team to learn not simply to provide the board with what it thinks the board will accept most readily. To be sure, the team can learn from the board and should not often persist in courses of action which the directors have marked as unacceptable. However, management is more closely in contact with actual market situations than the board is. Management is more informed and better able, in most instances, to formulate decisions. One sign of progress is that the team becomes more aggressive and more self-assured—presenting proposals to the board that derive from the team's own analysis and judgment; being ready to defend the proposals with vigor, reasoning, and evidence; and being ready to draw lessons for the future from the directors' reactions without being prepared to surrender autonomy to the board.

D. An Example of the Quest for Stability: The Development of Marketing Strategies

To show more clearly some of the things which happen as the team seeks control over its environment and its relationships with the board, let us look at how the marketing strategies of a firm evolve. The major stimulus for their evolution comes from the competitive challenge that the other two firms in the industry provide. Most of the means that management and the board have at their disposal for evaluating the firm's performance are relative rather than absolute. Such measures as net profits, return on assets, growth in sales or assets, and operating expenses as a percentage of sales act primarily in a relative sense as indicators of a firm's performance. In general, absolute standards tend to give way to an evaluation of the firm against its competition since the competitive approach of the firms together can greatly influence overall industry profitability. The board has all the problems of evaluating management's performance that are common to business practice. Consequently, the firm's performance relative to competition appears to represent the major basis for evaluation and, frequently, for team motivation.

The management team tends to focus upon ways to improve its competitive position. A good team will soon realize that its commonsense notions about the effects of various decisions on sales are not sufficient. To be sure, an increase in advertising expenditure or a decrease in price will tend to increase a firm's sales if all other factors remain constant. But the competitive environment will seldom if ever remain unchanged. Increased sales do not guarantee increased profits. Each decision variable has a decreasing marginal value, in the sense that the increment of profits resulting from increments of expenditure declines with increasing expenditures. There is, in effect, a saturation phenomenon which at some point will cause an increase in sales exactly equal to the increase in expenditure (and hence no increase in profits). It is no simple trick, however, to find this value for any given variable. Furthermore, the effect of a change in any given decision variable also depends on the levels of the other merchandising variables of the firm and on the actions of competitors. Thus, the marketing manager must consider the interactions of such elements as price, advertising, sales force effort, product characteristics, retail allowances, existing levels of retail distribution and manufacturing, and storage and shipping costs in terms of their effects upon profits.

How should these activities be coordinated? What strategy will be most effective in a given competitive situation? If other firms are lowering prices, can the marketing manager counteract these effects through increased advertising? Or is his best response also to lower prices? What are the long- and short-term goals of the firm? How will the actions of the firm influence subsequent competitive strategy and tactics? In the long run the competitive position of a firm can also be greatly influenced by the quality and variety of products marketed by each firm. Product innovations require both a product research policy and a plan for the introduction of new products. If little money is spent for research to develop improved products, the firm may find itself in a poor competitive position in terms of the basic appeal of its products. This would tend to reduce the relative effectiveness of its advertising expenditures. Consequently, the advantages and costs of a continuing research program must be evaluated relative to a policy of attempting merely to duplicate competitors' products through crash research efforts. Repeated changes in the product line result in excess production costs and may also serve to alienate some consumers if the old product being replaced better served the needs of some segment of the population.

A third element dealing with the effect of present decisions on the future is that of pricing, advertising, and sales force policies. If prices are allowed to fluctuate greatly from period to period or if retail allowances are used continuously, wholesalers may be induced to speculate on inventory, causing accentuated sales cycles for the manufacturer. The decay of advertising carryover effects, the "training" of salesmen, and habitual behavior on the part of consumers all serve to cause current marketing decisions to influence future sales.

The development of "optimal" strategy is also hindered by the fact that competitors' actions are uncertain. An increase in advertising expenditures in the face of an advertising increase or a price cut by competitors will not be as effective as the same advertising increase given no change in competitive behavior. The impact which a firm's marketing decisions have on its sales and profits very much depends upon the actions being taken by the other two firms in the industry.

The previous discussion has pointed to four considerations which complicate play of the game: diminishing marginal returns from expenditures, complex interrelationships between the various decision variables, effects of future considerations on present decisions, and uncertainty about competitors' actions. These considerations make it imperative for management to study the environment in which they compete in order to have some understanding about the probable effect of their decisions upon sales and profitability. The environment includes both the computer (the "world") and competition. The value of any given strategy will depend upon the strategies that competitors follow.

Most students start by believing that a simple method of developing an understanding of the computer model would be through controlled experimentation and the analysis of results. They thus attempt to establish the effects of individual decision variables by holding all but one of the variables constant from period to period (for instance, increasing advertising expenditure in one region while price and sales force are unchanged from the previous period), and then analyzing market results relative to results observed in regions in which no changes were made. Over a period of time such experimentation may give the firm some "feel" for the relative effectiveness of various market variables. But as in the real world, no experiment can assure control in all relevant dimensions. The effects of competitive actions, in particular, are frequently difficult to evaluate. Consequently, what is needed is a framework within which to analyze the results of complex sets of decisions so that growth in understanding can be attained through modification and development of decision procedures.

Experimentation is of more value in some areas than others. The effects of retail allowances and the probable performance of new products are areas in which experimentation can be particularly useful. It is also useful in the production area to determine a desirable level of maintenance expenditure and the effects of overtime on productivity. In many areas of marketing, however, attempts at controlled experimentation are unlikely to be successful. The firm might better study markets in all their complexities as part of their routine marketing operation. A firm can learn from the performance of its competitors whether or not the performance is studied in an experimental context. The purchase of adequate market research data is important here in order to establish the nature of competitive activities and the observed market results. The ultimate value of such research information, though, is completely dependent upon the firm's ability to analyze it, to reach improved understanding of market influences, and to implement improved decisions.

Because experimentation is important in providing data needed to analyze certain facets of operations, it should be an integral part of the firm's marketing and production planning. The cost of planned experimentation is often minimal. As a substitute for some other decision, its "cost" depends upon the effects of those decisions. For instance, an experiment to test the effect on sales of a 5 percent price cut might be considered as a substitute for a decision to make no change, or to increase advertising, or to combine a smaller price cut with an increase in advertising expenditure. Evaluation of the alternatives with respect to their effects on profitability is not a simple task. In many cases, evaluation is difficult, if not impossible, even after the experiment has been run. Thus both the costs and the results of experimentation are difficult to assess. A judgment must be made as to whether the information expected is worth the costs and risks involved. Sometimes, in order to gain valuable information, it might even be advisable to conduct an experiment which it is believed *a priori* will harm the firm's position. Again, though, the key to the value of experimentation is the analysis of market actions and results. A competitor with an organized, sound approach to market analysis is likely to learn more from another firm's experimentation than is that firm itself. Experimentation and research expenditures do not insure success. Frequently firms do not even market the most promising products developed by their research laboratories because they lack understanding of consumer wants and desires.

To minimize risk, most marketing experimentation done by players of the Game has been conducted in one region, for short durations, and under relatively stable competitive conditions. Abnormal situations, as when the firm or its competition cannot meet consumer demand due to inventory shortages, complicate the analysis of effects of merchandising variables.

So far we have been focusing upon experimentation and market analysis as a means for understanding the computer environment. For those who have the interest and the capability, the results of such analyses can be incorporated in a market simulation. Simulation involves the construction of a mathematical model which is representative of the process studied, in this case the "world" of the Game model. Based upon knowledge gained from market analysis, supplemented by common sense, it may be possible to construct a relatively simple mathematical model which would be useful for predicting the outcome of various decisions the firm might make. Such a model could be very useful in directing the strategic decisions of a firm.

In several years of play at Carnegie Tech, only one team has thus far developed what appeared to be a reasonably accurate simulation model of the Game environment, and then it came too late to be of much value to the firm involved. Better models are likely, though, as Game play is continued from year to year, with each new team taking over from its predecessor.[5]

Another direction which enterprising players have taken is to learn

---

[5]One such model is described in Section III.A of Chapter 8.

as much as possible about what competitors are planning. A well-planned, well-executed intelligence activity on one firm's part can frequently reveal much of another's firm's policies and strategies.[6] This information can be very important to planning the firm's own course of action. Knowledge that a competitor has a new product with superior characteristics may stimulate increased research activity. Likewise, knowledge of an impending price cut may prompt a state of readiness for retaliatory action. Because of the possibility of competitive reaction, each firm in planning its strategy must consider alternative competitive responses, the likelihood of each, and its probable impact upon the success of the firm.

How does management go about assessing its competition? Balance sheets, income statements, market survey data, and news announcements contain information which should be analyzed. Graphical plots of market statistics will often reveal evidence of a competitor's policies. Does the price level of a particular competitor appear to be leading the industry? What patterns do competitors display in allocating their expenditures? What ratio of advertising-to-retail-sales are they maintaining? The firm may usefully derive new data by simple numerical calculations. For example, dollar sales divided by average price per case will give a close approximation to a competitor's case sales for a quarter. By assuming that retail sales lead wholesale sales by approximately one month, the market manager can derive estimates of monthly case sales for each competitor. The balance sheets also contain valuable information. What are competitors' inventories, cash positions, and overall financial strength? News announcements or quarterly reports may provide information on new construction or other plans of competition. Study of recent market events may also provide tips to impending moves. By observing how a firm has reacted to situations in the past, one may get an idea as to how they are likely to react to a new situation. Management may also be able to predict competitive action or reaction by their knowledge of the managers of other firms. In the Game context the other managers may be classmates or co-workers. Knowledge of their personalities may aid the team in anticipating reactions to their decisions. Will the competitors follow a price lead? What action are they likely to take to combat a new product? Accurate answers to such questions frequently appear to hinge on the personalities of those making the decisions.

---

[6]A corollary to this observation is that the firm should maintain close control over its own reports, records, work sheets, and the like. Also slips of the tongue are to be avoided. Some firms have gone one step further and "planted" misleading memoranda in locations (for instance, wastebaskets) where competitors were thought to be collecting intelligence data in order to mislead the competitors' intelligence efforts and, presumably, market strategies.

The foregoing discussion has emphasized that knowledge of both the computer environment and of competition can be of great help to successful play of the Game. Knowledge of the market influence structure (that is, the computer environment) is perhaps the more important of the two under most circumstances. Accurate identification and evaluation of marketing alternatives is the major key to success. The probable actions of competitors, however, cannot be ignored. A price increase which is followed by competition has quite different consequences from one which is not. In simultaneous play of two industries (with identical parameters), the industrywide results have frequently differed very substantially in terms of overall profitability because of different orientations of competitors to long-term success. Some firms battle long and furiously in the attempt to gain high market share while firms in other industries are more inclined to "live and let live."

V. EXERCISING IMAGINATION AND INGENUITY IN THE GAME

The fact that firms may achieve a reasonably stable competitive position by midsemester does not mean that challenge of the Game is over. One consequence of the complexity of the Carnegie Game is that there are many possibilities for defining problems and opportunities that offer "break-through" potential for improving a team's competitive position. There are many kinds of decisions which teams can make in relatively unsophisticated ways to begin with, but to which they can return with increasingly sophisticated approaches as play progresses. The nature of these opportunities is best illustrated by some examples: the problem of controlling maintenance expenditures, approaches to a decision to build a new warehouse, and ways of delegating routine tasks to the computer.

A. Controlling Maintenance Expenditures

The problem of controlling maintenance expenditures shows the many levels by which a decision can be approached. Production downtime tends to vary from period to period. In any month it is a function of the percentage of plant capacity utilized that month as well as the level of maintenance expenditures in earlier periods. Past maintenance expenditures influence the general state of repair of plant facilities and equipment. As in an actual plant, neglect of maintenance leads to excessive downtime and resultant loss of production. Production managers frequently find that when they are scheduling production near theoretical plant capacity after a period of lower production (and lower maintenance expenditures), the plant does not produce the amount scheduled. Unanticipated downtime is the villain. The immediate result of this situation may be shortages of salable product; since disappointed customers may turn to competitors' products, the ultimate result may be lower sales and profits in future periods.

By increasing the firm's expenditures for maintenance in periods prior to anticipated capacity production, management can reduce the amount by which actual production falls behind theoretical (scheduled) production. Economic theory tells us that to maximize profits, the firm should equate marginal revenue and marginal cost. Under the simplest possible assumptions, namely, that (1) the firm can sell all additional available product at no increase in selling costs, and (2) the extra sales achieved in the current period will not represent additional sales volume in future "slow" periods as a result of the carry-over effects of habit in consumer buying behavior, the firm should act so that its marginal expenditure for maintenance to reduce machine breakdowns is just equal to its marginal gain in gross margin (revenue less variable manufacturing and shipping costs, exclusive of maintenance) from the sale of the additional product available as a result of reduced downtime.

Let us illustrate what a few teams have worked toward as they tried to establish a relationship between maintenance expenditures and marginal profit in the Game. When management takes over the firm, they have some history of earlier decisions and outcomes. If previous management has not been experimentally minded, particularly with respect to maintenance expenditures, these expenditures will have been constant (or nearly so). Conseqently, if a graph of percentage downtime versus maintenance expenditure per unit of theoretical plant capacity (measured in man-hours to allow for variety in product mix) were constructed, the firm should be able to plot at least one point.[7] A firm which has maintained a constant expenditure for maintenance month after month and has not expanded its plant (thereby changing its man-hour capacity) will tend to have its percentage downtime stabilized at some level. This is shown on Figure 4–2 as a point for the highest of three levels of maintenance expenditures.

Even if previous history is unavailable or is not constant, over three to four periods the firm can approximate with reasonable accuracy one point on the curve. By continuing a planned experiment using different levels of maintenance expenditure over the next four to eight periods, one or two additional points of the curve could be established, pro-

---

[7]Note that in the short run, that is, without plant expansion, theoretical plant capacity in man-hours of production is a fixed quantity dependent only upon the size of plant. The number of units of product produced under capacity operation is then a function of the productivity characteristics (man-hours per unit) of the product mix scheduled for production.

viding a rough approximation to the actual relationship between downtime and maintenance expenditures. This is illustrated in Figure 4–2.

The next step of the analysis can be performed using either an
equation approximating the relationship between percentage downtime and maintenance expenditures or a graphical approach. The graphical method is quite acceptable in this case, since extreme accuracy is
probably not possible in light of the particular estimation procedures
employed in constructing the curve of Figure 4–2 from two or three
points.

FIGURE 4–2

Effect of Maintenance Expenditures on Downtime

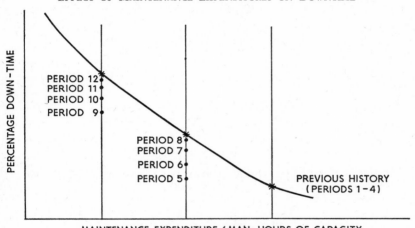

It is possible to change scales in Figure 4–2, multiplying both the
vertical and horizontal axes by the present plant capacity (in man-
hours), to obtain a graph showing the amount of lost capacity (that
is, percentage downtime multiplied by plant capacity) which will result from any level of maintenance expenditures. Since the amount
of available capacity is simply the total plant capacity less the amount
of lost capacity due to downtime, a graph can easily be obtained showing the amount of available capacity which will result from any level
of maintenance expenditures. If the horizontal and the vertical axes
are reversed on this last graph, the result will have the form shown in
Figure 4–3.

The slope of the curve in Figure 4–3 represents the increase in maintenance expenditures required to obtain a unit increase in available
capacity, that is, the marginal cost of obtaining additional capacity by
means of maintenance expenditures. This marginal cost is plotted as a
function of available capacity in Figure 4–4.

FIGURE 4–3

RELATIONSHIP BETWEEN MAINTENANCE EXPENDITURES AND AVAILABLE CAPACITY

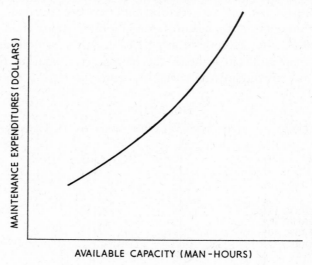

FIGURE 4–4

MARGINAL COSTS OF OBTAINING ADDITIONAL CAPACITY BY MAINTENANCE
EXPENDITURES

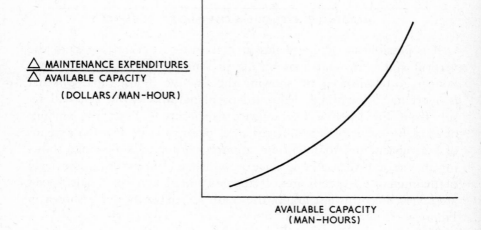

Assuming that the output produced by utilizing any increased available capacity can be sold at a constant price, a series of "iso-price" curves which represent the marginal "gross profit before maintenance expenditures" per available man-hour of capacity can be determined

for each level of product price. Since average variable production costs in the Game are rather insensitive to the quantity produced, the marginal "gross profit before maintenance expenditures" curves will be horizontal lines, intersecting the marginal cost curve of Figure 4–4 at points dependent only upon the level of the relevant product price. These conditions are are illustrated in Figure 4–5. It can be seen from Figure 4–5 that it becomes profitable to have additional capacity available, that is, to spend more for maintenance to reduce downtime, as the price of the product increases. This graphical analysis establishes the level of available capacity (and consequently, from Figure 4–3, the level of maintenance expenditures) which will maximize profits under various market price conditions, given the assumptions previously stated.

FIGURE 4–5

MARGINAL REVENUE VS. MARGINAL COST

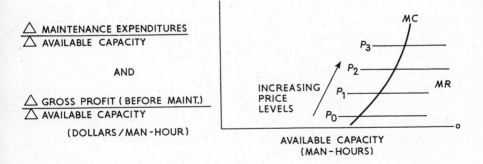

Similar analyses have been made by teams in the Game under a variety of conditions other than those assumed above. The economics of increasing output through increased maintenance expenditures have been balanced against the costs of overtime and investment in plant and equipment to increase theoretical capacity. Increasing production in periods of low demand and storing product to meet peak demands has also been recognized as an alternative to be evaluated. The costs of maintaining a stable work force have been studied in depth as a result of "union" demands for a guaranteed annual wage.

B. A Decision to Expand the Factory Warehouse

Much of the art of making good decisions comes from asking the right questions. An entirely unsophisticated team, faced with the knowledge that inventories are exceeding the capacity of the factory warehouse for finished goods, may make a number of arbitrary and potentially foolish decisions: cut back production on this basis alone in order to reduce inventory levels, continue production but automatically pay the higher charges for goods stored above the capacity limit, transfer more of the inventory to rented space in the regional warehouses, or build an addition to the factory warehouse that will provide more capacity than the firm is ever likely to require.

It does not take much understanding of how business operates to recognize that the matter is considerably more complicated. There are questions of how much inventory is really needed at the factory and in the regions, both now and in the future. Costs of storage at the factory and in the regions, costs of construction, and costs of transshipment between warehouses must all be considered. But even with a great deal of cost data (most of which is immediately available in the *Player's Manual*), the question of whether to construct new capacity is still not readily answered.

Without trying to show how the decision should be made, let us review two approaches that one team actually took: the first, when they brought the matter to the board; the second, after the board had expressed dissatisfaction with the initial approach.

As the team first approached the issue, they began with a question of costs. They found that the cost per case of capacity for expanding the warehouse was only 20 cents more than they would pay in a year's time as excess charges for storing a case of detergent in an overcrowded warehouse. Neglecting the fact of seasonality in detergent sales, which means that the period when peak warehouse capacity is needed may be only a few weeks each year, they concluded that it was automatically better to expand the warehouse rather than to overutilize it and pay excess storage charges.

Next they tried to determine how much capacity they needed. To simplify calculations, they projected an average monthly sales figure that they expected to maintain (2.2 million cases); figured the minimum inventories they needed to have on hand in regional warehouses (.96 million cases); and by subtraction, determined that they needed a factory warehouse which could hold 1.24 million cases (or .84 million cases more than the present warehouse would hold). They then calculated that the *annual* savings in storage and shipping costs would exceed construction costs by nearly $200,000; thus, warehouse expansion should be a very good investment.

The directors did not contest the team's general conclusion to build a larger facility, but they were not convinced that the projected size of the expanded warehouse was better than other sizes which might have been considered. They wanted to see alternatives, and they wanted to incorporate the effects of the strong seasonal pattern of sales on the calculations of costs and savings. They wanted to know more clearly the criteria by which an expansion was to be judged a good or poor investment.

The team went back to work. They charted more explicitly what sales rates would be at different seasons of the year. To their estimates of the minimum inventories that they would require, they added a buffer against emergencies that equalled 10 percent of monthly sales. They considered not just one, but five possible levels of expansion—ranging from expansion that would provide sufficient capacity only for the slowest period of sales during the year to expansion that would provide sufficient capacity for the month of peak demand. For the smallest of these five alternatives, they calculated the addition to the capacity of the warehouse that would be required, the associated costs and savings, and the rate of return on investment (in this case, 90 percent). For each successively greater level of warehouse capacity, they computed incremental costs, savings, and rates of return relative to the next lowest level of expansion. The incremental rate of return decreased as the projected capacity increased. While a 90 percent rate of return could be obtained by expanding the warehouse so that it would completely meet the needs of the firm only during the months of minimum sales demand, the incremental rate of return obtainable by going from a warehouse size sufficient for the second and third highest months of sales demand to a warehouse size sufficient for the highest month of sales demand would be only 7.5 percent.

Thus, in a second approach to the problem, much sounder conclusions were reached. The team had looked more clearly at the pattern of sales through the year and at the implications of seasonality in sales for possible levels of warehouse expansion. They had introduced rate of return considerations and included their judgments about what they considered an adequate rate of return. Finally, in comparing alternatives they had applied a fundamental lesson of economics: when comparing a larger vs. smaller expenditure, it is the marginal rate of return, not the average rate of return, on which the decision should be based.

C. Delegating Analysis and Decisions to the Computer

A third example of opportunity for players to exercise initiative and imagination in the Game comes from our experience with "player programs." Since the first runs of the Game we have encouraged players to use the computer to free themselves from many routine tasks of analysis, report preparation, and decision making. In writing programs, they increase their powers to understand and use the computer as a management tool. They may get better and more complete information on which to base their decisions; and when player programs are used as an adjunct to two- and three-month moves, teams test their ability to specify decision rules which a computer or a subordinate can apply without leading the firm to ruin.

At the simplest level, teams have used the computer to transform the information that is presented on the regular output forms into data that are more immediately useful from a managerial point of view. Simple programs can be written to derive, from market survey information and other data, estimates of the firm's retail share of market and of industry advertising expenditures; to derive, from balance sheets and income statements, sets of financial ratios; and to reinterpret general cost information by products or regions. Using the computer for such calculations is both faster and more accurate than doing them by hand.

At a more advanced level, during two- and three-month moves, teams have used player programs to make interim adjustments in the original decisions for the second or third months. For example, if a firm gets more than three new product possibilities from its research laboratory during the first month of a three-month move, it may want to shift some of the money it intended to spend on research for the final two months to advertising expenditures. If cash balances climb above a certain level, the firm may want to invest the excess cash in government bonds. If competitors change their prices in unanticipated ways, a player program lets a team respond before the end of a multiple-move cycle.

The next stage beyond conditional programs to adjust decisions during the second and third months of a multiple move is for teams to develop analysis and decision programs that can be trusted over a longer period to interpret past results and estimates of future prospects and generate decision proposals reasonable enough for the players to accept as their own. Samples of what might be produced by enterprising teams are shown in Chapter 5, Appendix 5.B, and in Chapter 8, Sections II.B and III.A.

Experiments with player programs, at a minimum, require only that players have access to a computer and a sense of care in specifying what they want. To make the player programs most effective, though, we are now incorporating them as additions to the main Game program for the move in which they are run. Teams turn in programs along with decisions, referencing variables by the same labels that the Game model uses and observing certain basic constraints that are necessary to make their programs compatible with the main program.[8] The programs are run along with the main program, and any special output that they generate is returned to the team along with the regular set of forms that the computer produces.

It is obvious that ingenuity must be tempered with caution for teams who write decision programs. Such programs must be based on a thorough understanding of the environment in which the firm operates; they should be written with built-in safeguards; they should be thoroughly tested; and they should be easy to revise or scrap if they do not work well. There are several teams at Carnegie who have helplessly stood by while the computer sold government bonds when it should have bought them or raised prices when it should have lowered them—mistakes made sometimes for complicated reasons, sometimes for simple reasons like the insertion of a "$+$" instead of a "$-$" sign in a key program statement.

We might describe other ways in which teams have used the Game to explore and test a variety of interesting approaches to management problems. These three examples, though, should suggest what can be done and, at the same time, leave much for the new teams which play the Game to discover and develop for themselves.

VI.   RUNNING THE GAME

To assure a reasonable environment for the development of players' interests and skills, a great deal depends on the administrative arrangements by which the Game is run. Administrative arrangements for starting the Game were briefly discussed in Section I of this Chapter. Here we shall provide some further comments on the administrative

---

[8]To insure compatibility with both the main computer model and a tight time schedule, we have instituted several controls:

1. All programs must be written so that they conform to the features of the the main Game program and so that they do not contain elements which might modify or destroy any part of the main Game program.
2. Only the data which are provided by (or derivable from) the firm's regular information and decision forms in the course of play are available to a firm's programs. In particular, a firm cannot submit a program which utilizes portions of memory which have been reserved for other firms or for the Game model.
3. Programs must be debugged using a special checking program before they are submitted for running.
4. Programs which cannot be incorporated readily into the main program by the Game staff, which will not run properly, or which violate the above constraints are discarded. As an alternative in case this happens, teams must always submit regular sets of decisions which can be used in place of the programs.
5. Programs, like decisions, must be submitted by the regular administrative deadlines.

procedures we have followed at Carnegie while running the Game for graduate students.[9]

Proper organization is the key to running the Carnegie Tech Management Game successfully. Procedures must be established for collecting decision forms from the firms, for keypunching and checking (or verifying) the input data, for computer processing, and for distributing the output reports. The actual computer processing is the least of the problems if the input data are prepared accurately. At Carnegie Tech, two graduate students, supervised by a faculty Game administrator, are responsible for all phases of this operation except the initial keypunching (which is performed by a clerk in the statistical laboratory). The Game administrator seldom becomes involved in the actual routine running of the Game because the students are capable of performing this function with little guidance. The only time that the Game administrator enters this phase of the operation at Carnegie Tech is when changes or adjustments in some accounts are required because of special extraneous circumstances—for example, because a firm has been struck by its union for one week of the month, or because a merger or cross-licensing agreement between two firms in different industries has been consummated.

The Game administrator bears overall responsibility for the operation of the Game. He establishes a schedule both for play and for such related educational exercises as wage negotiations and accounting-management audits. He also organizes and is a member of a three- or four-member faculty Game committee. This committee plays the roles of the banker and judiciary (labor law, antitrust actions, and so on). The committee also investigates and resolves Game results which appear questionable to players (and which could represent key punch errors, errors in processing, or errors in the Game program). Finally the committee may provide an independent evaluation of the competitive prospects of the teams at the end of the Game (for use by the boards of directors in evaluating team performance and as a balance against the directors' tendencies to identify too closely with their own teams). Once student assistants are trained to handle the routine operation of the Game and the Game committee is functioning properly, the administrator's role revolves primarily about the coordination of activities and, possibly, rescheduling due to extraneous factors (computer downtime, unscheduled holidays, and such).

---

[9]For more details, prospective users are referred to Kalman J. Cohen, William R. Dill, Alfred A. Kuehn, and Peter R. Winters, *Administrator's Manual for the Carnegie Tech Management Game* (Homewood, Ill.: Richard D. Irwin, Inc., 1964). For additional comments on administrative procedures when the Game has been run in executive programs, evening programs, and universities other than Carnegie, see Chapter 6.

The procedural steps to be followed in running the Game are outlined in great detail in the *Administrator's Manual*. A large number of comment statements have been included in the computer program to direct the attention of the operators to potential data input errors and to operational setup errors. The prime sources of difficulty in operation are likely to be input errors and, if the Game administrator is so inclined, special adjustments to past operating results can be made to correct for past input errors (or other special considerations) without rerunning the time periods involved. While procedures for making such changes have been incorporated in the program and are well documented, nevertheless they are not routine.

The basic parameters of the marketplace have not been varied *during* any play of the Game at Carnegie Tech. While such changes could be made with little difficulty, they are undersirable from an educational standpoint. The players have a great deal of difficulty attempting to establish the nature of market influences when they are stable, let alone shifting or fluctuating. Interestingly enough, many players believe that some of the parameters are being changed even when they are not. It is likely that they also overestimate the instability of basic market mechanisms, attributing changes in the market positions of brands to changes in consumer tastes when they reflect, for the most part, the influence of new methods of appealing to existing, but latent, tastes.

Some parameters are, however, changed almost routinely in the course of the Game. Wage negotiations generally lead to increases in the cost of labor. Similarly, suppliers may change prices for the raw materials used by a firm. Shipping and storage costs are also subject to change. The productivity of a firm's labor force may be modified to reflect the state of its labor relations. Also, interest costs and the availability of capital from the equity market are established separately with each application for funds. When changes in these parameters occur in the course of actual business operations, they frequently lead to the reevaluation of a firm's past decisions. In the Game they should lead to a similar reappraisal of alternatives by the players.

VII. CONCLUSION

This chapter and the one that preceded it are intended to show some of the facets of Game play that have developed in the graduate program at Carnegie Tech. From a discussion in Chapter 3 of ways in which the faculty has embellished the basic Game as a competitive management exercise with a variety of role-playing assignments and has embedded it into a total educational program, we have tried to switch in this chapter to a discussion of the Game as it is experienced by the players and to a brief consideration of some of the administrative tasks associated with running the Game. We look next in Chapter 5 at the ways by which we have tried to tie the Game experience to other courses in the graduate curriculum at Carnegie.

INTEGRATING THE GAME WITH OTHER GRADUATE COURSES

The Game is one of five courses that students take in the third semester of Carnegie's M.S. program in Industrial Administration. The Game itself provides a valuable educational experience, but one of its most attractive features is its accessibility for work in other courses. As the previous two chapters suggest, the Game offers opportunities for "field" experience that has more realism, more interpersonal dynamics, and more feedback on the quality of ideas and proposals than most cases and problem assignments do. At the same time it does not involve the costs, the complexity, and the slow time scale of real field investigations. Students do not have to worry about problems of getting access to crucial kinds of data or building effective relationships with several layers of company personnel who are not involved in the main part of the study. The Game situation is easier for students to familiarize themselves with. To the extent that its realism is acknowledged, the Game lets them look at something more akin to top-level management problems than they can usually get access to in a real company.

This chapter describes six experiments which we have tried at Carnegie to relate the Game to other courses in the M.S. program in Industrial Administration. Specifically, we look at the Game as an adjunct to a course in accounting, taken before students actually play the Game; to courses in administration, operations research, and marketing research, taken while the Game is in progress; and to courses in electronic data processing and business policy, taken after the Game experience is completed. The chapter which follows this one describes similar efforts to build the Game into the curriculum at other schools than Carnegie and efforts to use the Game in special programs at Carnegie and elsewhere.

I. THE AUDIT AS PART OF A FIRST COURSE IN ACCOUNTING[1]

The audit is unique for us as an experiment in which students work with the Game before they actually play it. How this was handled and

---

[1] The audit experiment is treated only briefly in his book. For more detail, we recommend that readers consult Neil C. Churchill, Merton H. Miller, and Robert M.

(Continued on next page)

some of its consequences for play of the Game have already been discussed in Chapter 3, but it is appropriate here to mention some of the results of the experiment for the teaching of accounting.

The audit reports which the teams prepared provided valuable feedback to the instructors on the degree to which their teaching about the philosophy and methods of auditing had gotten across to the students. The auditors took to their task with relish and ingenuity. Their thoroughness in conducting the audit and their ability to defend what they did before the boards and the Game teams also provoked a useful discussion among faculty and second-year students about the auditors' role in business and their responsibilities in filling this role.

The audit not only provided experience in checking routine accounting statements for accuracy, but also experience essential for modern management in checking the output of the computer for accuracy and in assessing the overall degree of knowledge and control that management had over the performance of their firm. The problems of working with management and of reporting on management's behavior to the boards of directors posed in a direct way ethical considerations which auditors must face in real life. There was some real friction between first-year auditors and second-year managers because of the way in which these decisions were handled.

The audit seems to have helped students in general to learn more about accounting. They were able to make cogent criticisms of the practices which the students followed, and they learned enough to improve these practices greatly when they played the Game. In particular, the audit sharpened understanding of the relations between auditing practice and financial analysis and the understanding of the rationale of cost accounting. An example of the sophistication and completeness of the audit reports is shown by the excerpts in Appendix 5A.

The audit also provided valuable experience with problems of human relations. The managing partners in particular reported how much they learned about trying to elicit cooperation in group efforts. All concerned found that their early notions about the incentives which would make a group of peers get a job like the audit done were too simple and naive. The notion that some members of the class would not pull their weight was hard for them to accept initially. The interaction with the boards was often lively, and the standards that most

---

Trueblood, *Auditing, Management Games, and Accounting Education* (Monograph #2 in the Carnegie Institute of Technology Series on Management Education; Homewood, Ill.: Richard D. Irwin, Inc., 1964). Also see Kalman J. Cohen and Merton H. Miller, "Management Games, Information Processing, and Control," *Management International,* Vol. 3, No. 3/4, pp. 159-87.

boards imposed in judging the reports were stringent. One board member called the confrontation with the auditors the most dramatic and exciting example of role playing he had ever seen.

II. THE GAME AS A LABORATORY IN ADMINISTRATIVE PROCESSES[2]

The Game has proved to be an effective laboratory in organizational behavior. It provides many organizational problems which have important real-life counterparts—the problem of maintaining a hierarchy without strong sanctions in a group which does not accept it easily, the problem of getting full-scale action executed when a decision to act is made, the problem of keeping planned relationships superior to and consistent with informal ones, the problem of maintaining effective communication and controls within the team, the problem of keeping all members of the team working under the same set of goals, and the problem of getting each member of the team to do his share of the work. The Game as a laboratory in administrative processes allows the student to put into practical use the theoretical framework he receives in the classroom.

Most second-year students who are in the Game also are enrolled in a course in The Administrative Process. This course follows a semester of intensive study, in the first year, of the behavior of individuals and groups, with an effort to set this analysis against the problems which students experience as they begin in graduate school, and against some of the major problems of supervision, influence, and communciation that managers face in industry. The second-year course moves ahead to consider the nature of business and public organizations as going systems and the problems of organizational design: the administrative means by which one achieves goals in an organization. The course in The Administrative Process is meant to help men acquire an ability to handle problems of organizational behavior in a precise and sophisticated way.

The skills that a student needs to develop to solve problems of individual and organizational behavior can be divided into two categories. The first is the skill of being aware of and sensitive to the interpersonal relations in which he participates or which are going on around him. "Sensitivity" is the ability to infer the underlying reasons and motives for behavior from observing the available clues that other

---

[2]Prepared by Kenneth E. Knight, now on the faculty at Stanford University. As a doctoral student at Carnegie, Knight worked with Herbert A. Simon and James G. March to develop an integration between the Game and the second-year Administrative Process course.

people give. Being able to understand what is going on in a complex organizational situation is like being able to explain the internal workings of a watch where you can see only its face and case. Doing this, however, for organizational and social behavior of human beings is more difficult—and far more important—than doing it for an inanimate mechanism.

The second category of problem-solving skills is that of designing, synthesizing, or modifying organizations to make them effective instruments for achieving goals. Sensitivity—understanding and diagnosis—is a preliminary to action—the revision and improvement of organizational designs.

The readings,[3] lectures, and class discussions provide a basic theoretical framework by which to describe and discuss organizations. The schedule of topics in the course includes:

Organizational description.
An organization as a political system.
An organization as a decision system.
An organization as an adaptive system.
Organizational design.

Students have been able to master the theoretical frameworks that have been presented in the course and to use these skillfully in examinations and discussions of other people's problems. On the other hand, when asked to describe situations in which they themselves have been involved, they often presented superficial and inconsistent analyses. The primary difficulty in the course has been to show students how to use theory and research findings to increase their understanding of organizations in which they are participants.

Case problems and readings about field studies[4] were used as supplements to the theoretical material in order to give the student a good idea of the problems they will have to solve in industry. These materials still tended to leave the students feeling that the principles of

---

[3]For example: Chester I. Barnard, *The Functions of the Executive* (Cambridge, Mass.: Harvard University Press, 1938); Peter M. Blau and W. Richard Scott, *Formal Organizations: a Comparative Approach* (San Francisco: Chandler Publishing Co., 1962); James G. March and Herbert A. Simon, *Organizations* (New York: John Wiley & Sons, 1958); Albert H. Rubenstein and Chadwick J. Haberstroh, *Some Theories of Organization* (Homewood, Ill.: Dorsey Press, Inc., 1960); and Herbert A. Simon, *Administrative Behavior* (2nd ed.; New York: Macmillan Co., 1957).

[4]For example: Meville Dalton, *Men Who Manage* (New York: John Wiley & Sons, 1959); William R. Dill, Thomas L. Hilton, and Walter R. Reitman, *The New Managers* (Englewood Cliffs, N. J.: Prentice-Hall, Inc., 1962); John D. Glover and Ralph M. Hower, *The Administrator: Cases in Human Relations in Business* (4th ed.; Homewood, Ill.: Richard D. Irwin, Inc., 1963); Paul R. Lawrence *et al., Organizational Behavior and Administration* (Homewood, Ill.: Dorsey Press Inc., 1961); William F. Whyte, *Money and Motivation* (New York: Harper & Bros., 1955).

administration were only applicable to "isolated instances" and "troubled organizations."

Given these problems in the Administrative Process course, the great benefit of the Game is as a laboratory in which to facilitate the students' transferring abstract definitions and theories into concepts that they apply to their everyday situations. The Game provided an atmosphere to develop the first of the problem-solving skills—sensitivity. A series of written assignments and exam questions were given that had the students analyze their team's activities. The impact of the assignments was enhanced by asking each team, meeting outside class, to discuss its behavior in the light of the material presented in the reading, lectures, and class discussion.

Five of the major assignments using the Game were the following:

1. An early written report in which each Game participant was asked to describe the process by which his team defined jobs and assigned members to them and to explain this in terms of modern organization theory.

2. A question on the midterm examination asking players to describe and evaluate, for the first half-semester of Game play, the development of the team organization with particular stress on the interplay between individual and group motivation. (The students were told at the beginning of the term that a question of this nature would represent 50 percent of the midterm examination.)

3. A written report in which each Game participant was asked to draw a detailed flow chart of a decision program that he or another team member was using. Special attention was given to information requirements, information sources, and the complex decision routines (judgmental decisions) that could be completely programmed.

4. A later report, at the time when teams were preparing to make their first "three-month" move, which required each team (a) to tape-record the meeting at which they debated the policies they would follow for the three-month move, (b) to listen to the tape and to discuss what it revealed about the functioning of their organizations, and (c) to prepare a report summarizing ways of improving their organization.

5. A question on the final examination, counting for half of the total examination, asking each man to recommend a plan of organization and policies to guide action for a group that would take over the company from his team.

Execution of these assignments and arrangements for discussing them with individuals and teams were facilitated by assigning an advanced doctoral student to work with the course instructor. Since this student had once been president of a Game team, he was in an especially good position to help develop meaningful assignments and to give useful comments to the participants. He was also helpful in showing teams links between Game experiences and real business problems.

The Game has provided students with an opportunity to see themselves in a realistic business environment where they faced difficult organizational problems that had to be solved. It has provided this opportunity in a way that no comparable exercise or case discussion has done. Comparisons of the several papers that are submitted covering the activities of each team have provided an excellent means of giving useful feedback to each student about his effectiveness as a team member.

III. USING THE GAME WITH A COURSE IN OPERATIONS RESEARCH[5]

As part of their education in general management all Carnegie Tech students have been required to take an introductory course in Operations Research.[6] This is followed by a second course which can be elected by students wishing to obtain further, more specialized, training.

The second course generally organizes students as a "mock consulting firm" which undertakes "client engagements" on problems actually confronting firms in the Pittsburgh area. This approach has proved to have several virtues from an educational standpoint. It motivates students to learn more about operations research methods on their own; and, at the same time, it helps to bring this learning into sharper focus by reference to one or more actual problems. Opportunity for imaginative applications of a variety of operations research approaches are supplied in a context that generally requires a blending of these approaches with other managerial skills in every aspect of an engagement—from making the initial identification of problems to securing the cooperation of company personnel and then assuming responsibility for all phases of the final report, including presentation to the company, preparation of manuals, computer codes, and so on. The students acquire some "feel" for actual problems, but, even more important, the classroom discussions and faculty-student conferences can also be utilized to discuss the kinds of professional responsibilities which might well devolve upon these students as practitioners in operations research and as members of a continuing firm of consultants which is, in turn, part of another organization (in this case, the Graduate School of Industrial Administration).

---

[5]Prepared by William W. Cooper.

[6]This course, previously called Advanced Business and Engineering Economics I, was given as the first semester of a two-semester, second-year graduate sequence. The curriculum has now been revised to fit this course as the middle course in a three-course sequence which commences with a required course in Management Mathematics. The third course, a more advanced seminar in operations research, can then be taken as an elective.

A. Using Operations Research Students as Consultants to Game Teams

The success of this educational experiment for the elective course in operations research made it natural to look for some way of creating a similar educational environment for students in the required introductory course as well. It did not seem prudent, however, to expose students in the introductory course to the full complexity and size of actual business problems. Hence, partly at the suggestion of Richard M. Cyert, recourse was made to the Carnegie Tech Management Game. Since 1960–61 students in this course have been assigned the role of consultants to "firms" engaged in playing this Game. Thus far the experiment has been successful. Use of the Game has avoided the kinds of difficulties—and responsibilities—which would inevitably be associated with assigning these students to engagements with actual business firms. At the same time, the complexity of the Game has supplied a surprisingly rich and challenging array of problems. The results of the experiment have allayed our fears that only rather simple applications of operations research techniques would be made and that students might derive only mechanical and superficial exercise of their skills in operations research.

The row headings in Table 5–1 show the kinds of problems which have been studied and reported upon to date. The first number entering into each cell sum refers to reports prepared in 1960–61, and the second number in the sum refers to reports prepared in 1961–62. The data are presented in this way to show the influences, if any, which might result from the fact that all reports—including faculty commentaries and criticisms—are placed on reserve in the library so that succeeding students may have access to them. This same procedure is followed in the advanced (elective) course where students work for real business firms. In that case there are compelling reasons for adopting this procedure because each succeeding group of students is required to know how their "firm" has operated in the past, the kinds of previous studies made, and the commitments or other obligations incurred in dealing with various clients.

Such continuity is not nearly so compelling for students in the introductory course. On the other hand, access to work that previous classes have done seems to provide a benchmark for students in forming their expectations, in providing them with insight about how to approach problems, and in gauging the kinds of standards that might be applied in evaluating their reports. Some students might be tempted merely to lean upon these previous reports instead of striking out on

TABLE 5–1

CLASSIFICATION OF GAME-BASED REPORTS PREPARED BY STUDENT TEAMS IN AN
OPERATIONS RESEARCH COURSE

Total reports: 29   Total Students: 63

Problem Selected	Linear Programming (Including Piecewise Linear)	Game Theory	Statistical Decision Theory, Bayesian and Subjective Probability	Quadratic Programming (Modified Neyman Allocation)	Markoff Process	Approximate Model or Solution Method
Inventory, production and employment	9+1=10					
Locating concentration centers						1+0=1
Transportation, including transshipment	3+4=7					
Lot sizes with variable prices			1+0=1			
Pricing strategies		1+1=2				
Sales forecasting under constraints	1+0=1					
Multiple managerial goals						0+1=1
Finished goods inventory			0+1=1			
Emergency production	0+1=1					
Funds for market survey tests				0+1=1		
Hiring and layoff strategies	.		*0+1=1			
New product introduction					0+1=1	
Accounting and financial planning	0+1=1					
Totals	13+7=20	1+1=2	1+2=3	0+1=1	0+1=1	1+1=2

*Hypothetical research report only. Not applied or tested on actual firm data.

their own. This danger, though, seems not to have materialized except, possibly, in the case of the transportation (plus transshipment) models. Even here no really serious copying tendencies have been detected although it cannot be denied that a reading of previous reports in this area might have served to suggest this as a relatively easy topic.[7]

It was recognized that students in this course would be more heterogeneous than those in the more advanced course. Allowance was thereforce made for this fact and indeed some of the "teams" consisted of only one individual. Most teams consisted of two or three individuals although in one case a team of four was permitted. A further deviation was permitted when two doctoral students preferred to pursue a topic for its research interest and potential rather than to engage in a study that was supposed to be directed toward an immediate, practical application and which would therefore involve negotiations and commitments to others who might not share all aspects of these same interests. Students could consult for their own teams. No student was permitted to serve as a consultant to a team in the Game if he was engaged, at the same time, as a member of the staff of another firm playing in the same industry. The two-industry structure of the Game runs at Carnegie has made it possible to circumvent the latter difficulty. In none of the 29 reports refered to in Table 5–1 was there any case where possible conflicts of interest could not be resolved.

B. Guiding the Work to Get Managerial as Well as Technical Quality

In this course it was desired to emphasize managerial as well as operations research aspects of the studies that might be undertaken. Each report was evaluated and graded with respect to: (1) the kind of problem selected, including its possible managerial significance as well as its operations research challenge; (2) the quality of the solution effected, including the possibility of its practical implementation; and (3) the kind of report which was prepared, including both its intelligibility to management and its professional content and quality as judged by, say, an operations research practitioner who might be called upon to evaluate the report or to aid in its implementation. To lead students toward these standards, arrangements were made at a very

---

[7] In general, the second group of students tended to extend their studies more in the direction of dynamic transportation models of a multiperiod variety, along with inventory and storage features and more extensive uses of dual evaluator and sensitivity analyses.

early stage in the course for periodic reviews and conferences with the students.[8]

A minimum of three conferences was scheduled for each student group. First, each student or group of students was required to submit a brief two- or three-page memorandum outlining the proposed study. This was reviewed with the instructor, then revised, and reviewed again so that when finally approved, it served as an authorization to undertake an engagement along the indicated lines.

The initially stated proposals commonly had two failings: (1) many involved problems of almost heroic dimensions such as "forming a mathematical model covering all phases of the firm," and (2) many were so vague that they could not be readily understood as recommendations for study and action. The latter weakness, in particular, was criticized severely to impress students with the need for orderly and precise writing not only as a matter of documentation but also as a matter of meeting the needs and pressures of management (represented here by the instructor).

With their approval in hand, the students could then open negotiations for an actual engagement with one of the teams in the Game. Sometimes further conferences with the instructor were then required as the negotiations progressed. In all cases, students had to prepare and submit a final memorandum summarizing the negotiations so that no misunderstanding could arise concerning the record of the obligations that they were thereby assuming.

Of course, many further conferences about special problems were also needed. The nature and number of these conferences varied greatly according to the quality of the student groups, the nature of the problems encountered, and other factors. Wherever possible, the instructor kept emphasizing the kind of management report that might result from the approaches that were suggested. He pointed out that in many instances one mode of attack might be preferable to another from a technical but not from a managerial standpoint. Emphasis was placed on the desirability of exploring more than one approach in depth, not only as a means of acquiring a more solid background for evaluating the potential value of each but also as a means of presenting management with a variety of alternative possibilities rather than with only a yes-or-no choice. Although the presentation of alternatives to a management group almost inevitably compounds the difficulty of report

---

[8]The library file of previous student reports also helps in this respect since it contains detailed commentaries as well as evaluations by the teacher on all aspects of the previous reports.

preparation, the instructor wanted again to emphasize that report preparation itself is an integral part of technical operations research work.

C. The Technical Approaches Used

The studies that the students have done involved recourse to a variety of techniques. The columnar classifications in Table 5–1 show the main operations research method (or model) utilized. Although it would be interesting to discuss each of these reports in some detail, we cannot attempt it here. It must suffice to say that in most cases the problems and their solutions would be regarded as sophisticated, and indeed, only a few years ago many might have been welcomed for publication in standard professional journals.[9] Of course, allowance must be made for the fact that these students were encouraged to use relevant published research. It is doubtful that they would have been able to achieve equally high levels of sophistication without drawing on work that others had done.

Some of the students' results were surprising in a variety of ways. For instance, prior to effecting these studies it was "common folklore" among the students that the Carnegie Game was predominantly a "marketing game." Hence the usual operations research approaches— which were thought to be mainly for "production type" problems— could not be expected to yield much return for the hard work that was likely to be involved in synthesizing a mathematical model, devising computer codes· and so on. This myth was exploded, however, even by the very first group of studies. As Table 5–1 shows, they were heavily concentrated in the area of inventory-production-employment scheduling. Using data available from past records of particular firms to check and illustrate their models, the student reports showed that substantial cost reductions and profit increases could be achieved by improving this aspect of firm operations. Indeed, students discovered that one firm had already accumulated so much inventory early in its career, that it could have ceased production completely and still could have supplied all likely levels of demand from already available stocks.

Referring to Table 5–1 again and bearing in mind that only the major emphasis is designated by the column titles, it is interesting to observe some of the methods that students did *not* use. Simulation attacks and heuristics did not figure as the major approach in any study, but they were employed in many reports to check and validate the data or models or to identify parts of a total problem that might otherwise

---

[9]Parts of one report which has been published in the *Journal of Accounting Research* are reprinted in Chapter 8, Section III.B.

be overlooked. Among other methods used in a secondary, but not a primary way, we would list classical statistical techniques such as regression and correlation analysis as well as less classical ones like exponentially weighted averages or linear programming (absolute deviation) regressions. There were no attempts to utilize such standard operations research techniques as queuing theory or dynamic programming. Most surprising, however, is the fact that none of these studies reported any attempt to use gaming—as distinct from the theory of games—even for exploratory purposes, although the studies were all conducted in the context of a business game and although gaming, as such, is well recognized as an operations research tool. Although some of the problems—or approaches—would not materially yield gaming methods, studies which could rather naturally have moved in this direction did not do so. For instance, the report labeled "multiple managerial goals" required some way of ascertaining the various goals of the management of one particular firm. The early part of this report seemed as if it might have moved toward a gaming experiment. Instead the students did only a statistical analysis of past records and adopted a preference or utility theory approach that evidently had its source mainly in classical economics and modern psychology, adjusted only by reference to the theory of games—not gaming!

D. Future Objectives

In at least one respect the timing and the introductory nature of the Operations Research course has been unfortunate. By the time that student teams complete their consulting assignments to the Game teams, it is too late for the "client managements" actually to use the results in the Game.[10] If the reports could be finished earlier in the semester, there would be a better opportunity to test whether the results are practical as well as sophisticated, interesting, and original. So far, the only real evidence of practicality is nebulous. It appears mainly in informal conversations with subsequent management teams in the Game—the year following the study. Some of these teams apparently have read the previous year's reports and have tried to experiment in using some of the models and results for operating their firms.[11]

---

[10]The models developed in many of these operations research reports were incorporated, however, in some of the management information and control systems formulated the following semester as term projects in the Electronic Data Processing course. See the discussion of the latter in Section V.

[11]Reports were also circulated to faculty who had served as members of the boards of directors for the client firms. Their comments were solicited on the relevance of the reports to each firm's total operations. We hoped to use the comments in further conferences with students who had prepared the reports, but unfortunately this plan was frustrated by lack of time.

IV. THE GAME AND A SEMINAR IN MARKETING RESEARCH[12]

In the teaching of marketing, the Carnegie Management Game has been used particularly in conjunction with an elective second-year seminar that is concurrent with the play of the Game. Depending upon the previous training or experience of the players in marketing, the Game can be used to acquaint them with the institutional character of the packaged grocery and drug industries, the types of market data available, the nature of the decisions to be made, and the interactions among such market influences as price, advertising, distribution, and product characteristics. The Game also provides an environment within which players can develop their skills at model building and in applying analytical methods to the solution of business problems.

Many students in Carnegie's M.S. and Ph.D. programs elect an advanced course in marketing which is focused around the objectives and methods of market research. This follows a first course, making extensive use of cases and projects, whose purpose is to introduce students to the marketing function and to give them experience in solving marketing problems. The advanced course builds on the introductory work in marketing as well as on what students have learned about statistics, computer programming, and human behavior in other first-year courses. Largely through seminar discussions of on-going research and practice, and through major term projects which the students undertake, the advanced course helps students learn to define problems for analysis, to build models, and to use them on real-world data to find out whether they work.

Of what benefit is the Carnegie Game to students in marketing? Apart from the desirable features cited for virtually all games (that is, student motivation and recognition of the interaction between such functions as production and marketing), we have found the Carnegie Game to be useful in developing a much deeper level of interest on the part of students in (1) the application of analytical techniques to the study of data, (2) the planning of market experiments, (3) the evaluation of models in the literature which might be of help in solving such problems as to how to budget advertising or establish prices, and (4) speculation as to the nature of the real world. The students are asked to play the Game and not the real world. They are to learn the characteristics of the Game as they play it and are told to take maximum advantage of their knowledge. If they find an apparent flaw

---

[12]For an earlier account, on which this section is based in part, see Alfred A. Kuehn, "Realism in Business Games," in Willian R. Dill, James R. Jackson, and James W. Sweeney (eds.), *Proceedings of the Conference on Business Games as Teaching Devices* (New Orleans: Tulane University, 1961), pp. 56-60.

in the Game, they are to exploit it. Thus they obtain experience in working with data quite similar to that available to their counterparts in industry and, like their counterparts, can achieve success by better understanding their environment and adapting to it.

In addition, during feedback sessions after the play of the Game, the student comes to realize that much which he believed to be true about the Game was, in fact, erroneous. For example, in an early play of the Carnegie Game the consumer product preferences in the four market regions were identical. Through variation in marketing activity among competitors, however, the shares of market of individual brands varied substantially. The players found it hard to believe that these differences were not due largely to regional differences with respect to the product charatceristics that consumers desired. Such experiences have a significant impact on the student and, we believe, provide a maturity in analyzing data not easily obtained from the study of cases or from on-the-job-training in industry.

The researcher who teaches theories has much to gain from observing the behavior of players and the response characteristics of a game that is based upon his theories. The Game becomes a vehicle for expressing the logical and mathematical relationships of his theory and forms a synthetic experimental environment for testing and extending the theory.

The instructor's efforts with the Carnegie Game have been directed at developing an understanding of the dynamics of consumer behavior and the influence of advertising, price, retail availability, and product characteristics. There has been a determined attempt in the Carnegie Management Game and the closely related CIT Marketing Game[13] to describe these processes realistically. Much of the basic marketing information available to management in the packaged detergent industry has been replicated by the two games. Although the Game still falls short of a complete simulation, the market structures of both the Carnegie Management Game and the CIT Marketing Game are built upon the results of empirical research in the marketing of a variety of proprietary drug and grocery products.[14] This realism and complexity

---

[13]The CIT Marketing Game has been programmed for the IBM 704, IBM 7070, IBM 7090, and IBM 1620 computers. Further information about this Game is available from Professor Alfred A. Kuehn, Carnegie Institute of Technology, Pittsburgh, Pennsylvania, 15213.

[14]The marketing functions of the Carnegie Management Game and the CIT Marketing Game are not identical. The simplicity of the latter in the areas of finance, production and accounting, and, consequently, the greater amount of computer storage available for the marketing function, has facilitated its use as a research tool in the study of market behavior. The Marketing Game thus provides a testing ground and source of future modifications of the marketing function in the Management Game. These functions

allows advanced marketing students to participate in research of the type summarized below.

A. Studying Consumer Behavior and Market Influences to Improve the Game Model

The research which resulted in the development of the model underlying the marketing functions in the Mark 1.5 version of Carnegie Management Games was initiated to develop decision rules for use by management in the budgeting of advertising.[15] Theoretical considerations and empirical evidence led to a model describing consumer brand-shifting as a probabilistic process. Price, advertising, retail availability, and product characteristics were treated as influencing the probabilities of consumers shifting their purchasing among various brands being marketed. Students in the market research seminar have drawn on their experiences in the Game and have carried out empirical studies to improve this early model.

The implications of the model were examined under the assumption that the managements of competing firms would reach advertising and pricing decisions independently and would seek to maximize their operating profits. These implications were then studied in the light of available theory and confronted with empirical evidence. Some of the assumptions about consumer behavior underlying the model were also tested with sequential brand purchase records available from consumer panels. This research has led to continued improvements in the model of consumer brand-shifting and in the overall marketing model incorporating the influences of price, product characteristics, advertising, and retail availability upon consumer purchasing behavior.

The examination of empirical evidence in the foregoing research suggested that the marketing variables in the system interact strongly with each other. Much of the difficulty researchers have had in identifying the effects of price and advertising may be a result of the way in which marketing problems have generally been partitioned. Most researchers have used models which either ignore certain important marketing influences or treat their effects as independent of one another.[16]

---

will most likely never be identical, however, because of the different uses being made of the games, the Marketing Game focusing upon only a single area of business training and research, the Management Game providing a broad view of management and organizational problems.

[15] A. A. Kuehn, "A Model for Budgeting Advertising," in Frank M. Bass, *et al.* (eds), *Mathematical Models and Methods of Marketing* (Homewood, Ill.: Richard D. Irwin, Inc., 1961), pp. 315-53.

[16] A. A. Kuehn, "How Advertising Performance Depends on Other Marketing Factors," *Journal of Advertising Research*, Vol. 2, No. 1 (March 1962), pp. 2-10. Excerpts from this paper are reprinted in Chapter 8, Section IV.C.

Subsequent refinements in the model were achieved through the process of building submodels, testing assumptions, evaluating implications, and comparing results with empirical data on consumer and firm behavior. Some shortcomings uncovered by this research, however, could be corrected only by complicating the model to such an extent that an analytic solution no longer appeared feasible.

To incorporate the new complications into the model so that their effects might be researched, a computer model was developed to simulate the market of the detergent industry.[17] This model has been incorporated into the CIT Marketing Game and also provides the basis for most of the marketing functions in the Mark 1.5 version of the Carnegie Management Game. Since several phases of the detergent market have not yet been studied in complete detail, however, some assumptions have been required to fill gaps in existing knowledge. For example, the inventory behavior of retailers and wholesalers was inferred from limited data on levels of inventory and reported ordering behavior. Similarly, some aspects of sales promotion activity common to the detergent industry (for instance, couponing, price, and merchandise packs) are not yet included in the model or in the games. Improvements in these aspects of the simulation model can be expected to result from current and future research. Some of the students participating in the advanced marketing seminar will contribute to this research.

B. Using the Game to Evaluate Marketing Strategies

With only minor changes in parameters, the Game model is capable of simulating a wide range of market conditions. Students in the marketing seminar have participated in research to determine the implications of the Game model with respect to its equilibrium characteristics under the assumption that firms act independently of each other so as to maximize their profits. This type of analysis is being done for market situations in which competitors sell identical products and for situations in which products are differentiated in terms of physical characteristics. The latter results are being compared with the behavior of Game players marketing identical sets of different products. The sensitivity of these equilibrium results to various parameters in the model (for instance, industry and interbrand price elasticities, degree of habitual purchasing behavior, and so on) are also being examined.

---

[17]Doyle L. Weiss, "Simulation of the Packaged Detergent Industry," in Charles H. Hindersman (ed.), *Marketing Precision and Executive Action* (New York: American Marketing Association, 1961).

Answers to the following questions should come directly from this research:

1. What is the most profitable marketing strategy to follow in the framework of the Game given distributions of consumer preferences for the physical product characteristics of a particular brand and those of its competition?
2. How should players in the Game allocate resources among several brands competing in the same or different submarkets of the industry?
3. How should a new product be introduced to the market? What effect does the timing of an introduction have on success?
4. What size of investment is justified in establishing a market position for a new brand? How does the answer to this question depend upon future product developments within the industry?

The above questions are being studied within the framework of the simulation model underlying the Game. The results obtained from this research will be compared with real industry experience to see if it is consistent with this experience. The model can also be studied by simulating past market behavior. Such testing will provide the means with which to improve the model, suggest areas for additional research, and, quite likely, suggest new marketing strategies which warrant field testing. Perfection in a simulation model is not needed for industrial application. All that is required is a model which can help management reach improved decisions. Whether the simulation model underlying the Game proves to be of operational value is yet to be demonstrated. It seems certain, however, that much will be learned in the course of this research—findings which should lead to a better understanding and improved models of market behavior.

V. THE GAME AS AN ENVIRONMENT FOR DEVELOPING MANAGEMENT INFORMATION AND CONTROL SYSTEMS[18]

Of the attempts to integrate the Game with other courses that we have described so far in this chapter, one (the audit assignment) takes place before students have played the Game. The other three (the assignments in organizational analysis, operations research, and marketing) take place while students are participating as members of Game teams. We now look at two courses, Electronic Data Processing and Business Policy, which students take the semester following Game play and in which students have been asked to reflect back on their experiences as participants.

The course in Electronic Data Processing has been one of the most popular second-year electives in the M.S. program at Carnegie. This is not a course in the identification of equipment or in the elements of

---

[18]This section is adapted from Kalman J. Cohen and Merton H. Miller, *op. cit.*

programming as it is in many schools. Students come into this course with a knowledge of, and some practice in, computer programming. The course concentrates on the uses of computers in management. It is built around the problems of designing computer-based management information, decision, and control systems.

Those graduate students in the Electronic Data Processing course who had the experience of playing the Game in the previous semester were asked in a term paper to design a man-machine information-processing and decision-making system that could be used by a firm playing the Carnegie Tech Management Game. For this purpose, they were to assume that the firm would no longer receive the regular printed output from the computer, but, instead, would receive each simulated "month" only a deck of punched cards or a magnetic tape containing all the information from which the regular printed output was derived. The students' specific task was to design the best possible system for taking the computer output at the end of one move and transforming it into a complete set of decision inputs for the next simulated move. The system would, of course, have to make at least some minimal use of the computer, if only because the information comes on punched cards or on tape. It would also have to make at least some minimal use of human components since the players were to be assumed to have the responsibility of reporting to and dealing with their boards of directors. Within these limits, however, the students were free to balance the man and the machine components as they saw fit, subject only to the restriction that the machine portions of the program had to be specified in sufficient detail so that it was clear how they might be programmed for a modern large computer such as our CDC G–21.

Although all the students had played the same Game and had virtually identical training in systems design, there is surprising diversity in the systems that were developed out of essentially the same raw material. However, in general, it is quite clear that the students had learned: (1) how a computer could be used to transform unorganized raw data into meaningful management information; and (2) how to devise sensible divisions of labor, based on the principle of comparative advantage, between the man and machine elements at the decision-making as well as the clerical level. This is not to say, of course, that equally thoughtful papers might not have been produced by some other type of assignment. However, using the Game had two important advantages. First, it encompassed a wider range of information-processing and decision-making problems than the students could ever hope to encounter within the same time limits in the context of any real firm.

At the same time, the students were able to draw on their own firsthand observations and experiences in a way that would be impossible with an armchair case or textbook problem.

In regard to the specific learning content of this exercise, we were particularly impressed by several features of these papers. While the students recognized the comparative advantages of electronic computers for the clerical side of data processing as well as for applying mathematical techniques for decision making, most of them did not overlook management's ultimate responsibility for the conduct of the enterprise. Programs were set up in such a way that management readily and at all times could monitor the important decisions produced by the computer models and could intervene to modify these decisions whenever appropriate. Furthermore, the underlying mathematical models typically incorporated parameters intended to reflect specific company policies in a way which permitted easy change whenever these basic policies were altered.

All of the management information systems designed by the students divided the decision-making tasks between management and the computers on the basis of the extent to which each decision could be programmed economically and the degree to which each decision variable interacted with the others. In those areas where management was asked to make the decisions, the computers provided printed copies of the relevant background information, suitably organized and displayed, to aid management in these tasks. In addition to the regular information and decision reports which were routinely printed by the computer, most of these management information systems provided easy procedures by which management could obtain special reports from the computer on request, should they ever feel the need for more extensive information about past operations or for more detailed forecasts about the probable consequences of future actions.

So that the reader may judge the content and quality of these papers more fully, excerpts from one are presented in Appendix 5B.

VI. THE GAME AS PART OF A BUSINESS POLICY SEQUENCE[19]

We regard the time that M.S. students in Industrial Administration spend playing the Game in the third semester of their program at Carnegie as the first half of a two-term Business Policy sequence. With the readings, problems, and cases in the second half of the sequence, the

---

[19]In part, this section is based on William R. Dill, "Management Games and Business Policy," a paper prepared for the Conference on Business Policy at the Harvard Business School, April 8–11, 1963.

Game is viewed as helping students acquire some very basic top-management skills such as:

1. The ability to understand different institutional settings for policy making—differences among firms in their position in the "life cycle," in their competitive environment, in the resources on which they depend for success, and in their ability to operate as private vs. quasi-public enterprises.
2. The ability to distinguish basic kinds of policy decisions and to understand their interdependence with one another—decisions about basic goals or fields of endeavor, decisions about strategies for matching the firm's choice of mission with opportunities and constraints in the environment, decisions about programs of action within the firm, and decisions appraising the firm's performance and potential for the future.
3. The ability as an executive to plan one's own behavior and the efforts of others in the organization in order to make and carry through policy decisions and in order to learn from previous experience.

A. Advantages of the Game in the Classroom

The Game frees us from the rigid framework imposed on the design of the Business Policy course by those who believe that it can only be taught via cases.[20] Both games and cases are efforts to compress processes and events with which it might take students years to gain acquaintance in business. Hence, any case or game is necessarily an "artifically simple" approximation of the world it tries to describe or simulate. The degree of complexity in a case or a game reflects the goals for which it has been developed and the "state of the art" more than any inherent limitations in the medium. Whether you measure complexity by the number of inches of printed materials that students must read, by the variety of problems that are posed, or by the length of time that students stay interested in working on the problems, the Carnegie Tech Game is more complex than even the most elaborate case series (the Hilton Hotel series, for example) that are being developed for use in policy courses.

To review the tasks that players in the Game must handle, we find that each team has total responsibility for the management of a simulated company with multiple products and multiple markets. In addition to the gross decisions involved in setting and coordinating basic policies in marketing, production, finance, and research, teams have to coordinate these basic policies with hundreds of specific decisions that must be faced within the functional areas. Teams may have to plan

---

[20]For example: "[Business policy] obviously must be a case course; we can imagine no other way." Robert A. Gordon and James E. Howell, *Higher Education for Business* (New York: Columbia University Press, 1959), p. 207.

and build new production or storage facilities or go to the bank or into the markets for new capital. They have to deal in person with union representatives about grievances and demands for new contracts that develop from their handling of the simulated work force. They may have to fight their way out of bankruptcy, or they may find themselves initiating or responding to proposals for a merger with another team. Their financial accounts and their decision procedures must be good enough to survive a critical audit by students from the first-year accounting course. Over the semester, they are required to develop decision rules which will allow their firm to run two or three periods of play at a time without further team intervention. All their activities are subject to periodic questioning and appraisal by a board of directors made up of faculty members and one or two business executives who have had actual board experience.

All of this is relatively simple in comparison to the real world, but it provides an excellent test of students' ability to realize in their behavior the attitudes, the problem-solving strategies, and the sensitivity to questions of implementation that we look for when we ask them to analyze a case.

In several respects, the Carnegie Game has been better than cases for providing a realistic introduction to what the world is like. Consider four kinds of experience which most of us would like a business policy sequence to provide.

1. *The Game has been better than cases for giving students the challenge of working with ill-structured, fragmented, and time-sequenced information about the state of the firm and its environment.* Except perhaps in Pigors' incident method[21], which so far as we know has not been used extensively in teaching business policy, cases present information in an unrealistically predigested form. For the Game, we start students with some general background information about the company, its competitive environment, and some of the traditions and constraints which may be relevant to their decisions. We then give each team a file of company reports for the last couple of years' operations (some 500 pages of data). As in the real world, the data is not complete. Much of it is poorly organized; some of it is trivial; some of it is inaccurate. As in the real world, the teams can only get some of the information that they would like to have about customers and competitors by buying estimates of what they would like to know or by engaging in industrial espionage.

---

[21]Paul Pigors and Faith Pigors, *Case Method in Human Relations: the Incident Process* (New York: McGraw-Hill Book Co., 1961).

In cases, companies are often unwilling to let more than balance sheets, income statements, and other "public" information be published even though additional data are essential for making realistic management decisions. In the Game, there are no clearance problems. Detailed information about what has been going on in marketing, production, and finance can be simulated for the management team.

Further, with respect to the kinds of information provided, the older cases on which we rely in business policy seldom give students the types of output which a modern computer-based information, decision, and control system would generate. In the Game, you can generate the kinds of information which will provide a fair test of whether students can apply modern analytic techniques in their efforts to solve policy problems. It would be hard, for example, to try out some of Mr. Mc-Namara's techniques for running the Defense Department using the kind of case materials that Mr. Wilson's or Mr. Stimson's aides would have supplied.

2. *The Game has been a surer means than cases for demonstrating the overall, integrated nature of the process of making and executing policy.* With cases, it takes a very skilled instructor to push students hard enough and long enough that they understand that policy making encompasses more than goal setting and general planning—that it also encompasses the elaboration of these plans into specific competitive strategies and programs of action, and the supervision of arrangements for their implementation. The computer, unlike some less skilled instructors, is intolerant of generalities and ruthless when students overlook a key decision or make a mistake. A Game team may start by a general agreement that their firm should increase its advertising expenditures, but before they are done, they must decide when, by how much, for which products, and for which regions of the country.

Also, the Carnegie Game situation provides a more vivid demonstration than most cases that the merits of any policy decision are relative, dependent on what competitors decide to do. In the Game, each team is continually aware that two other teams are working to thwart whatever they decide to do.

3. *The Game has provided better opportunities than cases to see feedback from decisions and to test skills in diagnosing and adapting to a new environment.* Too often in a policy case discussion, the instructor is both forecaster and judge—he listens to student proposals for action, helps them guess what the actions would lead to, and then uses these subjective forecasts as a basis for evaluating the worth of the proposals. His forecasts and evaluations must be tentative because he is seldom in a much better position than the students to know what their proposals for action would lead to.

The feedback in a game is impersonal. Students can estimate what they will accomplish for their company by a series of decisions, and then they can observe the outcomes. By letting them replay decisions, they can test whether another strategy would lead to better or worse results, or test whether the same strategy would work as well under different competitive positions. They learn to infer results, not from the instructor's reactions and comments, but from the kinds of reports that a real company president would use to judge how well he had done.

4. *The Game has provided a better medium than cases for letting students learn their own capacities and limits in managerial roles.* Sharp and experienced graduate students are often conceited in their approach to case problems. They learn intellectually to recognize the problems that cases present, but they cannot imagine themselves ever being as stupid or as unlucky as the principal figures in the case were. Even if we ask students to role-play the case, we are asking them to assume someone else's personality characteristics and to live with problems that someone else created.

One of the most valuable outcomes of our experiment with games has been the new awareness that students acquire of their own ability to *mis*manage a task which requires agreement on goals, advanced planning, coordination among different functions, incentives to keep team members productive and happy, and control to see that plans are executed. In their contacts with one another, with members of the board, with the bank, and with union representatives, the students on a team face many of the demands of real managerial roles. Most teams develop some of the same organizational problems that business policy cases describe. But in the Game, students have no one else to blame the problems on. The origins, and the cures, lie in their own behavior. The ability of the Game to give each student a sense of how he must develop his own skills and motivations to meet the demands of a top-management job may be the most distinctive and the most important contribution of the Game to the Business Policy course.

It is interesting that the cost of developing games and of installing the computers that are needed to run them is often regarded as "expensive," while the costs of further proliferation of case materials are seldom mentioned. It is important to recognize in our educational programs that computers and computer-based information and decision systems are going to be an increasingly important aspect of policy formulation and administration in business and government within the coming decades. It is also important, from the standpoint of achieving the revolution in policy formulation that organizations in our society must bring about in order to cope with the problems that we face, to put less emphasis on training young policy teachers to be good journalists and more emphasis on making them better analysists and theory builders.

In the major casebooks on business policy,[22] there are no cases which really pose students with designing and evaluating computer-based information and decision systems from the top-management level. Such cases would be very hard to collect and present. Yet it is possible with the Game to do some of these things—to let students, for example, write specifications for the kinds of data summaries and reports that they want to receive to control their operation or to let them write and program decision rules whose repetitive application within marketing or production is supposed to be consistent with overall company objectives. After some Game experience, students can be asked to develop simulations of the behavior of competitors or of customers that may be useful for testing the effects of proposed changes in strategic policies. The Game is equally useful in demonstrating to students the limits of computers as an aid to simulation, forecasting, and decision making. Direct experience with a management system in which computers are an important element seems essential to prepare students for top-level positions in a world where the use—and control—of computers will pose very different questions from those which company presidents faced in 1940 and 1950.

B.   The Transition from the Game to Cases and Readings

In the second semester of the Policy sequence, so far, we have made only limited references back to the Game experience. In part, despite the things which the Game does accomplish, the goals of the Policy sequence call for us to test students' analytic, creative, and organizational skills on a broader range of problems and institutional settings than the Game model and its accompanying role-playing exercises encompass. In part, because several other courses are closely integrated with the Game, it has seemed politic not to overweight the time allocated to the Game experience in the total curriculum.

During the second semester of Policy, where it is appropriate, both students and their instructor are encouraged to bring their experience from "the detergent industry" to bear on issues from the assigned cases

---

[22]For example: Edmund P. Learned, C. Roland Christensen, and Kenneth R. Andrews, *Problems of General Management* (Homewood, Ill.: Richard D. Irwin, Inc., 1961); Thomas J. McNichols, *Policy Making and Executive Action* (New York: McGraw-Hill Book Co., 1959); George A. Smith and C. Roland Christensen, *Policy Formulation and Administration* (4th ed., Homewood, Ill.: Richard D. Irwin, Inc., 1962); and L. L. Waters, W. G. Broehl, Jr., C. H. Spencer, and R. M. Powell, *Administering the Going Concern* (Englewood Cliffs, N. J.: Prentice-Hall, Inc., 1962).

and readings. If to solve a case, a particular choice of goals, strategies, or action programs seems appropriate, students can draw from their experience to make preliminary estimates of whether the proposed choice is a good one, to suggest measures for a more systematic evaluation, and to develop solutions for problems of implementation and control that may arise.

One effective assignment based on the Game in the second semester of the Policy course for 1962–63 was one which asked students to review their experience, to restate the explicit and implicit policy "guidelines" under which they began their operations as a team in the Game, and to indicate what they would do differently if they were to begin play again. The best of these papers treated the assignment both from the point of view of the Game as a simulated management exercise and from the point of view of the Game as a course for which grades would be assigned. Excerpts from some of the papers are presented in Appendix 5C. The lessons learned varied according to the problems which each team had faced during the Game.

The even more demanding analysis of Game experiences required of students in Business Policy for 1963–64 follows:

Strategic Variables in the Carnegie Tech Game

The purpose of this assignment is to analyze top-level decision making and its original implications in a firm which operates within a stable product-market scope.

The Problem

As the participants in the Carnegie Tech Game found out, day-to-day operations of a firm require management to make a multitude of decisions. A few of these are of critical importance to the success of the firm; a large variety has at most a moderate effect on performance. And yet the latter, by their sheer number, tend to submerge the former, producing a lack of management perspective—an inability to see the woods for the trees. In the real world a competent top manager seeks to isolate the critical or "strategic" decision areas. He then focuses his activity on the strategic decisions and seeks to delegate and make routine and nonstrategic ones. This is what has become known as the management principle of the "strategic variable."

Procedure

Each team of game participants will consider itself an *ad hoc* committee of senior executives appointed by the president of a Game firm. The mission of the committee is to advise the president on improvements in profitability of the firm which can be attained through improved and better organized decision making. The committee will study the operating histories of the firms in the Tech industries and supplement the quantitative data with their own management experience.

Each of the management committees will prepare a report to the management containing analysis of the firm's decision-making process and make recommendations. These, to the maximum extent possible, should be supported by analyses of actual performance of the firms in the Tech Game.

Recommendations will be made on the following points:

1. With respect to the decision process
   a) The decisions which must be considered of primary importance to to the firm and which must be given major top management attention.
   b) The decisions which can and should be delegated.
   c) Specific policies and standard operating procedures which should be adopted for making routine the second class of decision.
2. With respect to organization
   a) Assignments of areas of decision responsibility which will expedite (1) above.
   b) Organizational structure which is appropriate.

C. Projections for the Future

There are other ways of making greater use of the Game in the second semester of Policy which would still not result in its dominating the whole sequence. As individuals or as teams, for example, students could be motivated to take over one of the companies at a "crisis point" that had actually occurred during the previous semester's play. They would be told a little about how competing firms would behave— either the kinds of decisions that would be made or the kinds of rules that would be applied to generate decisions. Then, with the same model for competitors' behavior locked into the computer to apply against all of the students, the students would compete to see who could do the best job of improving the fortunes of the company that they are managing. Credit might be given not only for absolute level of accomplishments, but also for ability to set and then to meet specific performance objectives.

Similarly, as students begin to generalize from cases or readings about the ways to approach particular management problems of a kind that can be posed in the context of the Game and as differences in approaches get crystalized by class discussion, the Game can be used as a laboratory to test alternative proposals. By varying the parameters of the computer model and the kinds of strategies we assign to competing firms, we can create a large number of environments for managerial action. Again, students would be judged not only on the performance of their strategy proposals but on their ability to predict the outcomes of the experiments that they undertake.

We feel that the present rough balance of 50 percent emphasis on the Game and 50 percent emphasis on readings, cases, and other kinds of projects is a good one for the Business Policy sequence. The effectiveness of either approach depends, of course, on how it is used. It is clear that in the teaching of Business Policy, we need more clearly defined objectives for the course and more basic research underlying our teaching, as much as we need a new kind of problem environment with which to challenge our students. The search for new frameworks for the teaching of Policy is going on at the same time as our efforts to improve the Game, so that by the time we achieve the kind of blend that Cohen and Rhenman describe as a "business game case,"[23] we should have better ideas for how they are to be formulated and used.

VII. CONCLUSION

In bringing the Management Game into the M.S. curriculum in Industrial Administration at Carnegie, the first set of issues were those discussed at the end of Chapter 3. How much time should be allotted to the main Game experience? When should this experience occur during a four-semester graduate program? How should the experience be scheduled and the students' work be evaluated in order to make it consistent with the other courses they were taking? The faculty has worked hard to agree on answers to these questions.

We have not spent as much faculty time, though, deciding how the Game experience is to be exploited in other courses. There have been enough entrepreneurial faculty members to insure that experiments would be undertaken in courses concerned with topics as different from one another as accounting, organizational behavior, and operations research. There has been good enough communication among faculty members and between faculty and students to identify unsuccessful experiments that ought not to be repeated. And there is enough willingness within the School to accept change to insure that even successful experiments, like the audit project, will not be continued if the enthusiasm of the instructors responsible for carrying them through disappears. There is, with all this, an issue of overall balance. Whatever the merits of each single reference to the Game experience, students object to having too many projects in other courses tied to the Game. They recognize, as the faculty should, that at least in its present form the Game cannot be the only environment in which they practice solving managerial problems.

The attempts to exploit the Game in other courses that we have described in this chapter have been regarded as successful by the faculty members who initiated them, and generally, as well, by less partisan

---

[23]See Ch. 9, and Kalman J. Cohen and Eric Rhenman, "The Role of Management Games in Education and Research," *Management Science*, Vol. 7, No. 2 (January 1961), pp. 155–58.

observers who have compared the experiments with other teaching approaches. On the other hand, these experiments can be borrowed for use in other programs only with appropriate caution. The evaluations we have made are tentative, subjective, and local. What has been appropriate at Carnegie in our M.S. program may not be appropriate in other educational settings, and what has worked well as an experiment may not look good when it becomes a routine element in the curriculum. We have had more years of experience with the audit experiment than with any of the others described in this chapter. We find that when the instructors in Quantitative Controls I and the Game boards of directors have not given the assignment their full support, the level of student involvement and the quality of the audit reports have dropped.

When the novelty of exploiting the Game wears off, the successful integration of the Game with other courses is revealed as plain hard work. In his comments on the use of the Game with the Operations Research course,[24] William W. Cooper details the many hours which the instructor must spend in conference with the student project teams if they are to formulate their problem well and develop solutions that will stand the scrutiny of both managers and operations research professionals. While Professor Cooper's aspirations for the quality of the final reports are unusually high, so are the intelligence and the resourcefulness of the students with whom he has been working. The instructors in Quantitative Controls I, the Marketing Research seminar, and Electronic Data Processing have also worked closely with students on projects related to the Game; the instructors in Business Policy will clearly have to if the Game experience is to become integrated in a major way with the second half of the Policy sequence.

The faculty members who have been most successful in exploiting the Game in their courses are those who have been active participants in its development and administration or those who have compensated for this by the same kind of analysis of Game experience that they would put into the analysis of cases or readings.

Effort invested to understand and exploit the Game, though, is good for the faculty. It is an important and powerful way to further the knowledge of the new ways which we have for describing business situations, for predicting the dynamic consequences of business decisions, and for specifying procedures for making such decisions. The essence of cases and readings is too often the capturing of yesterday's experience for tomorrow's managers. Commitment to working with games is, frankly, more revolutionary and more oriented toward the

---

[24]Above, Section III.B.

future needs of management. It is a commitment to develop an understanding of the new techniques and theories that managers have to work with.

Development and administration of a game exercise, like preparation of a case, requires contact and familiarity with the business world. The essential difference between the tasks is that neither the case writer nor the case user needs so complete an understanding of the phenomena that each observes. If the efforts of the case writer provide a lively basis for analysis and discussion, that is enough. Work with a game, though, requires that the faculty member know much more intensively the way in which his students are behaving as members of management teams and that he know the basis on which the simulation against which they play has been constructed. The understanding gained in close work with the Carnegie Game as a simulated managerial environment has helped many of our faculty to be better observers, better analysts, better model builders, and better teachers in relation to real-world business problems.

I. REVIEW OF FINANCIAL STATEMENTS AND INTERNAL CONTROL

A. Financial Statements

1. *Balance Sheets.* *a)* The thousands digits were revised to eliminate statistical error both in the Month 12 balance sheet and truncated errors for months throughout the year. A figure of $25,000 was inserted under "Deferred Charges" when it was discovered that the firm was liable for this amount of financing expense whether or not it chose to take the debenture issue. Credit was made to "Accounts Payable." The footnote concerning debentures seemed essential for full disclosure.

b) Expenditures of $270,000 for the construction of a new warehouse have been authorized. Expenditures on this project through Month 24 amounted to $135,000. Due to the proximity of the completion date, we determined that the warehouse could be shown on the balance sheet in its full amount with the remaining expenditure of $135,000 expressed as a current liability.

2. *Income Statement and Reconciliation of Earnings.* *a)* Federal income tax had to be adjusted since management had not considered the increased tax liability that the year-end accrued interest revenue brought.

b) A tax credit of $59,664 from the first quarter had to be resubtracted from tax liability. This had to be done to correct a misunderstanding of Game rules that former credits were not carried over from quarter to quarter. Such credits are carried over and machine figures were found correct.

---

[1] These are excerpts from the letter of recommendations submitted to the management and board of directors of team B-1 in the 1960-61 play of the Carnegie Tech Management Game, by an audit group consisting of David R. Bamberger, Lawrence J. Brewer, George H. Daggett, C. R. de la Brousse, Thomas C. Gilmore, Donald M. Johnson and Matthias E. Simon, Jr. The letter was part of the material required in an audit project assigned in the course, Quantitative Controls in Business. These excerpts presented here have been chosen to give some of the flavor of the full document on matters pertinent to this book and have not been edited by the authors except to remove some minor errors of style.

Summary of Adjustments (a) and (b):

As submitted............................ $12,483,968
Plus: Liability for interest revenue............   17,500

                                        $12,501,468
Less: Recorrection of tax credit..............   59,664

                                        $12,441,804

c) Profit and retained earnings figures were adjusted to reflect above adjustments.

3. *Sources and Uses of Funds.* Although not submitted by management, we prepared this statement and recommend its use.

*   *   *   *   *

B.   Internal Control

1. We recommend that the internal control system document be formally adopted by the Board of Directors with consideration being given to the following modifications:

a) A good costing system (such as modified standard process costing) would be an aid to the company. It would aid both in control and decision making.

2. We also recommend that the raw material inventory be costed on the basis of Last In—First Out (LIFO) in place of the present average cost method.

This would result in substantial tax saving, assuming the past increase in prices is indicative of the future. If it had been installed at the beginning of this past year, the LIFO system would have saved approximately $130,000 in taxes.

*   *   *   *   *

II.   REVIEW OF MANAGEMENT AUDIT

A.   Management Organization

In general we found the overall effectiveness of Firm B–1 management to be excellent. Our observations disclose the following:

—they have been unusually successful in bringing profits to the firm;
—they are getting decisions out that are effective in competition;
—they appear to employ an active strategy in capitalizing on the shortcomings of the rivals;
—they have had good, cooperative relationships with the Board of Directors and the Auditors;
—they have prepared outstanding agendas and memoranda for the Board;

—they have been active innovators in quickly bringing out the outstanding product "B" and in trying out other products from their research and development efforts . . .

*   *   *   *   *

At the time we were engaged by you, your chairman stated that the Board was aware of the relative success of Firm B—1's management but was interested in whether its operations might be even better. From our observations we have concluded that definite improvements could be made, and we will summarize the evidence that brought us to this conclusion.

Before we begin, we would like to emphasize that our main purpose was to *survey* conditions as we found them and to make basic recommendations as part of our audit. Extensive recommendations and aid in their implementation would more properly fall under the area of management services, where we would propose a separate contract.

1. *Definition of Officer Responsibilities.* *a)* *Opinion.* In its responsibility to the stockholders of Firm B—1 the Board of Directors should promote added stability in its management organization by requesting management to submit a delineation of officer responsibilities for the Board's approval. Control of the management by the Board should thereby be also enhanced.

b) *Evidence.* (1) Interview with the President indicated no definitions of officer responsibilities were set up. Original organization was in three committees in the functional areas of finance, production, and marketing. Changes since have moved Mr. Pondy from Chairman of the Finance Committee to President (coordinator) and Mr. Ishler from Chairman of the Production Committee to Finance Officer.

(2) Examination of minutes of Board of Directors meeting of September 20, 1960, disclosed essentially the same information. In addition, the Board gave only its temporary approval to the original setup. The matter was apparently to be taken up at the next Board meeting.

(3) Examination of minutes of the next Board of Directors meeting, October 11, 1960, disclosed that this subject was not taken up during this meeting nor subsequently.

c) *Conclusions.* (1) There are no formal definitions of officer responsibilities.

(2) There is no evidence that the Board of Directors has followed through in its desires for delineation of responsibilities.

2. *Minutes of Meetings.* *a)* *Opinion.* Inasmuch as minutes of Board meetings often contain authorizations for management to take certain actions (e.g., the sale of debentures), a record of approved projects (as well as the approval of the minutes themselves) would seem essential in any responsible firm. A file of the minutes should be established for ready access by the management, the Board of Directors, auditors, and other legally interested parties. The Board of Directors should review the minutes for completeness and accuracy, and they should signify their approval on the file copies.

Extensive minutes of management meetings may be impractical in the Game situation, but past decisions and bases for past decisions should be readily available for the aid of management, both present and future; auditors; or any other parties (such as management consultants) to whom they would be useful. Summaries or extractions of significant proceedings in management meetings should be recorded and filed.

*   *   *   *   *

3. *Filing of Records and Reports.* *a) Opinion.* An elaborate and extensive filing system is considered impractical and cumbersome in the context of the Game. However, a simple system of filing *what* and *where* should be established by management so that all properly interested parties can have ready reference to any significant history, including past forecasts.

A program of review should be established to insure that all essential records are maintained and no more.

b) Evidence. (1) Game output (operating data). One complete set was found with the President. Partial files were kept by other members but were found incomplete.

(2) Forecasts, Analyses. Files of these were found inadequate and incomplete. There was no central company file or President's file. Functional area files were nonexistent or incomplete.

c) Conclusion. A working history of the firm is not available. Records of past decisions, analyses, forecasts, and analyses of forecasts are not readily available to individual officers, the Controller, the President, the Board of Directors, or to the auditors.

*   *   *   *   *

B. Decision Making

1. *The Decision-Making Process of the Firm.* *a) Opinion.* Management has a good plan for decision making. Efforts should be made to ensure that the plan is carried out completely each month. A program for evaluation of the system and how it works should be established.

*   *   *   *   *

2. *Decision Rules.* *a) Recording.* We recommend that all important decision rules related to the firm's operations be recorded in

writing and filed. Present practice does not include the recording of decision rules, but rather, the decision rules are particular to the decision maker. If the firm has adequately recorded decision rules, it will be in a position to (a) replace key individuals without greatly jeopardizing its operations and (b) improve consistency of decisions. A particular example of a decision rule that should be recorded is: The company should lay off employees only if it intends to do so for a period of at least two months.

b) *Reviewing.* We recommend that the practice of a continued analysis and reevaluation of these decision rules be established. Previously there have been no recorded decision rules; therefore, no periodic review has been made. The practice of analyzing and reevaluating these decision rules as situations change would serve as an internal check on the firm's operation, and would force the managers to reappraise present rules in hope of determining improvements.

Returning to the previous example: If conditions were to change such that the wages of employees double while laying-off cost remained substantially the same, then it would surely pay to lay off the man for a shorter time period. Changing conditions, therefore, may change the substance of the decision rule.

C. Special Area Problems

1. *Finance — Long-Range Planning.* a) *Long-Range Capital Planning.* We recommend that there be a greater emphasis placed on long-range planning. Capital planning for a six-month period has been the standard practice observed. An extension of this planning period would supply information on the long-term intentions of the firm for future investors and creditors as well as being useful for the Board and for management. A company of this size, we feel, should have long-range investment plans and capital budgets reaching at least two or three years into the future.

b) *Operations and Future Position Planning.* We recommend that a projected income statement and balance sheet be made every quarter for a period of a year ahead. Presently, projections are made for six months ahead. The quarterly review should enable the management and Board frequently to evaluate its actual operations and position against these plans. Corrective actions could be taken if necessary. The projected income statement in the form of a budget is particularly valuable in controlling expenses of operation during the period as well as permitting frequent financial analysis of the firm.

2. *Production.* a) *Active Participation.* The Production Officer should take more initiative in participating in the decision-making

process. Our observations showed that Production has taken a subordinate level to Marketing and Finance in most decisions.

  b) Production Records. Our general recommendations under Filing of Records and Reports apply most heavily in this area. No records were immediately available to the Production Officer. This includes production plans for the near and far future as well as past decisions and operating data. We were directed to the operating data records of the President and the Finance Officer in examining operations of the Production Department.

  c) Inventory Problems. The problems in raw materials and finished goods inventories are well known to you. Very possibly the conditions in *(a)* and *(b)* above have contributed with forecasting difficulties to producing frequent inventory runouts.

  We recognize that there is no one single remedy to the firm's inventory problems. Efforts have apparently been made to better stabilize the inventories in the face of wide-ranging demand, but we believe even stronger efforts should be made. The use of ranges rather than single values in Marketing's forecasts could greatly aid the Production Officer. At the same time the Production Officer should prepare ranges and mixes of production that he can produce over time. He should demand *and* use longer-reaching sales range potentials and keep checks himself on how results match up with forecasts. An active, aggressive Production Officer, adequate records for analysis, and stronger communication links between Marketing and Production appear to be prerequisites to a satisfactory attack on the inventory problems.

  3. *Marketing.*   *a) Price-Advertising-Demand Analysis.*   Pricing and advertising decisions, along with the competitors' decisions and market demand, determine sales. We recommend that a careful study be made of the interrelationship between these variables. A correlation analysis might prove quite useful.

  b) Adequate Records. We recommend that more complete records of decisions, decision rules, and other significant information be efficiently stored for use in self-evaluation and decision making.

  c) Probability Sales Forecasts. We recommend that the feasibility of sales forecast techniques using probabilities and ranges (subjective and/or from past data) be studied. This may disclose decision risks not apparent from the use of a single number.

*   *   *   *   *

To the Board of Directors and the Stockholders of Firm B–1

  We have examined the balance sheet of Firm B–1 as of End of Month 24 and the related statements of income and retained earnings for the year then ended. We did not observe the inventory at the beginning of the year, but we are satisfied that it appears reasonable after testing against sales and other operating data. In other respects, our examination was made in accordance with generally accepted auditing standards and accordingly included such tests of the accounting records and such other auditing procedures as we considered necessary.

In our opinion, with the foregoing exceptions of inventories, the accompanying balance sheet and statements of income and retained earnings present fairly the financial position of Firm B–1 at End of Month 24 and the results of its operations for the year then ended, in conformity with generally accepted accounting principles applied on a basis consistent with that of the preceding year.

GILMORE AND COMPANY

Pittsburgh, Pennsylvania
February 25, 1961

| Appendix 5B | An Information-Processing and Decision-Making System for Top-Management Players of the Carnegie Tech Management Game[1] |

I. INTRODUCTION — OUR CONCEPT OF SYSTEM DESIGN

This paper presents a comprehensive description of an information-processing and decision-making system that can be used with the Carnegie Tech Management Game, Mark 1.5. It describes primarily the machine portion of the total man-machine system we envision, while also detailing the roles and actions required of man.

This system has been designed to make routine, monthly decisions which carry out policies of top managers playing the Game and to provide useful information to these managers over and above the regular Game output.

A summary description is presented in Section II. Detailed descriptions, the models employed, flow charts, variable dictionaries, and portions of the 20—GATE computer program for the system are presented in the technical appendices.

Month-by-month play of the Management Game can be described by a simple feedback system diagram, as in Figure 5–1.

Our proposed decision-making and information-processing system can also be usefully expressed in terms of control system technology, as is done in Figure 5–2. The machine system is intended to prepare the bulk of decisions going into the Game. The feedback loop to management now occurs only once every three months. Players remain an important part in this man-machine system, and can concentrate on

---

[1] These are (slightly revised) excerpts from the introductory sections of a term paper for the Electronic Data Processing Systems course at Carnegie written in the spring semester of 1962. The authors are David R. Bamberger, John D. Chase, I. Edward Fraser, Thomas C. Gilmore, Richard C. Lyon, and Matthias E. Simon, Jr. The remainder of the paper, which has not been reproduced here because of space limitations, contains detailed descriptions (in verbal, mathematical, and computer flow chart form) of each of the models referred to in these excerpts. Extensive excerpts from another term paper, "A System for Making Decisions in the Carnegie Tech Management Game," written in the spring semester of 1961 for this same course, may be found in Appendix A of Kalman J. Cohen and Merton H. Miller, "Management Games, Information Processing, and Control," *Management International*, Vol. 3, No. 3/4, pp. 159-87.

FIGURE 5-1

FEEDBACK SYSTEM IN MONTH-BY-MONTH PLAY OF THE MANAGEMENT GAME

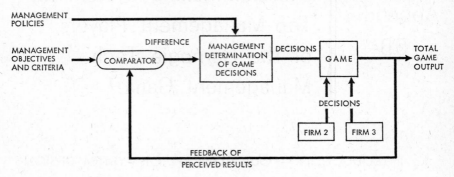

top-management functions, which include controlling the "controller" —the computerized, monthly decision-making system.

II.   SUMMARY DESCRIPTION

A.   Overview of the System

This system has been designed and programmed to be run on the CDC G–21 computer between monthly runs of the Carnegie Tech Management Game, Mark 1.5. When the system is properly debugged, it could run independently and prepare decisions for an indefinite number of months. Despite this capability, we have sought not to replace but to assist top managers. Moreover, our system *requires* the direction and guidance of managers to maintain or improve the *quality* of decisions being made.

Properly termed a computer subsystem, our program in essence acts as middle-management functional organizations whose members may be thought of as capable and systematic but limited in experience, guidance, and viewpoint. Man and machine in this system must interact and learn together from experience much as top and middle managers new to a company must do to keep the company going and to drive it toward the objectives selected.

The players of the Game using this system can devote more time to top-management functions: setting objectives, installing policy, requesting special analysis reports, and monitoring the decisions and information produced by their subordinates. Long-range corporate planning, decisions to expand, and decisions to obtain long-term financing are still considered exclusively top-management (i.e., man's) functions. Occasionally, as in real-world situations, top management may need to step in to make other specific Game decisions for a particular month, and

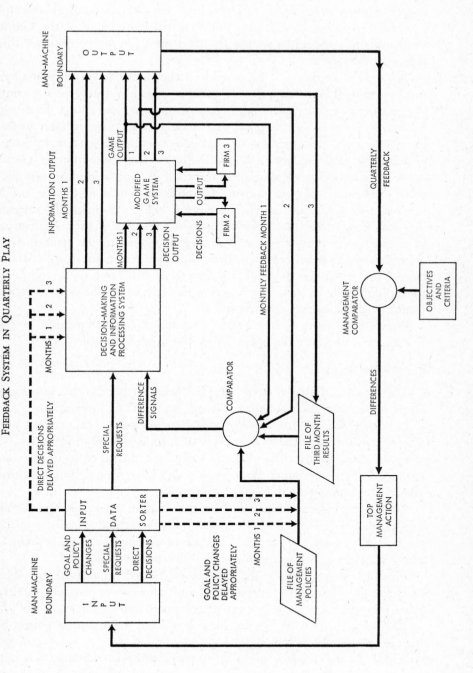

FIGURE 5-2

FEEDBACK SYSTEM IN QUARTERLY PLAY

this perogative is maintained. However, over time, as the players and computer system gain experience and refined knowledge of the Game environment, the players should find less need for intervention of this type.

The computer system is designed to accept input from top managers just before the beginning of every quarter. This input may be any combination and quantity of policy changes, requests, and direct decisions. Moreover, portions of this input can be delayed to come in later in the quarter as management directs. Management receives system information at the end of a quarter along with the regular three-months' Game output. (A schematic drawing of the total system, including our machine system, the players, and the Game is presented in Figure 5–2.)

This system, as well as its description below, is definitely divided into functional areas of marketing, production, and finance. Each area, in effect, makes reports to a top manager assumed to be tending that area. Communication between areas within the system is spelled out below, but it is expected that top managers will have to act together to resolve problems such as conflicting objectives or policies, production limitations, and budget constraints.

Freed of the more routine tasks, players can spend more time as top managers in directing the operation of the firm as a whole.

B. Marketing

The functional area of marketing has been further divided into long-range marketing, short-range marketing, and product innovation.

1. *Long-Range Forecasting and Evaluation.* The primary purpose of this subsystem is to provide basic forecasts of retail sales, wholesale sales, and selling costs. A secondary purpose is to collect sales data to provide a basis for long-range reports and for refining the forecasting and market strategy models.

Total retail sales are forecasted for each region separately and for all the regions together by the exponentially weighted moving-average method. These are reconciled in a manner directed by management to provide a 12-month forecast for each region at the retail level.

Projected shares of these markets are calculated for each of the firm's products by a multiple regression model considering product quality, price, advertising, and previous shares of the market.

Wholesale sales forecasts are then developed for a similar period by the use of seasonal factors.

All of the above information is tied together to provide sales forecasts and marketing budgets for the production and financial areas. Some changes in the forecasts and budgets may be made as part of the short-run strategy or product innovation subsystems.

Improvements to the prediction models may be desired after further experience in the market. A weight-search program for the exponentially weighted moving-average models and a multiple regression program are available in the system for management to use. A four-year file of market data is collected and maintained for such testing or special reports.

A quarterly summary of marketing operations is regularly prepared, which can be used with a quarterly forecasted summary for management's evaluation of longer-run forecasting capability.

When this program is completed, control passes to the short-range marketing strategy area, which is discussed in the following section.

2. *Short-Range Marketing Strategy.* The total decision-making system includes both this computer subsystem as well as management responsibilities. Although all decisions are made by the computer subsytem, management has not been relieved of the responsibility for control of both the management and the computer components of the total system. This is particularly important in the ill-structured area of marketing strategy.

To control the total system, management establishes policies in the form of boundaries in which the computer system may operate. Management must specify minimum and maximum price boundaries, minimum and maximum advertising boundaries, and both promotion goals and the rate of movement towards these management-determined promotion goals. In addition management may make any specific decisions if it chooses to and may change the computer system boundaries (or policies) at any time.

The marketing area may have both share-of-market and profit goals. Thus the computer system uses the previously discussed regression model to select several advertising and pricing strategies and predict share of market and profits by product and by region for each strategy for the following month. Management specifies relative weights which may be changed at any time to be attached to share of market and to profits. The computer system then selects the price and advertising strategy which will give the "best" value of the sum of weighted share of the market and weighted profits. Provision is also made, as previously discussed, to update the regression model both to obtain a better mathematical formulation for prediction and to reflect recent experience in the market.

If management is to make any specific advertising decisions, it should be noted that the regression model has tentatively indicated that advertising in the previous month is the most significant advertising variable on sales this month. Advertising this month, then, will create demand for sales next month.

Management specifies percentage distribution goals (by product and by region) and the rate of change in salesmen to achieve these goals. The computer system then calculates the appropriate changes in salesmen by product and by region for the coming month.

In addition the computer system will handle several special situations. Should inventories be low, marketing strategy will adapt to these constraints within the management-specified boundaries. In the event of significant stockouts, the marketing strategy is revised in the following month to avoid stockouts if possible within the management boundaries. In both of these cases an alarm is printed to call management attention to these problem areas.

If a product is to be closed out, the marketing strategy is revised to attempt just to run out of regional warehouse inventory at the end of the closeout month. This avoids opportunity costs associated with product dumping.

The long-range market plan (forecasts of unit sales, price, advertising, salesmen, and market research expenditures) is modified by the short-range plan. The modified plan forms the basis for coordination and feedback between the functional areas. The financial area receives planned receipts and disbursements for cash-flow planning and for product-profitability analysis. The production area receives forecasts as a basis for setting production schedules.

On a short-run basis (during a quarter) the feedback and coordination rests on the accuracy of the regression model and on the management-determined boundaries or policy parameters for the computer system. If, for instance, the maximum advertising boundary is ten times the forecast level of advertising, it would be possible to run into a cash bind. Thus management must exercise judgment in establishing the computer system boundaries or policy parameters, in conjunction with the reports generated by the computer system, effectively to discharge the management responsibility for total system control.

The short-range marketing computer subsystem prints out monthly Game decisions. In addition, predicted share of market, retail sales, and regional warehouse sales by product and by region are printed. Alarms are printed when inventories are too low to make "best" decisions within management-established computer system boundaries—indicating the need for increased inventories or changes in computer system boundaries. An alarm is also printed when stockouts occur.

In brief, the short-run marketing strategy is to move toward management-established goals as rapidly as management or the competitive environment will allow.

3. *Product Innovation.* The product innovation area includes

product research, product comparison testing, and product introduction. Management control of this area is accomplished by establishing policies. The policies include the type of research project to use, when to test a product, and when and how to introduce a new product. All details involved in carrying out these policies will be handled by the program. Management will be supplied information on the decisions the program has made, plus sufficient information in order to review how the decisions were made. The program will also handle directly any overriding decisions that management may make.

Product introduction occurs when a product is sufficiently profitable as determined by management policy. The program operates by estimating the expected dollar value of a product to management. The expected dollar value is determined from the relative quality preference of a product against the current market of competitors' products. This information is supplied to management on each product as it is developed.

Product research is handled by estimating the probability of developing a product with a given dollar profitability. Each month management will be informed of the probability of developing a product better than the current best product, using each research project type. An estimate of how much better the product will be and, given current management policies, of how long it will take to develop the product will be made.

Information inputs to this area are obtained from the previous months' decisions. Information made available to other areas includes (1) the current market of products, (2) any expected change in products, (3) the quality of all products on the market, (4) sales volume and promotion for 12 months for all products being introduced, and (5) a 12-month cash flow forecast of the product innovation area.

C. Production

This section of the program can be used to make all decisions (except construction) that are required of the production manager in the Carnegie Game. Using the results of previous play and the sales forecasts generated in the marketing section, the program follows a set of heuristics to determine the decisions for the next month and forecasts of production activity for the next 12 months. The decisions that are made include destination of production, number of workers, maintenance expenditures, fraction overtime authorized, raw materials ordered, and transshipments. It also provides data for analyzing plant and warehouse expansion.

The decision rules that were developed were of the form: do not hire a man for seasonal needs unless he can be fully used for six months. The rules that were developd were an effort to tell what should be done in all cases in order to minimize the costs of production consistent with the policies of marketing and finance. These rules incorporated the various costs such as holding inventory, overtime, hiring and firing, etc. The program then follows the rules and makes the decisions that the production manager would make if he followed these rules. There is a cost computation section at the end that computes and totals costs over the desired period. These costs are then sent to finance or used in evaluating policies and in estimating cash requirements.

The program allows management to set buffer levels, factors of safety, minimum levels and maximum levels, as well as several other policy factors. If major changes in policies are desired, the program can be changed. It can also be used separately to evaluate changes in policies or costs.

The initiation of new construction rests solely with top management, but the program will carry out these decisions (as well as any other specific decisions that top management deems necessary to make) in any month.

D. Finance

Under policy direction from management, the finance program is capable of making all decisions necessary for month-to-month operation. This program collects information from other functional areas, anticipates cash requirements 12 months into the future, and meets these requirements by purchasing or selling government securities as well as by obtaining 90-day notes. Applications for term loans and equity financing are not made by the program. These remain strictly as top management responsibilities.

In addition to its operating capabilities, the program is able to print several information reports of value to management:

1. *Pro forma* income statements and balance sheets.
2. Anticipated cash flow statements for 12 months into the future with information as to the advisability of obtaining long term financing.
3. Profitability forecasts—by region and by product—for six months into the future.

Appendix 5C

Selected Papers on Policy Guidelines for the Management Game Teams

The excerpts below are taken from papers written after the Game by students in the Business Policy course at Carnegie. The assignment was to draw on their experience to prepare a revised set of policy guidelines for their team if it were to begin play of the Game again.

I. A PAPER WRITTEN BY THE PRODUCTION MANAGER[1] OF THE MOST PROFITABLE TEAM IN THE 1962 RUN OF THE GAME

The success of a Game team is largely dependent on the sets of policy guidelines made in two major areas—organization of the team and Game-play objectives, strategies, and operations. Decisions regarding how to organize the team should be made before considering Game-play strategies. If a member knows he is solely responsible for a certain activity area, I feel his motivation to come up with "winning" strategies is greatly enhanced. Also there may be a tendency for a team to organize on the basis of an adopted strategy policy with the consequence that at a later date, the team will find it difficult to incorporate changes in strategy made necessary by competitors' actions.

Recommended guidelines for both major policy areas are presented and discussed below.

A. Team Organization

The organization of the team should be based on functional area assignments. The responsibilities falling under each functional area should be precisely defined. Preferably, each member should be delegated specified tasks and held responsible for making decisions in that area. In the delegating process, the team should be careful not to break up highly interdependent decision areas. To avoid conflict, the team member who is given the assignment of advertising expenditures should also be responsible for the other marketing factors upon which advertising performance depends (price, salesmen). Also, when delegating the decision areas, members' special qualifications, abilities, or interests

---

[1]Burnham H. Baker, Jr.

191

should be considered. Take advantage of a member's summer experience or previous contact with some area of the Game.

Each man in addition to making a specified set of decisions should be held responsible for whatever coordination or information transfer with other team members is required for a consistent set of team decisions in total. Coordination and joint discussion are required only to the extent necessary to insure that individual decisions are compatible. For example, has the production manager ordered the long-lead-time raw materials in sufficient time to allow the new product to be introduced on schedule? The team president should have the final say when decisions of functional area managers are in seemingly unresolvable conflict.

B. Game Play

1. *Objectives.* I feel it is desirable if all members of the team view an "A" grade as their objective in the Management Game as long as the team perceives the board of directors as being sufficiently benevolent to consider this as a possible outcome in grading. Fortunately, this was the situation for my team. Two excellent subgoals for becoming an across-the-board "A" team are to make lots of money in Game play (maximize profits) and to allow each member an equal opportunity to participate or be "visible" at the board meetings.

Once a policy is adopted an effort should be made not to vacillate from it. My team adopted the policy of profit maximization, stuck with it, and was most successful. I would recommend the same policy guideline if Game play were to be resumed. A comparison of our performance with that of the leading team in the other industry shows that profits do not necessarily correlate with market share.

2. *Competitive Strategy.* My recommended profit maximization strategy is to get a comparable market share with the least number of products. For example, given a comparable market share, a team with one product should have lower costs than those teams having two or more products. Since its promotional expenditures can be concentrated on one product, it can realize equal effectiveness at less cost compared to the multiproduct team. Also, having only one product facilitates better planning and control procedures in factory operations leading to further reduced costs.

To obtain and keep a comparable market share the team should have a product equal to or better than its competitors as well as sound promotional activity. To maintain a superior product requires a great deal of R and D activity. What effective R and D strategies are, must be learned from experimentation. Also, since the effectiveness of a promotional move is highly dependent on competitors' action, the possible strategies here are numerous. However, for continuous success in promotional activity, it will be necessary to "feel out" one's competitors as well as to have a feeling for the structure of the Game variables involved.

3. *Operations.* A marketing → production → finance decision sequence should be followed. The production manager should use a sales forecast from marketing as a basis for his decisions, while the finance manager must know production decisions (raw material ordering, etc.) before he can determine cash flows. This suggests that time constraints must be placed on each decision maker to facilitate such a sequence. If noon Thursday is the due date for a team's decisions, then the marketing sales forecast should be available by noon Monday, the production decisions by noon Tuesday and the finance decisions by noon Wednesday. This allows sufficient slack time to adjust for any incompatibility in member's decisions.

In their decisions, the team members should take advantage of slack by experimenting to determine the structure of the Game variables. This could be anything, from having a small quantity of a special product in a region upon which to try various promotional strategies, to having the production manager drastically cut maintenance expense when scheduled production is well below capacity in order to collect data for determining optimal maintenance expenditure. The team should, however, avoid price cutting if at all possible. Price cutting is generally considered a sign of weakness. It usually gains the team little but the wrath of its competitors, and it can lead to harmful retaliatory action affecting the overall health of the industry.

II. A PAPER WRITTEN BY THE PRODUCTION MANAGER[2] OF THE MOST PROFITABLE FIRM'S LEADING COMPETITOR

In light of the experience obtained in participating in the Management Game last semester, I would recommend the following goals and procedures for a team playing the Game under similar conditions:

1. Maintain profitable operations.
2. Secure and maintain a slight lead in market share.

These goals are considerably different from those stated by the team at the beginning of the Game, which were:

1. Maximize profits.
2. Maximize market share.

---

[2]Edmund C. Glover.

The new goals which I am recommending may seem at first just to be watered down versions of the original goals, but they lead to a very different set of operational procedures. These goals are more "operational" than those they are to replace in the sense that they are measurable. It is possible to say whether the firm's operations are profitable and whether it has a lead in market share, although it is not possible to say that profits or market share have been maximized.

The goal of profit maximization and the goal of market share maximization are conflicting goals in the context of the Management Game. A team seriously attempting to maximize its market share would cut its prices and raise its advertising expenses in an attempt to draw more sales from its competitors. This would lead to a retaliation by the competing firms and the resulting price war and advertising race would eventually reduce the industry profitability to zero or below. If maximizing profits is to be the team's goal, a choice must be made between "short-run" and "long-run" profits. "Short-run" profits can be increased by sticking to one product, cutting research expenses, and following other policies which would eventually hurt the competitive position of the firm. On the other hand, maximizing "long-run" profits is as far from being an operational goal as "do a good job" or "make optimal decisions."

Maintaining profitable operations and maintaining a lead in market share are not easy goals to achieve. While it is possible for all of the teams in an industry to be profitable, it is obvious that only one team can lead in market share. I recommend the following procedures or means toward achieving these goals:

1. Have a Liberal Product-Development Policy

The success of a team depends to a large extent on the products it has. Not only can a product with superior characteristics be sold with less advertising, but a product with a good productivity level can be made cheaper and in greater quantities. A small cost advantage in the production of a product can lead to substantial differences in the profits of the team, and the ability to produce large quantities can be very important when introducing a replacement product or reacting to an increase in peak sales.

2. Maintain a Two-Product Line

There are some advantages in having a single product. A given amount of advertising is more effective when concentrated on one product. Introducing a second product has a rather high initial cost. Production decisions are much simpler to make with only one product being produced. A two-product line has even more advantages in a highly competitive situation, however. The biggest advantage is the ease with which a new product can be introduced. Whenever a new product is developed which is superior to one of the existing products, production is immediately switched to the other product, materials ordered for the new product, and production is begun on the new product when the inventory of the product being dropped is reduced to one month's expected sales. With only one product, changing products must be done by dumping a large quantity of the old product, which can be very expensive. Having two products also increases the ability of the firm to carry on effective marketing research. Having three products increases the disadvantages of a two-product policy without increasing the advantages significantly.

3.   Keep Production Plans Flexible

To be able to take advantage of the benefits of a two-product policy, production plans must be kept flexible. That is, raw material inventories must be kept high enough and in the right proportions to allow any change in product mix to be made while continuing to work the labor force at the most economical level of overtime.

4.   Keep Financial Forecasts and Plans Up to Date and Continually Try to Improve Accuracy of Forecasts

A good financial forecast is essential to sound planning. If financial needs can be forecast ahead of time, spending can be adjusted to fit the supply of money, and/or a bank loan can be arranged with much better terms than would be possible for a team already in financial trouble.

5.   Keep Sales Forecasts and Production Plans Up to Date and at Least Six Months Ahead

Financial planning and production planning both depend primarily on the sales forecast. With an accurate sales forecast, financial plans can be made which will greatly help in the overall control of the team, and production plans can be made to minimize cost of goods sold. Production costs rise rather rapidly when, due to poor sales forecasts, inventories depart from planned levels and must be brought back into line by hiring or firing workers.

6.   Keep Industry Advertising Levels Low

This is rather more of a subgoal than a policy, since one team obviously does not control the industry spending levels. However, the team should do all it can, short of actual collusion, to prevent an advertising "war." High levels of advertising do not increase the industry sales, but they do reduce profits of all teams involved.

7. Develop and Use Definite Control Procedures to Maintain Division of Responsibility and Standard Communication Procedures

Most of the conflict within a team is due to disagreements over the limits of each member's responsibility and over the quality and timing of intrateam communications. The team will be most effective if this conflict can be minimized.

III. A PAPER WRITTEN BY THE PRESIDENT[3] OF THE THIRD TEAM IN THE INDUSTRY

Estimate of the Situation

Firm A–3 earned profits last year of about $320,000. This sum represents less than 1 percent of either sales revenue or stockholders' equity. A commercial bank savings account would have been a better investment. Considering the risks in the detergent industry, the firm should expect a profit rate of *at least* 10 percent of stockholders' equity. If this goal can't be achieved, the firm should retire from the industry as fixed assets wear out.

Other firms in the industry are in similar straits. The detergent industry has overexpanded its productive facilities to the point where prices have been seriously depressed. Prospects are dim for significant improvement of industry conditions in the near future. The total market demand for detergents is not increasing very rapidly. The possibility of having more "sensible" pricing practices is not likely either. There is lack of trust in the industry. Detergent industry executives frequently expound on the need for higher prices, but when a price rise is attempted the rest of the industry tends to hold the original price and attempt to gain share of market.

Any realistic strategy to improve the firm's profits must be based on improving our *relative* performance. We are essentially engaged in a zero-sum game.

General Strategies

It is obvious that profits may be increased by either decreasing costs or increasing revenue. The area of cost reduction does not seem very fertile. Our costs of production are pretty inflexible. It is difficult to imagine substantially cutting operating expenses. The big part of

---

[3]M. Eugene Carlisle, Jr.

operating expense is advertising and sales force expense. If we reduce these our share of market will fall.

Increasing revenue by raising price isn't sensible for share of market will again suffer. Increasing advertising to raise sales isn't feasible, for experience indicates our competition will simply follow us.

We need a strategy which can't be easily or quickly counteracted. The most promising area is in new product development and introduction. The development of new products is an uncertain business. If we can get a jump in innovation in the product area, we shall be hard to catch. Product preference may be exploited by higher market share or higher price or by lower selling and promotional expenses.

Organization

The firm's hierarchical structure will be designed to emphasize the importance of the marketing and product development functions. An executive vice president will be appointed to which both field sales and product research and development will report. This will facilitate the coordination of development and marketing activities but still retain individual responsibility for each function.

Product Introduction

The firm presently has several new products in its library. The best of these in the medium sudsing range will be substituted for A as soon as possible. We shall market only one product to make most efficient use of our sales force and our advertising. However, the one product will always be the best we have available.

Product Development

The firm will double its present expenditure on research and development to $400,000 per month. All of this will be spent on basic research (project 1).

Finance

The firm presently has working capital of roughly $5,000,000. This seems insufficient in view of the erratic nature of the detergent industry. Also, considerable investment in basic research may be necessary before a payoff results. Thus, application for a long-term loan for $5,-000,000 will be made at the bank.

Comparison with Original Plans

The above policy guidelines differ in several respects from those presented orally at our first board meeting.

Our estimate of the situation was not so explicit. We didn't set a goal for profitability below which it wasn't worthwhile to stay in the business. We didn't make the specific decision that industry conditions weren't likely to improve and that only by taking profits from other firms could we hope to improve our own position. We originally held a vague hope that somehow more "realistic" prices could be established.

Our consideration of general strategies was not so complete. We rather confused our plans for new product introduction with our choice of product distinction as the means to improve market position. We didn't single out the area of research and development for strong emphasis.

Our program of action was considerably different. We didn't allocate our personnel in a special way to implement policy as was suggested above. We didn't establish a general plan for the introduction of new products. The shift to the one-product plan (we originaly planned a multiple-product line) is based on experience with the Game. Since we didn't originally establish a policy of strong activity in research and development, this shift is also based on experience in playing the Game.

Chapter 6	USE OF THE GAME IN OTHER EDUCATIONAL PROGRAMS

One problem in offering a general evaluation of the Carnegie Tech Management Game as an environment for learning is that most of our experience has come from its use in the M.S. program in Industrial Administration at Carnegie. In this chapter, we try to broaden our perspective by offering reports on the use of the Game in several other settings. From Tulane University and the University of Pittsburgh, we have reports on two other efforts to use the Game with graduate students as part of a course sequence in administration and business policy. In fitting the Game to such a course sequence at the graduate level, Tulane and Pittsburgh have varied their approach from that used at Carnegie in order to suit their own resources, curricula, and students. Tulane has also used the Game with undergraduates.

The University of North Carolina reports chiefly on their use of the Game as an elective course for undergraduate seniors with superior grade averages and on ways in which they have moved, on their own, to reprogram and improve the Game model. These efforts include elaborations to make the production manager's task more complex and more realistic and preparation of a computer simulation of a team, so that one or more of the player teams can be simulated in research runs of the Game.

Finally we include reports on three efforts to use the Game with businessmen: first, with upper-level managers in our nine-week Program for Executives; second, with Bell Telephone Company executives in a special program at the University of Pittsburgh; and third, with junior to middle-level engineering and technical personnel in an evening program at Carnegie.

All of these reports were prepared especially for inclusion in this volume by people responsible for running the Game in the various settings. To preserve the differences in experience and in point of view that they represent, they are published here with a minimum of editorial revision. Some of the problems that they describe having with the Game are problems that we feel we have eliminated with the Mark 1.5 version of the Game model and with the documentation for the Game which this book and the accompanying *Administrator's Manual* provide. Some of the conclusions about the educational benefits of the Game, like some of the ones we have drawn in previous chapters, may be premature. We have put our own reactions and comments into a few editorial footnotes and into Section VII, at the end of the chapter.

I. EXPERIENCES WITH THE GAME AT TULANE UNIVERSITY
(By Clinton A. Phillips[1])

Management games have been used at Tulane at both the undergraduate and graduate levels since the academic year 1958–59. Initially, the games employed were relatively simple. In the academic year 1960–61, the Mark 1 Carnegie Tech Game was introduced and made an integral part of our required second-year, one-semester M.B.A. course in Administrative Policy. In this course, students' attention had been directed largely to cases—to get them to analyze the subsystems of a business, to help them learn to put them back together, and to help them learn through induction about the judgmental processes that are important in the real world.

In 1961–62, four Carnegie Games were run simultaneously in the spring semester and another during the summer session which followed. In the spring semester, one Game was used in connection with the M.B.A. course in Administrative Policy; and the other three were integrated into an undergraduate management seminar required of all seniors. In the summer session, the Game was again used in connection with the latter course.

Since the Game's introduction here, we have had faculty members serve on boards of directors for each firm. In the spring session of 1961–62 when four games were run, three boards were established, each of which served four firms. Thus, one group sat as a board for all four *"One"* teams, another for all *"Two"* teams, and a third for the *"Three"* teams.

A. The Game in the Policy Course

The Game is an integral part of the Administrative Policy course, with the students' time roughly allocated one third to typical policy cases, one third to readings and discussions in the general area of management, and one third to the Game. Approximately one third of the course grade originates from a student's performance in the Game.

The faculty member in charge of the course is the administrator

---

[1]A few paragraphs have been inserted from another paper prepared by C. Jackson Grayson, also of Tulane, for the Conference on Business Policy at the Harvard Business School, April 8–11, 1963.

of the Game. Other faculty members serve on various boards of directors of the teams.

Students are introduced to the rules of play of the Game in the month prior to the Policy course and are asked to make one or two practice decisions. When the actual Policy course begins, students can therefore begin the play immediately. Moves are made once a week for the first two months of the semester. Later, this is stepped to two moves a week. Meetings are held between boards of directors and team members as often as the respective parties desire. Financial charts are maintained in a student lounge illustrating the relative financial behavior of industries and teams.

Some useful learning undoubtedly takes place just in the normal "unattended" play of the Game. This alone, however, would not justify such a heavy investment of faculty and student time. We explicitly introduce more formal relationships between the Game and the curriculum through classroom discussions, faculty-student role playing, and experiments with the game structure designed to direct the student's attention to concepts that we believe he should experience and think about in a more formal fashion.

We also discuss the Game play in formal class sessions in the policy course. For example, early in the play of the Game, students are asked by their directors to submit to them written policy statements for the operation of their firm. While these are in preparation, the class is directed to readings concerning formation of company policies; and a policy case is discussed with emphasis on this point. Later, some team statements are stripped of identity and brought in for class discussion. This kind of interaction between a class and the Game also occurs during course discussions of organization, staffing, planning, decision making, and controlling. Some difficulty is encountered in teams' desires for secrecy regarding their operations, but this problem causes much less difficulty than anticipated. Because of heavy demands on time caused by Game play, the Policy class meets fewer times in formal sessions than before we used the Game. However, we believe that advantages of heightened interest in readings and case discussions caused by involvement in similar Game situations outweighs loss of class time used in more traditional ways.

In another variation, we asked students to write a set of policies which, in their opinion, would convey to decision makers sufficient guidelines for operation of the firm. Resulting policy statements ranged from broad "general welfare" statements to specific decision rules. Then we asked another set of decision makers (students in another industry) to study the policies and team history and make decisions in accordance with their interpretation of the stated policies. Actions were usually, as would be expected, at wide variance with the wishes of the policy writers. The policy statements were allowed to be revised, and the cycle was repeated. This experiment was costly in terms of student time, and we would have to revise it before doing it again. However, it was an excellent way to demonstrate very vividly the problems of written policy statements, communication of policies, and implementation.

B.   Integration of the Game with Other Courses

The Game has been used as an integral part of other courses in management wherever possible. Intrateam experience provided a background for players in courses where human relations problems and, particularly, conflict and its resolution were discussed. Of particular interest, perhaps, was the spontaneous development in one class of team member evaluations as a result of a discussion of personnel rating forms. The suggestion that each team member evaluate his fellow members was made by the president of what was generally regarded as a successful team. Many opposed the suggestion on the ground they had not been forewarned they would be required to do this. Another team president argued that the instructor, who also happened to be the administrator of the Game, was being paid to do the evaluating—that this was not a student responsibility. Inevitably came the rebuttal that responsibility cannot be avoided forever and that now was as good a time as ever to begin playing God with merit ratings. Eventually, it was decided to develop and distribute rating sheets to each team to be filled out and returned to the instructor but with the important proviso that he not look at them until after team and individual grades had been determined for the course.[2] Summaries of his fellow team members' evaluations were made available for those who wished to have them. By and large, the resulting evaluations were thoughtful and frank. Had we been able to use them for grading purposes, we could have done a better job of evaluating individual performance. We shall probably use these rating sheets again, but not without warning the students before play begins. In this event, it may be necessary to permit individual team members to transfer from one team to another during play so as to give a team member an out if he finds himself in an intolerable situation.

---

[2]Teams and individuals within each team were graded by their respective boards. These grades were turned over to the appropriate instructor. Thus, each team member received two grades for the Game, one his team grade, and the other his individual grade. These two grades combined constituted 25 percent of his grade in the course. Needless to say, all concerned had misgivings about the validity of these grades.

The Game was also integrated into another course which was introduced into the undergraduate curriculum in 1962. This course, required of all seniors, is entitled Management Information and Control Systems and covers such topics as cybernetics and information theory, goal setting, planning, and systems design and implementation.[3] Its goal is to help students visualize a business as a total system. Virtually all undergraduates playing the Game were also taking this course; thus the instructors were able to use the Game as something of a laboratory. Among the term projects required of students in this course were flow diagrams of the various decision processes in the Game. In making the diagrams for information and control, the students are even more forcibly made aware of functional dependencies, advantages and shortcomings of programmed decision rules, effects of uncertainty on decision functions, and the areas where heuristic problem solving is really essential. We require that these flow diagrams be in such a format that they could be programmable conceptually, and in some cases, students actually program subsystems of their networks and control segments of the Game with computer program routines. Class discussions both in this course and in Business Policy have been heightened concerning the role of computers in man-machine networks of the future. We anticipate that this course and our Administrative Policy course will draw closer together over time.

Another important way whereby the Game may be integrated with course material is through the boards of directors. It is important that board members be selected to represent a cross section of disciplines. Acting in their various capacities as accountants, economists, or experts in marketing, finance, and operations research, board members can and should request forecasts, budgets, analyses of demand, rationales of advertising expenditures, production programs, and the like. To satisfy these requests, team members find it necessary to review materials covered in previous courses. A frequently heard comment from students is that they never really understood a concept until they were forced to use it in playing the Game, and particularly to explain it in defending their actions to their boards.

Our board members have tried to play their roles as realistically as possible. At times, conflict situations have been deliberately engineered to see how team members would cope with them. On one occasion, team members appeared for a board meeting poorly prepared. The board chairman expressed indignation and not too gently chastised the team generally, and the president particularly. Another board member

[3]The basic text used was Jay W. Forrester, *Industrial Dynamics* (New York: John Wiley & Sons, 1961).

moved for immediate adjournment. The motion was quickly seconded and passed. At subsequent meetings, the team was prepared.

In our judgment, we have achieved some success in integrating the Game with course material. The Game has acted as a strong catalyst for learning, even though the direction of learning cannot always be predicted or controlled. Naturally, we have not done as much as we would have liked. That we have been as successful as we have is due in no small measure to the excellent cooperation and interest exhibited by our faculty.

C. Experience with Extra-Game Activities

The Game can be used as a basis for related activities. One of our most interesting experiments in this area involved labor negotiations. Teams were informed that their labor contracts were about to expire. The role of union bargaining agent was played by a professor of industrial relations with long experience as an arbitrator. Each team met with its board to decide on bargaining strategy. Thereafter, a series of meetings was held with the union agent and eventually each team made a settlement. Terms of settlement varied depending upon the bargaining ability of the various teams. The various wage increases were then plugged into the Game.

Of particular interest was the dilemma faced by one team which had been ordered by their board not to sign a labor contract without prior ratification by the board. After negotiating what they regarded as a favorable settlement, they informed the union agent they could not sign a contract until they had board approval, whereupon the agent, who also felt he had negotiated terms favorable to the union, told them if they walked out without signing he would withdraw all of his concessions. Finally, they signed. Some hours later, the president of the team picked up his telephone and listened to a lengthy tirade from his board chairman. The next day, at a special board meeting called by the chairman, the tirade was continued. Presumably, something was learned from the experience.

Our second major experiment involved a stock market game. In the academic year 1961–62, when four Games were played simultaneously, an instructor in finance devised a game to be played by undergraduate juniors taking finance courses. Each student was given a number of shares of each of the twelve Carnegie Game firms and a hypothetical sum of cash. Certain students were designated brokers and assigned a number of accounts to handle. Brokers were permitted to buy and sell securities but only through another broker. Trading sessions lasting one hour were conducted after the results of a set of

Carnegie Game decisions had been made available to the participants. (In addition to the quarterly income and balance sheet statements, monthly sales and net income figures were posted for each firm.)

The objectives of the stock market game were basically twofold. First, we hoped to provide a realistic mechanism for teaching finance students such concepts as principles of valuation, the mechanics of stock transactions, and the rights of corporate shareholders. Second, we hoped that teams playing the Carnegie Game would get some insights into the problems involved in management-stockholder relations, particularly as they might arise at stockholders' annual meetings.

Unfortunately, we were unable to use the stock market game very effectively. This was due in part to the sheerly administrative problem of getting students to keep accurate records. Also, operational problems with the Carnegie Games that semester slowed down the stock market game. However, we are confident the stock market game could be used effectively and we plan to try it again.

Other experiments have included formal introduction of rumors, antitrust suits, crises in the economy, organizational deaths, rotation of organizational positions, and deliberately irrational board behavior.

D. Operational Problems in the Use of the Game

We began by using the Mark 1 version of the Game, and had several problems with it, some technical and some organizational. The technical problems had to do with programming the Game for our computer, at that time an IBM 650. Frequent malfunctions arose in the bank loan workout function, for example. These may have been due to faulty programming or a failure to keep within certain mechanical tolerances in our tape memory system. In addition, we have experienced difficulties due to the inexperience of our machine operators. A final technical problem has stemmed from early versions of the player's manual, which was not as explicit as it might have been. Our main difficulty here was with the undergraduates.

Our organizational problems have been relatively minor. Because of student and faculty class-schedule conflicts, it was all but impossible to get a complete team and a full board together at one time. This problem was also most acute at the undergraduate level. Through better scheduling, we hope to avoid this problem in the future.

The cooperative spirit of the faculty members who served as board members and especially those who acted as chairmen had much to do with making these runs of the Game as successful as they were. A number of faculty members spent many hours not only in board meetings, but also as father confessors to team members. All felt they could have spent even more time profitably with their teams but competing demands prevented this. Ideally, board members, or at least board chairmen, should be given reduced teaching loads so that they may devote the time necessary for board duties.

E. Plans for the Future

We have come to regard the Game as a useful adjunct to our curriculum. Its ability to motivate students to put in long hours in cooperative endeavor is certainly impressive. And if carefully integrated into the total program, it can be a powerful device for the teaching of the concepts and skills needed for modern management. We intend to continue the use of games at both the graduate and undergraduate levels of instruction.

If gaming is to be exploited to the extent of its potentiality, then attempts should be made to relate the Game to every single course in the curriculum. Such a relationship requires a fairly heavy commitment to gaming on the part of the instructors affected. It also requires a careful sequencing of the entire curriculum.

In connection with this belief, we are now working at Tulane on a rather ambitious project to PERT our entire curriculum. That is, we want to state explicitly the course concepts and concept sequences, and tag them with estimated time requirements. Then, we hope to put the entire curriculum together with PERT techniques (1) to plan consciously for the development of appropriate tools before applications, (2) to indicate which concepts are on the critical path so intensive course work can be initiated early, (3) to plan for repeated applications for reinforcement of tools and concepts, (4) to build redundancy explicitly into the curriculum, and (5) to assure us to some extent that some concepts do not fall unattended between two outfielders because of a false set of expectations. Tentatively, we plan to use a complex game as a running laboratory that will begin play with the first day of classes and will increase and decrease in intensity of play as the curriculum progresses. The idea of smaller games or subgames within the complex games for separate courses is also being considered.

II. EXPERIENCES WITH THE GAME AT THE UNIVERSITY OF PITTSBURGH
(By Edward Sussna and C. Edward Weber)

The University of Pittsburgh has used the Carnegie Tech Management Game for two years, and plans are to extend and enrich its use. Our present direction can be understood best, perhaps, by describing and appraising the present role of the Game in the curriculum. The

M.B.A. program is built on a three-term calendar in which each trimester is the same length as a semester. The pervasive purpose of the M.B.A. program is to develop the bases for analysis in the first trimester, to apply the analysis to the functional fields in the second and third trimesters, and to integrate the functional fields in the third. Instead of the traditional business policy course, two courses are employed in the final term to attempt the integration: Business and Society, and Administration and Integrated Decision Making. The latter attempts the integration within the enterprise, and it is here that the Carnegie Game is employed.

A. The Game in the Policy Course

The role of the Game in Administration and Integrated Decision Making has differed in our two years of experience. In the first year, we attempted to give equal weight to policy cases, lectures on administration, and the Game. On the second time around, about half the time was assigned to gaming and the remaining time to cases and lectures. The lectures were designed to place the Game in a broad business policy context in the second year rather than to develop any field systematically. In addition to the Carnegie Game, a simpler game was played in the second year within the same course. The simpler game was introduced in order to see how bargaining might be incorporated into the course.

The initial design of Administration and Integrated Decision Making was intended to balance the traditional methods of pedagogy with the use of games, while less attention was given to the traditional methods in the second year. It was feasible to shift the focus to the use of a complex game, we believe, because of a change in the way the Carnegie Game was employed in the course. The emphasis in the first year was on the application of analytical techniques to problems arising out of the Game. The emphasis in the second year was on policy making and the role of judgment and bargaining within the context of the Game.

The organization of the instructional staff was modified in line with the change in emphasis. In the first year, the instructional staff consisted of a Game administrator, William Morgenroth, and a faculty coach, C. Edward Weber. The Game administrator coordinated the running of the Game, and the faculty coach advised the teams on substantive problems in the Game. The faculty coach received reports from the teams, guided them towards long-range problems, and encouraged them in the application of analytical techniques. In addition, Dean Marshall Robinson acted as the bank loan officer.

In the second year the coach concept was not used, and the banking function was performed automatically by the computer program. The instructional staff that year consisted of three faculty members: Peter Firmin, a visiting professor from Tulane University; Edward Sussna; and C. Edward Weber. The three faculty acted as the nuclei for faculty boards of directors. A faculty board of directors was assigned each team, and one of the instructional staff served on each board. The task of the instructional staff was to create a unity of effort among the boards since there were twelve faculty participating on the boards in addition to the instructional staff. The teams presented formal oral and written reports to the boards.

The Game administrator required a staff in order to run the Game. In the first year, he employed approximately ten hours of clerical time each week, four to five hours of IBM 7070 operator time each week, the services of a key-punch operator, and the services of a graduate assistant from Carnegie Tech. Most of the time of the 7070 operator was used in searching for errors which prevented the program from running. The FORTRAN version of Mark 1.5 was not ready to run when the course was taught the second year,[4] and the Graduate School of Industrial Administration at Carnegie Institute of Technology very kindly ran the Game for us on their equipment. Accordingly, we have no direct experience on the data processing staff required for running the Mark 1.5 version.

Twenty-eight students played the Game in the first year. They were divided into three teams of nine or ten and formed one industry. The number increased to fifty-five students in the second year, and the students were divided into two industries for which the teams were made up of nine or ten students. In the first year, there were eleven months of play; in the second year, seven. The decrease in the amount of play resulted from concentrating the course in the second half of the trimester in the second year and from having the Carnegie Tech computer shut down to be moved to another building. The eleven plays in the first year were made singly, at weekly intervals. In the second year, the first three plays were for single moves at weekly intervals, but the remaining four plays included two Game months at a time.

B.   Evaluation of Our Experience

An appraisal of the role of the Game in our graduate curriculum must be tentative in light of our limited experience. The number of

[4]This version has been used during the 1963 and 1964 summer trimesters at Pittsburgh. These runs have provide the first major "field test" for the FORTRAN program that is published in the *Administrator's Manual* which accompanies this volume, and we are grateful to the faculty and students at Pittsburgh for their patience while many of the final "bugs" were being identified and corrected.— (K.C.J., W.R.D., A.A.K., P.R.W.)

months played appeared to be too few for the students to obtain feedback from their decisions to introduce new products, expand facilities, maintain the level for their work force and other long-range decisions. Clearly, the number of plays needs to be increased substantially. At least twenty-four months seem to be necessary. The horizon can, perhaps, be extended beyond that by having successive classes take up the companies as they are left by the previous class. The teams would have access to the reports made by the teams which managed their company. This may give the students the sense of history which exists in an enterprise and which appears to be lacking in the way the Game is presently played.

The size of the teams appeared to be too large for the most effective use of the Carnegie Game. Pitt's M.B.A. class now has more than seventy students. Reducing the team size will increase the cost of the Game, but we believe that the benefits to the students would be sufficient to justify the reduction in team size to five or six. The large teams which we have used made it impossible to grade the performance of every student. We seemed to be able to identify performance of students only at the two extremes. More importantly, the size of the teams resulted in an uneven distribution of the work and the instructional benefits among the team members. Our impression was that this did not usually result from a lack of interest on the part of students, but rather from their intense interest. The desire "to win" seemed to drive the leadership within the teams "to take over" the operation of their companies. It does not appear to us that increased faculty supervision provides a satisfactory answer to this problem. The high motivation should be made a factor in distributing the work more evenly rather than less evenly. If the teams were made small enough, the task would become too large to be done effectively by only part of the group. In effect, every member would be essential to the operation of the company, we believe, only if the teams would be kept small. If each member is essential to the team's performance, there will be a better basis for grading each student.

The administration of the Game has been handicapped by a lack of know-how in the processing of inputs and the running of the program. We have had to rely on Pitt's Computation Center and Engineering School as well as on Carnegie. The task of assembling such human resources is sizeable; and, unfortunately, often they would leave before they could train their replacements. We need to develop a pool of persons where the more experienced members train the new members.

Most students appeared to be enthusiastic about the Game even though the plays were made under extreme time pressures. For example, students were required to digest the player's manual and histories and turn in a complete set of decisions within the first two days of the trimester. Deadlines for the teams to complete their decisions were consistently met with a minimum of errors. The high degree of involvement by the students could be seen in their willingness to perform Game-related assignments. Several volunteered the view that "the Game was exciting" and that "this was the first time in their education that they felt like managers of a going concern." Some of the students felt that improvements could be made in the following directions: the number of plays was too small to permit testing of any long-term policies; some students did less than their share of the work, but were not penalized accordingly; non-student errors (for instance, in keypunching or even an infrequent program bug) were demoralizing; and faculty boards of directors should be more active in guiding or coaching the teams.

C.   The Game versus Alternative Methods of Teaching

Business policy courses have relied usually on the case method as a vehicle for giving the student an integrated view of a business enterprise. This was our approach, but we no longer believe that it is an appropriate one for Administration and Integrated Decision Making. In the first place, the Game offers certain experiences which a case does not. Students must adapt to a dynamic economic environment under conditions of uncertainty. They must also adapt to a dynamic social environment. They are confronted with a sometimes hostile and sometimes encouraging board of directors. Bargaining among functions is necessary in order for the teams to complete their decisions. For example, the marketing and production managers in one firm almost came to blows before the board of directors because the production manager felt he was being forced to produce at high unit cost to satisfy an overly optimistic market forecast. Other experiences include group reactions to uncertainty and the processing of large flows of information.

Secondly, the students had been exposed to cases, sometimes of a very complex nature, before they reached the Administration and Integrated Decision Making course, but had not played a complex game prior to the course. The Game therefore was regarded as provocative and exciting, cases as rather dull. Some students suggested that cases be completely omitted in the future. By the same token, use of several types of games throughout the M.B.A. program might sour students on the educational benefits of games. It is our belief that the use of games should be restricted in the curriculum, perhaps, to the business policy course and to courses which draw from the students' experiences from playing the Game in the business policy course.

The relative advantage of lectures is difficult to appraise. In the second year, lectures were used for such topics as administrative theory, cybernetics, and accounting controls. The topics are appropriate to business policy and some aspects may not receive proper emphasis elsewhere in the curriculum. It seems that in choosing the proper mix of cases, lectures, and games, the main overlap resides in cases and games, for the kinds of substantive knowledge brought out in lectures is not developed in cases or games, even though such knowledge may be applied here. The conflict between the Game and lectures is in the allocation of time. At present, we are uncertain whether the benefits from the course would be increased by decreasing the time devoted to lectures.

The use of boards of directors had salutary effects on both the faculty participants and students. The faculty are prone to become more sympathetic to the Game when they get involved in it. Also, they may accept the high costs (in terms of student, faculty, and computer time) more readily. Students are impressed by the willingness of the faculty to devote so much time to the Game. In all candor, however, it should be pointed out that some faculty members did not become involved and they regarded the Game as just that—a game, very unrealistic.

There also is a problem of exactly how close the relationship between faculty and students playing the Game should be and whether the boards should be basically friendly or hostile to the student managers. Some students believed that there should be frequent board meetings and that board members should be available for consultation as problems arise. But clearly some limits must be established if participation in the Game, for which faculty board members received no teaching credit, is not to become a serious drain on faculty time.

D. Plans for the Future

There are several ways in which we hope to extend and enrich the educational benefits of the Carnegie Management Game. First, bargaining is a phenomenon present in a complex organization, but it is difficult to incorporate this within traditional methods of pedagogy. Perhaps bargaining within an organizational context can be more formally incorporated into the Game. For example, managers might be told that their performances would be evaluated both on the total effectiveness of the management and on how well individual functions were carried out. Each function can be assigned operational objectives, while total effectiveness can be determined by the board in terms of overall profits and competitive strength. The production manager, for example, would be forced to seek two sometimes conflicting goals—minimizing unit production costs (which would demonstrate how well he was discharging his individual responsibility) and contributing to increased firm profits. A considerable amount of bargaining would be involved in resolving differences among the several functions in the Game. Switching the emphasis to individual goal fulfillment makes the Game more realistic in demonstrating to the participants that the firm is not "one big happy family of systems analysts" and that the resolution of conflict with other managers of the same firm is essential.

Second, experience with the Game at Pitt suggests that Game presidents accept a disproportionately large amount of responsibility. They are policy makers, task masters, channelers of communications, and public relations men. In one case, shortly before the crucial final meeting with the board of directors, a president was rendered *hors de combat* by an accident. His unplanned absence threw the firm's managers into complete disorganization, from which they did not recover. To dramatize the need for greater delegation of functions, it might be helpful to pull out of action the key members of a team without advance notice, particularly where it seems that an individual or small clique is exercising undue influence in the firm's operations. As suggested earlier, we believe that team size should be reduced, and that the board chairman should be given greater investigatory responsibility.

Thirdly, in view of Pitt's experience, careful thought is being given to changing the mix among the Game, cases, and lectures in the Administration and Integrated Decision Making course. In particular, the elimination of cases to make room for richer use of the Game is being considered. Cases seemed to offer little challenge to the M.B.A. students because the cases did not lead as naturally to the application of analytic tools as did the Game and because the students have extensive experience with cases. Several students volunteered the view that the Game came closer to a real business situation in dramatizing organizational conflicts, time pressures, information processing, and human relations. It is unfortunate that we know so little about evaluating the effectiveness of alternative teaching methods, but on an intuitive basis, at least, a complex game seems to offer greater returns than do cases in a course where time is seriously limited.

Finally, several faculty members whose experience with the Game was gained mainly as directors offered suggestions for improvements which would entail elaboration of functional areas, covered too briefly in the professors' opinions or not at all. As examples, they recommend a money market which would permit far greater investment opportunities than now afforded, a more detailed transportation decision which would require choice among competing modes of transportation, and a risk management function which would involve various forms of insurance decisions. All of these could be added to the Game. Presumably, such addenda would become part of the work in the student's specialized courses, rather than a part of the Administration and Integrated Decision Making course.

III. EXPERIENCES WITH THE GAME AT THE UNIVERSITY OF NORTH CAROLINA
(By Richard Levin)

The Mark 1 version of the Carnegie Tech Management Game was introduced at the University of North Carolina as the result of a conference on management games held at Carnegie in March, 1961. Based on reports returned from our representatives at that meeting, the decision to use a complex management simulation was made late in the spring and reprogramming was begun immediately for the Univac 1105 available at the University of North Carolina.

Reprogramming was completed shortly before the fall semester began, and due to time limitations, faculty pre-Game experience was limited to three quick decisions. The Game was introduced first at the undergraduate level in place of a senior elective course within the school of Business Administration. Enrollment was limited to 21 students with "B" averages or better. At the time it was felt that if the Game was to be successful at the undergraduate level, this type of preselection was necessary. Introduction of the Game for the M.B.A. group was considered; however, the one year M.B.A. curriculum then in effect did not appear to offer the time considered necessary by the administrators for successful play of the Game.

A. Impressions after the First Run

We would suppose that our first reactions, once rigorous play had commenced, would be similar to any complex game experience. There were, of course, the inevitable "bugs" to be removed from the program; occasional lapses of play while the computer staff became familiar with the language; and finally, *ad hoc* decisions that were required of the administrators concerning situations "not covered by the manual."

Out of the early period of play, comprising several Game months, several distinct impressions were formed by the faculty administrators. Some decision was obviously necessary concerning the degree to which students were to be allowed to create their own environment as opposed to a situation where the administrators "fixed" the history to create a particular problem situation. (This could be called *unattended* play versus *programmed* play).

It was obvious that lack of sufficient financial history of previous play was a weak point.[5] It precluded the type of analysis which the Game, in its complexity, can demand, and it tended to restrict policy making and implementation. It soon became obvious that the marketing function was the major determinant of team success, to the exclusion of other functional area decisions in certain cases. This may indeed be the case in the detergent industry; however, for teaching purposes in a complex management simulation, a better distribution of workload was required. The cost structures of the three competing firms were changed basically to a flat unit cost curve throughout a wide range of outputs, conditions which allowed profits at very low output levels. The cost structure did not reward proportionately those firms aggressive enough to carve out large market shares.

The role of the faculty administrators was a critical one. If they were to achieve for the student maximum educational benefits, they could neither adopt the role of oracle nor allow the play of the Game to move ahead unattended. Faculty answers to student questions that revealed information about the Game model tended to be a problem. Finally, in this regard, some pertinent questions were raised concerning the proper distribution of faculty directors; for instance, whether the same group of faculty members should act as directors for all teams or whether each team should have its own personal directors.

Critical to the success of the Game experience was the making and implementation of long-run operating policy. "Playing the Game" without planning would give the student one type of experience while conceiving, implementing, and controlling long-run policy through the use of the Game would give a more desirable kind. More ways to stress long-range actions were needed.

It was obvious at an early date that grading the Game activity as a course would indeed be an onerous task. The preselection process for student participants had narrowed the range of competence among the players, but from looking at previous course grades it was also soon obvious that performance in the Game was not wholly dependent upon past academic standing.

The early period of play was a rewarding experience with respect to existing methods of teaching business administration. In some cases, it pointed up the need for additional quantitative work since the number

---

[5]The same problem arose at Carnegie in the early runs, where players had at most three to six months of prior history. We now provide 12–40 months of prior history (some of it condensed but most of it derived from actual student play), and we plan at some point to put the Game on a continuing basis wherein one year's teams would begin where the previous year's teams have ended their work and wherein many years of decisions, outcomes, and traditions of play would be available to the new teams.— (K.J.C., W.R.D., A.A.K., P.R.W.)

of factors to be considered left team members searching for new techniques. Often lack of adequate controls forced a team into an embarrassing situation. It was heartening to see how quickly the techniques and tools learned from previous work were brought to bear on many problems. In any event, both the strong and weak aspects of the "business curriculum" were showing up in what the students did.

B. Student Reaction

Student reaction to the Game during the initial period was excellent. Most students accepted the Game for what it was—a simulation—and criticisms of the degree of reality achieved or lost were at a minimum. Problems of division of work among team-members and of unwillingness to work were minimal. A great aura of secrecy developed concerning team plans and actions, and there was intense intercompany competition. There was initial criticism of the amount of work involved per decision, but this decreased once the team members began to learn how to routinize their decision-making processes. There was no problem with maintaining a schedule of decision making as far as the teams were concerned.

Most of the participants felt that the Game was a rewarding experience. There was wide general agreement that the major lessons taught were: (1) the absolute requirement for intracompany coordination between functional areas and (2) the value of planning and controlling the decision-making process. Student comments indicated to the faculty administrators that other valuable lessons were also being learned— lessons of team organization, small group dynamics, and, even at this early stage, company politics.

C. Revisions after One Year's Play

Student reactions after a year of play prompted several changes in the Game model and in the administration of the simulation. The more important basic changes will be treated briefly here.

1. *Boards of Directors.* At the University of North Carolina, we have concluded that a board of directors which is common to all three teams in the simulation functions best. If the same board is able to hear the problems, discuss alternatives, and maintain close communication with all of the teams in the industry, the simulation becomes more effective. For that reason, three faculty members are appointed to act as a board of directors common to all of the teams in the industry. These faculty members receive a reduction in their course load for serving in this capacity.

2. *Operating Policy.* Each competing firm is required to formu-

late a set of operating policies at the end of the fourth week of play. From that time until the end of the semester, the Game is operated largely on the basis of these policies. Succeeding decisions are made by the Game administrators solely on the basis of policies previously turned in by the participants. These policies may be changed at any time by the teams, thus changing the rules by which the administrators make decisions. In this manner, we emphasize a long-run approach to the Game problems.

3. *Speed of Play.* The frequency with which the moves are made after the first few weeks of the semester appears to be critical to the success of the Game as an educational simulation. The greater the number of moves played, the more effective is the simulation. Obviously, being able to play through a simulated period of 30 months in one semester makes it incumbent upon the players to tailor their thinking toward long-range goals, decisions, and control.

4. *Stability of Sales.* The seasonal index of sales has been altered so that it goes through two cycles per year. That is, there are two peaks and two troughs. The magnitudes of the changes in each cycle are different. Though this is merely a mechanical change in the model, the extra planning it requires of the participants appears to make it a worthwhile revision in the basic Game model.

5. *Grading Procedures.* After being "in the woods" with respect to grading for a year, certain practices have evolved which enable grading to be done on a fairly rational basis. Each of the directors grades the contribution of each student at each of the board meetings (roughly once a month). In addition, the combined team performance is graded at each meeting. A comprehensive final examination is also administered. The final grade of each participant, then, is a weighted average of these three measures.

6. *Team Organization.* Originally our policy was to require rotation of team members into each of the three functional areas on an arranged basis. After some experience with the Game, we have now changed our requirement and allow the team to organize as it sees fit. We require all participants, however, to be familiar with the operating decisions and long-range planning that are currently taking place in all three functional areas. In this manner, continuity of functions is maintained and more severe requirements can be imposed upon the players' performance within their function.

D. Plans for the Future

As a result of two years' experience with a complex management simulation we are convinced that it offers a valuable tool for use in business administration education both at the undergraduate and graduate levels. By the same token, the speed of play makes it impossible for the participants to treat each decision as a new problem since time will not permit such a fragmented view. Efficient decision-making routines (including forms, meeting schedules, organizational specifications, etc.) become essential to continued team participation in the Game at this accelerated rate of play.

1. *Previous History.* After a year's experience where no previous history was available for the participants it became obvious that an ample financial history is an absolute necessity for an effective simulation. The primary advantages of having such a history are (1) that it affords a good opportunity for students to apply data compilation and synthesis techniques learned in other courses, and (2) that it markedly shortens the "learning" or "wandering" period which would otherwise be experienced at the start of each new semester. With adequate history, many of the basic relationships in the Game models can be explored to a point where the decision making takes on a more rational character from the outset of the Game.

2. *Cyclical Nature of the Market.* A period of one semester representing about 25 to 30 months of simulated play would normally take the teams through two cyclical movements in the product market. These cyclical fluctuations represent a strong point in the simulation; that is, careful forward planning and controlling become critical to continued team success. For this reason and in order to increase the number of instances where production balancing and inventory control must be carefully exercised, the number of cyclical fluctuations per year has been increased.

3. *Other Projected Changes.* Our staff is committed to use and develop a complex simulation as an integral part of our curricula and plans are going forward accordingly. In addition to the changes we have already noted, other developments are in progress.

The entire Carnegie Tech Game program has been rewritten in GATT for the Univac 1105, with complete flow charts and documentation to permit any parameter in any segment of the program to be changed as a routine matter. In this manner, the business environment represented by the Game model may be altered by the administrators at will to offer additional problems or study areas for the Game participants.

A program which will be able to "play the Game" has been written and is being tested. This program, while not designed to make perfect decisions, will in fact operate the three firms in the industry on a profitable basis. This project was undertaken to enable the game administrators, and other persons interested in the Game as a research tool, to test the effects of various policies over a fairly long period of time without having to make each succeeding decision "by hand." With this program we can test the effects of changes of individual parameters within the Game model and changes of existing policy for firm operation over an extended period of time. With the current "Game-playing program," individual decisions for 12 successive months can be made and printed out by the computer in a matter of a little over one hour.

The production segment of the original Mark 1 Game is being altered in several ways so that the decision making in that area becomes as challenging as that required by the marketing function. These changes include (1) the creation of several factories, one in each selling district, to allow greater use of allocation theory in the shipment and transshipment of finished goods; and (2) a nonhomogeneous production process which requires formal routing, scheduling, and in-plant dispatching for the production of individual products. Thus, cognizance must be taken of individual line setup times for a production run of any single product, and individual machine-center time restrictions present additional constraints to production. This change will, of course, present further opportunity for the use of mathematical techniques in production scheduling and plant operation.

Research is being undertaken on the decision-making process followed by the Game participants in an effort to design, test, and validate the Game experience on a formal basis. It is anticipated that the research will require several years to complete.

E. Conclusion

The Carnegie Tech Game has been successfully played by both undergraduates and M.B.A. students for a period of two years at the University of North Carolina. During this period, intense interest has been generated on the part of the faculty administrators in the area of gaming and simulation. One of the first projects to result from the Game experience is the UNC Retailing Game, a complex retailing simulation to be published soon.

We are convinced that the type of simulation represented by the Carnegie Game offers to the student a unique advantage not available through more conventional methods of business administration education. The game administrators look upon games as the best currently available method of teaching the value of planning, coordination, and control in a complex environment. A game offers an excellent laboratory for the application of knowledge gained from formal classroom work, and represents an ideal vehicle for training students in the problems of leadership and in the awareness of the importance of small group dynamics.

Although, when compared to other course offerings, the game represents a disproportionate investment in terms of faculty time and school funds necessary for its continued operation, we are convinced that the additional investment has a definite payoff for those students who participate in the experience. Plans now underway call for an even greater involvement of a complex maangement simulation in both the teaching and research programs of the School of Business Administration at the University of North Carolina.

IV. THE BUSINESS GAME IN EXECUTIVE DEVELOPMENT PROGRAMS

(By Melvin Anshen[6])

Business games have been introduced in many executive programs in recent years. Programs reporting game experiments include several conducted by universities, as well as a number sponsored by individual companies and by general and specialized management organizations.

The recorded experience indicates that many of the educational values of games for student players are also present when the players are mature, experienced managers. Along some dimensions, indeed, the educational values may be even greater for executives than for students. Along others, the values are somewhat less.

Experienced managers place demands on game design and administration that exceed and differ from those that arise in student play. It would appear, therefore, that fully effective use of games in executive development programs requires imaginative design (1) to accommodate the intellectual content and operational structure of a game to the executives' intensive "real-world" experience, (2) to minimize or remove clerical detail that students accept and often benefit from executing, (3) to structure the relationship between faculty and players in ways that are consistent with the executives' concept of their status and the faculty's concept of their educational role, and (4) to control the investment of players' time and energy so as to assure a reasonable balance between the demands and attractions of the game and the requirements of the other planned components of a development program.

Much more than student players, executives are likely to be critical of elements in a game that are clearly inconsistent with their knowledge

---

[6]Formerly Professor of Industrial Administration at Carnegie, now on the faculty at Columbia University.

of the world of business. Their negative reactions may be expressed with respect to artificial characteristics in a game's general economic and business environment (as in unrealistic fluctuations in seasonal sales or impossible time horizons for the accomplishment of investment in plant and equipment), or to distorted behavior in the specific industry setting of a game (as in demand-price interactions that depart from market experience). They are reluctant to accept gross simplifications that run counter to their knowledge of the complexity of actual operating procedures or management performance. They are likely to rebel against any substantial volume of mandatory clerical work, such as hand calculations and detailed posting of decision forms. They are impatient with rules that impose stiff penalties for what they regard as low-order mistakes (as in suffering loss of production because of failure to indicate appropriate raw material procurement in the correct box of a complex decision form).

On the positive side, executives as a group are often quicker than students to respond to the intellectual challenge of a game. They are strongly disposed to extend their planning into the future, to select specific targets, and to implement their plans with appropriate marketing strategies and financial and production programs consistently sustained through time. Their administrative experience encourages a mental attitude that places a high value on purposive action related to defined objectives. They are highly stimulated by a game's management problems and its competitive pressure.

When these favorable responses are awakened by a game that is complex enough to challenge their managerial thinking and realistic enough to win their cooperation as participants, the educational values compare favorably with those associated with student play. Since most participants in executive programs have had only limited exposure to management problems in more than one business function, the Game presents a stimulating opportunity to think at the level of top management's comprehensive overview, to analyze the position of the total enterprise in relation to its environment and the activities of competitors, and to design strategies and programs that express a balanced and coordinated commitment of resources in all functional departments. The unique contribution of the game as an educational instrument—in contrast to the case method so widely used in executive programs of all types—is its dynamism with consequent necessity for the players to live within the constraints of their own past decisions. In addition, executives have an opportunity to solve problems related to the creation and maintenance of team organization, to exercise their analytic skills in complex settings, and to draw from their game experiences insights and materials that can be exploited in other parts of their development programs and in their personal careers.

A. The Management Game in the Carnegie Program for Executives

Few of what were later judged to be the special features desirable for effective use of the Carnegie Management Game in executive development programs were built into the Game in its first trial in the Carnegie Program for Executives. Game content and procedures generally followed the pattern set for the initial student play. The Game manual prepared for student use was distributed to the executives without editorial modification. Company histories provided to the executives at the start of their play reported actual student performance in an earlier Game run. The operating requirements for executives—calculations to be made, decision forms to be completed, etc.—were identical with those imposed on student players. As with students, the executives, divided in five-man teams operating in two parallel three-firm industries, were given neither instructions nor guidance with respect to internal company organization for decision making. The computer program was that used in the last preceding student Game.

The single major divergence from the rules governing student play was the introduction of a device to limit the time that executives could give to the Game. Alerted by evidence in student performance that the intrinsic interest of the Game's management problems and the challenge of its competitive pressures readily encouraged unduly large investment of time by at least some participants, the administrators of the executive program were concerned about preserving a balanced effort across all work areas in the concentrated nine-week program. They anticipated that the Game would be a valuable addition to the program, as well as contributing the liveliness of a novel activity to change the pace of the normal routine of study, lectures, and discussions. But they did not want the Game to claim more than a reasonable and predictable share of each week's work hours. For this reason, a single afternoon each week was assigned to the Game. Results of the preceding week's decisions were not revealed to the executives until one o'clock on the afternoon scheduled for Game play and decision forms were required from the teams by five o'clock. While is was possible for the executives to use other unscheduled time during the week for assessment of past Game results and design of future plans and policies, the absence of specific information on current operating performance held this kind of activity within acceptable limits.

Assessments based on close monitoring of the executives' play and on post-Game evaluations by the players revealed a number of special problems related to both the content and the operating procedures of the Game in executive use. Some of these had been anticipated, although at a lower level of significance than the assessment suggested. Others came to the attention of the Game's designers and administrators for the first time.

1.   As a result of errors and occasional hapless administrative moves by preceding student managers of the firms inherited by the executives, some of the executive teams took over firms in unusually weak or awkward positions. They were able to extricate themselves from these difficulties only in the course of several weeks' play, amounting to as much as half the decision periods in the nine-week program. The executives criticized this state of affairs as unduly limiting their ability to maneuver and to realize the full benefits of what they judged to be the sounder management policies that they were able to institute in the latter part of the program after rectifying earlier management errors. The criticism was particularly sharp from those who believed that their competitive performance in the Game was seriously disadvantaged by the ineptitude of prior managers.

2.   For reasons associated with the foregoing situation, some executives found their company histories of only limited value in revealing essential facts about the nature of the economic environment and the strategic significance of particular marketing and pricing decisions. Since the purpose of the histories was to provide background for judgment and planning, those who found little meaning in the record—or, even worse, a misleading record—were far from enthusiastic about the volume of historical material made available to them, which they had been encouraged to study in advance of playing the Game.

3.   Many executives became impatient with the amount of clerical work they were required to perform. This included, for example, routine translations of production decisions into raw material purchase orders. Much more than students, executives distinguished between making management decisions determining basic policies and the means for implementing them, on one side, and pencil-and-paper work, on the other. They were intrigued by the Game's challenge in the former area, bored by its detailed requirements in the latter. They observed that in real-world company operations, managers did not occupy their time with clerical work, and they concluded that the limited Game hours were not well invested in this kind of activity.

4.   Against the background of this view, many executives criticized the penalties imposed by Game procedures for clerical mistakes of both commission and omission. Failure to order a raw material or in-

scribing a procurement action on the wrong line of a decision form might interrupt or distort operations for one or more months. The executives' view was that this situation was inconsistent with their own experience with internal controls. In the real world such errors could be corrected at a cost considerably short of the loss of one full month's production. They regarded it as unduly punitive of a low order of carelessness or, as was claimed on occasion, inadvertent misunderstanding of Game procedures.

5. The executive schedule provided for only seven decision sessions. The Game period in the first week of the program was used for general orientation and in the ninth week for evaluation. Since each set of decisions determined a firm's operations for one month of Game time, the stretch of administrative play covered seven months. Within this limitation, there was little incentive for players to extend their planning horizon into the longer-term future and to think through the related problems in marketing, production, research, and finance. The evolution of plans and of cross-functional links could not be accomplished in the time available for play. Even with artificially shortened construction periods for plant addition, expansion programs could not be brought to fruition, nor could new products be introduced and fully exploited. The Game's interesting problem potential in the area of financial planning and capital structure also went largely unexplored. The players found themselves limited to short-range marketing maneuvers. Even here they lacked an opportunity to confront the full cycle of seasonal fluctuations in demand. There was criticism of this entire time constraint.

6. Executives with a background in marketing believed the demand-price relationships determined by the computer program to be unreasonable and contrary to "real-world" experience.[7] Here, as elsewhere in the Game, executives were much more inclined than students to be impatient with gross departures from what they knew or judged to be reality. Most students would accept an artificial constraint and proceed to play the Game within its limits. Most executives were unwilling to accept such a constraint without protest. They expected a Game based on the detergent industry to have performance characteristics at least roughly consistent with those they believed to prevail in that industry.

7. Wisely or otherwise, in the first attempt at executive play, it was

[7]A good deal of the problem lay not in unrealism of the Game model, but in poor choice of parameter settings. For example, market demand was allowed to run far ahead of industry capacity—with the result that firms could raise prices drastically without losing sales. Better parameter settings have been achieved in later runs of the Game.— (K.J.C., W.R.D., A.A.K., P.R.W.)

not judged feasible to establish boards of directors with their explicit monitoring function and authoritarian relation to the executive-players. Nevertheless, the Game's administrators were concerned to find some mechanism for helping the players to assess their total performance in terms of planned objectives and actual accomplishment, and to evaluate the Game experience as a basis for decisions affecting the use of the Game in future programs. The adopted mechanism was a terminal mass meeting of the entire group with the program faculty. The meeting opened with a review of competitive performance in the two industries and then undertook to move into a discussion of each team's objectives, policies, and operating results. The discussion ended with a critical appraisal of the Game as an educational experience within the context of the total executive development program. This mechanism for review and assessment did not function effectively. The executives were reluctant to discuss their management performance in the presence of competitors. Even the critical observations on the Game's content and procedures tended to be superficial. At the same time, a variety of comments suggested that the players would have welcomed an opportunity in a different setting to talk about the total experience.

As a result of the initial play of the Game in the executive program, a number of changes were introduced in subsequent years. Many of these were specifically designed to alleviate or remove the causes of critical reaction described above.

1. Executive teams were launched in business with company histories that represented sensible and effective management performance. It was not judged essential, for morale or other reasons, to start the three competing teams in an industry in identical positions. However, an effort was made to open the competitive play with teams in reasonably proximate postures, with none in an unusually strong or weak situation in the market place, in financial resources, in product availability, or in production and warehousing facilities.

2. To reduce the burden of clerical work and to minimize the possibility of costly error resulting from ignorance or misunderstanding of Game procedures, each executive team was assigned a student assistant available throughout every weekly decision period. The assistant's role was carefully defined to him and to his executive team. His job was to complete the necessary decision forms in a manner that would execute the executives' policy determinations and to serve as advisor on Game rules and procedures. In no circumstances was he permitted to participate in decision making, to serve as a member of the management group for his firm, or to counsel on policy.

3. The limitation on Game time imposed by the constraint of seven

decision sessions and the one-decision-per-month structural design of the Carnegie Game was relieved by providing that, after the first two decision sessions, teams would be required to make decisions at a single decision session that would cover two, and later three, successive months. In effect, this amounted to devising decision rules governing strategy and tactics in a variety of possible situations. The result was to extend the Game time from seven months to over one year, and thereby to open up new possibilities for product innovation, brand strategy, expansion of production and warehousing facilities, and long-range financial planning and its implementation.

4. Adjustments were made in several of the critical marketing parameters, in response to the allegation of gross departure from common market experience.

5. Although the Game's administrators still hesitated to set up formal boards of directors, provisions was made at the conclusion of play for each team to meet with two members of the faculty who were briefed with a complete record of the full detail of the team's performance throughout the Game. Team members had an assigned mission to report on objectives, plans, and policies, with such supplemental review of performance results as they might choose to present by way of explaining their competitive success or failure. The faculty pair were authorized to raise questions designed to get under the surface of the team's performance and generally to strengthen the educational values of the experience in several areas, including analysis of external and internal problems, consistency of programs with plans, flexibility in adjusting to unexpected turns of events, coordination of the functional departments of the firm, and economic use of capital and other resources. The meeting was also used to solicit evaluations of the Game within the context of the total program.

These adjustments in organization and procedure went some distance toward removing the sources of earlier criticism. It seems clear, however, that there remain substantial opportunities for adding to the value of the Game in executive play. In the area of the Game's time horizon, for example, the device of requiring simultaneous decisions for two or three consecutive months is open to valid criticism. From the executives' viewpoint, it is an unrealistic procedure. They object to making decisions for future time periods in the absence of specific information on conditions that will prevail immediately prior to those periods. They would greatly prefer to make decisions for calendar quarters considered as a block of time. This, too, is unrealistic, of course. But it would permit, at least, a decision to be made with full knowledge of a firm's position at the start of the decision period. A number of adjustments in the underlying Game program would be required to implement this change, but many observers would find it a useful modification in terms of opening possibilities for managements to administer affairs through periods extending up to two years of Game time.

In addition, there are extensive opportunities for enlivening and enriching the play through in-basket and role-playing mechanisms. While these have been at least partially explored in student play, as reported in Chapters 3 and 4, they have not yet been introduced in the executive Game, principally because of the constraints imposed by (1) the relatively short duration of the whole executive program, and (2) the currently prevailing belief that the Game should not be permitted to claim significantly more time than four to five hours a week. Beyond this, it is by no means sure that executives' notions of status would be outraged by the necessity for reporting as managers to a board of directors. Some observers believe that this device would make an important contribution to the seriousness of executives' application to tasks in the Game, as well as strengthening some of its educational values. Finally, there are untapped opportunities for drawing on selected aspects of the Game's operations as raw material in other parts of the executive program—in the work in human relations, for example, and in the work in quantitative techniques for decision making, as well as in business policy.

B. Educational Values of Games for Executives

The foregoing description of the evolving Carnegie experience with the Game in several annual executive development programs suggests some general observations on the contributions of this type of instrument to the development of managers. These observations are usefully set against the background, reported in Chapters 3, 4, and 5, of specific educational values of the Game when used in student programs: (1) experience in analyzing complex problems at the general management level, (2) experience in handling diplomatic problems of personal interaction with individuals and groups outside the management team, (3) experience in designing and working with organizational structures marked by hierarchical characteristics and functional division of labor, (4) experience for the individual in allocating time and handling relations with associates, and (5) use of Game materials and experiences as teaching input in other courses.

While the Game offers a parallel set of educational opportunities to mature managers, their extended administrative experience leads to a different balance of gains and needs. Unlike students with their limited exposure to organizational activity and to the politics and diplomacy of relations with outside groups, junior and middle-level executives enter development programs with substantial experience and understanding in these areas. Most executives can benefit from an analytic and sophisticated study of organizational and diplomatic problems, to be sure. But they do not need to find the raw material for this study in the operations of a business game conducted for a brief period of time in association with strangers. On the other hand, executives whose administrative experience has largely been confined to one functional department of a business (as is generally true for most participants in executive development programs) can realize important benefits from the Game's challenge of managing the affairs of a company from the comprehensive viewpoint of top management. The assignment of responsibility for developing balanced and coordinated action programs in research, production, distribution, and finance—in a context which compels forward planning and the flexible implementation of plans through successive action periods—can be a novel and valuable experience.

It would therefore appear that the dominant educational contribution of games for executive players is the opportunity to practice decision making at the general management level. Simple games, even when designed to encourage company-wide thinking, are of limited value. At least they fail to take advantage of the rich educational potential that a game situation can present. Much more valuable are complex games, rich in problem materials that compel probing analysis of the intermesh of functional relationships. It is particularly important to expose executives to games that emphasize long-range planning and the phased conversion of such plans into action programs that touch operations in all parts of a business. This kind of game inevitably leads the players into financial analysis and planning, forces them to deal with the constraints and costs of money as a scarce resource, and encourages them to face up to investment and pay-back problems. If the game is so designed and structured that the players accept its complexities as close to reality within the institutional setting—rather than simply devised for their torment and confusion—the combination of natural interest and intellectual challenge creates an educational situation of the highest potential.

In such a context, the Carnegie Game can be a useful adjunct to the business policy cases which serve as the usual approach to the task of helping executives to think at the general management level. Cases present an opportunity to expose executives to top management problems in a variety of institutional settings. They can be employed in planned sequences that permit the instructor to move from relatively simple to relatively complex situations, to explore problems of implementation in depth through several organization layers and in headquarters-field relationships, and to follow the history of policy and its execution through changing environmental conditions. They have a major deficiency, however, now rather widely recognized: they are static in relation to the students' decision process. In the popular phrase, they do not force students to live with the results of their own decisions, to face a future that is under continual evolution as a result of present actions.

The Carnegie Game has a happily matching set of educational characteristics. It may lack machinery for exposing students to general management problems in the variety of institutional settings described above; on the other hand, it has a built-in dynamism. The players must live with their decisions over time. They are confronted by circumstances which evolve from their own and competitors' policies, the strategies that they implement, and planned changes in the economic environment. Beyond this, the Game's designers and managers can introduce shock elements (changes in raw materials prices, or a major fire in a plant or warehouse), opportunities for role-playing negotiation under pressure (bargaining out a wage contract or securing short- and long-term financing), and comparable experiences to test the teams.

These observations contemplate an important contribution to the study of business policy—analysis and decision making at the level of general management—represented by a complex management game. It can be used concurrently with policy cases, with each educational instrument matching strength against its companion's weakness. An added advantage of the Game is its potential for strengthening the motivation of participating executives through the competitive pressures generated among the players.

A second significant educational contribution of the Game in executive development programs is the encouragement it gives to the study and application of quantitative techniques of analysis. In this thrust, the Game may be even more valuable for executives than for students, although it urges the latter in the same direction. This follows from the fact that the normal bite of academic discipline may be sufficient to push graduate students through a prescribed program of quantitative work. With executive groups, the principal reliance must be on self-motivation. In this circumstance, the capability of demonstrating within the Game context the operational uses of quantitative analysis, its specific relevance to practical management problems, and the continual generation of fresh problem materials can be powerful motivating influences.

V. THE MANAGEMENT GAME IN A MIDDLE-LEVEL EXECUTIVE PROGRAM

(By Neil C. Churchill)

The experiences with the Carnegie Tech Management Game in executive development programs, including those cited by Professor Anshen in the preceding section, have been limited primarily to programs designed for upper-level executives. More recently, the Carnegie Tech Management Game has been used in a middle-level executive development program with positive results. This report deals with the results of this experience: (1) by evaluating the experience and generalizing the results, and (2) by describing the manner in which the Management Game was used in this program.

A. Goals and Results of Using the Game in the Program

The primary difference between middle- and upper-level executive development programs lies, for the former, in the participants' younger age and lack of experience and in the heavier emphasis placed on the development of techniques and managerial skills. In addition, where the development program is essentially of an "in-plant" nature, the breadth of the group's experiences are limited primarily to those in one industry and perhaps even to one company. In many respects middle-management programs are closer to those of graduate business education than they are to programs designed exclusively for upper-level executives. The participants are more willing to accept abstractions, in the Game context at least, and are less likely to have broad experiences or deep-seated convictions that are violated by the conditions of the Game. They are more willing to dig into the detailed aspects of the Game and are less upset by the clerical requirements it imposes on them. The overall executive roles of planning and coordination required by the Game are newer and hence more interesting to middle-level executives than to men who have experienced such problems in a real context. Finally, middle-management participants are somewhat less experienced with group activities and have less well-developed interpersonal skills than more senior executives. A further consideration for in-company training programs is the increased motivation that the evaluative nature of the program provides. This stimulus is not present in most upper-level programs.

As has been pointed out, a large, complex management game emphasizes overall company planning, necessitates functional interactions, contains dynamic aspects of extended play, and requires interpersonal interactions for effective performance. A desire for these features led to the decision to use the Carnegie Tech Management Game in a six-week, middle-management development program at the University of Pittsburgh. This program was a joint effort between the Bell Telephone Company of Pennsylvania and the University of Pittsburgh.[8] The participants ranged from 30 to 39 years of age and were all drawn from the same managerial level.

This program, entitled "Management Perspectives: A Development Program," met five and one-half days a week for a six-week period. The Management Game was introduced at the beginning of the second week of the program, and the play extended over approximately four and one-half calendar weeks. During this period, the teams made 15 sets of decisions: three single-month moves, three two-month moves, and two three-month moves.

1. *Evaluation of the Game Experience.* The Game experience in the Management Perspective program was considered a success by a majority of the participants, the directors, and the faculty.

The participants devoted a considerable amount of time and a great deal of energy to playing the Game. In return, they obtained a broader picture of the business enterprise, gained an overall viewpoint of company operations, experienced the need for interactions between functions, developed increased understanding of interpersonal relations, and even had some chance to apply to the Game what they were being taught in other segments of the program.[9] They enjoyed the experience although the tensions created by reporting to a board of directors containing a top executive from their company was, at times, considerable.[10]

The program faculty felt generally that the results warranted the time expended. While only five (or 9 percent of 55 formal sessions were devoted to the Game, the participants spent more than a proportionate amount of their time making the decisions (on the average, 7–15 hours a week). The Game is complex, competitive, and challenging, and the effort that can be spent on it, at least initially, is almost unlimited.

---

[8]We are indebted to the coordinators of the program, Marshall Robinson, Dean of the Graduate School of Business of the University of Pittsburgh, and to D. G. Tolley, Assistant Vice President of Personnel Relations, Bell Telephone Company of Pennsylvania, for reviewing the paper presented here.

[9]In answer to a questionnaire administered some six months after the Game experience, thirteen of the participants indicated that they felt they had learned better interpersonal relations by working in and with other people in groups; eight noted that they had learned to make better decisions; and five or more each cited (a) they learned that decisions should be based on facts not feelings, (b) they developed new concepts of the importance of planning or working toward a goal, (c) they had learned more about their individual fellow members, and (d) they had learned more about themselves.

[10]Each team reported to a board of directors consisting of one faculty member and one executive from the Pittsburgh office of the Bell Telephone Company. Further details are contained in the second part of this report.

An attempt was made to minimize the interference of the Game with other subjects by using it as the basis for explicit assignments in the other courses and by scheduling the Game decisions to be due, as much as possible, on Saturday afternoon or after a scheduled Game session. In retrospect, this did not always succeed, but at least half of the excess time devoted to the Game seemed to come from time that would have otherwise been spent by the participants in nonacademic pursuits.

In general, these were the results of using the Game in the program:

1. A major benefit that the participants received was an overall, company-wide point of view of a business operation. Although all of the participants had had experience with differing activities in their own company, this experience had been mostly at the operating rather than at the planning level. In the play of the Game, the opposite was true and the broader aspects of corporate management were not only in evidence but were dominant.

2. All of the participants were from the Bell Telephone Company of Pennsylvania. Most, if not all, had had little experience with other companies. Thus the Game, based as it is on the consumer-directed, packaged detergent industry, presented them with a new environment in which to manage. The Game environment made them examine the beliefs, preconceptions, and rules of behavior that they held valid about the business environment, ethics, and management. These rules and beliefs, often sound but equally often couched in terms appropriate only to a narrow segment of the world, were now subject to scrutiny in a totally different environment—an environment which forced them out in the light for examination and evaluation. The need to operate in an environment where few "rules of thumb" were known required the collection of evidence and its analytic evaluation for successful operation. The Game provided many instances where holding to preconceptions in spite of evidence to the contrary resulted in costly mistakes. Thus it taught logical evaluation, the ability to sense change, and to react and adapt to it.

3. Since the Game provided a complex environment, tools and techniques taught in other sections of the program could be tried out in a relatively cost-free situation, but one, nonetheless, representative of the business world. This advantage is lessened in a short six-week program such as this one was. It is also difficult to integrate the Game fully with the other courses in an initial program. Consequently more coordination is needed, and is contemplated in the future.

4. The Game provided a dynamic opportunity to recognize mistakes, to analyze their consequences, and subsequently to adapt strategies to them. This is an attribute that is not available in case discussions and has an immense value in demonstrating to the participants how a mistake in one area of operations has implications in many others; for instance, failure to order raw material in the production area would influence pricing policy and advertising expenditures in the marketing section. In this respect, what may, in one sense, be an unrealistic or severe penalty for a "clerical error" is, in another sense, necessary to emphasize functional interrelations and to aid in developing adaptability to unforeseen occurrences.

5. Finally the Game provided an opportunity to learn to work with groups under pressure and with delegated responsibilities. This may be of less importance with senior executives who have had many such experiences than it is with graduate students and even with middle-management personnel. Most participants found it challenging to deal with a group of peers under pressure—particularly in a situation where they possessed no sanctions that could be invoked—and many of the participants gained significant insights into their own patterns of behavior.

Since the Management Game was successfully used in this program, more successfully than had sometimes been the case in Carnegie's regular Program for Executives, a comparison is in order. It was (1) the same game, (2) played over the essentially same time span, and (3) administered by essentially the same staff as at Carnegie Tech. The differences were:

1. The composition of the participants involved middle- rather than upper-management personnel. Further, they were all from the same company.
2. The participants in the program were being evaluated (in the same manner as most in-plant training programs).
3. The Game structure required each team to report to a board of directors.
4. More time was allocated for the participants to play the Game.
5. The staff had tried to avoid problems that had arisen in earlier runs.

Which of these differences were determining is, of course, not known. Certainly the age and experience of the participants seemed to be a factor.

Time available for play was important,[11] and the necessity of having to report on plans, strategies, and their consequent results certainly had an effect on behavior.

In extending the results, it must be realized that while the first two factors vary with the type of program, items three and four above can be created in any game situation. A board of directors can be formed even if it is composed only of faculty members or perhaps a mixture of participants and staff.[12] Time to play the Game is also important, but time alone does not effectively contain the interested and yet motivate the disinterested in the nonevaluative environment found in most executive development programs.[13] Finally we might pose some questions

---

[11]One participant who played the Game in the Program for Executives at Carnegie Tech stated to the author (who was also in charge of the Game there), "We were given the [Game] manual the night we arrived and spent a lot of time learning the rules. Then we were told to play the Game Wednesday of each week from 1:30 until we went home. In that case it took only two people in the group who didn't care for it to shoot it down."

[12]Several executives who have played the Game at Carnegie Tech expressed the desire for feedback from knowledgeable persons to help guide Game performance.

[13]Perhaps the experience with the Game in nonevaluative executive programs is typical of behavior in other parts of the same programs where a few do not wish to, and in fact do not, participate in specific activities or courses. Yet this nonparticipation may not be evident except in intensive group efforts.

about the characteristics of the participants. Is it that young, middle-level executives are more willing to put up with the abstractions of the Game and less reluctant to participate in a potential status-reducing experience? Or is it that the Game itself offers them relatively more in education and experience so that they will work harder and question less? We really do not know.

2. *Summary.* If the experience examined is representative, the following conclusions can be made:

1. A complex general management game can be a useful part of an executive development program.
2. The advantages of a game in such a program seem to be greater for middle management than for top management—and perhaps particularly useful in in-house training programs.
3. A game requires ample time for play and involvement; otherwise it will be viewed as an ancillary, make-work experience.
4. It is desirable to have a board of directors for the team to report to and to explain their strategies to.
5. Properly structured, a complex management game can provide a rich environment for developing broad, general understanding of the company-wide problems and interactions involved in operating a modern business.
6. Finally and perhaps most importantly, it provides a business-oriented environment where attitudes, interpersonal skills, and mechanisms used in decision making can be examined, evaluated, and improved at relatively little cost when compared to on-the-job experience.

B. Implementation of the Management Game in the Program

This six-week management-development program was the outcome of a joint effort between the Bell Telephone Company of Pennsylvania and the Graduate School of Business of the University of Pittsburgh. This program combined the advantages of highly motivated participants in an in-company training program with the intellectual resources and the academic environment of a major university. The program is of interest in its own right, but the comments here will be limited to those pertaining to the use of the Game.

The Game was one half of the section entitled "Integrated Decision Problems." The other half of the section was devoted to detailed analysis of several cases involving the establishment and implementation of managerial policy. The Game was introduced in the second week of the program. The final evaluative session was held on Thursday of the sixth week of the program. Thus actual Game play extended over only four and one-half calendar weeks.[14]

1. *The Participants.* The participants consisted of 20 men of demonstrated ability and above average managerial potential drawn

---

[14]The participants lived together on the University of Pittsburgh campus for the six weeks of the program. The work week was five and one-half days in length, with one long weekend break at the end of the third week of the program.

from throughout the Company. They were all at the same level of managerial responsibility and many knew each other through job assignments or through common training experiences. These men were, in a sense, in competition with each other. They knew that their performance in the program and in the Game would be evaluted.[15]

2. *The Structure of the Game.* The Game orientation meeting took place on the first day of the second week of the program. The participants had been given the player's manual the week before. Prior to the orientation meeting, they had been grouped into three teams of six to seven men each and provided with histories of their firms' actions for the preceding 12 months of play. The groups were chosen essentially at random, but an attempt was made to distribute men with similar functional experiences evenly between the teams.

A board of directors was formed for each team. This board consisted of one Bell executive and one faculty member from the University of Pittsburgh who was familiar with the Game. The boards were matched with teams so that no participant had as his director a person for whom he was currently working.[16]

The board members attended the orientation meeting with the participants. The composition of the teams and their specific assignments were given to them at that time. After the orientation meeting, the boards and the teams met for lunch and held the first of three board meetings. The second board meeting took place after the first six Game-months of play. The final meeting took place the day of the final evaluation.

The second of the five scheduled Game sessions took place two days after the orientation meeting. At this meeting, the Game structure was developed more extensively, general questions were answered, and teams were given time to make their first moves. During this latter part of the session, the Game staff circulated among the teams, answering specific questions relating to each particular team's problems and strategies. The results of the first move were returned to the teams the next day and the second set of decisions was due at the end of the week. The third set of single decisions was due just prior to the long weekend.

The third formal Game session took place on the first day of the fourth week, just after the long weekend and just prior to the first "multiple move." The results of the first quarter of play were made

---

[15]The type of evaluation made, its purpose, and the criteria used were made explicit to the participants and were accepted by them prior to the start of the program.

[16]However, there was a high probability that a participant would work for one of these men at some time in the future.

available and the teams were in a position to evaluate themselves and one another. In order to compress the time devoted to the Game, the participants were now required to hand in, as a single package, decisions for two monthly moves. These moves were processed without the Game teams being permitted to alter their decision for the second month in response to the results obtained for the first. To mitigate the lack of realism such multiple moves entailed and the possible consequences that the corresponding lack of response might produce, assistance was provided the participants in the form of "player programs" which instructed the computer to modify, in preset ways, the decisions of the second month in response to results of the first. The Game staff made themselves available to assist the players in writing such programs, but the content of the programs was the responsibility of the team itself.[17] The third Game session was devoted in part to explaining this multiple-move capability and in part to elaborating on the nature of the Game and answering questions on a confidential, team-by-team basis.

Throughout the play of the Game, the Game administrator and his staff were available by phone or by appointment to answer questions and to explain the Game environment. In addition, the staff was available for an hour or two prior to the collection of each set of decisions to clear up last-minute questions, to interpret the Game rules and the Game environment, and to assist in the preparation of player programs.

The fourth Game session was scheduled at the end of nine months of play and just prior to the three-month decision moves. Again some time was devoted to aiding firms in formulating strategy and in helping them understand further the Game environment and the competitive positions in which they found themselves. This was done without attempting to tell them "how to play." This is necessary several times in any complex Game situation since the students gain knowledge and raise more insightful questions as the Game progresses. In this session help was also given in writing player programs for the two three-month moves, one of which occurred at the end of the fifth week and the second at the beginning of the sixth week of the program.

The fifth and final Game session was devoted to an analysis by the Game staff of the manner in which the teams played the Game. Details of the Game environment were explained and related to the real world.

---

[17] The Game staff served as "human compliers" who translated the teams' explicitly stated goals, objectives, or strategies, into computer code and then onto punched cards. Thus, the participants did not need to have a knowledge of computer programming. They did, however, have to learn to be explicit in formulating the statements they wanted implemented.

The ending position of each team was evaluated,[18] as well as their revealed strategies and the critical points of their behavior. The purpose of this was (1) to reveal the structure of the environment in which the teams operated, (2) to indicate ways in which features of this environment could have been discovered, and (3) to show instances where preconceptions led the participants to persist in inappropriate behavior even in the face of evidence that demonstrated a need to change.[19]

Following the staff evaluation session the teams met with their boards of directors for a final review and discussion of their performance.

3. *Recommendations.* If the Game were to be played again in such a program, the following changes seem advisable:

1. The Game should be integrated with the rest of the program—particularly the human relations, organization, and analytic areas.
2. The Game should be introduced in the first week of the program. This would permit either the same number of Game months to be played at a less intense pace or else two to six additional months of Game play.

---

[18]One direct result of this evaluation was the allocation of some $1000 worth of books purchased for the program. The participants had decided that the allocation of these books would be governed by Game performance, and they had chosen the following criteria to determine the winner:

1. Profits made during play of the Game—40 percent
2. Market potential at the end of the Game (affecting the future in the short run)—20 percent
3. Potential of product library (determining long-run positions)—20 percent
4. Financial and managerial ability to capitalize on items 2 and 3—20 percent

The Game staff evaluated each team by each of these preselected criteria.

[19]An indication of the involvement, and perhaps of the tension, that the Game engendered is the following song composed for the closing Game session. Obviously Firm 3 was considered the loser. Only the names have been changed to protect the participants.

BALLAD OF FIRM THREE

Oh we didn't make a barrel of money
Maybe we're ragged and funny
But we'll struggle along
Singing a song—side by side.

Through all kinds of meetings
What if the stock should fall?
As long as Barlow is laughing
We really didn't mind it at all.

Oh we've had Mooney's charts and we've parted
We're worse off then we started
But we'll struggle along
Singing a song—side by side.

'Tho Harris and Chadwick watched the money
We lost so much it was funny
Still we'll struggle along
Singing a song—side by side.

3. The involvement of the participants with the Game should be more closely regulated. This does not mean that involvement would be lessened, but only that the assigned preparations for other courses and the requirements of the Game would be coordinated more explicitly in order to level the demands placed on the participants.
4. An evaluation of the firms' competitive positions might be made at the midpoint of the program as well as at the end.
5. Game manuals and histories might be provided to the participants before the program begins.

With or without these changes, the Carnegie Tech Management Game, requiring integrated group effort devoted to company-wide planning and coordinating activities, can provide a useful environment for management development.

VI.   EXPERIENCES WITH THE GAME IN AN EVENING PROGRAM

(By Richard W. Deckmann and Thomas P. O'Mara[20])

One session of the Carnegie Tech Management Game was played in the spring semester of 1962–63 in the Carnegie Institute of Technology Evening School Industrial Management Program. This program is a special three-year baccalaureate course of study primarily for individuals who have completed Bachelor's degrees in science and engineering. The Game was substituted for the second semester of a third-year Business Policy Course.

As previously taught, the course was an attempt to integrate the disciplines of marketing, finance, production, statistics, and managerial psychology in a case-oriented, problem-solving experience. In addition, reading assignments and lectures in the five areas of business analysis, planning, organization, staffing, and control ordinarily consumed about 40 percent of the class time and somewhat less of the preparation. In the first semester, primary attention was given to analysis, planning, and business organization. Staffing and control were usually treated in the second semester.

Previous sessions of this class had shown certain problems with this teaching technique. The more obvious ones include an irregular level of preparation, biases of both student and teacher, and single-valued perceptions of case problems—often based on a real-life identification

---

[20]Part-time members of the faculty of Carnegie's Evening School and members of the Commercial Research Department of the United States Steel Corporation. The actual running of the Game was handled under the direction of Neil C. Churchill, with Samuel Beaird and Arnold Kaplan, graduate assistants, running the program and answering questions for the players.

with a particular area.[21] Other shortcomings of the case method as we experienced it include differences in students' verbal ability, which may influence the teacher's perception of the student's understanding; and differential degrees to which students comprehend the discussional nature of the class room experience. Here the extremes are individuals who hesitate to verbalize anything of which they are not absolutely certain, and individuals who continually introduce extraneous material in the small hope that it may have some merit. Lastly, there is the short-range time orientation of the case discussion itself. The student senses that when the class discussion is ended, the problem area—resolved or not—will never be reopened. Hence, in some minds there may be a premium established on achieving an *ad hoc* solution without much anticipation of its long-term consequences. Perhaps this last is the response of some students to the instructor's unwillingness to prescribe specific regimens for case problem ills. Through the Game we hoped to overcome at least some of these shortcomings.

A.   Organizing the Teams

Among our 26 students, 21 already held Bachelor's degrees in engineering or science. Many had received these degrees in the Evening School at Carnegie. The group was divided into three teams (firms) of eight or nine members. In selecting the teams we attempted to put approximately equal numbers of superior, average, and below-average individuals in each firm. A second pattern was also established. One team, #2, was largely composed of the more highly opinionated and argumentative members of the class—as viewed by the instructor during the first semester's work. (A student observer from a business psychology course attended the first five class sessions of this team.) Another team, #3, was composed mostly of the more recessive personalities, and the last team, #1, was made up of the more verbose individuals who contributed freely but not necessarily usefully in previous case discussions. The reasons for this arrangement were that the instructor believed that the real contributions of individuals would be more easily elicited within the group and measured by him if this equation of temperaments was achieved. He also wished to observe the degree to which these personality characteristics influenced efficiency of communication and personal interaction. Effort was also made to insure that people living in the same geographic areas of the

---

[21]See DeWitt C. Dearborn and Herbert A. Simon, "Selective Perception: A Note on the Departmental Identification of Executives," *Sociometry*, Vol. 21, No. 2 (June, 1958), pp. 140–44.

city were associated. Thus, the problem of out-of-class meetings was minimized, but certainly not eliminated.

Each firm had two directors who were, in all cases but one, alumni of the two-year daytime M.S. program in Industrial Administration at Carnegie. The other director was a superior student who had graduated from the Evening School Industrial Management Program the previous year. The directors met with teams for one organizational meeting in which the general outlines of the Management Game were explained and background material distributed. They then attended the sessions following the third and sixth months of play and the annual meeting at the end of the Game.

B.   Team Behavior during Play

The team members elected their presidents and appointed members to function in the areas of finance, production, and marketing. No influence was exerted on these selections. Play—that is, completion of the decision forms—took place in class each week. In the beginning, a one-month's move was made each week. After six such sessions, play was accelerated to complete two moves per week. Nine class sessions were used for making moves.

At least one meeting of each group outside of class occurred each week. They were scheduled by the students on Sunday afternoons or after some other evening class which all members of a team attended. In addition, meetings of the two or three individuals responsible for a certain functional area occurred frequently, and, apparently, innumerable telephone conversations ensued. Obviously, however, meetings were more difficult to arrange than they would have been in a full-time day program.

For the first few sessions, a graduate student with some experience in the Game was available during part of the session to answer procedural questions and to advise about some questions of substance concerning marketing, production, and finance in the Management Game. Class sessions were held on Thursday nights. The decision sheets were coded on punched cards on Friday, the computer run made on Friday or Saturday, and a complete print-out of the results mailed to each student and director on Sunday. Since many of the students had business mailing addresses in the city, almost all received the results of their play by Monday afternoon. This rapid and rather prodigious effort on the part of the School was one element in maintaining student morale during the Game. The students sensed a very real effort being made in their behalf.

After an initial drive to understand the constraints of the Game, some students began at attempt to structure and systematize their functional areas. Much attention was devoted in each of the three firms to obtaining a useful sales forecast. For instance, one individual who was employed as a computer programmer attempted to make a complete regression analysis of all possible variables influencing sales in the previous year's history of play; the results were not used by his team, however.

Morale and interest generally remained at high levels throughout the sessions. Considerable team identification and even emotional involvement occurred. (Several students later suggested that the Game be used in future classes, and two volunteered to act as directors.) However, occasional mistakes in coding made both by the students in completing the decision forms and in the machine analysis dampened team spirits. Where it was not possible to correct the errors because of the time loss involved, they had a significant negative effect on both morale and individual performance.

There was significant variation in the quality and quantity of student contributions, but probably no more than that experienced with this group in the first-semester case course. The three firms handled problems of varied levels of effort in different ways. In Firm #1, an organization pattern seemed to develop in which all requests for work and responsive contributions occurred between the president and the individual involved, with occasional diversion of communications through his one lieutenant. In this team, which was composed of the more verbose individuals, frequent acerbic exchanges occurred.

In the team comprised of the more opinionated members, Firm #2, the president lost control from time to time; and while he may have felt that he was deferring to the expertise of the individuals in each functional subgroup, it appeared to the instructor that he was being manipulated. The directors criticised the actions of the firm vigorously, occasionally telephoning the president to explain their position and request analyses. Offsetting these tension-producing circumstances was the fact that, largely through produce superiority, this firm soon achieved a superior market and profit position. Its members were highly frustrated from time to time, but remained highly motivated and extremely positively oriented toward what was happening to them.

The third group, Firm #3, generally very capable but less extroverted, held quiet and generally longer sessions, spent significantly more time hunting theoretical bases for their business judgments, understood their competitive position more thoroughly, and avoided acrimony in debate as far as could be observed. Partly because of product luck, they found themselves in the poorest competitive position and generally devoted themselves to attempting to maintain share of market with limited advertising resources and poorer products. At year-end they had generated only a small net profit.

In part because of the limited amount of time that teams could spend together between classes, student reaction to the attempt to play two months in one evening was uniformly negative. They also could not anticipate the results of the first month's play in order to play the second intelligently. They were instructed in the beginning that they would not know how many months would be played—that they would be graded on the basis of market position, success in product development, financial (profit) position, and development of production resources. They were specifically cautioned against "end play" in order to get them to emphasize long-run rather than short-run objectives.

Each firm submitted quarterly reports to its board of directors after the first and second quarters of play and an annual report at year-end. The last two of these were mailed to the directors for their study before the respective meetings.

C. Performance Results and Student Reactions

At the end of the twelfth month of play, each student completed in class a questionnaire[22] rating himself and his firm members in terms of six specific performance measures—effort, achievement, communication ability, group influence, cooperation, and management perspective—and in terms of total performance. Each of these terms was defined and associated with an eight-place linear scale. The student marked a code letter for himself and each of his firm's members on every scale. Similar scales were used to rate the expectation of success for each member, social preference for each, and the anticipated average of all total performance ratings for the team. Other questionnaire entries asked the student to diagram the communication network and the influence network which he perceived operating most often during the firm's work sessions. He was also asked to rate his firm's performance in terms of the above measures and indicate, too, his opinion of it as a place to work. Lastly, each student prepared an individual critique detailing the contributions he made during the play and criticising the operation and content of the Game.

Actual business decisions and operations for all three firms were generally conservative. The directors of the firm with a distinct product advantage, for instance, were unable to induce exploitive price behavior (which they sincerely believed to be in the firm's best interest).

A major factor affecting management behavior was the difference in

---

[22]Included in this Chapter as Appendix 6A.

the characteristics of the products available to each firm. As it became evident to Firm #2 that their products were much superior to the others, their principal concerns were raw material inventory management, pricing, and, later, facilities expansion. Firm #3, on the other hand, soon realized that they were being penalized by a relatively poor product line, and, therefore, they placed emphasis on product research, developed a method for rating the overall market value of competitors' products, and adopted a strategy of attempting to conserve profits and market share. Firm #1, with an attractive product, probably did a slightly poorer job of "managing"—placed their emphasis less well and failed to capitalize on a greater number of commercial opportunities.

Analysis of the questionnaire results yielded some insights into the class's attitudes toward the relative importance of various performance and social factors in predicting total performance and business success. On a team-by-team basis, it yielded some very tentative indications of how individuals' perceptions of the relative values of various performance variables may be related to personality. In the first study, we did a regression analysis of each performance factor against total performance, predictions of business success, and social preference. We found high correlations between total performance and all the specific performance elements except cooperation, which apparently was not considered nearly so important. The high correlates with "success" were communications ability, group influence, and management perspective; achievement showed a notably low correlation. Almost all of the relationships between specific performance factors and social pref-

TABLE 6–1

CORRELATIONS BETWEEN QUESTIONNAIRE RESPONSES

	n = 26			
	Total Performance	Success Expected	Social Preference	Group Influence
Effort.....................	.936	.667	.745	.870
Achievement...............	.941	.364	.779	.937
Communication............	.972	.825	.495	.931
Group influence............	.991	.825	.787	x
Cooperation................	.551	.713	.647	.791
Management perspective......	.950	.807	.511	.725
Total performance...........	x	.882	.805	.991
Success....................	.882	x	.720	.825
Social preference............	.805	.720	x	.787
Anticipated total performance.	.966	.736	.751	.914

erence seemed less strong. Lowest were communications ability, management perspective, and cooperation. These correlations, together with similar relationships between performance factors and group influence are shown in Table 6–1.

While the smaller sample size of the individual teams did not permit regression analysis, it was possible to rank each team's total scores for each of the performance factors and compare them with scores for total performance, success, social preference and expected total performance. In this study, Firm #1 ranked its own cooperativeness lower than any other performance factor and lower than total performance, while Firm #2 ranked its cooperativeness *higher* than any other attribute. Firm #3 viewed effort and management perspective as its long suits.

Inspection of individuals' scores shows great consistency among the peer rankings and, except in a few instances, realistic self-concepts, as determined from close agreement between total performance ratings and the anticipated average total performance ratings. Many other comparisons of the questionnaire data are possible. The questions asking for patterns of influence and communication were poorly completed in most cases. It remains to be determined whether the questions were not understood or whether the students were unable to express these relationships.

D. Conclusion

In summary, introduction of the Carnegie Tech Management Game into the Evening School Industrial Management curriculum seemed to result in an intense learning experience. On the basis of student hours expended, it was also a very demanding one. Student comments throughout the Game were highly positive. The Game seemed to us to yield better results than cases had.

Because of differences in product characteristics, no firm generalizations can be made concerning relationships between personality or individual performance factors and team performance. However, interesting inferences can be drawn from student opinions and biases concerning these relationships as measured by questionnaire techniques.

VII. WHAT THESE APPLICATIONS OF THE GAME SHOW

The experiences reported by other users of the Game are valuable for many reasons. They show that even in its early versions, the Game has been adopted successfully by schools other than Carnegie, and more importantly, has been used imaginatively in ways that we did not anticipate and has often been improved in the process. They reemphasize some of the problems of administering the Game and some of the steps that must be taken to integrate it into the curriculum. They provide judgments and evidence about the educational effectiveness of the Game, and they suggest ways in which the Game can be made still better for teaching and research.

The contributors to this chapter have almost all introduced the Carnegie Management Game primarily as a substitute for work with cases and simpler games in business policy or related areas. They differ in what they try to teach. Tulane has put emphasis on teaching the concept of the firm as an integrated system; Pittsburgh, on teaching the use of analytic techniques and on the role of judgment and bargaining in managerial decisions; North Carolina, on the processes of long-range planning and policy making; Carnegie's Program for Executives, on the interrelationship of functional areas, on the need for forward planning, and on the importance of quantitative analysis.

All of the schools using the Game with graduates or undergraduates have adopted boards of directors as an important element of the simulation in order to help lend realism and educational focus to what the players experience. North Carolina has used the same board for all the teams in the industry, and Tulane has used the same board to serve equivalent teams in different industries when several Games are run at once. Such steps provide enough work to justify teaching credit for the faculty members who serve and, at the same time, minimize the number of directors who must be recruited and may contribute to greater uniformity in assigning grades. The executive program of the Bell Telephone Company of Pennsylvania provides strong evidence for the effectiveness of boards of directors when the Game is played by experienced managers.

Apart from agreement about the usefulness of boards of directors, ideas for embellishing the Game diverge. Tulane pioneered in building labor negotiations and a "live" stock market activity into the Game; and they have also related the Game closely to work in managerial controls, systems, and human relations. The Carnegie Evening School group sought ways to bring players into fruitful contact with other students in a managerial psychology course. Pittsburgh is looking for ways to incorporate problems of insurance and risk management into the Game. North Carolina has taken a different tack: rather than build role-playing exercises around the Game, they have sought to improve the Game model itself by complicating the set of decisions that the production manager can make and by lessening the predictability of consumer demand.

Notably at North Carolina, the Game has stimulated the faculty to develop simulations of their own: on the one hand, a separate retailing game (just as we have developed a separate marketing game at Carnegie) and, on the other, programs to replicate on the computer the plans and decisions of reasonable human Game teams.

The successes and failures at all the schools emphasize one of the most important things which we have learned at Carnegie, sometimes at considerable cost in player morale. It is critically important in adopting the Game to allocate enough time and enough resources to pretest the running of the Game and to orient faculty members and students to the Game's scope and limitations. Anshen's comments on our first use of the Game in Carnegie's Program for Executives presents the issue most clearly, but the other authors give the same advice. The early problems of inadequate instructions for the team members and insufficient histories have been overcome in this volume and in the materials which accompany it. Many of the problems of adapting the Game to your own computer facilities will be eased considerably, we hope, by the *Administrator's Manual* for the Game. But other problems can only be solved by thorough and unhurried local planning and preparation and by faculty and administrative support of the Game while it is in progress.

Persuading faculty people or outsiders to participate in the Game has not been a major problem for the schools reporting in this chapter. Clearly, though, for some faculty members, evidence of what the Game can do and credit for participating in it are prerequisites to their involvement with it.[23] Maintaining faculty and computation-center staff, though, who are familiar with the Game model and with how to run it, is a problem for all of the users, including Carnegie.[24]

The users report a variety of ways of selecting teams (including an attempt to group men on the basis of their aggressiveness in class discussions). Most seem to have decided as we have, though, that it is best to let the teams which are selected make their own allocations of job titles and job assignments to their members. Faculty imposition of organizational structure is resented. None of the users reports success

---

[23]For an extended discussion of the process of getting administrative and faculty support and participation in educational and research uses of gaming, see William R. Dill, James R. Jackson, and James W. Sweeney (eds.), *Proceedings of the Conference on Business Games as Teaching Devices* (New Orleans: Tulane University, 1961), pp. 30-34.

[24]As this book goes to press, we have just received inquiries from a school which wants to resume using the Mark 1 version of the Carnegie Game, but which has no one on the campus who knows how earlier runs were conducted. They have discarded the limited information that had been accumulated as documentation for the Mark 1 program, they have discarded the program decks and tapes, and they have lost the services of the people who had managed the earlier runs. Even with the better documentation that we are now offering for the Mark 1.5 version, efforts to insure continuity of knowledgeable staff remain important.

in getting members of teams to rotate job assignments although North Carolina does require each team member to be thoroughly familiar with the jobs of his teammates. Despite the complexity of the task, the reports show that part-time students can meet in large enough groups frequently enough to benefit from experience in the Game if some allowance for them to get together is made in selecting the teams and scheduling the sessions.[25]

Most users have decided that the advantages of a longer span of play outweigh the artificialities of asking men to make moves for two or three months at a time. Tulane and North Carolina have experimented, as we have, with ways of letting teams write "policies" and "decision programs" that will let them delegate routine decision making to the Game administrators or to the computer. The most difficult problems arise, perhaps, in short-term executive programs where, even with two- and three-month moves, it is difficult to let teams play long enough to see the longer-range consequences of their decisions.

All contributors regard the grading of team performance as a difficult task. Tulane and North Carolina report the most explicit solutions. Despite the problems which all early users encountered, enthusiasm is reported as high. The contributors to this chapter have differing ideas about the relative merit of the Game versus cases, but after trying mixtures of the two, all seem to be planning more rather than less emphasis on the Game in future programs.

Each contributor has his own estimate of the major educational benefits that students derive. They range from Deckmann and O'Mara's clinical observations of the changes in teams of evening students over the course of a semester to Levin's report from North Carolina on how the students' actions in the Game helped highlight strengths and weaknesses in other parts of the curriculum. Our next chapter is devoted to discussing the educational effects of the Game in more detail.

---

[25]In the view of observers who have watched both full-time graduate students and part-time evening students play the Game, though, it seems clear that full-time students have the advantage. They bring a more varied set of ideas and tools to the Game from previous courses, and even though special efforts can be made in evening programs to help students get together, it is impossible to provide evening students with the kinds of opportunities to work together in making decisions that full-time students have. Clearly a game like the Carnegie Game requires a large investment of player time if decisions are to be made on more than a crudely judgmental basis.

Performance

Rate the members of your firm (from highest to lowest, with a code letter) for their:

1. *Effort*

   | 8 (high)   (low) 0 |

   Initiative demonstrated, perserverence exercised and time expended.

2. *Achievement*

   | 8   0 |

   Success in understanding their particular business areas, in developing plans, and in devising techniques to manage their problems.

3. *Communication*

   | 8   0 |

   Ability to make their thoughts and plans *understood* by the group.

4. *Group Influence*

   | 8   0 |

   Success in getting their ideas *considered* and their plans *put into practice*.

5. *Cooperation*

   | 8   0 |

   Their willingness and capacity to understand the *other individual* problem areas and to work *outside* their own area of responsibility.

6. *Management Perspective*

   | 8   0 |

   Ability to relate the importance of the various management functions and to plan an act in the overall best interest of the firm.

7. *Total Performance*

   | 8   0 |

   Demonstrated ability to combine any or all of the above characteristics—and others which you found to be important—to contribute to the firm's effectiveness.

   What other factors did you consider in evaluating "Total Performance"?

8. Rate the firm members in the way you think the other members' rating will *average out*.

|
| 8 (high)   (low) 0 |

Communication

Here are some theoretically possible communications networks. Select one and modify it, or draw your own to describe the pattern of communication that usually occurred when your team met. Letter the circles. If a single pattern (or two) will not describe the communication in your group, omit this answer.

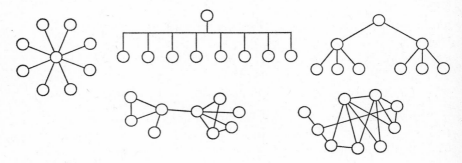

Influence

Draw another diagram to indicate how *influence* (orders, requests for information, judgments, decisions) flowed from person to person. Use arrowheads to indicate direction of flow. Letter the circles. Draw a double circle around the most influential person.

Rate the *team* performance, by a check mark, in the following areas:

1. Effort

|
| 8 (high)   (low) 0 |

2. Achievement

|
| 8   0 |

3. Cooperation

|
| 8   0 |

4. Management Perspective

|
| 8   0 |

5. Communication

|
| 8   0 |

6. Group Influence

|
| 8   0 |

Rate the members of your firm (from highest to lowest, with a code letter) to show your expectation of their probable success as business executives.

| 8 (high)   (low) 0 |

Rate the members of your firm to show your preferences for them socially.

| 8 (high)   (low) 0 |

In your opinion, is this firm a good place to work? (Check mark.)

| 8 (high)   (low) 0 |

Chapter 7

STUDENT REACTIONS TO THE GAME [1]

A complex business simulation like the Carnegie Game provides students with an opportunity to acquire useful experience in working in an organizational setting and in trying to solve managerial problems. The student papers reprinted in Chapter 5 and the discussions of how the Game fits with various courses and programs in Chapters 5 and 6 provide evidence of some of the kinds of learning that the Game experience produces. In this chapter, we look at the kinds of things which students themselves say they have learned from participating in the Game and examine some of the factors which affect their interest and involvement in it. The data of this chapter are from runs of the Game in the M.S. program in Industrial Administration at Carnegie. The data do not answer all the questions that might be asked about the Game's educational impact, but it is hoped they will stimulate further studies of the Game's effectiveness as a teaching device and additional experiments with its design and administration.[2]

---

[1] In preparing this chapter we have drawn freely on two papers: William R. Dill, "The Educational Effects of Management Games," in William R. Dill, James R. Jackson, and James W. Sweeney (eds.), *Proceedings of the Conference on Business Games as Teaching Devices* (New Orleans: Tulane University, 1961); and William R. Dill and Neil Doppelt, "The Acquisition of Experience in a Complex Management Game," *Management Science*, Vol. 10, No. 1 (October 1963), pp. 30-46.

[2] A variety of efforts to assess the effects of management games are underway. The subjective evaluations of many game developers and users are summarized in Kalman J. Cohen and Eric Rhenman, "The Role of Management Games in Education and Research," *Management Science*, Vol. 7, No. 2 (January 1961), pp. 131-66; and in Dill, Jackson and Sweeney, *op. cit.* For a study which compares a production management course based only on cases with a course based both on cases and participation in a game, see James L. McKenney, "An Evaluation of Business Games as a Learning Experience," *Journal of Business*, Vol. 35, No. 3 (July 1962), pp. 278-86. James Robinson of Northwestern is undertaking an experiment to compare games, cases, and problem papers as a means of teaching decision-making skills in political science. He summarizes the basic case for games this way:

—In contrast to other methods of instruction, games make students be more explicit about what they are doing, seeing, and hearing. Games give them quick feedback about the quality of their decisions. Games also heighten students' interest and motivation.

—As a result, games may be superior to other methods of instruction in producing learning which is general and structural and not bound to specialized content or issues, which integrates the processes by which decisions are reached with the substantive issues in the decisions, and which reinforces factual material provided through earlier reading or discussion.

From 1959–60 through 1963–64, there have been ten runs of the Game with second-year M.S. students at Carnegie. Organized in teams of six to eight men, these men played the Game for a full semester. Each year there have been six teams, organized in two parallel but separate industries. In 1959–60 and 1960–61, the Game was required as an ungraded supplement to a full schedule of courses. Since 1961–62, the Game has been graded and has counted as one course in the students' regular schedule. Team members averaged 6–12 hours of work per man during each week of play over the semester (although key members have reported spending 30–40 hours in key weeks).

I. A REVIEW OF THE GAME'S EDUCATIONAL OBJECTIVES

As part of the integrative stem of the M.S. curriculum, the Game was designed to challenge students to deal effectively with the kinds of problems that real executives face. The Game should help students realize that decisions made in different areas of management and made at different points of time are interrelated and that the organization and procedures for making decisions have consequences for the quality that results. In addition the Game should help students develop:

1. An ability to formulate strategic objectives and to derive from them operational targets against which performance can be measured.
2. An ability to seek out and evaluate information from the mass of data that a complex and diffuse environment makes available, and an ability to organize it so that it provides a useful guide to future decisions.
3. An ability to forecast, plan, and take action to achieve planned outcomes in a situation where there are hundreds, rather than dozens, of variables to be coordinated and controlled.
4. An ability to combine the role of generalist and specialist and to handle decision problems whose solution rests on imaginative and thorough analysis as well as those whose solution rests on fast, intuitive judgments.
5. An ability to work effectively with other people on the team and with groups outside the company.

To develop these skills, the Game is designed and administered to provide four major kinds of experience: competitive, negotiating, organizational, and reflective. *Competitive* experience refers to the job described in Chapter 2 of interpreting the history of the simulated company which a team runs and of making new sets of decisions which —in interaction with other teams' decisions and with the computer model—will insure the company's survival and growth. Here the students are working with qualitative and quantitative outputs of the com-

---

See James Robinson, "A Research Design for Comparing Simulation with Case Studies and Problem Papers in Teaching Political Science," in Dill, Jackson, and Sweeney, *op. cit.*, pp. 123–29.

puter and are trying to discover how they can set their decisions to generate the kinds of outputs they desire. The team has the opportunity to develop complex programs within each of the functional areas, but faces the continuing challenge of making the programs and proposals for action fit with each other and with the overall goals of the firm.

Negotiating experience arises from requirements that the teams deal periodically with the kinds of outside groups that the management of a real company would have to work with. The primary external group is a board of directors (made up of faculty members with, for teams since 1961–62, one or two executives from industry). Other outside groups with whom the teams have dealt have included auditors, union representatives, and bankers. The auditors do an audit of financial statements for the first "year" of play, evaluate management's decision-making and control procedures, and make a report to management and the board of directors. The union representatives can introduce grievances at any time and intervene near the end of the first "year" of play to negotiate a new wage contract with the teams. The bankers pass on company requests for loans and decide the conditions that firms must meet when loans are granted.

Organizational experience comes from the challenge of designing, setting up, and maintaining a team organization that can cope with the analytic and negotiating tasks and that can survive as a functioning unit until the end of the semester. The job is complicated because the boards of directors require the teams to define formally both a structure and rules of operation for themselves and expect the teams to justify their plans. The competitive task is complex enough to reinforce the boards' demands for organizational planning. All teams differentiate on the basis of function, so that different members are in charge of relatively limited areas of the company's activity. Most teams also establish a hierarchy, with a president or chairman who is expected to lead and to coordinate and with one or two levels of management below him. Boards may—but seldom do—ask for men to change job assignments midway through the Game. Rarely, boards have replaced presidents whose performance has been unsatisfactory.

Anticipatory and *reflective* experience during the Game comes largely from assignments made in other courses that build on what is happening in the Game. There are two kinds of reflective assignments to which most students have been exposed as they play the Game. One kind, in conjunction with a course in the administrative process, asks them periodically to discuss or write about the organization of their team: ways in which it has developed, the motivations of its members, its approaches to particular kinds of problems. The other kind, part of a course in operations research methods, asks them to take a problem from the Game which is amenable to an operations research approach and to develop a solution using the techniques that they have learned.[3]

Some early discussions of the educational effects of games[4] stressed the links between these effects and the basic design of the Game model, that is, the learning that comes from the competitive experience which a game provides. It has become increasingly clear, though, that the total design of a management game for educational purposes includes not only the computer model but the procedures for running it and for fitting it into the curriculum.

II. SOME OBSERVATIONS ON THE LEARNING PROCESS[5]

From observations by faculty directors and from questionnaire data that students provided in the 1960–61 and 1961–62 runs of the Game, we can describe some of the ways in which learning occurs in the Game. In this section, we summarize our major findings about what students learn; about changes in the pattern of learning as play progresses; and about relationships between learning and such variables as motivation, position of team, and prior experience of special kinds that students bring to the Game.

A. Observed Changes in Players' Behavior

It is clear that student performance within the Game improves during the semester of play. Much of the improvement is in their ability to handle the analytic tasks which the computer model and the actions of their competitors pose. They do become quicker and more sophisticated about abstracting, organizing, and using information from a complex and diffuse environment. They recognize better the differences between valuable and trivial information. They make more elaborate and subtle inferences about the relation of past results to future decisions. They coordinate information and actions more effectively between the separate functional areas of marketing, production, and finance.

Their forecasts generally improve in accuracy, and their plans are based on more rational assumptions. In a variety of contexts, such as planning market research expenditures, scheduling equipment mainte-

---

[3]A more detailed description of what the negotiating, organizational, and reflective tasks involve is provided in Chapters 3 and 5.

[4]For example, *Proceedings of the National Symposium on Management Games* (Lawarence, Kan.: Center for Research in Business, University of Kansas, 1959).

[5]In summarizing and interpreting questionnaire data for this section, most of which has been taken from Dill and Doppelt, *op. cit.*, we wish to acknowledge the help of William Fox of the University of Florida and Donald Burns of the Bell Telephone Company of Pennsylvania.

nance, budgeting advertising, or planning a new factory or warehouse, they learn how economic concepts like marginal analysis or return on investment apply to specific management decisions. They gain experience with the power—and the limits—of quantitative decision rules. They become more careful about testing specific decision proposals against general policies they have agreed on, and they see more clearly the interactions between current decisions and future competitive position.

In working with outside groups like the boards of directors, they get good practice in expressing themselves to a skeptical and sometimes hostile audience. Over the course of a semester, we usually notice improvement in the level of preparation for meetings, in the skill with which ideas are presented, in the tenacity with which ideas are defended, and in the subtlety with which teams control the agenda of meetings and the direction which discussion takes.

Within their organizations, students become more sensitive to the factors involved in establishing and maintaining effective working relationships with their teammates, and they get better at anticipating and solving the problems of coordination and control which the Game poses. They have varying degrees of success in setting goals and schedules, in meeting deadlines, and in handling the problems of motivation and influence that must sometimes be faced within the team.

The Game also has stimulated players to consider basic questions of judgment and value. They must constantly review and appraise the objectives which they have set for themselves and must justify their choices to the boards of directors. They must face issues of compromise within the team about goals, decision rules, and procedures. They sometimes must subordinate personal ties with classmates in favor of necessary decisions about organizational relationships, particularly with incompetent or lazy team members. Pressures to win raise issues of competitive ethics *vis-à-vis* other teams and the administrator of the Game.

B.   The Level of Learning

We had hoped that learning in the Game might be learning "in depth" that students could—and would—transfer readily to new situations. As Robinson points out,[6] many people have argued that games make students more explicit about what they are doing and produce learning that is "general and structural" rather than bound to specialized content or issues. Impressions that this is so are still held firmly by most faculty observers of the Game, but firm evidence has been hard to find.

---

[6]Robinson, *op. cit.*

There is no doubt that a great deal of what students learn is partial learning or pertains only to playing the Game more effectively. Without stimulation or assistance to make learning explicit or to generalize, they may not apply their experience outside the Game. After the 1961–62 run, we asked the players to write down what they had learned from playing the Game. We coded the answers, and as Table 7–1 shows, almost two thirds of the statements about what was learned simply reflected new recognition that certain problems exist for managers. This is an important kind of learning, to be sure, because many of management's failures are failures to recognize or acknowledge problems. But it can still be regarded as a lower level of learning than learning in a specific or general way how to deal with a problem. Only 3 percent of the statements were explicit, specific descriptions of the solutions or strategies that had been learned.

TABLE 7–1

CODED REFERENCES TO LEVELS OF LEARNING (1961–62 RUNS)

Level of Learning (Main Code Category)	Observed	Percent of References ($n = 126$)		
		Expected I (Equal Chance, Main Categories)	Expected II (Equal Chance, Subcategories)*	
Problem recognition.......	66%	33%	50%	
General solutions..........	31	33	38	
Specific solutions..........	3	33	12	
Totals.............	100%	100%	100%	

Results of chi-square test: p (Obs. same distribution as Exp. I) $< .001$
p (Obs. same distribution as Exp. II) $< .01$

*Computed because the number of possible subcategories into which an answer could be placed as an example of "problem recognition," as an example of a "general solution," or as an example of a "specific solution" were unequal. Hence if coding were done on an entirely random basis, by subcategories, 50 percent of the answers would have been coded as "problem recognition," etc.

Interviews with team members after several of the Game runs reinforce the questionnaire findings. It is easy to get good suggestions from players about how they would change their behavior if they were to play the Game again. It is much more difficult when you ask for more general kinds of learning to get players to move from statements of what they "learned about" to statements of what they "learned."

A desire to increase both the explicitness and generality of learning in the Game has been a primary motivation in our adding reflective assignments in other courses. These are "off-line" assignments as far as Game play is concerned, but they stimulate students to review and extend their Game experiences. The reflective assignments in both the administrative process and the operations research course have been judged by the instructors as very productive. The success of the operations research assignment stemmed from the motivation students had to choose complex problems whose solution was important to their performance in the Game, and from the experience students got with the difficulties of adapting operations research techniques to the problem they had chosen and the information they had to work with. The success of the administrative process assignments stemmed from the fundamental differences between students' approach to problems that are their own and problems that are someone else's. The teams had to contend with many of the classic problems of management organization that people have written textbooks and cases about. Frequently in a case discussion, students will argue that the best solution is to hire a more intelligent group of managers. But since, in the Game, their own attitudes and behavior had created the problems, they could not so easily dismiss the task of learning how to prevent or solve them.

While we would still like to find ways to increase what students take out of the Game, there is at least one dimension in which the Game has had more impact on future behavior than other devices, such as case studies and field projects, which we have used at Carnegie to give students experience with "the real world." Problems which the Game raises have caught the interest of many students and become the focus for further work in courses or on the students' own time. The yield so far is several published papers[7] and the beginning of several doctoral dissertations.[8]

C. The Dominance of Interpersonal Experiences as a Source of Learning

Although many kinds of learning occur in the Game and although students may spend more time working alone with data and decisions than in working with one another or with faculty directors, students remember what they learn from interactions with other people more vividly than they remember what they learn from working on the competitive tasks in the Game. For example, after the 1959–60 run, one of

----

[7]Of the research papers reprinted in Chapter 8, four of these were initiated and carried through solely by graduate students. A fifth—the paper by William R. Dill, William Hoffman, Harold J. Leavitt, and Thomas O'Mara—involved two faculty members as co-authors but originated with a study that Hoffman and O'Mara undertook in one of their second-year courses.

[8]Two of these have now been completed: Yuji Ijiri, "Goal Oriented Models for Accounting and Control" 1963; and George H. Haines, Jr., "A Study of Innovation on Nondurable Goods," 1964.

the teams met with its board of directors and with other interested faculty members for an intensive informal discussion of what they had learned. Of the six teams that year, this was the one which from the beginning had the best morale and the smoothest running organization. It was also the most profitable firm in the industry. Yet roughly half their comments pertained to organizational learning; for example:

I learned a great deal about coordination and what it really means and what is needed to get it done.

You must make definite decisions in a limited time—even when you have little time to work on them.

We had to be able to justify things [to the board] as well as to get them done.

One thing we naturally did ... was to establish routines and get things set up so that they would become easier. .... This allowed us to place greater emphasis on longer-range planning in all areas.

I have learned to look for influence patterns and have learned about their importance in a way which I don't think I would have done just from the courses only.

More evidence of the greater impact of interpersonal modes of learning comes from the 1961–62 runs. At the end, students were asked to write a brief summary of what they had learned. These summaries were coded on several dimensions, one of which was designed to assess how much of the learning was:

Team-derived; i.e., derived primarily from the experience of participating as a member of a small group.

Externally-derived; i.e., derived primarily from experiences with outside groups like boards of directors, auditors, and labor negotiators.

Model-derived; i.e., derived from experiences with the computer model, with the rules of play, and with the tasks of making good management decisions.

Of these three sources of learning, the first two are primarily interpersonal; the third is primarily impersonal.

Even if we allow for the fact that there were more subcategories for coding *T–D* learning (20 subcategories) than for coding *E–D* (9) or *M–D* (10) learning, most of the reported learning stemmed from participation in team activities. As Table 7–2 shows, only 12 percent of the coded responses[9] reflected impersonal, model-derived learning.

Looking at the same thing another way, of 42 students who had at least one coded response, 29 (69 percent) referred *solely* to learning that resulted from experiences within the team or with outside groups (see Table 7–3). No respondent referred solely to learning from expe-

---

[9]The median number of coded responses per student was 3; the range for 43 students was 0–5. Coded units could represent passages varying in length from a phrase to a paragraph or more.

riences with the Game model. Even allowing for the crudeness of the coding process used, the emphasis on interpersonal learning is greater than we would expect by chance alone.

TABLE 7-2

CODED REFERENCES TO LEARNING DERIVED FROM DIFFERENT SOURCES (1961–62 RUNS)

Kind of Learning (Main Code Category)	Percent of References ($n = 126$)		
	Observed	Expected I (Equal Chance, Main Categories)	Expected II (Equal Chance, Subcategories)
Team derived.............	76%	33%	51%
Externally derived..........	12	33	23
Model derived.............	12	33	26
Totals.............	100%	100%	100%

Results of chi-square test: p (Obs. same distribution as Exp. I) $<.001$
p (Obs. same distribution as Exp. II) $<.001$

TABLE 7-3

VARIETY OF STUDENTS' REFERENCES TO DIFFERENT LEARNING SOURCES (1961–62 RUNS)

Mix of Learning References	Percent of Respondents ($n = 42$)		
	Observed	Expected I (Equal Chance, Main Categories)	Expected II (Equal Chance, Subcategories)
Solely team or externally derived...............	69%	33%	46%
Mixed of team or externally derived and model derived.................	31	60	50
Solely model derived........	0	7	4
Totals.............	100%	100%	100%

Results of chi-square test: p (Obs. same distribution as Exp. I) $<.001$
p (Obs. same distribution as Exp. II) $<.01$

Although we might also expect that learning derived from interpersonal experiences would be more explicit than learning derived from interaction with the model, there was no evidence that this was true. We looked to see if $T-D$ learning and $E-D$ learning were more explicit than $M-D$ learning. All responses were coded to show whether they simply indicated learning that certain kinds of problems existed or whether they indicated that general or specific solutions to the problems had also been learned. Interpersonal learning was not more explicit, by this measure, than impersonal learning. Of 111 references to $T-D$ or $E-D$ learning, 38 (34 percent) reflected learning of solutions. Of 15 references to $M-D$ learning, 5 (33 percent) reflected learning of solutions.

D. Changes in Learning as the Game Progresses

On the 1961 questionnaire, as a supplement to asking players what they had learned, we asked them to indicate what they saw as their main challenges both at the beginning and at the end of the Game. One would hypothesize that the main challenges a team perceived would change as the Game progressed, and that in the Carnegie Tech Game, the progression might be the following:

—Initial focus on problems of organization. The boards of directors want a plan of organization; the team members want to agree on organizational arrangements to reduce the amount of ambiguity and uncertainty they have to contend with; and the magnitude of the total Game task relative to the time available for play requires that a team organize early if it is to do even an adequate job of running its company.

—Subsequent focus on problems of maintaining the firm as an operating entity. Once organized and once past the first two or three sets of decisions, teams are in a reasonable position to begin trying to outguess their competitors and the computer model and to begin looking for rational rather than random rules for selecting among decision alternatives. Teams are under pressure from their own leadership and from the boards of directors to build a strong, stable competitive position for their firm—usually to aim for 40–45 percent of the market and profits in a three-team industry.

—Still later, primary interest in challenges of experimentation and innovation. Once a team has organized and stabilized its competitive position, if it does not lose interest in the Game, its major challenges lie in seeking ways to enliven play for themselves and competitors and in exploring alternative strategies that it could not afford to try when it was trying first to understand and control is environment.

The difference between what students saw as challenges before and after the Game in the 1961–62 run reflect this sequence of challenges. Students were asked at both points to list the problems they saw for themselves (1) in making an effective personal contribution to the work of the team, (2) in helping the team achieve a good record of profits and growth, and (3) in dealing with the board of directors. Answers were coded in two ways.

The first coding was of the answer as a whole: To what does it give primary emphasis? Problems of personal adjustment and team organization? Problems of controlling interactions with the Game model and with competitors? Problems of relations with the board? Answers which stressed the first of these were judged to be stressing organizational issues. Answers which stressed the last two were judged to be stressing maintenance of the company's position and innovation to improve that position. (It was not possible in the answers to discriminate reliably between maintenance and innovation.)

As Table 7–4 shows, the heaviest pre-Game emphasis was clearly on organizational challenges; the heaviest post-Game emphasis, on problems of maintenance and innovation.

TABLE 7–4

PRE-GAME TO POST-GAME SHIFTS IN MAIN CHALLENGE OF GAME (1961–62 RUNS)

| Pre-Game: Number of Students Naming | Post-Game: Number of Students Naming | | | Totals |
	Personal and Team	Game Management	Relations with Board	
Personal and team challenge.........	6	17	3	26
Game management challenge........	1	6	0	7
Relations with board challenge......	1	0	1	2
Totals......................	8	23	4	35

Results of chi-square test: p (Post-Game same distribution as pre-Game) <.01

The second coding was a more qualitative analysis of answers to the three subparts of the question separately. This coding checked with the first. The stress on problems of individuals' fitting into the team or on problems of the team's working together effectively dropped off sharply during the Game both in numbers of people mentioning such challenges and in the length of the answers given. The stress on Game maintenance factors roughly doubled.

Both pre-Game and post-Game, the most frequently named personal challenges were those of living within the time constraints that the Game imposed and those of maintaining personal interest in the Game. Otherwise, the pre-Game personal challenges were mostly reflections of ambitions for self-development: the need to develop qualities like patience, sociability, tolerance, ambition, or aggressiveness or the need to acquire certain kinds of knowledge. After the Game, though, the secondary personal challenges had little to do with self-development. In their place were the problems of the "organization man"—how to submit gracefully to team objectives or team practices that you do not agree with.

The stress on team matters also shifted in nature. Before the Game players wrote about themselves as individuals in relation to the team: I must help avoid friction, I must take responsibility, and so on. They put high priority on the maintenance of harmony and on the avoidance of conflict. After the Game, they were more concerned with action than harmony. They were concerned about attitudes that the team had developed, about the effects of these attitudes on team performance, and about what they could do to change or control the behavior of others on the team.

With respect to challenges of maintaining their company's position, the post-Game comments differed from pre-Game comments mostly by reflecting a greater knowledge of how the Game worked and by describing problems and challenges in more detail. There seemed to be a slight trend in the post-Game comments toward more attention to problems of innovation—developing quantitative decision rules, reducing the amounts of routine analysis that have to be done, finding ways to be "more aggressive" with competitors, and seeking improved relationships with the boards of directors.

E. The Sources of Motivation and Interest

We tried to assess students' motivation before and after the Game by asking them to indicate on a five-point scale how likely they would be to participate in the Game if it were voluntary rather than compulsory. In retrospect this may not have been a very good measure. It is not clear from the data that the players with the highest interest post-Game worked any harder at the Game or learned any more from it on the average than the less-interested players.

Still, taking this measure of interest as one index of motivation, what affects interest levels of players in the Game? First of all, as studies of satisfaction suggest,[10] much of the motivation to take part in something like a management game has little to do with experiences in the Game. Initial expressions of interest tend to persist through the Game. Table 7–5 shows that a higher proportion of students than we would expect by chance did not change their level of interest between the beginning and the end of play. Fewer than we would expect by chance made large shifts up or down on the interest scale.

A second hypothesis about the factors affecting interest says that motivation will depend on team performance. Table 7–6 shows that post-Game interest ratings, averaged by teams, have a closer relation to the teams' profits than they do to pre-Game interest ratings. Persistent

---

[10]For example: Uno Remitz, *Professional Satisfaction among Swedish Bank Employees* (Copenhagen: Munksgaard, 1960).

experiences of failure, as one might expect, seem to be particularly damaging to interest in the Game.

TABLE 7–5

PRE-GAME TO POST-GAME SHIFTS IN INTEREST LEVEL (1961–62 RUNS)

Point Spread between Pre-Game and Post-Game Answers	Observed	Expected (Equal Chance, Given Initial Distribution)
0..............	12	7.6
1..............	18	12.2
2..............	5	8.7
3..............	2	6.5
4..............	1	3.1

Results of chi-square test: p (Obs. same distribution as Exp.) $<.01$

TABLE 7–6

PRE-GAME INTEREST, POST-GAME INTEREST, AND PROFIT PERFORMANCE (1961–62 RUNS)

Team	Mean Pre-Game Interest	Mean Post-Game Interest	Total Profit (12 Months— Millions of Dollars)
A1.............	3.5	3.8	$39.7
A2.............	4.0	3.0	18.8
A3.............	4.1	3.0	33.4
B1.............	4.2	3.9	67.5
B2.............	3.4	3.1	46.5
B3.............	4.5	4.0	71.6
	$r = .23$	$r = .86$	

Limited evidence from the 1962–63 runs of the Game suggests that being in last place and nearly bankrupt may not be as damaging to the morale as being in last place and profitable. At the end of the 1962–63 runs, two teams were struggling to recover from very precarious financial situations; the two middle teams were beginning to feel that they had a chance to overtake the leaders; and the two top teams were realizing that their dominance of their respective industries was not as sure as it had once seemed. In such a situation on an indirect, but quantitative measure of morale, there were no significant differences among the teams.

None of these hypotheses fully explains the wide variations in post-Game interest that show up among the individual players, though. Let us look further for links between interest and activities in the Game. To the extent that experiences in the Game do matter, is it the job that a man does which matters or is it the influence that is atributed to him by his teammates?

The answer seems clearly to be that job matters more than influence position. There is no relation between post-Game interest ratings and post-Game ratings of which men on each team were most and least influential. But it is clear from data gathered in both the 1960–61 and 1961–62 runs that while men going into different functional jobs had relatively homogenous degrees of interest before the Game, men in some jobs lost interest more rapidly than men in others did as the Game progressed. After the Game, presidents and marketing managers —the men with the most difficult and time consuming jobs—have consistently been happiest about their experiences. The finance, production, and research and development managers were next most satisfied. The controllers, operations research specialists, and executive vice presidents were least satisfied. The least-satisfying jobs are so in part because within the context of the Game they are regarded as routine and unchallenging—they offer the fewest opportunities to learn or to take actions that will affect the fortunes of the team.

Morale and involvement seem, finally, to depend a great deal on the way in which the faculty conducts the Game as a course. Where we have observed severe breaks in student interest, these can often be traced to instances where the faculty directors have been disinterested in the Game or have been casual, arbitrary, or unrealistic in some of their actions. If grades are assigned, the students expect that a reasonable effort will be made to make grading standards consistent across teams. Students have also been sensitive to features of the Game that add to the load of routine work they must do without adding to the educational challenge, to program errors and machine difficulties which disrupt the ability to schedule meetings of their teams on a regular basis, and to mid-Game decisions by the Game administrator or banker that may on the one hand solve an emergency like a bankruptcy but that on the other hand seem to change the rules of play or to give one team an unanticipated advantage over the others.

F. Relation of Learning to Activities in the Game and to Prior Experience

It is not clear from the limited range of our experience at Carnegie how learning in a game depends on the jobs that players perform, but it is clear that these relationships are very important and are worth further study. Each functional officer has his own set of tasks to perform. The president and two or three others on the team are likely to dominate interactions with the boards of directors, and the production manager and the president have the best opportunities to learn from negotiations with the union. The controllers in the 1961–62 Game run found that their experience as auditors of the previous year's teams was helpful in developing satisfactory systems of internal controls, but many others on the 1961–62 teams indicated that the audit experience had little or no effect on their Game play.

The data of Tables 7–7 and 7–8, although of questionable reliability, suggest some of the differences in learning opportunities that different positions may afford. From Table 7–7, it seems that presidents, executive vice presidents, and men in charge of marketing and production learn more than men in other positions do. Table 7–8 (based on data from the previous year, 1960–61) confirms this impression. On a list

TABLE 7–7

ASPECTS OF LEARNING VS. POSITION IN THE GAME:
AMOUNTS, SOURCES, AND LEVELS OF LEARNING (1961–62 RUNS)

Position	Amount No. of Codings per Man	Sources			Levels	
		Team Derived	Externally Derived	Model Derived	Problem Recognition	General and Specific Solutions
Presidents and executive vice presidents (8 men)...	3.4	63%	15%	22%	74%	26%
Vice presidents, marketing (6 men)........	3.8	87	9	4	61	39
Vice presidents, production (5 men)........	3.6	72	17	11	56	44
Vice presidents, finance (6 men)..	2.3	71	8	21	86	14
Controllers (5 men)........	2.2	100	0	0	73	27
Research & development men and marketing assistants (8 men)........	2.8	73	18	9	64	36
Operations research men and other assistants (4 men)........	2.0	80	10	10	50	50

of "factors" in the Game environment, the principal officers of teams were better able to recognize the differences in importance between relevant and irrelevant "factors" than the planners (mostly marginal team members) were. Tables 7–7 and 7–8 also suggest differences among positions in the sources, levels, and foci of learning.

TABLE 7–8

Aspects of Learning vs. Position in the Game:
Importance Ascribed by Men to Specific Factors in the Game Environment
(1960–61 Runs)

Position	Mean Degree of Importance Ascribed (Scale: 0, Low; 6, High)			
	15 Factors Relevant to Marketing	11 Factors Relevant to Production	2 Factors Relevant to Finance	9 Actually Irrelevant Factors
Presidents (5 men)...............	4.7	3.7	3.8	1.5
Marketing officers (8 men).........	5.1	3.1	3.3	1.2
Production officers (5 men)........	4.0	3.7	2.6	1.6
Finance officers (6 men)...........	4.3	3.0	2.9	1.0
Planners (5 men).................	5.1	5.1	3.6	3.0

A questionnaire administered after the 1962–63 run provides further evidence that at least perceived opportunities to learn are greatest for team presidents, next greatest for production and marketing men, and least for financial managers and controllers in the Game. Each man was asked to indicate on a scale how each of the 26 features of the Game had contributed to what he had learned from the Game. Table 7–9 shows the percentage of items which had a positive, neutral, and negative effect on learning for the men in the different positions.

TABLE 7–9

Perceived Contribution to Learning of 26 Features of the Game (1962–63 Runs)

Position	Average Percent of the 26 Features Rated as Contributing to Learning in a:		
	Very Positive or Positive Way	Mixed Fashion or in No Way	Negative or Very Negative Way
Presidents (6 men).........	53%	40%	7%
Production officers (5 men)..	43	49	8
Marketing and research and development officers (13 men)...................	41	46	13
Financial officers and controllers (9 men)........	26	64	10

What players learn also seems to depend greatly on the experience and attitudes which they bring to the Game. Trial runs show that for sophomores with little or no knowledge of business, it is a major task to read the information which they have to work with and to comprehend the basic dimensions of the decision problems that they face. With executives from industry who think they know how to manage firms, there is likely to be less varied experimentation with strategies and more consistent effort to maintain strategies which they are convinced from prior experience are good.

The men who do best in the Game or who seem to learn most from it are not necessarily the top men, intellectually, in the class. There is a significant correlation (.4 to .5) between scores on the Admission Test for Graduate Study in Business and course grades at Carnegie. But we have not found any correlation yet (1) between individual team members' scores on the ATGSB and individual measures of how much influence players have over their fellow team members, or (2) between team averages on the ATGSB and team measures of success (accumulated profits) in the Game.

G.   In Summary

The evidence of learning that we can summarize here is far from conclusive, but it is supported by other questionnaire surveys and by informal comments from many of the men who played the Game. It is also supported by the experiences that other users of the Game have reported in the previous chapter with quite different groups of students. While there are many problems to be solved before the full educational potential of the Game can be realized, the faculty at Carnegie is persuaded that a complex management simulation exercise is a valuable addition to its educational programs. The Game was the first of several innovations in curriculum that the faculty accepted when we last revised the graduate program; and after five years, we still are successful in persuading more than half the School's faculty and several outside business executives to commit 20–40 hours apiece to serve as directors, union negotiators, or bankers, during a semester's Game play.

The observations of how people learn support the opinions expressed earlier that the educational value of the Game depends not only on the computer model, but also on the role-playing assignments under which the Game is played, and on the integration of the Game with other courses. In the next section, we look more closely at some of the things that might be undertaken to improve the Game's value as an environment for learning.

III. IMPROVING THE GAME AS AN EDUCATIONAL EXPERIENCE

As an educational instrument, the Game is not a device for teaching. It is an environment for self-instruction. Learning the Game is very much akin to learning from day-by-day experience in real life. Players deal with stimuli from many sources, with quite variable relevance to the goals that they and the Game administrators have set. Even in the case of stimuli intended by the Game's designers and administrators to pose particular problems, there is no direct link between stimulus and action. Players pay no attention to much of the information to which they have access.

Teams use their past experience, their goals, and simple associative rules for tying information together to restructure the things that they see and hear into definitions of tasks to be performed. And when they take action, there is no clear external reaction or reinforcement to the response. One of the major challenges of the Game, in fact, is to discover what results actions of various kinds do bring. Reinforcement—or what teams perceive as reinforcement—comes from many sources, and it may not always be what the Game designers or administrators intend.

In any steps that are taken to enhance the Game's educational potential, then, we must recognize that each step will have indirect and unanticipated effects on learning as well as those which we want to bring about. We must recognize that under any arrangements, much of the total experience that players get lies beyond our control.

A. Issues of Complexity

Most problems that have arisen with the Game have not occurred because it was too complex. Students' response to the challenge of difficult problems has been good. They recognize that the complex situation is a closer prototype than simpler models are to what they will encounter in industry. They have usually wanted more complexity, rather than less. If efforts are made to complicate the Game, the central task is clearly to enlarge the opportunities that the production, finance, and control officers have to make these more nearly equivalent to the opportunities of the people in marketing. It is not to reduce the complexity of the marketing function.

More can be done, also, to enrich the Game in the later stages of play, when the making of basic decisions becomes routine. Role-playing assignments, if realistic and relevant to the rest of the Game task, are one useful way toward enrichment because something like a round of labor negotiations can be organized and held specifically for insertion when student interest begins to flag. Multiperiod moves and the opportunity to write analysis and decision programs provide new kinds of challenges.

In cases where we run two industries in parallel, we plan to relax some of the constraints that have kept these industries completely separate in the past. We shall announce rules under which teams may negotiate the sale of raw materials or products between industries and under which teams from the two industries might merge. We may introduce a "job market" of some sort under which teams could try to bid good managerial talent away from their competitors.

B.   Issues of Motivation

In most respects the Game does not pose serious motivational problems. The knowledge that participation is required, the expectation that it will be a challenging experience, and the hope that it will be a useful forerunner of later experiences—all provide motivation enough for most graduate students or most young men in management. Most participants take the assignment seriously, commit time to it, and try to profit from it.

Our experience also shows, though, that high levels of interest and effort are not inevitable and that one of the main tasks of the faculty who work with a game is to help establish and maintain a good motivational climate for the exercise. If the Game is at odds with the basic "flavor" of the program in which it is embedded or if it is spurned by the influential members of a school's faculty, it may be rejected by the students. Students get their evidence of faculty feelings from direct and indirect expressions of sponsorship and enthusiasm, from faculty attendance at board meetings and feedback sessions, from the faculty's familiarity with the Game and with what they are trying to do, from the way in which the faculty approaches its evaluation and grading responsibilities, and from references to the Game in other parts of the curriculum.

Whether students enjoy participating or not, almost all of them find the Game an intense and involving personal experience. They feel keenly the pressures of trying to master the competitive tasks, their relations with one another, and their relations with the boards and other groups. They usually react most strongly and most negatively to things which represent changes in their understanding of the climate and rules of play and which may represent threats to their strategies or their position. They look to the faculty to protect them against arbitrary decisions and actions.

One frequent motivational irritant comes from the difficulties men have in working with others on their team. A certain amount of experience with these kinds of interpersonal conflict is valuable. In order to minimize the chances that the faculty will be blamed for bringing it about, we have been moving at Carnegie toward systems for assigning men to teams under which the students elect the team presidents and the presidents then operate with considerable freedom of choice to select their own teams.

We would like to find ways of encouraging teams to experiment and innovate more after the initial organizational period and subsequent establishing of team position. We are thinking not only of experimentation that might improve a team's competitive standing, but also of experimentation that might help teams draw more explicit "lessons" from the Game. To get this, perhaps the boards of directors should relax their pressure for short-run profits and assign greater rewards for imagination and entrepreneurial efforts that do not pay immediate dividends. It is sometimes difficult to teach students that results count without at the same time stifling their venturesomeness.

We would like also to encourage teams to repeat key experiences more willingly. To the extent that the Game can be run in ways that will minimize students' expenditure of time for routine analysis and paperwork, it may be possible to induce teams to accept productive repetitions of work with central Game problems. Teams might learn a great deal by replaying series of moves. In the Game, as in most other learning situations, there is a gap between the number of repetitions of experience that most teachers think are desirable and the number that most students are willing to endure.

C. Issues of Feedback

If students are to learn effectively from experience, they probably need more explicit help than we have given to see how experience can be usefully analyzed, organized, and stored for later use. A partial solution to this problem would be more reflective assignments associated with the Game asking students to record and analyze what they have learned or to evaluate statements from others about what they have learned. Also, we could provide more opportunities in the Game for students to compare their experiences with others in the same functional roles. Without sacrificing too much of the excitement of competition among teams, and without teaching disrespect for antitrust laws, it is possible to hold occasional general discussion sessions during play to compare perceptions of problems, strategies that have been developed, and hypotheses about the outcomes of strategies.[11] Another kind of comparative experience might be obtained by periodically replaying a move or series of moves "off-line," so that players could experiment with different strategies for the same problem.

A third kind of experience, which departs even more strongly from traditions of "realism" in games, would be provided by arrangements under which teams could make moves that do not count, on an occasional or on a regular basis. Teams would, say, be allowed to submit two or perhaps more than two sets of decisions per move. They would designate, in advance of seeing the results, which set of decisions and outcomes they wanted to count in the recorded history of their firm and to serve as the basis for future moves. But because they could see the results which another set of decisions would have produced at no penalty to future profits, they would have both a greater encouragement to test innovative strategies and a better basis for evaluating what relations exist between decisions and outputs. If the Game administrators are worried that a team might use such a privilege too frequently, the number of off-line experimental moves permitted could be limited or teams could be charged for the privilege.

Satisfactory feedback arrangements should help to improve the quality of students' learning. We have seen what some of these problems are: (1) making learning that occurs from interactions with the computer as vivid and meaningful as learning which occurs from interactions with other people; (2) extending learning so that students learn solutions for problems in addition to developing a sense of problem recognition; and (3) exercising students' ability to extend and validate things learned in the Game in other kinds of situations.

IV.   CONCLUSION

This limited exploration of what students learn and how they learn from experience in the Game has been intended to define more clearly the problems which we face in future use of the Game. It has called attention to the need for new kinds of Game structure, incentives, and feedback arrangements to make Game experiences richer for all participants. This implies a particular effort to get better balance between the access that men in different positions on a Game team have to learning opportunities in the Game and an effort to add for all men activities of a reflective nature that may help them to solidify and extend the things they are learning in the Game to problems they will face in other settings.

---

[11]Tulane University has already done this to good effect. See Chapter 6, Section I.

To capitalize on the real educational potential of management games, we need to consider more explicitly questions of *how* people learn when we design games and plan their use. Further studies of what happens to students in games are needed, both of a cross-sectional type and of a more intensive longitudinal nature. The latter should focus more on the development of knowledge, strategies, and attitudes in individual students—trying to assess in detail the effect of previous experience on their style of play, the changes and developments that occur in the Game, and the kinds of changes that the Game brings in later behavior. We need to study more closely:

1. The processes by which players attend to their environment and translate the inputs of information that the environment presents into tasks for themselves to perform.
2. The ways in which players discover and conceptualize alternative ways of completing tasks and make choices among them.
3. The ways in which players use information from their environment and assumptions from prior experience to define "outcomes" or "consequences" of the actions they have taken.
4. The value systems by which outcomes are interpreted to become sources of satisfaction or dissastisfaction for the players and to reinforce or extinguish existing patterns of behavior.

This involves more intensive study than we have done so far of the goals, the expectations, and the action habits which players bring with them into the Game. It involves more analysis not only of the kinds of information that players pay attention to, but of the sources of information they attend to and of their heuristics for putting isolated pieces of information together. Since in a complex environment, players can attend only to a small part of the information that is available to them, different patterns of selection will lead to different perceptions of tasks, different definitions of action alternatives, different attributions of consequences, and perhaps even different systems of values.

Chapter
8

THE GAME AS AN
ENVIRONMENT
FOR RESEARCH

Management games can be useful not only as a training device in a business education program but also as a research tool. The developers of the Carnegie Tech Management Game have been interested in seeing it used as an environment for research as well as an environment for teaching. However, the research potential of this Game is still largely unexplored. Most of our energy has so far gone into getting the computer model to meet the standards which we originally set for it and into making the Game an effective part of our educational curriculum.

This chapter begins with a discussion of various approaches which can be followed in using business games for research purposes. Largely as a by-product of the business training uses of the Carnegie Game, several research papers have been published which can be regarded as pilot studies illustrating the challenges and the opportunities in using this Game for research. Seven quite different studies are reprinted in Sections II–IV of this chapter to show what can be done and to suggest types of research projects which other users of the Carnegie Tech Management Game might wish to undertake. To conclude this chapter, Section V presents an overall assessment of the research potential of the Game, including some suggestions to increase its effectiveness as a research environment.

I. SOME APPROACHES IN USING THE GAME FOR RESEARCH[1]

One reason for building complexity and institutional realism into the Carnegie Tech Management Game was to create an environment for research on behavioral, economic, and managerial processes that combines the advantages of laboratory experiments on small groups and highly artificial organizations with the strengths of field studies of business and industrial firms. The environment of the social science laboratory provides an opportunity for focus on a few clearly defined variables

---

[1] Some of the material in this section has been adapted from Kalman J. Cohen and Eric Rhenman, "The Role of Management Games in Education and Research," *Management Science,* Vol. 7, No. 2 (January, 1961), pp. 158–65; and from Alfred A. Kuehn, "Realism in Business Games," in William R. Dill, James R. Jackson, and James W. Sweeney (eds.), *Proceedings of the Conference on Business Games as Teaching Devices* (New Orleans: Tulane University, 1961), pp. 58–60.

and hypothesized relationships, for systematic manipulation of the things which are under study, and for control of the things which are not. Field studies provide fewer opportunities for systematic manipulation and for elimination and experimental control of irrelevant variables, but conversely provide information about more complicated patterns of behavior than most laboratory experiments do. Properly managed, field studies can be valuable guides to the behavior of total systems and can be used both to suggest critical relationships for study in the laboratory and to test the general relevance of narrowly based laboratory findings. As a rich and detailed environment, the determinants of which are known and subject to control, the Carnegie Game hopefully might play an intermediate role.

A.   Parallel Concepts and Developments

In a discussion of the use of the Carnegie Tech Management Game for research purposes, it is illuminating to compare this research tool with other parallel concepts and developments. The success of natural sciences like physics, chemistry, and biology in the use of laboratory experimentation has always been a challenge to social scientists. But the equipment of the latter for performing laboratory experiments has been meager, and this has often been thought to be one of the major reasons preventing more rapid progress in the social sciences.

Recent developments in electronic computing machinery and in mathematical model building have led to widespread interest in applying computer simulation techniques to the study of social science problems. It is beyond the scope of this book to evaluate the potential of simulation techniques in the social sciences.[2] However, since many people seem to make an incorrect identification between the fields of computer simulation and business games,[3] let us merely observe that these are quite different concepts, although they have a twofold interrelationship. As we have seen, computer simulations are integral parts of the Carnegie Tech Management Game, for they represent the economic and industrial environments in which the competing firms inter-

---

[2] A review of attempted applications of computer simulation techniques in economics and a discussion of the methodological issues involved may be found in Kalman J. Cohen and Richard M. Cyert, "Computer Models in Dynamic Economics," *Quarterly Journal of Economics,* Vol. 75, No. 1 (February, 1961), pp. 112–27. For a broad survey of simulation techniques in the social sciences, see Harold Guetzkow (ed.), *Simulation in Social Science: Readings* (Englewood Cliffs, N.J.: Prentice-Hall, Inc., 1962).

[3] In fact, the American Management Association attaches the name "simulation" to their three business games. Authors associated with the AMA, in writing about business games, frequently do so under some such heading as "Competitive Management Simulation." See, for example, Clifford J. Craft and Lois A. Stewart, "Competitive Management Simulation," *Journal of Industrial Engineering,* Vol. 10, No. 5 (September–October, 1959), pp. 355–63.

act. However, we can also look upon the Carnegie Game as an example of development beyond the type of computer simulation in which the entire relevant system is simulated by a computer program, to the more complex types of simulations that are possible when men and machines (preferably electronic computers) are allowed to interact in large-scale laboratory experiments. Although this type of man-machine simulation has to date mainly been used in the development of military systems,[4] the broader concept of simulation on which it rests should be kept in mind when we discuss the uses of the Carnegie Tech Management Game for the development of efficient business procedures.

Operational gaming is another concept which is also often, and easily, confused with business games. Like Thomas and Deemer,[5] we want to use the term operational gaming to emphasize the use of gaming to find an optimal solution to a game. Both operational gaming and business games have important roots in the development of war games. However, in contrast to business games, operational gaming has a direct root in the mathematical theory of games; operational gaming provides a method for attempting to solve games (in the strict sense in which solution is defined in the theory of games). We shall now briefly consider the extent to which business games such as the Carnegie Tech Management Game might be used in an operational gaming context, that is, for finding an optimal solution to a competitive business situation.[6]

B. Simulation of Business Operations

There have been relatively few attempts thus far to use an existing management game to discover either optimal or even improved patterns of business behavior.[7] The three papers by Kuehn and Day, by Weiss, and by Kuehn which are reproduced in Section IV provide indications of how the Carnegie Game can be used for this purpose in the marketing

---

[4]See William W. Haythorn, "Simulation in RAND's Logistics System Laboratory," *Report of the System Simulation Symposium* (New York: American Institute of Industrial Engineers, 1958), pp. 77–82; Robert L. Chapman, John L. Kennedy, Allen Newell, and William C. Biel, "The Systems Research Laboratory's Air Defense Experiments," *Management Science*, Vol. 5, No. 3 (April, 1959), pp. 250–69; and Murray A. Geisler, "The Simulation of a Large-Scale Military Activity," *ibid.*, Vol. 5, No. 4 (July, 1959), pp. 359–68.

[5]Clayton J. Thomas and Walter L. Deemer, Jr., "The Role of Operational Gaming in Operations Research," *Operations Research*, Vol. 5, No. 1 (February, 1957), pp. 1–27; on p. 6, Thomas and Deemer "define *operational gaming* as the serious use of *playing* as a primary device to formulate a *game*, to solve a *game*, or to impart something of the solution of a *game*." (Italics theirs).

[6]For a discussion of the relationship between operational gaming, Monte Carlo, and simulation techniques, see Thomas and Deemer, *ibid.*, pp. 4–6.

[7]The use of other methods of simulation for this purpose appears to be fairly common by now. Compare D. G. Malcolm, "Bibliography on the Use of Simulation in Management Analysis," *Operations Research*, Vol. 8, No. 2 (March–April, 1960), pp. 169–77.

area. There seems to be no doubt that this and other management games can be used to help develop good patterns of business planning and decision making if enough care is exercised to make the structure simulated by these management games sufficiently realistic and if the participants making the decisions are sufficiently well aware of good business practice to behave in a reasonably intelligent manner. Military war games have long been successfully used in this manner.[8]

There is a valuable research by-product in the simulation of business operations which may arise from working with business games. To the extent that the formulators of such games try to have realistic simulations of the industrial or economic environment programmed into the game, it is frequently necessary to extend our empirical knowledge. If one is trying to construct a quasi-realistic management game for the petroleum industry, for example, then one has to find out in fact how the different promotional and pricing policies adopted by firms in this industry will affect both the total market and their share of the market. While business games themselves certainly do not provide any answers to this question, the attempt to construct realistic games may lead to new areas of empirical investigation.

Many of the research efforts in marketing at Carnegie Institute of Technology have been directed at developing an understanding of the dynamics of consumer behavior and the influence of advertising, price, retail availability, and product characteristics on the sales of consumer goods. Mathematical models of various relationships have been constructed on the basis of empirical study and several management decision rules have been developed. Some of these decision rules have been used to help guide the advertising budgeting of major consumer products firms. Nevertheless, there are numerous gaps in our knowledge of the marketing system, gaps which became very evident when we attempt to construct as realistic a management game as the Carnegie Game was intended to be.

A complex and intentionally realistic game can provide a vehicle for expressing the current state of such a marketing theory. With it one

---

[8]The Germans in the present century used military games as a means for rehearsing their 1918 Spring offensive in World War I; and in World War II preliminary studies based on war games were used in planning the invasions of France in 1940, the Ukraine in 1941, and the potential invasion of England which never did take place. See Clayton J. Thomas, "The Genesis and Practice of Operational Gaming," *Proceedings of the First International Conference on Operational Research* (Baltimore: Operations Research Society of America, 1957), p. 68.

The Japanese, in a series of war games played in 1941, very carefully rehearsed their entry into World War II and their forthcoming campaigns in the Pacific theatre of operations. For a detailed discussion of these Japanese efforts, see Robert D. Specht, "War Games," P-1041, The RAND Corporation, March 18, 1957, pp. 1-4.

can examine the theory's dynamic characteristics, test the effects of alternative management strategies, and observe management behavior in the game environment. Analytic techniques can be developed and tested, deficiencies in the theory underlying the game can be uncovered, and specific principles of recognized value can be taught. Such uses of the Carnegie Game are examined more fully in the three papers by Kuehn and Day, by Weiss, and by Kuehn reproduced in Section IV.

The researcher has much to gain from observing the behavior of players and the response characteristics of a game based upon his theories. Perhaps of most interest are the deficiencies in theory which become evident. For example, the original version of the Carnegie Game did not respond realistically to large variations in a firm's price level. It became clear that an important (although simple) function was missing in the Game. We had never come across a need for such a function in analyzing actual marketing data for grocery products since competitors generally maintain some semblance of price stability. A subsequent search of actual market statistics for the rare, isolated instances of large variations in price from period to period supported the need for an additional function to correct the deficiency uncovered in the Game by the players.

Several other benefits from using the Carnegie Game that can accrue to the teacher-researcher are: (1) the results of after-the-Game discussions with the players as to how certain marketing relationships should be constructed; (2) ideas for research, stemming largely from the recogized gaps in one's knowledge when attempting to develop an even more realistic game; and (3) a laboratory setting for the pretesting of analytical techniques or decision rules which might later be tested in an actual marketing situation. The last item is of particular interest. If we cannot make effective use of a research tool in estimating the parameters of the model underlying the Game, then we certainly would not be able to make effective use of it in solving actual marketing problems. The Game thus can provide an inexpensive screening device for experiments which might be very expensive in actual practice. In the Game we can determine how suitable various procedures are for estimating the underlying parameters; this was in fact done for the technique for estimating consumer preferences presented in the Kuehn and Day paper reprinted in Section IV.A. In the world, deviations of the model from reality accompany the errors in estimates of parameters, frequently making it difficult or impossible to determine whether the model or the estimating procedures are responsible for deviations between predictions and observations.

C.   Research in Economics

Since management games are generally structured so that firms are competing with each other in an economic environment, it is quite natural to think of using business games for some areas of economic research relating to the theory of the firm. The particular area of microeconomic theory in which the present state of knowledge is least satisfactory is oligopoly market structures. Business games are frequently formulated in terms of a relatively small number of competing firms, and the participants are generally acutely aware of the influence that their actions have in calling forth reactions by their competitors. Hence, general management games represent typical oligopoly situations, and they might conceivably be used to explore some of the unsolved problems of oligopoly behavior.[9]

Relatively complex and realistic management games, such as the Carnegie Game, can be exceedingly useful in exploring various aspects of oligopoly behavior. For example, the effects on individual firms' price and output behavior of such variables as number of competing firms, relative size of competing firms, price elasticity of the market, geographical locations of firms, ability to introduce new products, extent of product differentiation, and so on, can all be explored much more easily through laboratory play of such a game than they can be explored through observations, interviews, and statistical studies of actual business firms.

Another class of economic problems which could be explored through research with the Carnegie Tech Management Game would be problems in the area of the "behavioral theory of the firm."[10] This newly developing area of microeconomics focuses on the impact of or-

---

[9]A few publications in this area have already appeared. See Austin C. Hoggatt, "An Experimental Business Game," *Behavioral Science,* Vol. 4, No. 3 (July, 1959), pp. 192–203; Lawrence E. Fouraker and Sidney Siegel, *Bargaining Behavior* (New York: McGraw-Hill Book Co., Inc., 1963); and Martin Shubik, "Some Experimental Non-Zero Sum Games with Lack of Information about the Rules," Cowles Foundation Discussion Paper No. 105, 1961. Two papers were presented at the 1960 National Meeting of the Operations Research Society of America reporting on some further interesting developments in the use of business games for oligopoly research. For abstracts of these talks, see George J. Feeney, "Experiments with Man-Machine Decision Systems," *Bulletin of the Operations Research Society of America,* Vol. 8 (1960), p. B–25; and Austin Hoggatt, "Business Games as Tools for Research," *ibid.,* p. B–96.

The Carnegie Tech Management Game model itself has provided the basis for a new model of oligopoly behavior which has been discussed in Alfred Kuehn and Timothy McGuire, "A Model of Consumer Behavior and Its Implications for a Theory of Imperfect Competition," presented at the Econometric Society's National Meeting in Pittsburgh, Pennsylvania, on December 29, 1962.

[10]See R. M. Cyert and J. G. March, *The Behavioral Theory of the Firm* (Englewood Cliffs, N.J.: Prentice-Hall, Inc., 1963).

ganizational and institutional factors on business decision making within firms. By suitably manipulating the organizational structure of firms competing in the Game, it would be possible to try to determine the effects of different organizational structures on price and output policy. Again, in principle, these effects are determinable through analysis, observation, and interviewing of actual firms in industry, but as we know, these latter are all exceedingly time-consuming and costly operations. Hence, it is certainly worth exploring the possibility of being able to investigate such phenomena within the confines of a laboratory, at least to the extent of providing preliminary validations of some specific hypotheses which can then be tested more thoroughly in the real business world. This methodological approach has been adopted in the Haines, Heider, and Remington paper which is reprinted in Section II.B.

D.   Research in Organization Theory

Organization theory is another area in which the Carnegie Tech Management Game should prove to be an extremely useful research tool. Since World War II, great advances in the study of organizational behavior have been made. Not only has a fairly well-defined theory of organizations begun to emerge, but a number of interesting laboratory experiments for analyzing particular organizational questions have been devised.[11] One problem usually raised in connection with laboratory experiments designed to explore the effects of changing organizational structure or communication patterns on behavior is the question of how transferable are the results determined in such a laboratory situation to the world of business, military, or governmental organizations in which researchers are more fundamentally interested. In this regard, management games may have a significant advantage over previous laboratory experiments. It is quite obvious that the structure of even relatively simple business games, such as the AMA, UCLA, or IBM Games, resembles much more closely the objective task environment found in business organizations than do the simple experimental situations which have hitherto been used to study organizational phenomena.[12] A more complex game, such as the Carnegie Tech Management Game, goes even further in the direction of providing a laboratory

[11]See James G. March and Herbert A. Simon, *Organizations* (New York: John Wiley & Sons, 1958), and the references cited therein.

[12]See Anatol Rapoport, "A Logical Task as a Research Tool in Organization Theory," in Mason Haire (ed.), *Modern Organization Theory* (New York: John Wiley & Sons, 1959), pp. 91–114; and Donald F. Clark and Russell L. Ackoff, "A Report on Some Organizational Experiments," *Operations Research*, Vol. 7, No. 3 (1959), pp. 279–93.

situation endowed with a large degree of face validity with respect to the actual business organizations in which we are interested.

Again it will obviously be necessary to find a compromise between realism—which may facilitate the transfer of results from laboratory to real life—and tolerable complexity—which makes it possible to draw any conclusions at all from the experiment in the laboratory. It is therefore likely that the simpler laboratory experiment and the more complex situation that the Carnegie Game presents will supplement each other in the same way as do the chemist's laboratory test and his pilot plant study. When collecting empirical data to test his fundamental theories, the scientist accepts the artificial test tube experiment. But when he wants to test a complex production process these simple laboratory experiments are not regarded as reliable. He knows that what works in the laboratory might cause him considerable trouble in the full-scale plant. This is why he wants to test the process in a pilot plant designed to make experimentation possible. Considering its size, cost, and purpose, a laboratory for experimental games like the RAND Logistics Systems Laboratory[13] really is a pilot plant test station. But even with their limitations, organizational "pilot plant tests" should be very valuable. A simple test which shows that an organization works in a tolerable way provides valuable knowledge. This is especially true when these tests may come about at very little incremental cost when they are by-products of regular educational runs of the Carnegie Tech Management Game. This was the case for the research by Haines, Heider, and Remington described in Section II.B.

By varying the procedures according to which teams of players are selected and organized in playing the Carnegie Tech Management Game, it is possible to explore a great many features of organizational behavior. It is possible, for example, to study the effects of variations in team size on performance, morale, and adaptability to change. By changing the hierarchical nature of different firms' organization structures, we can explore the effects of such hierarchies both on external performance in the market and on such internal features as goal formation, organizational identification, goal conflict, influence, and others. The paper by Dill, Hoffman, Leavitt, and O'Mara which is reprinted in Section II.A illustrates the type of research which can be done along these lines.

It is easy to suggest a great many other types of organization theory research projects which can be carried out using runs of the Carnegie Tech Management Game which are primarily intended to serve an edu-

---

[13]Geisler, *op. cit.*

cational function. For example, we can alter the amount of time allowed for players to make decisions and try to get some notion of the effects of time pressure. As time pressures are increased, will we get a shift from long-range planning to "putting out the fire" behavior? To what extent can problems of time pressure be traded off by establishing more complex organizations with a greater amount of work specialization? Are there differential effects of time pressures which come early, in the middle of, or late in Game play?

The pattern of information flows within the Carnegie Game firms can also be manipulated experimentally. By restricting the amounts of information that flow to particular team members, it is possible to study the effects of such information flows on team performance, goal formation, and so on. Finally, another obvious area of organizational research would be the effects of stability of team membership on performance and morale.

E. The Research Papers Included Here

The studies which are included in Sections II–IV are of three kinds. Section II contains two papers which are attempts to use the Game to test the limits of commonly accepted propositions about organizational behavior. Some of these are propositions which have been developed with small, *ad hoc* groups in laboratory settings. For these the question is whether they still have validity in the larger, more task-oriented, more long-lived groups that one finds as Game teams or as management teams in the real world. Others are propositions which have been developed from observations in industry. For these the question is whether they can stand up in the more clearly defined, more controlled environment of the Game. The Game serves a useful purpose in this type of research because it provides a new setting in which to study how organizations develop and how they function. In this environment we can reassess the general applicability of hypotheses that are suggested by the results of other research.

The two papers in Section III illustrate how the Game can be used as a medium for developing improved methods of business planning and decision making. The Haines study in Section III.A was based on observations of teams making marketing decisions for the Game. It developed a computer model which simulated this behavior and which could be used to make marketing decisions in future Game plays. The study in Section III.B by Ijiri, Levy, and Lyon shows how modern mathematical methods can be applied to budgeting and financial planning problems in the Game. Both of these papers were based on observations made and problems arising in actual plays of the Carnegie Tech

Management Game. The authors had easier access to the Game than they would have had to real-world business situations. However, there is little doubt that the decision-making processes that were observed and the problem situations studied are very much like those in real firms, and that the techniques developed in these studies are applicable in real firms.

The third kind of study (represented by the three papers in Section IV) takes advantage of the institutional realism and the compressed time scale of the Carnegie Game model to obtain an improved understanding of real-world marketing problems. These studies use results from repeated plays of the Game as ways of determining the properties of the Game model and as ways of finding out the comparative merits and weaknesses of different strategies which businessmen use or which advisors to business recommend. What works best in the Game model may not necessarily work best in the real world, but tests with the Game are a cheap and fast way of determining which alternatives deserve more detailed examination in a real business context. The Kuehn and Day paper in Section IV.A develops a technique for estimating consumer preferences which can be used in the real world as well as in the Game. In Section IV.B the Weiss paper suggests how the Carnegie Game can be used for operational purposes as a simulation of the packaged detergent market. The paper by Kuehn in Section IV.C indicates how experience gained in plays of the Game can be used to evaluate different advertising policies. In principal, similar approaches could be used to evaluate decision strategies in other areas of marketing, in production, or in finance.

Some of the papers which are reprinted in this chapter might have been improved had they been planned and executed solely as research projects, with more elaborate controls and with more replications. In their present form, however, they illustrate two important points about the Carnegie Tech Management Game's ability to stimulate research. The first four of these studies (those in Sections II and III) were built around actual student runs of the Game, where the runs were planned as educational rather than research ventures. In the remaining studies (those in Section IV), the authors also derived valuable insights from similar student runs. It is thus clear that opportunities to gather meaningful research data are consistent with our educational objectives in using this Game. The second point is that five of these seven studies (the papers by Kuehn and Day in Section IV.A and by Kuehn in Section IV.C being the sole exceptions) were written or coauthored by M.S. or Ph.D. students at Carnegie. The research for these five papers was actually initiated by graduate student authors. Except for the one paper (Section II.A) in which Dill and Leavitt collaborated, they were carried through and published substantially without faculty participation.

II. STUDIES OF ORGANIZATIONAL PROCESSES

The two papers which are reprinted in this section both illustrate ways in which the Carnegie Tech Management Game can serve as a useful research tool in the areas of organization theory.

A. Experiences with a Complex Management Game (by William R. Dill, William Hoffman, Harold J. Leavitt, and Thomas O'Mara)[14]

During the first run of the Carnegie Tech Management Game with graduate students in the 1959–60 academic year, we were able to collect data that bear both upon problems of education for management and on questions of social research. This paper reports our findings, first, on educational aspects of the Game and second, on the implications of our data for some current issues in organizational research.

In the administration of the Game reported here, players were required to play, but they were give no course credit or other extraneous reward for playing or winning. Two industries, A and B, each consisting of three teams, played the Game starting from identical positions. Teams A0 and B0 were given complete

FIGURE 8–1

ORGANIZATIONAL PATTERN IMPOSED ON TEAMS A1, A2, B1, AND B2

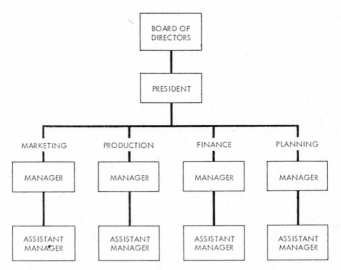

ORGANIZATIONAL PATTERN IMPOSED ON TEAMS A1, A2, B1, AND B2.

[14]This is a modified version of William R. Dill, William Hoffman, Harold J. Leavitt, and Thomas O'Mara, "Experiences with a Complex Management Game," *California Management Review,* Vol. 3, No. 3 (Spring, 1961), pp. 38–51.

freedom to develop their own structures. Teams A1 and B1 were given organization charts (Figure 8–1) and asked to appoint their members to the positions on the chart. Teams A2 and B2 were given the same charts with individuals already appointed (by the faculty) to all the jobs thereon.

Each team was assigned a "board of directors," made up of several faculty members. Teams reported to their boards periodically. Different boards defined their roles quite differently, so that some were more demanding of elaborate rationales for team decisions than others, and some took a firmer hand in determining team policy than others. Board activities and attitudes were not subject to experimental control.

1. Data and Methods. *Before* the Game, we were able to collect data on:

1. The "attractiveness" of the Game to prospective players. These data took the form of a rank assigned to the Management Game as a voluntary activity among these alternatives: Carnegie Management Game, written cases, oral cross course cases, field observation in industry, seminar in writing and speaking, study of ethics and values in business, free time for reading and research, involvement in organized faculty research.
2. The average intellectual capacities of the team as measured by scores on the ATGSB (Admission Test for Graduate Study in Business).[15]
3. The "personality types" of individual players as measured by scores on the Myers-Briggs questionnaire.[16]
4. Players' predictions about which members of their teams would be most influential.

During the Game, we were able to gather data on:

1. The overall performance of each firm in the Game, measured by gross profit figures.
2. Certain aspects of morale and attitudes, measured by questionnaires following each quarter of play (i.e., after every third decision). Our morale measure was the sum of the answers to the following nine questions, each scaled from 1 to 9:

    Evaluate the following: (1 = worst possible; 9 = best possible)
    1. Your team's current organizational setup.
    2. Your team's current leadership.
    3. The quality of teamwork in your team.
    4. The overall quality of your team.
    5. The personal relationship now existing among team members.

    Evaluate the current direction of change in the following:
    (1 = deteriorating very fast; 9 = improving very fast)
    6. The morale of your team.
    7. The personal relationships among your team members.
    8. The quality of your team's analysis of problems in the Game.
    9. Your team's status in the eyes of other teams.

---

[15]Validity data on the ATGSB are available from Educational Testing Service, Princeton, New Jersey.
[16]Published by Educational Testing Service, Princeton, New Jersey.

After the Game we were able to gather data, by interview, on:

1. The influence of individual players on one another.
2. The degree of dispersion of influence within teams.
3. The degree of "consonance" (agreement among players about who was influential) in each team.

These three measures require additional explanation. The influence of individual members on one another was measured from responses, after the Game, to the question: "Who (on your team) influences ———?" Into the blank went the names of all members of one's team, one's self included.

The answers to this question were tabulated in matrix form to display first-order influence relationships (e.g., X influenced Y). Each team matrix was then squared, using techniques reported by Festinger[17] to discover second-order relationships as well (e.g., to show that if X influenced Y, and Y influenced Z, then X indirectly influenced Z, too).

2. Influence Index. An influence index was computed for each team member by adding together: (1) the total number of men whom he was reported to have influenced directly, and (2) the total number of men whom he was reported to have influenced indirectly through a second person. The first-order and second-order influence totals were weighted equally.[18]

The standard deviation of the distribution of these indices for each team is the influence dispersion index. The greater the standard deviation, the greater were the differences in power among team members.

Our measure of consonance was derived from the difference between a team member's (X's) own perception of who influenced him, and the perceptions of all other team members about who influenced X. Consider, for example, the A01 row in the matrix for Firm A0 shown in Table 8–1. The circles under

TABLE 8–1

EXAMPLE OF DERIVATION OF FIRM CONSONANCE INDEX

Data from Firm A0 Based on Question: "Who (on Your Team) Influences____?" (Circles, When Read across Rows, Indicate Responses to: "Who Influences You?")

	A0 1	A0 2	A0 3	A0 4	A0 5	A0 6	Total	Individual Indices	
A0 1	x	②	1	0	2	④	9	6/(9 + 4)	= .462
A0 2	④	x	1	①	1	③	10	8/(10 + 7)	= .470
A0 3	3	1	x	⑤	③	4	16	8/(16 + 2)	= .445
A0 4	③	①	②	x	②	⑤	13	13/(13 + 12)	= .518
A0 5	3	1	2	5	x	②	13	2/(13 + 3)	= .125
A0 6	1	1	1	1	1	x	5	0/(5 + 0)	= .000

Total for Firm   = 37/94   = .394

---

[17]See L. Festinger, S. Schachter, and K. Back, *Social Pressures in Informal Groups* (New York: Harper, 1950).

[18]Hoffman and O'Mara originally computed an influence index suggested in L. Katz, "A New Status Index Derived from Sociometric Analysis," *Psychometrica*, Vol. 18, No. 1 (March, 1953), pp. 39–43. This weights second-order and higher-order influence relationships according to the probability, *a*, that higher-order links will in fact be used. It is a more sophisticated measure than the one we finally decided on, but it was not feasible to estimate the *a* in Katz's equations empirically, or to choose a single value of *a* on *a priori* grounds that would yield solutions to Katz's equations for all the teams.

A02 and A06 mean that A01 says he was influenced by those players only. The numbers in the circles, 2 and 4, mean that two (of a possible five) other team members agree that A01 is indeed influenced by A02, and four others agree that he is influenced by A06.

Our index for each member is the ratio of agreeing votes to the total of (1) votes cast by other members, *plus* (2) the votes that could have been cast, but were not, in the circled areas. Thus for A01 our consonance index equals $6/(9 + 3 + 1)$. The 9 in the denominator is the row total; the 3 is for votes that could have been cast for A02 but were not; and the 1 is for a vote that could have been cast for A06, but was not. The firm's index in this case is 37/94 or .394.

This firm's consonance index, then, measures the extent to which members perceived the influence structure in the same way at the end of the Game.

The overall relationships among all of these pieces of data are summarized in Tables 8–2 and 8–3. Table 8–2 summarizes the data by firm; Table 8–3, by individual member.

3. *Educational Effects of the Game.* During these first plays of the Carnegie Game, we looked for answers to several questions that we and others have raised about the role of our Game—and games in general—as a setting for teaching managerial skills. These were the questions:

1. Will a complex game encourage teams to adopt the hierarchical patterns of organization which are so familiar in industry? Working with simpler games, we had had difficulty getting students—or even executives—to differentiate clear leader-follower roles in their groups.

2. Who plays the Game well? Can the most influential team members be identified, *a priori*, by their intelligence or by other traits of personality? For the team that makes the most profit, is sheer analytic skill more characteristic than other managerial qualities?

3. Does the high morale and high involvement reported by the early users of management games carry over in the extended play of a more complex game? Student teams in this study made moves at roughly weekly intervals over a six-month period, as an addition to an already heavy course load. Deadlines for decisions were imposed, but scheduled times to meet and make decisions were not provided.

4. *Patterns of Organization.* In designing the Carnegie Game, we put a high value on giving players realistic experience in the functioning of hierarchical organizations. Normally, among graduate students or among executives-on-campus, there are strong egalitarian norms. Men are reluctant to assume either superior or subordinate roles on a continuing basis, especially in situations where their acceptance of these roles becomes a matter of record among faculty and peers.

Our efforts to encourage hierarchical organization with the Carnegie Game included a variety of steps:

1. The very size and complexity of the Game was intended to make it difficult for a team to operate as a "committee of the whole," with each member equally expert about each of the major fields of activity.

2. Large teams—initially with eight or nine members—were set up in hopes that the frustrations of arranging and conducting meetings would build

TABLE 8–2

Summary of Several Measures by Firm

(Means of Firms)

Firm	ATGSB Score	Attractiveness (Pre-Game)	Influence Dispersion Index (Range)	Consonance Index	Morale After			Profits after Taxes								
					Q2	Q3	Q4	Q1	Rank	Q2	Rank	Q3	Rank	Q4	Rank	Total
A 0....	591.0	2.9	3.2	.394	45.2	37.2	40.6	801	1	9,121	3	11,835	1	1,292	3	23,049
A 1....	520.4	2.8	4.2	.586	36.4	39.4	55.5	17	3	9,158	2	11,197	2	4,200	1	24,572
A 2....	552.5	2.3	2.3	.209	46.2	44.2	32.9	57	2	12,986	1	9,684	3	1,359	2	24,086
B 0....	567.5	3.1	N.D.*	N.D.*	49.7	42.7	44.3	260	1	9,470	3	12,350	2	5,340	2	27,420
B 1....	548.7	2.9	5.1	.510	38.5	42.4	51.0	(60)	2	11,695	2	19,074	1	8,290	1	38,999
B 2....	538.5	2.1	1.1	.333	28.7	40.4	43.6	(538)	3	11,790	1	11,870	3	3,800	3	26,922

*Team B0 was so decentralized, its members professed that questions about influence could not be sensibly answered.

TABLE 8–3

SUMMARY OF SEVERAL MEASURES BY INDIVIDUAL PLAYERS

(Ranks of Individuals within Firms)

Firm	Player	Predicted Influence	Consonance Index	ATGSB	Actual Influence
A 0	A	1	6	4	1
	B	4.5	3	1	2.5
	C	4.5	2	3	4
	D	3	1	5	5
	E	2	5	2	2.5
	F	6	4	6	6
A 1	A	2	2	3	1.5
	B	4.5	3	1	1.5
	C	3	1	2	3
	D	1	4	5	4
	E	6	6	X	5.5
	F	4.5	5	4	5.5
A 2	A	2	2	3	2
	B	1	1	5	1
	C	5	3	6	3
	D	5	6	4	4
	E	3	5	2	5.5
	F	5	4	1	5.5
B 0	– – – – – – – – – – – – – No Data – – – – – – – – – – – – – –				
B 1	A	3	4.5	5	1
	B	4	3	1	2
	C	1	4.5	3	3
	D	6.5	6	4	4
	E	2	1.5	2	5
	F	5	1.5	7	6
	G	6.5	7	6	7
B 2	A	1	1	6	3
	B	2.5	5	4	1.5
	C	2.5	2	5	1.5
	D	5	3	1	6
	E	6	4	2	4.5
	F	4	6	3	4.5

pressures to differentiate roles and to break the organization into functional subgroups.

3. Each team was supervised by a faculty board of directors. In dealing with the teams, the directors tended to channel communications through the president (or through a few top officers). The president was expected to present most reports and recommendations, and he was held responsible for the whole team's operations.

4. Hierarchical organizations were imposed by the boards of directors on four of the six teams at the start of the Game. Two teams (A0 and B0) were given complete freedom to organize as they pleased. Two teams (A1 and B1) were asked to appoint men to fill the jobs in the organiaztion chart shown in Figure 8–1. The final two teams (A2 and B2) were set up in accordance with the chart in Figure 8–1, and the board announced whom it wanted to fill each of the positions.

What happened? We were successful in getting a substantial degree of hierarchial organization in two teams, A1 and B1 (See Table 8–2). The influence dispersion index (Table 8–2) at the end of the Game was 4.2 for A1 and 5.1 for B1. There was a moderate amount of influence spread in A0 and very little in A2 and B2.

By the time students had played the Game for twelve decision periods, the complexity of the task had decreased considerably. Many decisions had become more or less routine. Profits, even for the weakest team, were quite high; consequently there was not much pressure for strong leadership or radical change. The teams had shrunk in size to six or seven members because some men were excused at the beginning of the spring semester. To a large extent, interest in rotating job assignments among team members had operated against the long-term stability of organizational hierarchies.

The way in which the boards of directors approached their jobs may help to explain why A1 and B1 did develop hierarchies. At the start of the Game the directors of both A1 and B1 clearly saw their role as an active one—to call student attention to various problems, to goad them on performance, to evaluate and criticize what they had done, and to offer positive suggestions and advice on what the group might do. The directors of B0 and B2 also saw their role as an active one—but not as completely so as the directors of A1 and B1. The directors of A0 and A2, in contrast, defined for themselves a much more passive role—primarily to answer questions, to listen, and to observe.

The initial conditions of organization may also have had some effect. A1 and B1, the two teams which showed the most differentiation in the influence of team members, were the two which had been required to use a particular organization pattern but were also free to decide for themselves who would take each job.[19]

In summary, it was more difficult than we had expected to simulate the experience of life in a hierarchical organization for the teams. The Game program has since been adjusted to sustain the level of complexity of the team's job through a long period of play, and further changes are being incorporated into a new Game,[20] which is currently under development.

Much of the success in promoting hierarchical organization seems to depend on the arrangements under which the Game is played and the attitudes which

---

[19]We were more successful in establishing formal divisions of work among functional specialities in using the Carnegie Game with five-man teams from our Program for Executives than we were playing the IBM Game with five-man teams in earlier years of the same program. (The executives were free to organize themselves as they pleased, and they did not have to report to boards of directors.) It is not clear in the executive runs of the Carnegie Game, though, that hierarchical relations were any stronger than they were in runs of the IBM Game. In the Carnegie Game, the chief executive did have a more substantial agenda planning and coordinating job to do than in the IBM Game.

[20]The Mark 1.5 version of the Carnegie Tech Management Game.

the boards of directors take. In the future, the fact that two hierarchically organized teams were the most profitable and had the highest end-of-Game morale may influence new teams' approaches to organization.

5. *"The Compleat Gamester."* The Carnegie Game is intended as a general management game which will be appropriate for educating men who aspire eventually to managerial, rather than specialist staff positions. The difference between it and simpler general management games is one of depth of simulation rather than one of basic purpose. Nonetheless, it may be that the added complexity of our Game and the possibilities for attacking some problems in it by relatively sophisticated analytical techniques makes it more amenable to mastery by the intelligent analyst than by the good manager.

The issue involved is an important one. If high intelligence and related analytic skills are sufficient for success in the Game, the Game is probably not a good simulation of real managerial situations.

Using data about players which we already had in hand, we have explored the relationship of intelligence and four personality traits to success in the Game—success as measured by the individual influence of team members and by the team's relative profit records.

As a measure of intelligence, we used the Admission Test for Graduate Study in Business (ATGSB), a general test of quantitative and verbal aptitude developed and administered by the Educational Testing Service and very similar in form to the aptitude sections of the Graduate Record Examination or the College Board examinations. Despite its name, the ATGSB is not a test of knowledge of business and related areas.[21]

Within the teams, there is no relationship between total scores on the ATGSB or between the verbal or quantitative subscores and the amount of influence which members had at the end of the Game. Neither is there any relation between ATGSB score average for a team and the amount of profits it earned over the course of the Game.

Since there is a significant correlation in most business schools between ATGSB scores and course grades—usually between .4 and .6, but occasionally as high as .7—the Game appears to do better than courses in calling forth nonintellective skills.

We do not yet know what the nonintellective correlates of personal influence or team profitability are. We tried to relate scores on one personality instrument, the Myers-Briggs questionnaire, to influence and profitability data; but the findings were all negative. The Myers-Briggs test is based on Jungian theories. For anyone who takes it, it yields one of 16 profiles, based on two-way classifications on each of four dimensions. The dominant side of his personality may be:

1. Extroversion (E) or Introversion (I): a primary orientation to the world outside himself or to the world within.
2. Judging (J) or Perceiving (P): a primary tendency to make judgments and evaluations of what he experiences or simply to perceive and store his experience.

---

[21]The intercorrelations between scores for the same men on the ATGSB and the aptitude section of the GRE are in the .7 to .9 range in studies that we have done at Carnegie.

3. Thinking (T) or Feeling (F): in his judgments, a tendency to use a rational, analytic approach or to use an emotional approach.
4. Sensory (S) or Intuitive (N): in his perceptions, a tendency to rely literally on direct sensations or to make use of hunches and intuition.

We looked both at the distribution of overall profiles on the test and at the distribution of scores on each of the four dimensions. From neither approach could we detect any relationship to individuals' influence on their team, to individuals' ability to agree with their teammates on what the influence structure looked like, or to teams' profit performance in the Game.

Further work needs to be done with instruments that measure attitudes, values, and skills that are more closely related to the tasks that a Management Game player or a real-life manager faces. For the moment, though, we are encouraged that the problems of predicting Carnegie Game performance (like the problem of predicting managerial success) seem to be quite independent of the problems of predicting success in normal academic pursuits.

6. *Morale Improved with Teamwork.* Playing the Game over an extended period of time, as an overload, might not be viewed as especially conducive to good team morale. We did not hope to generate the high level of excitement and involvement that can be generated when games are played full time for a period of one to several days, without direct faculty supervision, and with strong competitive spirit among teams.

Given the list of activities described above, players indicated (before the Game started) a higher average preference for participating in the Game than for any of the other alternatives. Morale was never exceptionally high for most of the players, but for the players who were preparing for careers in management (men in the School's M.S. program), morale increased steadily throughout the Game.

The determinants of morale need more study, but a few things are clear. Students responded not only to their own profit performance, but to their successes and tribulations as an organization and to the arrangements under which the Game was played.

Many people associated with the development of management games feel (without evidence as yet) that games can serve as a rich medium for organizational research. The second purpose of this paper is to present some findings about the organization and social structure of these Game teams, and to try to relate those findings to some current issues in organizational and small group research.

7. *The Game Is a Tool for Research.* As the reader will see, our findings are not at all conclusive, but they are suggestive enough to make us believe that the Game can indeed be usefully exploited as a research tool.

Although our data are not definitive, they have direct relevance for some current questions about organizational behavior. Here are several questions and the relationship of our data to them:

Let us consider first the general issue of *egalitarianism* versus *hierarchical differentiation* in organizations.

One can argue that an egalitarian social structure makes for free and clear intercommunication, and hence for high morale and for effective group problem solving. But one can argue, conversely, that a group needs a differentiated power structure to perform effectively. It needs to have some members holding greater power than others, so that someone will take responsibility and make decisions.

Table 8–2 shows the influence dispersion index for the five teams on which we were able to gather end-of-Game influence data. The data indicate that the two highest-morale, highest-profit firms, A1 and B1, show the greatest dispersion of influence, suggesting that egalitarian distribuiton of influence is neither necessary for successful problem solving nor for high morale in these Game firms.[22]

Our data also bear upon the issue of *perceptual consonance.* The point has often been made that mutual understanding of differences in people's power may be more important for a group's morale and readiness to work than equality of power. Our influence index tells us which members are seen to be most influential, but it does not provide information about the extent of agreement among members about who was influential. The team consonance index in Table 8–2 is intended to do that job.

A1 and B1, the teams with the greatest morale and profitability, had the highest degrees of consonance. Our data are consistent with the hypothesis that groups whose members agree about the state of their internal relationships are more likely to be "successful." But high consonance in this case is also associated with high influence dispersion; this suggests either that people can agree about who influences whom when there are big (and hence more visible) differences in influence, or, alternatively, that members of "good groups" see things the same way, even if what they see is a hierarchy of influence.

If we turn now to data about individual firm members in Table 8–3 we make contact with some other current research issues.

Consider, for example, the general question of the *predictability of influence.* In this study, members made predictions about who would be influential in their firm. Months later they were asked to indicate who had actually been influential. The relationship (Table 8–3) is positive. To show it more lucidly, examine Table 8–4, which shows the average actual rank in influence (over five teams) of members of each predicted rank. The orderings match almost perfectly.

TABLE 8–4

PREDICTED AND ACTUAL INFLUENCE

(5 Firms Averaged)

Predicted Influence (Rank)	Actual Average Influence (Rank)
1	2.4
2 (including 2.5)	2.3
3	3.6
4 (including 4.5)	4.2
5	4.9
6 (including 6.5)	5.4

[22]Ghiselli and Lodahl report a high correlation between *skewness* in the distribution of certain traits among group members and group effectiveness, a finding which seems supportive of the one reported here. See E. E. Ghiselli and T. M. Lodahl, "Patterns of Managerial Traits and Group Effectiveness," *Journal of Abnormal and Social Psychology,* Vol. 57, No. 1 (July, 1958), pp. 61–66.

It is clear that team members were able to predict influence with considerable accuracy, a finding consistent with some other ongoing research about the reliability of observations of influence in groups.

8. *What Are Influential People Like?* Finally, on another part of the question: "What are influential people like?" our data provide some material on the relationship between actual influence and individual consonance indices. The individual consonance index (Table 8–3) can be thought of as a measure of the extent to which an individual's statement about who influences him is corroborated by his fellows. It turns out (Table 8–5) that in general the more influential people may perceive their own influence more accurately than their less influential teammates do, though the degree of relationship is not very high at all.

TABLE 8–5

RELATIONSHIP BETWEEN INDIVIDUAL CONSONANCE INDEX AND
ACTUAL INFLUENCE

(5 Firms Averaged)

Consonance Index (Rank)	Average Actual Influence (Rank)
1 (including 1.5)	3.2
2	2.3
3	3.0
4 (including 4.5)	4.0
5	3.8
6	3.8
7	7.0

9. *Conclusion.* This experience with one run of the Carnegie Tech Management Game demonstrates that it is quite possible: (1) to evaluate certain educational aspects of the Game, and (2) to gather data from the play of the Game about some questions of organizational and group behavior.

In this instance we were able to investigate relationships between Game performance and (1) individual ability (no relationship); (2) personality variables (no relationships); (3) dispersion of power (influence) within teams (more dispersion, better performance); and (4) consonance of perceptions of influence within teams (more consonance, better performance). We were able also to show positive relationships between predictions about influence made before the Game and actual influence measured just after the Game, and between one's personal influence and the consonance of one's perceptions with the perceptions of his teammates.

B.   The Computer as a Small-Group Member (by George H. Haines, Jr., O. Fred Heider, and Daniel Remington)[23]

Recent years have seen a growing proliferation of forecasts involving the future of computers and automation in business firms. This literature has fore-

[23]This is a modified version of George H. Haines, Jr., O. Fred Heider, and Daniel Remington, "The Computer as a Small-Group Member," *Administrative Science Quarterly,* Vol. 6, No. 3 (December, 1961), pp. 360–74.

cast the kind, extent, and effect of computer use. For example, H. A. Simon has predicted that "the kinds of activities that now characterize middle management will be more completely automated (in the years to come) than the others, and hence will come to have a smaller part in the whole management picture."[24] Other forecasts in a similar vein have been made by Leavitt and Whisler.[25] A more cautious examination of the coming changes has been made by Anshen.[26] Emphasis has been placed on heuristic programming of computers as the key method that will spur this technological change.[27]

Although several heuristic programs are now in operation,[28] in none of these has the computer become part of an organization. However, computers using other tools, such as algorithmic decision rules, have actually been used in organizations.[29] No claim for innovation is made here for the mere use of a computer; what is new is the way in which the computer operated. The critical elements in the program were that the management of the firm retained control of the parameters, and that the program was not guaranteed to produce usable answers (although the program did not fail in this respect during its use). It is not clear, however, that these differences from an algorithmic decision maker matter to the human members of the group.

Successful use of computers as information processors and decision makers depends upon an understanding of the interaction processes of human beings and computers. Most questions about this process are at present unanswered. Before the study reported here was begun, four specific questions were asked in an attempt to give structure to the events observed: (1) How can such an alteration in decision making be facilitated or hampered? (2) What kinds of effects (if any) would this change have on organization structure? (3) Will there be a "subtle withdrawal of support"[30] for emotional reasons? (4) Would the time sequence of the change in this study follow the phases suggested by previous observers of industrial change?[31]

This paper will report on a field study of the introduction of a heuristic computer program into a small group in an attempt to give tentative answers to these questions and to suggest specific problems in this area for future study. The particular task the group dealt with was the Carnegie Tech Management Game.

The heuristic program was written as part of a continuing study of the organization of a task-oriented small group operating in a stable environment.

[24]M. Anshen and G. L. Bach (eds.), *Management and Corporations, 1985* (New York: McGraw-Hill Book Co., Inc., 1960), p. 50.

[25]H. J. Leavitt and T. L. Whisler, "Management in the 1980's," *Harvard Business Review,* Vol. 36, No. 6 (November–December, 1958), pp. 41–48.

[26]M. Anshen, "The Manager and the Black Box," *Harvard Business Review,* Vol. 38, No. 6 (November–December, 1960), pp. 85–92.

[27]H. A. Simon and A. Newell, "Heuristic Problem Solving: The Next Advance in Operations Research," *Operations Research,* Vol. 6, No. 1, (January–February, 1958), pp. 1–11.

[28]F. Tonge, "Summary of a Heuristic Line Balancing Procedure," *Management Science,* Vol. 7, No. 1 (October, 1960), pp. 21–42.

[29]See Feeney, *op. cit.,* for an abstract of a previous study of this phenomenon in a controlled situation.

[30]Anshen, *op. cit.*

[31]For a description of these phases, see R. Lippitt, J. Watson, and B. Westley, *The Dynamics of Planned Change* (New York: Harcourt Brace, 1958), chap. 6.

The program, which made decisions in the marketing area of the Game, was developed from a study of how marketing decisions were actually made in the Game. The decision program and the preliminary results of this study are reported in Section III.A. Here we merely need to note that the program is characterized by control parameters, which allowed the team using the program to set marketing policy (for instance, whether a product would be high priced, medium priced, or low priced).

The field study thus had a dual purpose: to test the performance of the program, and to observe its impact upon the group processes. To obtain this test a group was induced, not forced, to use the program as its decision maker in the marketing area. Tapes were taken of discussions between the marketing manager and the president during the course of phasing the computer program into the group. These tapes were then transcribed, and used in writing the description of the program's use below.

This paper will attempt to give tentative answers to the questions previously posed by a study of what actually happened in the firm that accepted the computer as a member. It first describes the events that occurred and then discusses the events critically to shed some light on what might be expected if heuristic programs are introduced as decision makers in actual practice.

1. History. The Mark 1 version of the Carnegie Tech Management Game was played over most of the 1960–61 academic year by six teams of graduate students. They were required to play, but given no course credit or other extraneous reward for playing or winning. The teams were composed of five to seven members. The following describes the relevant chronological events for the team of five participating in this study.

a) Phase 1: "Development of a Need for Change."[32] The first meeting of the firm was to organize. The members decided to pattern their areas of responsibility along the functional lines outlined in the Game instructions. They assigned people to functional areas on the basis of personal interest and experience. The firm then drew up an organization chart (Figure 8–2).

The members of the firm set to work to try to learn their jobs. As part of this process, they held a group meeting to analyze the past performance of the "company" they were taking over. At this meeting, which was before any operating decisions had been made, the firm was approached to see if it would be willing to use the marketing program for its decisions and agree to use the program's decisions as long as they appeared reasonable to the firm. Just what the term "reasonable" meant was not further defined at that time.

The marketing manager of the firm recommended to the group that it accept the offer. He argued that he knew and had worked with the person who had written the program (hereafter referred to as the consultant), and had confidence that the program would be acceptable. The group tentatively accepted. It was decided that the team would make all decisions for several periods in order to give management experience in the Game. As soon as it was convenient, the firm would shift to computer-made decisions in the marketing area.

In the early "months" of the Game, data from the past month became available Wednesday noon, and decisions were due Friday morning. The team made

---

[32]The phases the change process followed corresponded so clearly with those outlined in Lippitt, Watson, and Westley, *op. cit.* that their terminology was chosen for the phase headings.

it a practice to meet in a classroom on Wednesday evening to make decisions as a group. A stable pattern of information processing (see Figure 8–3) quickly evolved. The president would outline goals for next month. The finance and production officers outlined very generally the constraints they had

FIGURE 8–2

INITIAL ORGANIZATION CHART OF THE FIRM

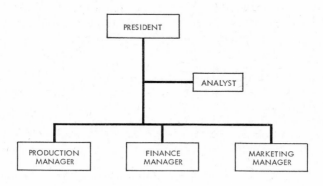

FIGURE 8–3

INITIAL COMMUNICATONS NET OF THE FIRM

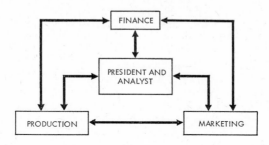

to apply to their decisions.[33] Then the president, the analyst, and the marketing manager would work out predicted sales and make the marketing decisions. Meanwhile the production and finance officers would set up their records. The marketing group would then submit their decisions to the production and finance officers, who would check the feasibility of the decisions. If any restrictions in funds or inventory were felt, the group would argue the point and arrive at a modified decision. Generally these meetings ran about three hours.

During these first few decisions, forecasts of case sales proved uncannily accurate. The firm evolved a policy of low price, low advertising, low distribution, and minimum excess inventory, until such a time as product research provided a good product. They set as a goal maximizing gross profits, and felt they had an operational policy to achieve this goal. The team members felt that the

---

[33]The finance officer was concerned with limited funds and the production officer with a high inventory.

team had high morale and were satisfied with the results of their operations, since profits exceeded expectations. During this period they formed no long-range strategies in the marketing area but did attempt to plan ahead in production and finance, making the assumption that the future market would be roughly the same as the present one.

b) *Phase 2: "Establishment of a Change Relationship."* The consultant appeared at a special meeting prior to the fourth decision meeting to explain the program. At this time, the team became disillusioned about the computer program. The group had thought the program would be an algorithmic one which would somehow maximize profit and yield unbeatable decisions. Instead, they were told that the program was a heuristic one, based on how previous teams had actually made decisions. The members of the team felt the heuristic rules incorporated in the program were naïve and extremely simple. They further believed that their heuristics for case sales forecasting were more complete than those of the program and would "beat it cold."[34]

A team that had been studied previously in deriving the program had experienced great success. The present firm was surprised to hear the consultant admit (when questioned) that he thought much of the success of the previously studied firm had come not from its marketing rules but from its having superior products.

At this stage the firm felt frustrated, first because they believed the consultant was late in getting to their problems, and second because they learned that the program would not be completely operational initially. At this time, the firm indicated that "if we had known how things were going to develop, we would certainly have prepared an alternate strategy to use if we decided not to accept the program." As it was, they felt "they were stuck with it." The general consensus, however, was that the firm would not use the program if it did not show "satisfactory" results in two months. Satisfactory was defined as positive net profit. Beyond this, the members felt, the question of continued use could be argued in the future. Before this time the decisions had been made but not analyzed. Now the firm set up a review board consisting of the president and the analyst, and the marketing manager was forced to justify the computer's decisions before this somewhat critical board.

The members of the firm were also very much concerned because they believed that the core of the marketing program was based on the firm's share of the total market.[35] This method was, they felt, quite different from the method they used in making these decisions.

As already indicated, the firm believed that it had achieved a working procedure for (at least approximately) maximizing long-run profits. When questioned, the consultant said that his computer program could also accomplish this objective. (In truth, however, the consultant had personal doubts that anyone could really maximize long-run profits, whatever this phrase meant.) The

---

[34]Further experience with the part of the program forecasting case sales did disclose a serious flaw in the heuristics which allocated case sales among products when a new product was introduced.

[35]This was not true. It is worth noting that at this time the firm felt that market share as reported in the Mark 1 version of the Carnegie Game was based on actual sales. In reality, this figure was based on potential sales. (No direct estimates of market shares are available in the Mark 1.5 version of the Carnegie Game; instead, estimates of retail case sales may be purchased.)

firm members accepted the consultant's expressed statement, although they were not really sure they believed him.

At this point, the firm's attitude toward the "black box," as the program was called, was one of cautious distrust. They decided to continue the Wednesday meetings and make marketing decisions in the usual manner for use in case the program was not successful and for comparison so that the firm would not accept decisions blindly.

The consultant also had some doubts about whether the firm would really use the program. All the talk about maximizing, which the consultant felt was not a description of the firm's actual goals, left the consultant wondering if the firm was seeking an excuse to evade its promise to use the program.

c) *Phases 3–5: "Working toward Change."* The first task was to try to simulate past decisions in an attempt to get the control parameters in the program set according to the firm's desires. At first only the advertising decisions were thought to be acceptable. The following month the programs for the price decisions and case sales forecasts became operational, and the firm began to use these decisions. The next month the program for distribution expenditure decisions went into operation, and the firm had shifted completely to machine-made marketing decisions.

This change in the place where actual month-to-month decisions were made was not accomplished without difficulties. Although no changes in the organization structure were formally planned, the introduction of the computer actually altered the firm's system of information processing considerably, as shown in Figures 8–3 and 8–4.

FIGURE 8–4

COMMUNICATIONS NET OF THE FIRM AFTER THE
INTRODUCTION OF THE COMPUTER
MARKETING PROGRAM

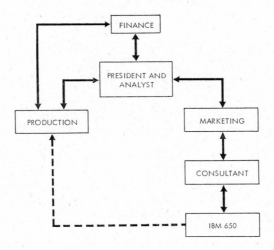

In addition to the communication and organization changes reflected in Figure 8–4, there were effects on the timing and sequence of decisions. Initially, as mentioned, the decision process was: (1) to set broad objectives to guide the analysis, (2) to communicate constraints found in the production and finance areas to define the field in which the marketing manager could operate, (3) to analyze alternatives and make tentative selection of marketing decisions, and (4) to analyze alternatives and make decisions in production and finance. This entire process had been carried out in one room with a great deal of cross-functional group communication at every stage in the development of the alternatives and decisions. Now with computer availability determining when the marketing decisions could be made, the order in which the decisions were made was variable from week to week. The firm found that it had to alter its system of information processing to deal with this change.

Most of the difficulties that occurred in introducing the program arose from the firm's attempts to adapt to the changes in the system of information processing. In particular, the marketing manager no longer spent any time in coordinating results with the production and finance officers, and he continued to operate under the assumption that the previous constraints (restricted funds and excess investory) still applied. Similarly, the production and finance members of the firm believed that there was little control to be exerted over the program. The method of control of the program was not fully understood. As a result the problems that arose reinforced the notion that the program operated independently of factors in other functional areas.

The marketing manager also felt that his concentration on the computer kept him from knowing what competitors were doing and made him lose sight of long-range objectives. (The computer did, of course, do a great deal of work in keeping up with the competitors' activities as part of its decision-making process.) The marketing manager remarked that he "did not really see how these side effects could be avoided, as it took a great effort to get the program working and phased into the firm." For instance, the firm's share of the market was going up, yet the marketing manager did not point out to the production manager that this would imply that past forecasts of case sales should be raised. Some shortages resulted. Further, the marketing manager became lax in reporting marketing results to the finance officer.

The inventory shortages precipitated a major crisis. This crisis demonstrated to the firm that its structure had really altered and led the firm to knowledge of how to deal with the new structure.

d) Phase 6: "The Generalization and Stabilization of Change. On the basis of its case sales forecasts, which had previously been very accurate, the firm continued to reduce inventory. At the same time that the computer's decisions were increasing the firm's share of the market, however, a competitor experienced severe shortages because he forgot to order raw materials. The firm felt that this combination of events had caused them to run out of finished goods to sell. This information showed up in the production sheets, and (because of the new structure) did not filter through to the marketing manager in time for him to consider altering marketing strategy. With unchanged parameters, the computer continued with an aggressive marketing strategy of low price and increased advertising.

When the president of the firm saw the marketing decisions, he held that they were completely unreasonable in terms of the situation at the time. It was then two hours before the decisions were supposed to be turned in. He argued that the inventory shortage was a special case and that the computer was undoubtedly unable to handle such a special and unusual problem. The president's reaction at this point was to suggest that they give up the computer and return to making decisions as they had previously. When the marketing manager finally understood what had happened, he argued that the computer had merely been misinformed, and that the firm would do better to use its decisions rather than to make decisions on the spur of the moment by themselves. But the president found this unacceptable.

After a little discussion, the president called the consultant to inform him that the firm intended to alter some of the computer's decisions. The consultant became aware of the problem for the first time. After listening to the president, he suggested that the firm correct their policy statements to allow for shortages and run the program again. The firm agreed, and reran the program with the correction.

The firm accepted the new decisions and stated that they were very much satisfied, since the month's results coupled a rise in price with an increase in market share. Although the marketing manager had previously been a strong supporter of the program, this incident convinced him fully of the capabilities of the program. The president still expressed reservations, stating that "there should be someone within the firm questioning 'black box' decisions." It is notable that at this time the rest of the firm expressed varying degrees of positive satisfaction with the program.

The president, in summing up the communication problem, said that at first under the new system it seemed that marketing decisions were made without the management group present or controlling and without regard to timing. The incident of the competitor's shortage points out the initial difficulty of the other operating departments in adapting to changes in marketing decisions. This difficulty undoubtedly arose because the communication flow and perceived control system of the firm had been altered. As the marketing manager gained experience and skill in using the program, his feelings that the firm could not control the computer gradually diminished.

e) *Phase 7: "Achieving a Terminal Relationship."* The timing of decisions remained a problem, because limitations in computer time did not always allow the program to be run when most convenient for the firm's decision-making sessions. Nevertheless, the firm felt enough confidence in the computer program to allow it to make decisions over a three-month period during which management was absent.

A review of the three-month period indicated that the computer program was an effective tool in retaining a basically healthy position under what management considered to be extremely unfavorable circumstances. Management recommended continued use of the program.

2. *Overview of the Group's Final Feeling.* The management of the firm was quite satisfied with the program at the end and stated, "After this experience we feel much happier with the heuristic program, because it allows the firm to set marketing policy." Because they retained basic management control over marketing decisions, the firm met with little opposition from its board over its use of the computer.

Recently the firm had meetings with an auditor group and its board of directors. Although there was still some skepticism within the firm about the program, in these meetings the group members emphasized the program's good points and in all cases strongly supported it.

The marketing manager felt that the short-run decision problem was solved, and he was next trying to engage in long-run planning, for he realized that use of the program gave him a powerful tool for evaluating different policies.

3. *Discussion and Conclusions.* This study has indicated the feasibility of having a heuristic computer program actually be a member of a decision-making group. While this may not be surprising, this is the first time such a project has actually been conducted. It is believed that this first investigation can shed some light on specific problems worth studying in this area and on the questions raised in the introduction.

The observations recorded above appear to be consistent with the theory that any successful change will pass through a set of clearly defined phases in a particular order. This consistency with previous theory and observations[36] allows the conjecture that the study has captured an essence of change in the real world.

The second notable feature was the absence of any overt emotional reaction. Occasionally one hears that human beings confronted by such a program would have an extremely negative emotional reaction. There was not open evidence of such a reaction in this study.

One could, however, expect people to mask such a reaction and substitute for it verbal rationalizations aimed at undermining the computer. For example, in the history it appears clear that there was a tendency for the computer's decisions to be evaluated more critically than those of the human being who had previously performed the task, as indicated under Phase 2. Of course, this effect could be abetted because the computer cannot argue back. There is also the tendency to demean the computer's ability to handle special cases, although it is by no means clear that this derogation arose from an emotional source.

Further, this case is actually somewhat special in that the people involved felt they had control over their own fate. Another question to raise is: Did the school environment, which prevented severe penalties for failure, affect the existence of emotional reaction? These questions suggest two hypotheses worth future exploration:

Hypothesis 1: Negative emotional reaction will be more extreme with definite punishment for failure than without.

Hypothesis 2: Negative emotional reaction will be more extreme if the people involved in the change do not feel they have control over the program than if they do.

The third effect is how the organization structure changed. Specifically, there tended to be one (human) member of the firm with whom the computer did most of its communicating. The temporary difficulties the firm ran into because it had not planned ahead organizationally for the computer are a further reflection of the alteration in structure. Figures 8-3 and 8-4 demonstrate that the organization structure did change, and that the introduction of the computer increased the centralization of the organization. This supports the hypothesis put forward by Leavitt and Whisler, although one must be cautious about extrapolating results from a small group of five people to a large corporation.

Given the present state of communicating with computers, the history presented above would suggest that any introduction of a computer into such an

---

[36]Lippitt, Watson, and Westley, *op. cit.*

organization could be facilitated first by providing for such special communication links and secondly by openly and officially altering the organization structure to make the new information flows clearly understood within the organization. Indeed, these considerations might have some applicability whenever a computer is used.[37]

Together with the historical record, this suggests a third hypothesis:

Hypothesis 3: For any such heuristic program to be actually used, it is necessary that an influential member of the group strongly support the computer.

In the group studied, the marketing manager served such a function. His support of the program was a key to the program's acceptance and to the firm's continued use of the program during the inventory crisis.

Of course we cannot, from a single sample, be sure that conditions such as those listed would be requisite for the successful introduction of such a tool, but it does seem that both setting up an organization structure to facilitate communcation with the program and having an organization member responsible for the success of the change can facilitate the transition.

The case reported also suggests some of the mechanisms which may enter into attempts by human beings to resist the change. It appears that such action is not a blind, emotional hatred or distrust of change, but rather rational behavior by human beings trying to do their job. It may be hypothesized that people not intimately familiar with the computer program will tend to demean the program's ability to handle special cases. With a problem not considered in setting up the computer program, it is reasonable to expect that the search for a solution to it would be directed outside the program. The inventory shortage problem discussed is an example of this reaction.

If the computer does not have strong support, one could expect the special cases to multiply until the computer has, in reality, no job. This does impose on the author of such programs the requirement that the decision rules formulated be capable of handling special cases or be quickly adapted to such exceptions. One should also desire of such a program the ability to rerun and alter decisions, if top management decides to alter its policy, which is exactly what would be expected of the human being it replaces.

This completes the discussion of the questions originally raised. During the course of the study, however, an interesting observation was made of the firm's behavior toward outsiders. Even at a time when certain members of the group were suspicious and critical of the computer program, the group told outsiders only about the advantages of using the computer. Thus it seems reasonable to expect that other groups adopting such a tool might make only favorable reports, which suggests a fourth hypothesis:

Hypothesis 4: The more internal dissension, the more the group using the computer would give favorable reports to other groups.[38]

---

[37]It appears that such considerations were evident in at least one actual case. See F. C. Mann and L. K. Williams, "Observations on the Dynamics of a Change to Electronic Data-Processing Equipment," *Administrative Science Quarterly,* Vol. 5 (1960–61), pp. 215–56.

[38]The hypothesis suggests an analogy to the Simon model of Festinger's theory of the dissident group member. Cf. H. A. Simon, *Models of Man* (New York: John Wiley & Sons, Inc., 1957), p. 133.

This report also raises some other questions. Would some other communication structure be more effective in facilitating the change? Would innovation be facilitated by introducing such tools in all areas of the firm, rather than in just one, as was done here? What would the result have been if the program had possessed a learning program above the heuristic one used, so that the program would have set its own control parameters with only general guidance from human management? All of these questions seem important, and all of them are as yet unanswered.

III.   STUDIES OF PLANNING AND DECISION-MAKING TECHNIQUES

In this section, two research papers are reprinted which show how the Carnegie Tech Management Game can be used as a reasonably realistic, but very accessible, environment in which attempts can be made to develop improved methods of business planning and decision making.

A. The Rote Marketer (by George H. Haines, Jr.)[39]

The purpose of this paper is to discover the decision processes used by members of a specific task-oriented group. The task is that of producing the monthly marketing decisions required in the Mark 1 version of the Carnegie Tech Management Game.

The specific theory presented below is consistent with the general concepts of Newell, Shaw, and Simon.[40] In particular, it is postulated that there exist: (1) a memory, (2) search and selection procedures, and (3) a set of rules or criteria which guide the decision-making process. One way of specifying precisely these three elements is by use of a computer program. This is the device adopted in this study.[41]

Usually heuristic computer programs can modify their behavior by eliminating unsuccessful procedures and adapting to changing conditions in the "environment." This is true of the model presented here, also. The present study postulates that the basic organization of such decision-making procedures is epicyclic in nature.

The "upper level" of this performance structure is the part which performs the overall planning function—which learns in the sense indicated above. The output of this program takes the form of a set of policy parameters. The policy parameters control the general behavior of the "lower level" program.

The "lower level," which is the part of the process studied in greatest detail in this paper, accepts as inputs the policy parameters set by the "upper level"

[39]This is a modified version of George H. Haines, Jr., "The Rote Marketer," *Behavioral Science,* Vol. 6, No. 4 (October, 1961), pp. 357–65.

[40]See A. Newell, J. C. Shaw, and H. A. Simon, "Elements of a Theory of Human Problem Solving," *Psychological Review,* Vol. 65, No. 3 (1958), pp. 151–66.

[41]For a more complete discussion of the issues involved in using a computer program in this manner, see A. Newell and H. A. Simon, "The Simulation of Human Thought," RAND Corporation Report P–1734, 1959. An extended example of the way in which a computer program can be used to express a theory of trust portfolio selection can be found in Geoffrey P. E. Clarkson, *Portfolio Selection: A Simulation of Trust Investment* (Englewood Cliffs, N. J.: Prentice-Hall, Inc., 1962).

program plus the necessary data from the world. It then proceeds to make decisions in a set, mechanical way. Although this program responds to the environment, the decision structure it uses is fixed. For this reason it can be termed a rote program, using "rote" to imply a set, mechanical way of making decisions. This general type of decision-making process is not inconsistent with certain propositions in organizational theory, as will be noted below.

By definition, all goals are influential in decisions. One particular goal of the teams studied seemed to be of particular relevance, however. The teams tended to set two operational goals. The first was continued existence. Such a goal and its implications have been discussed for actual firms by Fellner.[42] The second goal of the team (if they perceived no danger of going out of business) was doing as well as the other teams in the industry. This goal is characterized by statements such as "B0 is our chief competitor, so let's set all prices next period equal to their prices this period." The essence of such a mechanism is a simple response to the environment. For example, policy may be set to make the nature of the simple response move in the same direction as everyone else.

It is easy to note in the ensuing discussion that in such rote performance programs very few features of the "complex environment" are used in making the decisions. It is not sufficient to leave the analysis at this point. Above the rote performance program lies a fairly sophisticated analysis—a program with the ability to calculate consequences and deal with uncertainty by imagining alternative responses to the environment. This more complicated planning program appears to be only infrequently invoked, however.

The actual performance of people reaching decisions in plays of the Carnegie Tech Management Game was studied in four cases. In one case shorthand notes of the decision process were taken; in another some formal, taped protocols were obtained; in two cases no formal notes of the decision process were taken.

As protocols of the upper level of decision are not easy to obtain, it was decided to study first the rote program. Through this a clearer understanding of how and where the planning function enters into the total process of decision making could be gained. Once this is known, the rare chance of observing a planning decision could be made more fruitful by having an understanding of what the outputs of the planning program were. Thus this report will deal primarily with the rote performance programs.

1. Performance Program Structure. The performance programs fall into the following clearly defined areas:

   a) Advertising Decisions
   b) Price Decisions
   c) Case Sales Forecasting
   d) Distribution Expenditure Decisions

For each of these areas a detailed program was developed. The programs were written in GATE, an algebraic computer language for the IBM 650 with disc storage.

a) Advertising Decision Program. This program produces advertising decisions for the next month. It is an example of the response-mechanism type of decision making discussed previously. A flow sheet is shown in Figure 8–5.

---

[42]W. Fellner, "Average Cost Pricing and the Theory of Uncertainty," *Journal of Political Economy,* Vol. 56, No. 3 (June, 1948), pp. 249–52.

FIGURE 8-5

ADVERTISING FLOW DIAGRAM (*Control Variables Shown as* $X_1 - X_t$)

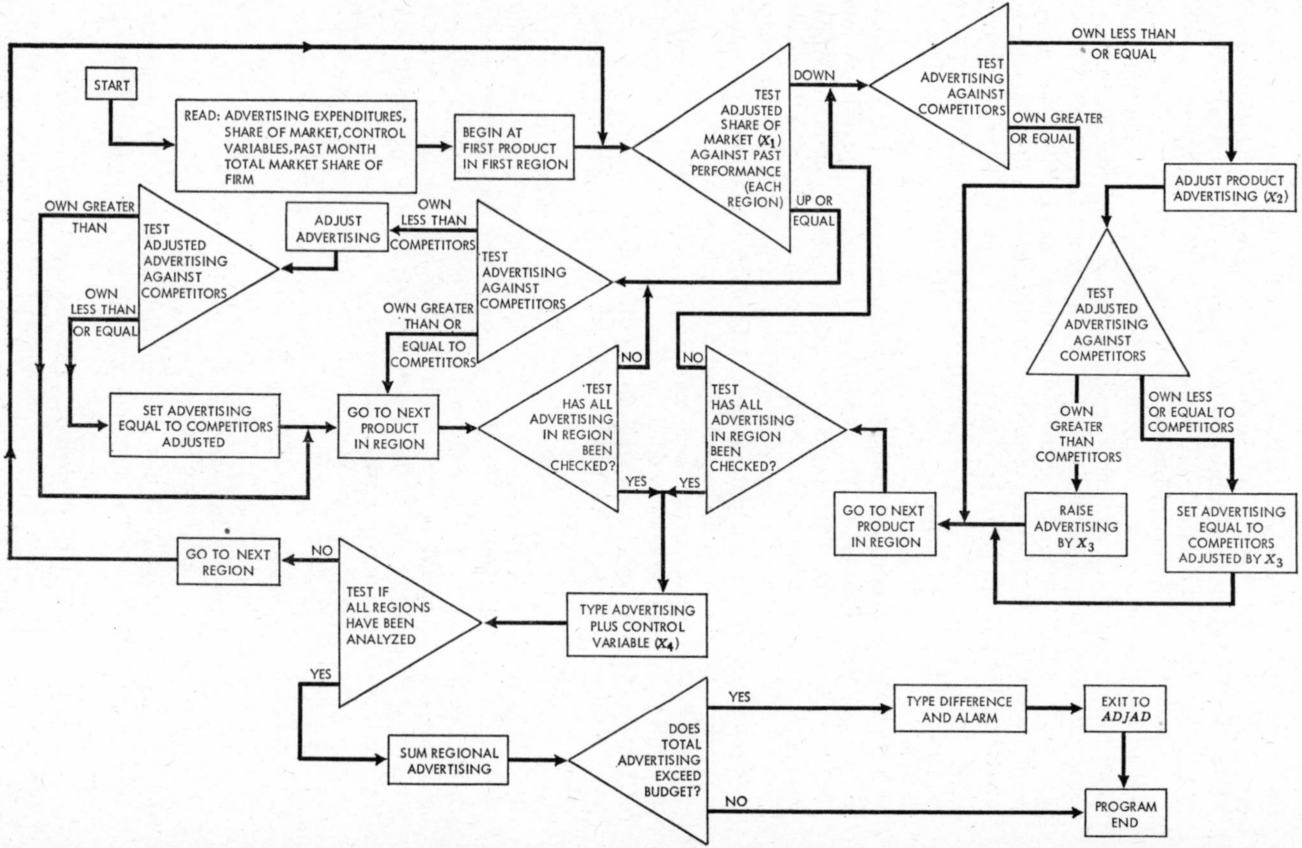

In the process outlined in Figure 8–5 the program responds to the environment differently according to certain cues. For purposes of exposition, let us assume that all control variables are greater than zero. Then we can discuss the qualitative behavior of the program. First, it tests whether "share of market" is increasing. If "share of market" has fallen, the response mechanism is more likely to increase advertising expenditures than if "share of market" has risen.

After this, the program tests the firm's advertising expenditures for the past month against its competitors. Usually, the sensitivity of this test is controlled by a variable set by the planning program. If advertising is too low, it is raised to meet the competitors' adjusted advertising. Only if "share of market" has fallen is there a chance that the rote program will raise advertising above the competition. This type of behavior should not really be too surprising in view of the satisfying type of goals explicated previously. The planning program, however, can initiate aggressive action if this is deemed necessary. Such action can be taken directly through setting a "dollar amount of advertising" control variable greater than zero (X_4 on the flowsheet).

Finally, the program checks "desired advertising" against the amount budgeted. If the amount desired is too large, the program recognizes this by producing an "alarm" output and computing the amount by which "desired advertising" exceeds the budget. This information does not go to the financial officer. Instead it causes the "adjust advertising" program to be evoked, and in the forecasting program it reduces forecasted sales for the next month.

The outputs of the advertising decision program will in general either leave advertising unchanged or else alter advertising upward to meet competitors' increases. The essence of this mechanism is very similar to an economist's kinked demand curve: it will raise advertising to meet competition, but not lower advertising if competitors lower theirs.

The interested reader can obtain a clear picture of the complexity of outputs which this program allows by setting various control variables negative or null and working through the qualitative behavior of the program, as was done above for the case when all the control variables are greater than zero.

As described above, the "adjust advertising" program shown in Figure 8–6 is invoked whenever the advertising decision program requires that more money

FIGURE 8–6

"ADJUST ADVERTISING" FLOW OUTLINE

1. Start.
2. Read: Desired advertising, each region.
            Amount desired total exceeds budget.
            Control variable (C_{50}).
            Share of market.
            Past month regional total market share.
3. Determine in which regions market share has risen.
4. Subtract C_{50} from desired advertising in each region in which market share has risen. After each subtraction, check to see if amount budgeted minus desired advertising is now positive. If so, go to 6. If not, go to 5.
5. Apportion the remaining amount to be cut in 4 parts, cut this much from each region.
6. Program end.

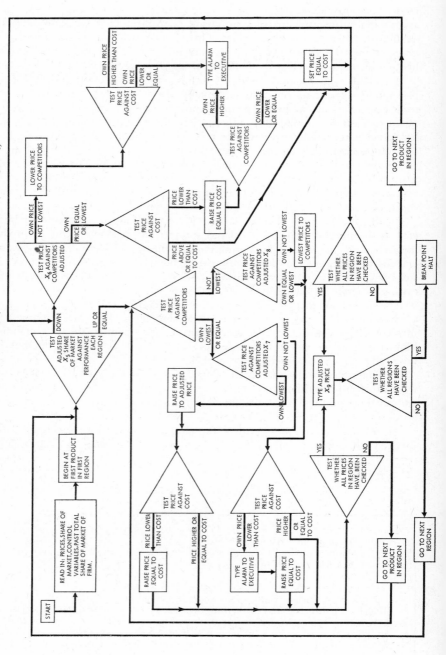

FIGURE 8-7

PRICE DETERMINATION FLOW DIAGRAM (*Control Variables Shown as* X_5—X_9)

be spent on advertising than the group (or the finance manager) wants to spend.

The "adjust advertising" program first sets up a list of all areas in which the firm's share of market has risen. From the "desired advertising" in each such area it subtracts an amount set by the planning program, testing after each subtraction to see if desired advertising now equals or is less than budgeted. If more money remains to be deleted, the program arbitrarily cuts one fourth of the amount left from the desired advertising for each area.

The program then outputs the new "desired advertising," which is now equal to or less than the amount budgeted for advertising on the product under consideration.

b) Price Determination Program. The bulk of the mechanisms used in this program are analogous to those used in the advertising program. Two differences should be recorded.

First, the program can follow price cuts and price increases made by the competition. Whether it does or not depends, of course, on the size of the price difference, the sensitivity of the program to price differences (set by control variables), and how "share of market" has moved for the firm (see Figure 8–7).

Second, the program also contains a standard cost mechanism. The standard cost mechanism, referred to in the flow sheet simply as "cost," is a markup variable. That is, the "costs" used in the program represent direct costs with a percentage markup. The program will not allow price to fall below this "cost" under any circumstances. If competitiors are selling a product at a price sufficiently less than this "cost," the program lowers price to "cost" and outputs an alarm to the planning program.

The role of this particular alarm to the planning program is clear. It exerts pressure for the planning program to: (1) lower the percentage markup, (2) put pressure on the advertising program to raise advertising, and (3) increase the search for new (better) products.

FIGURE 8–8

CASE SALES FORECASTING FLOW DIAGRAM

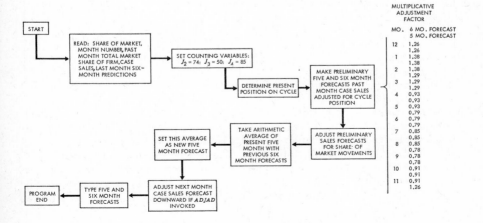

c) Case Sales Forecasting. The case sales forecasting program has a fairly simple appearance because sales are well structured by the Game. The cyclical pattern is rigidly given; thus numbers appear where otherwise control variables would possibly enter.

The program predicts sales five and six months ahead, based on the cyclical pattern, present sales, and share of market movements. The mechanisms are clearly outlined in the flow sheet (see Figure 8–8). Notice that the program also adjusts forecasts for the effects of insufficient advertising.

Probably the most interesting aspect of this program is the tremendous amount of uncertainty it absorbs. Because the factory needs stable forecasts on which to base production, shipping, and raw materials orders, the program makes no changes in predicted sales for five months save for a possible downward adjustment due to low advertising. This may seem unreal; it may seem that "nobody would do this." The only defense for it is that this is precisely the mechanism used by the teams observed.

d) Distribution Expenditures Program. This program, which determines distribution expenditures on the basis of the cyclical pattern and past month case sales, is represented in Figure 8–9. One team which was observed at first

FIGURE 8–9

DISTRIBUTION EXPENDITURES FLOW OUTLINE

1. Start.
2. Read: Month number.
           Product and policy control variables.
           Past month distribution expenditures.
           Case sales.
3. Test: Are we in high part of sales cycle?
           a) No—Go to 4.
           b) Yes—Go to 8.
4. Adjust distribution expenditures (X_{12}).
5. Test: Adjusted distribution against competitors.
           a) Higher—Leave distribution the same, go to 10.
           b) Lower—Go to 6.
6. Adjust multiplicative factor by X_{10}.
7. Set distribution equal to past month case sales times multiplicative factor plus X_{11}, go to 10.
8. Adjust multiplicative factor by X_{13}.
9. Set distribution equal to past month case sales times multiplicative factor plus X_{14}.
10. Type distribution.
11. Program end.

used advertising expenditures instead of past month case sales, but later switched to using past month case sales "because they felt it was better." The question of how people evaluate alternative heuristics is not explored further in this paper, although it is clearly an interesting one. The program does not respond in any matter to competitors during the peak months; during the low sales months (months 8, 9, 10, 11, 12, 1, and 2) it can lower distribution expenditures if competitors have set their expenditures sufficiently below the firm's own previous level.

2. Testing the System. Before discussing the implications which can be drawn from the above system, we shall consider the validity of the cognitive processes represented by the above programs. Two different methods of testing were used.

The first was simulation of actual decisions made by various firms. Tables 8–6 to 8–9 report the results of these simulations. It is obvious from examination of the figures that the simulation results come "fairly close" to the actual decisions the firms made.

TABLE 8–6

ADVERTISING SIMULATION

(In Thousands of Dollars)

		Predicted	Real	Random	Naïve
Product A	E	19.8	20	308	26
	S	19.5	20	319	20
	C	64.0	20	848	20
	W	28.0	30	563	30
Product B	E	380	330	481	380
	S	300	300	1	300
	C	553	500	588	550
	W	507	500	276	500
Product C	E	51	50	267	50
	S	0	90	430	90
	C	204	50	161	50
	W	158	90	97	90

$$(1)\ \Sigma\ (\text{Real-Predicted})^2 = \quad 43,737.25$$
$$\Sigma\Delta_1^2 = \quad 25,399.35$$
$$(2)\ \Sigma\ (\text{Real-Random})^2 = 1,847,199.0$$
$$\Sigma\Delta_2^2 = 532,346.92$$
$$(3)\ \Sigma\ (\text{Real-Naïve})^2 = \quad 5,036.0$$
$$\Sigma\Delta_3^2 = \quad 4,099.67$$

H_0: (1) = (2) $\hat{F} = 20.96$ Reject H_0 ($\alpha = .05$) for $F_{11,11} = 2.82$

H_0: (1) = (3) $\hat{F} = 6.20$ Reject H_0.

The question which arises is whether this supposed closeness is real or not. We propose a simple-minded test to attempt to answer this question. This test is based on an alternative model. The alternative model asserts that the actual decisions can be better explained by assuming the numbers used by the firms were generated randomly. The reason for doing this is simple. The entire discussion of this paper is based on the assertion that the decision-making process of the firms studied is nonrandom. If, however, randomly drawn numbers come closer to the actual decisions than the results of the theoretical model described above, it seems clear that we should become suspicious of the validity of the proposed model. Therefore, a list of random numbers with a uniform distribution was drawn[43] and set down in the column headed "Random."

---

[43]From A. Duncan, *Quality Control and Industrial Statistics* (Homewood, Ill.: Richard D. Irwin, Inc., 1955), p. 633.

TABLE 8–7

Pricing Simulation

(In Dollars per Case)

		Predicted	Real	Random	Naïve
Product A	E	6.10	6.17	7.73	5.97
	S	6.17	6.27	4.24	6.07
	C	6.10	6.05	6.08	6.00
	W	6.14	6.13	2.20	6.04
Product B	E	5.90	5.92	9.15	5.78
	S	5.90	5.98	6.49	5.78
	C	5.90	5.82	3.66	5.75
	W	6.00	6.05	2.21	5.90
Product C	E	6.48	6.22	9.21	6.38
	S	6.30	6.29	3.47	6.39
	C	6.58	6.48	3.47	6.48
	W	6.30	6.36	6.40	6.42

(1) Σ (Real-Predicted)$^2 =$ 0.1445

$\Sigma\Delta_1^2 =$ 0.0955

(2) Σ (Real-Random)^2 = 76.8947

$\Sigma\Delta_2^2 =$ 20.7779

(3) Σ (Real-Naïve)^2 = 0.2268

$\Sigma\Delta_3^2 =$ 0.0384

Ho: (1) = (2) $\hat{F}$ = 217.57 Reject Ho ($\alpha =$
.05) for $F_{11,11} = 2.82$

Ho: (1) = (3) $\hat{F}$ = 2.49 Cannot reject Ho.

TABLE 8–8

Case Sales Forecasting Simulation

(Sales in Thousands)

	Predicted	Real	Random	Naïve
Month 19	1,855	2,891	6,539	2,669
Month 20	2,531	2,272	8,764	2,891
Month 21	1,949	2,183	861	2,272
Month 22	2,119	2,286	852	2,183
Month 23	2,246	2,507	8,986	2,286
Month 24	2,326	1,893	4,230	2,507

(1) Σ (Real-Predicted)$^2 =$ 1,478,632

$\Sigma\Delta_1^2 =$ 526,616

(2) Σ (Real-Random)^2 = 106,697,018

$\Sigma\Delta_2^2 =$ 28,128,528

(3) Σ (Real-Naïve)^2 =   876,812

$\Sigma\Delta_3^2 =$ 295,242

Ho: (1) = (2) $\hat{F}$ = 53.41 Reject Ho ($\alpha =$
.05) for $F_{5,5} = 5.05$

Ho: (1) = (3) $\hat{F}$ = 1.78 Cannot reject Ho.

TABLE 8–9

DISTRIBUTION EXPENDITURES SIMULATION

		Predicted	Real	Random	Naïve
Product A	E	151	208	258	120
	S	143	116	453	120
	C	147	50	113	120
	W	141	201	897	120
Product B	E	87	61	88	90
	S	90	89	60	90
	C	87	151	67	90
	W	88	40	50	90
Product C	E	28	0	77	20
	S	35	20	27	40
	C	31	38	54	40
	W	30	0	11	40

(1) Σ (Real-Predicted)^2 =   25,654

$\Sigma\Delta_1^2 =$ 8,388.67

(2) Σ (Real-Random)^2 = 619,535

$\Sigma\Delta_2^2 =$ 454,564.25

(3) Σ (Real-Naïve)^2 = 28,688

$\Sigma\Delta_3^2 =$ 10,591.67

H_0: (1) = (2) $\hat{F}$ = 54.19   Reject H_0 ($\alpha =$

.05) $F_{11,11} = 2.82$

H_0: (1) = (3) $\hat{F}$ = 1.26 Cannot reject H_0.

A second alternative model is to say that next period's results will be the same as the last period's. The predictions this model would make are listed in the "Naïve" column. This is a fairly strong test, and we would hope that our theory can account for the results as well as the naïve model does. The point is, of course, that such a naïve model does not help in explaining why existing decision patterns exist, while the theoretical model presented above does.[44]

To test the closeness of fit, the difference between the three models and the actual decisions are tabulated, and from these numbers the three relevant variances are calculated.[45] The results of these tests are reported at the bottom of each table. In all cases, our model comes closer to the actual decisions than does the random number model. Our model does as well as the "naïve" model in all cases except the advertising simulation.

This type of simulation, however, raises another question: could such relatively good fits have been obtained by varying the control parameters to fit the one case? In other words, are these programs spurious in the sense that the control parameters would have to be varied for each decision period to achieve sensible decisions?

[44]For a discussion of this type of test, see I. R. Savage and K. W. Deutsch, "A Statistical Model of the Gross Analysis of Transactions Flows," *Econometrica*, Vol. 28, No. 3, (July, 1960), pp. 551–72.

[45]See Duncan, *op. cit.*, for the F–tables used and (p. 405) for the graph of the operating characteristics curve for the test.

Rather than attempt to run simulations over a long period of time, a slightly different test was proposed. This test was to let the program be used by one team which actually was engaged in playing the Carnegie Tech Management Game and to allow them to reject the program if they felt that its decisions were unsuitable. If the program was used, they would be free to alter the control parameters as they saw fit, and as much as they saw fit. This was actually done.[46]

The team used the program for six "months" (a month is the decision unit in the Carnegie Tech Game). The team accepted the program, used it, and continued to use it as long as the computer in which the program was run was available to the team. During this time the control parameters remained unchanged, except for the introduction of a new product. At this time some (but not all) control parameters were altered. Also, the value of one control parameter in the pricing program (X_9 on Figure 8–7) was made contingent upon whether or not inventory run-outs had occurred in the past month. We can conclude that once set, the control parameters are exceedingly stable.

This test had the additional feature of testing the reality of the program by throwing it into competition with humans. At any time the team could have dropped the program, but they did not do this. The conclusion is that the program is actually useful in the "real world" of the Game. The team members believed that use of the program aided them because it forced them to think in terms of strategies, not month-to-month decisions.

As part of this test, a modified Turing test was performed. The competitors of the team were asked whether they could tell in what month the firm had begun to use the program (this fact previously being kept secret). They were unable to do so. This is not really a very strong test, as almost any adaptive program would give this kind of result.

There is no evidence to deny the proposition that the program does appear to have captured the essence of the actual rote (that is, nonlearning) part of the decision-making process. It must be kept in mind, however, that probably none of the tests used have great power.

3. *The Game and the Real World.* The program presented above represents a theory of how Carnegie Tech Management Game players make decisions. This theory consists of a structure of salient facts about the environment, through which the program processes the appropriate data from the real world in its decision making. In this it resembles the metaplan of Miller, Galanter, and Pribram.[47]

The structure itself, one may conjecture, arises out of a search for and recognition of patterns in the real world. For example, in the pricing program the list of prices which is set up is composed of four areas, nine products per area: a structural aspect of the Game. If we compare this with a study of how such decisions are made in the real world, striking similarities occur.[48]

An analogous decision-making procedure appears in the Cyert, March, and Moore study of a department store.[49] The case sales forecasting programs are essentially the same in structure, and in the heuristics used. Further, the pricing process outlined in the department store study follows an almost exactly similar

---

[46]For a detailed report of the effects this had on the team, see Section II.B above.

[47]G. A. Miller, E. Galanter, and K. H. Pribram, *Plans and the Structure of Behavior* (New York: Holt, 1960).

[48]See Cyert and March, *op. cit.*

[49]R. M. Cyert, J. G. March, and C. G. Moore, "A Specific Price and Output Model," in Cyert and March, *op. cit.,* chap. 7.

pattern to the theory outlined above for Management Game players. In both programs, a standard cost is a key variable in the pricing decision process; the type of attention paid to competitors' prices is very similar also.

The differences in the two programs seem to come from structural differences in the real worlds under consideration. This is not surprising if we believe the underlying postulates to be the same, for then environmental differences would cause different actual behavior. For example, the department store study contains a subprogram to deal with sale pricing; this is absent in the Game program. The reason for this is simply that "sales" are not allowed in the Mark 1 version of the Carnegie Tech Management Game.

4. Relation to Organization Theory. The general model developed here from observations of the "real" Game world provides some interesting illustrations of some propositions in organization theory.

First, the general model built here is not just epicyclic in nature. The higher level affects the lower-level program in only a few places, through the control variables. The essence of the mechanism used has been described by March and Simon as follows: "Limitation of high-level action to the recombination of programs, rather than the detailed construction of new programs out of small elements, is extremely important . . ."[50]

Similarly, organization theory predicts that "in organizations where various aspects of the whole complex problem are being handled by different individuals and different groups of individuals, a fundamental technique for simplifying the problem is to factor it into a number of nearly independent parts, so that each organizational unit handles one of these parts and can omit the others from its definition of the situation." The model presented here of marketing decision making precisely illustrates this contention.

Furthermore, we are here faced with a relatively stable environment, namely, the rules of the Game. Thus it is not surprising that there is only limited communication between the specialized subprograms. The coordination which does exist between the subprograms is largely coordination based on preestablished plan.[51] Moreover, this communication is measurable; in theory, at least, more or less communication could be used and the effect of this discovered by experiment. The above program also illustrates the structure of programs for handling recurrent events, and the organizational aspects of such programs.

It is obvious that the program presented in this paper, which is concerned largely with programs to respond to sequences of situations requiring short-run adaptive behavior, exhibits the form hypothesized to exist in organizations in general. This in itself is an interesting fact. The question arises as to whether such a fact can be used to push into the area of testing hypotheses in organizational theory. As of yet, no statistical answer to the question has been proposed.

B. A Linear Programming Model for Budgeting and Financial Planning (by Yuji Ijiri, Ferdinand K. Levy, and Richard C. Lyon)[52]

This paper reports on an experiment in applying modern mathematical methods to management problems in budgeting and financial planning. In this

---

[50]March and Simon, *op cit.,* p. 150.

[51]*Ibid.,* p. 143 and p. 150.

[52]This is a modified version of Yuji Ijiri, Ferdinand K. Levy, and Richard C. Lyon, "A Linear Programming Model for Budgeting and Financial Planning," *Journal of Accounting Research,* Vol. 1, No. 2 (Autumn, 1963), pp. 198–212.

experiment the techniques of linear programming and double-entry accounting are joined by means of suitable models and interpretation in order to see what might be gained in the way of a unified approach to total enterprise planning.

Two very general aspects of this study may be identified. Starting from an initial statement of the balance sheet accounts, the first aspect of this study was concerned with devising ways of planning (and identifying) the transaction flows that would, in terms of some relevant objective: (a) bring the corporation into the best possible end-of-period balance sheet position, and (b) make due allowance for other aspects of management policy, technological limitations, and so on. The second aspect of this study was concerned with synthesizing information that could be utilized by management to evaluate all aspects of the problem. That is, it was desired to erect a model which could be used to supply information by means of which a company's management might readily determine the dollar consequences that could be expected to flow from altering the firm's policies or the environment in which it operated, and so on.

To accomplish both of these study objectives simultaneously, the so-called direct and dual aspects of a linear programming approach were utilized.[53] Briefly, the direct linear programming model was used to synthesize an optimum program under given conditions (or constraints) in order to achieve a best end-of-period balance sheet as outlined under the first of the study aspects noted above. Then the dual linear programming model was utilized to provide information on how the initially stated conditions might be altered, as outlined above, for the second aspect of this study.

It would have been desirable, of course, to test or otherwise validate (and study) this kind of application in the context of an actual business firm. This was not done. Instead, an application was made in the setting of the Carnegie Tech Management Game. Fortunately, this Game is sufficiently complicated so that it will bear the weight even of the applications of modern operations research techniques, like linear programming, in more than trivial or unchallenging ways. Thus, the application was made in the following manner. Acting as a hypothetical operations research group[54] within one of the functioning firms, various aspects of a model were synthesized and tested against data that were assembled for this purpose. In particular, electronic computer runs[55] were made and compared with actual operations for a representative period of months. Significant improvements were noted, but since this involved an *ex post facto* comparison it cannot be considered a wholly valid test of the model under the conditions of the Game where large amounts of uncertainty, the need for coordinated action (as contrasted with coordinated plans), and like considerations must also be handled. For this reason, and also because it will permit us to simplify parts of the (direct) model, we do not propose to emphasize this aspect

---

[53]For an explanation and a managerial interpretation of "direct" and "dual" linear programming models, see A. Charnes and W. W. Cooper, *Management Models and Industrial Applications of Linear Programming* (New York: John Wiley & Sons, Inc., 1961), chap. 1.

[54]This was actually done as part of an assignment for Carnegie Tech's graduate course in operations research taught by Professor W. W. Cooper and described more fully in Section III of Chapter 5. This present paper by Ijiri, Levy, and Lyon is based largely on the OR report to the firm in question, prepared as part of that assignment.

[55]Carnegie Tech's CDC G–21 computer was used for this purpose.

of the study here. We shall try, instead, to emphasize the possible managerial uses of the so-called dual evaluators—which emerge from any such model—after first developing the direct model in sufficient detail to provide a basis for understanding: (a) the actual operating problem that was studied, and (b) the kinds of interrelations that obtain between any pair of direct and dual linear programming models.

1. *Synthesizing the Model.* In order to synthesize the one-period model with which we are here concerned, it will be convenient to commence with the balance-sheet shown in Table 8–10. This is the actual balance sheet for an operating firm, at the relevant beginning-of-period date. Note that certain accounts have been combined in order to achieve some desirable simplifications in the model that will be utilized.

TABLE 8–10

BEGINNING BALANCE SHEET

C:	Cash	$ 7,260,000	*P:*	Accounts payable	$ 3,592,000
B:	Securities	12,000,000	*D:*	Dividends and taxes	
R:	Accounts receivable	6,999,000		payable	2,922,000
G:	Finished goods	4,032,000	*L:*	Loans payable	4,400,000
M:	Raw materials	1,499,000	*E:*	Stockholders'	
F:	Fixed assets	26,000,000		account	46,876,000
		$57,790,000			$57,790,000

Attention is now called to the letter codes that appear alongside the account captions. By means of the "spread sheet" conventions of double-entry accounting,[56] these letters will be paired in a way that admits of the debit-credit relations that are needed for accounting interpretations of the resulting transactions. For instance, refer to Table 8–11 (see page 321), and observe that the letter pair CB refers to the class of entries debit Cash, $C,$ and credit Securities, $B(=$ Bonds). In each case we shall employ the variable X to refer to the "amount" of the transaction. Thus, in Table 8–11, $X_{CB} = \$9,703,000$, the amount which is debited to Cash and credited to Securities. In every case the debit entry will be symbolized as the left member of a letter pair and the corresponding credit entry will be symbolized by the letter appearing on the right in exactly the same manner as was just explained for X_{CB}.

2. *Model Constraints.* These debit-credit letter pairs for the transaction flows need to be supplemented by symbols for the balance sheet (stock) amounts. To represent these figures, we shall use the symbol K with an appropriate subscript. For instance, $K_C = \$7,260,000$ refers to the opening Cash balance while $K_B = \$12,000,000$ refers to the opening balance of the Securities account, and so on.

The balance sheet accounts and the transaction flows will, of course, be related by the usual accounting identities. In addition, we need to impose certain

---

[56]These are explained in A. Charnes, W. W. Cooper, and Y. Ijiri, "Breakeven Budgeting and Programming to Goals," *Journal of Accounting Research,* Vol. 1, No. 1 (Spring, 1963), pp. 16–43. See also the references cited therein, and especially Eric L. Kohler, *A Dictionary for Accountants* (Englewood Cliffs, N.J.: Prentice-Hall, Inc., 1952).

conditions (or constraints) which limit the transactions. As a case in point, for this one-period model, we impose:

(1) The firm's sale of securities cannot exceed the beginning balance in this account—namely,

$$X_{CB} \leq K_B \tag{1}$$

where, of course, $K_B = \$12,000,000$ in this case, and the inequality symbol "$\leq$" means that X_{CB} can equal, but cannot exceed, this amount.

In addition to *inequality* constraints, like (1), we also wish to incorporate *equations* which we now illustrate by means of one part of the data for the Game:

(2) Interest on securities, as earned, is received in cash for the securities on hand at the *end* of the period. The monthly interest rate is 0.229 percent. Hence

$$X_{CE} = .00229 \, (K_B + X_{BC} - X_{CB}) \tag{2}$$

To see what this expression means note that K_B is the opening balance for Securities while X_{BC} refers to securities purchased during the period by offsets to Cash. Similarly, X_{CB} refers to the Cash debits realized by sales of securities during the period. Hence $(K_B + X_{BC} - X_{CB})$ correctly states the ending balance when, as is true under the conditions of the Carnegie Tech Game, all such transactions are effected only in cash. Thus applying the indicated interest rate of 0.229 percent we obtain exactly X_{CE}, the amount which is debited to cash and credited to the stockholder's account.[57]

In the model that we shall use, direct reference to income account details will be avoided. This greatly simplifies the model and does so with no great loss since supplementary analyses of the transactions, with the aid of the model (and its associated spread sheet), can always be undertaken to synthesize an income statement whenever it is wanted. (See Table 8–13, page 322.)

The point to be emphasized is that the model with which we are concerned will be one in which *all* constraints must be *simultaneously* satisfied. Thus, for example, the X_{CB} which appears in (1) is exactly the same as the one that appears in (2). It will perhaps serve to illustrate our intended meaning by rearranging terms in (1) and (2) and positioning the constant, K_B, on the right to achieve the pair of expressions:

$$X_{CB} \qquad\qquad \leq \qquad K_B$$

$$.00229 \, X_{CB} + X_{CE} - .00229 \, X_{BC} = .00229 \, K_B \tag{2.1}$$

Note, in particular, how the variable X_{CB} has been positioned in these expressions. This is intended to reflect the simultanity aspect of the constraints for this model. If, in any solution, an amount is assigned to the variable X_{CB} in one of these expressions then this same value must be assigned to this variable in the other expression. The admissible values for the variables must therefore satisfy *all* of the constraints simultaneously.

---

[57] In the Carnegie Tech Game, all interest income is realized as immediate cash income, and the price of the bond is held constant throughout the Game periods.

Bearing this in mind we now proceed to formulate the remaining constraints as follows:

(3) Since the firm's terms of sale are 30 days net, its maximum collection of receivables during the month is given by the beginning balance in the Receivables account.

$$X_{CR} \leq K_R \tag{3}$$

(4) The beginning-of-the-period Cash balance limits the purchase of securities.

$$X_{BC} \leq K_C \tag{4}$$

(5) The firm's selling price during the period studied was $9.996/unit, while its standard cost of production was $2.10/unit. The following constraint represents the gross profit on a unit sale in terms of the corresponding deduction from finished goods inventory. Note that $3.76 = (\$9.996 - \$2.10)/\$2.10$.

$$X_{RE} = 3.76 \, X_{RG} \tag{5}$$

(6) Standard cost of finished goods ($2.10/unit) includes material cost ($X_{GM} = \$1.00$/unit) and conversion cost ($X_{GE} = \$1.10$/unit), which consists of direct labor cost and direct overhead.

$$X_{GE} = 1.1 \, X_{GM} \tag{6}$$

(7) Production capacity limits conversion during the period. Production capacity is expressed here in terms of the value of raw materials (at standard cost) that can be converted.

$$X_{GM} \leq 1,300,000 \tag{7}$$

(8) Conversion is limited to raw materials on hand at the beginning of the month.[58]

$$X_{GM} \leq K_M \tag{8}$$

(9) Market conditions limit sales in the coming month to 2,000,000 units[59] ($4,200,000 at standard cost).

$$X_{RG} \leq 4,200,000 \tag{9}$$

(10) Sales during the month are further limited to the completed units on hand at the beginning of the month.[60]

$$X_{RG} \leq K_G \tag{10}$$

---

[58]In this case $K_M = 1,499,000$ so that the preceding constraint, (7), is controlling. We have, however, represented both constraints for the sake of completeness in cases where $K_M < 1,300,000$.

[59]Obtained from the relevant market forecast, determined as an expected rate, a maximum, and a minimum. The maximum is entered here as an exact upper limit for subsequent study by reference to the relevant dual evaluators.

[60]Cf. footnote 59. It should also be observed that this constraint is intended to reflect the lag on shipments from the plant to the relevant distribution centers.

(11) Repayment of loans is limited by the outstanding loan balance at the beginning of the month.

$$X_{LC} \leq K_L \tag{11}$$

(12) Because the firm is allowed 30 days for payment of materials purchased on credit, it has adopted a general policy of not paying the accruals incurred on accounts payable that result from material purchases during the month. Thus, the payment of accounts payable is limited to the sum of the beginning balance of accounts payable plus expenses accrued during the month.

$$X_{PC} \leq K_P + X_{EP} \tag{12}$$

(13) Monthly depreciation charges are .833 percent of the net fixed assets owned at the beginning of the month.

$$X_{EF} = .00833 \, K_F \tag{13}$$

(14) Expenses to be incurred during the coming period, including both manufacturing cost (other than material cost) and operating expenses, consist of the following four items: (*a*) fixed operating expenses, \$2,675,000; (*b*) variable conversion cost, X_{GE}; (*c*) effective interest penalty for discounts not taken on accounts payable (3.09 percent per month); (*d*) interest (monthly rate, .291 percent) on loans payable at the end of the month.

$$X_{EP} = 2,675,000 + X_{GE} + .0309 \, (K_P + X_{EP} - X_{PC})$$
$$+ .00291 \, (K_L + X_{CL} - X_{LC}) \tag{14}$$

(15) Income tax is accrued at 52 percent of the net profit. In addition, the firm's policy is to declare a dividend equal to \$83,000 plus (minus) 5 percent of the excess (shortage) of what it considers a standard net profit after taxes, \$1,860,000.

$$X_{ED} = .52 \, (X_{CE} + X_{RE} + X_{GE} - X_{EF} - X_{EP}) + 83,000$$

$$+ .05 \, [.48 \, (X_{CE} + X_{RE} + X_{GE} - X_{EF} - X_{EP}) - 1,860,000]$$

Simplifying,

$$X_{ED} = .544X_{CE} + .544X_{RE} + .544X_{GE} - .544X_{EF}$$
$$- .544X_{EP} - 10,000 \tag{15}$$

(16) Company policy is to maintain a minimum cash balance of \$4,000,000 at the end of each period.

$$K_C + X_{CB} + X_{CR} + X_{CL} + X_{CE} - X_{BC} - X_{PC}$$
$$- X_{DC} - X_{LC} \geq 4,000,000 \tag{16}$$

(17) Because of an impending price rise in the following period—that is, in the period following the one under study—the firm requires that

the end-of-the-month finished goods inventory be at least as great as the minimum sales expected during the next month ($3,570,000 at $2.10 standard cost/unit).[61]

$$K_G + X_{GM} + X_{GE} - X_{RG} \geq 3,570,000 \qquad (17)$$

(18) The firm expects to produce 1,200,000 units in the succeeding month. Thus the raw materials on hand at the end of the month must be sufficient for this production. (At $1.00 raw material cost/unit, the end-of-the-month raw materials balance must be $1,200,000).[62]

$$K_M + X_{MP} - X_{GM} \geq 1,200,000 \qquad (18)$$

(19) All outstanding income taxes payable and dividends declared, including those accrued or declared during the month, have to be paid by the end of the coming month.

$$K_D + X_{ED} - X_{DC} = 0 \qquad (19)$$

In addition to these constraints, all transaction variables (X's) are required to be nonnegative. This is done to avoid any confusion between the debit and credit entries which would otherwise have to be given a reverse (credit-debit) interpretation for negative values of any X. Either way of proceeding can be elected, but, for the present purposes, it simplifies the exposition merely to arrange the model so that the nonnegativity condition can be enforced on all variables.

3. Statement of Objectives and Completion of the Model. As already indicated, it was decided to eliminate any explicit statement of the profit-and-loss accounts (in their usual sense) in the model that we are synthesizing. Thus, in place of assuming that profit maximizing is controlling, we can consider that this firm wishes to maximize its Net Addition to Retained Earnings.[63] This is given by

$$\text{Net Additions to Retained Earnings} = X_{CE} + X_{RE} + X_{GE} - X_{EF} - X_{EP} - X_{ED} .$$

Because the objective is maximization we can refer to the preceding constraint details and set forth the full linear programming model as:

$$\text{Maximize } X_{CE} + X_{RE} + X_{GE} - X_{EF} - X_{EP} - X_{ED}$$

---

[61]Note that this amount too is subject to treatment by means of the dual evaluators. For instance such an analysis will show how much is being lost from current profit opportunities in order to provide for the future in this manner.

[62]The comment in note 61 applies here as well.

[63]It is not proposed to enter into a statement of whether this is the proper objective or whether any *one* objective is ever proper for a business. If, for instance, breakeven or other objectives are wanted, then recourse may be had to the devices discussed in Charnes, Cooper, and Ijiri, *op. cit.* Some caution may be needed in considering *multiple* objectives since policy conditions (like "stable employment," etc.) can be reflected in the constraints. On the other hand when multiple objectives are really wanted, then recourse may be had to approaches like those given in Charnes and Cooper, *op. cit.*, chap. 9.

subject to

$$X_{CB} \leq K_B \tag{1}$$

$$X_{CE} - .00229\, X_{BC} + .00229\, X_{CB} = .00229\, K_B \tag{2}$$

$$X_{CR} \leq K_R \tag{3}$$

$$X_{BC} \leq K_C \tag{4}$$

$$X_{RE} - 3.76\, X_{RG} = 0 \tag{5}$$

$$X_{GE} - 1.1\, X_{GM} = 0 \tag{6}$$

$$X_{GM} \leq 1{,}300{,}000 \tag{7}$$

$$X_{GM} \leq K_M \tag{8}$$

$$X_{RG} \leq 4{,}200{,}000 \tag{9}$$

$$X_{RG} \leq K_G \tag{10}$$

$$X_{LC} \leq K_L \tag{11}$$

$$X_{PC} - X_{EP} \leq K_P \tag{12}$$

$$X_{EF} = .00833\, K_F \tag{13}$$

$$X_{EP} - X_{GE} - .0309\, X_{EP} + .0309\, X_{PC} - .00291\, X_{CL} + .00291\, X_{LC}$$
$$= 2{,}675{,}000 + .0309\, K_P + .00291\, K_L \tag{14}$$

$$X_{ED} - .544\, X_{CE} - .544\, X_{RE} - .544\, X_{GE} + .544\, X_{EF} + .544\, X_{EP}$$
$$= 10{,}000 \tag{15}$$

$$X_{CB} + X_{CR} + X_{CL} + X_{CE} - X_{BC} - X_{PC} - X_{DC} - X_{LC}$$
$$\geq 4{,}000{,}000 - K_C \tag{16}$$

$$X_{GM} + X_{GE} - X_{RG} \geq 3{,}570{,}000 - K_G \tag{17}$$

$$X_{MP} - X_{GM} \geq 1{,}200{,}000 - K_M \tag{18}$$

$$X_{ED} - X_{DC} = - K_D \tag{19}$$

$$X_{CB}, X_{CR}, X_{CL}, X_{CE}, X_{BC}, X_{RG}, X_{RE}, X_{GM}, X_{GE}, X_{MP}, X_{PC}, X_{DC},$$
$$X_{LC}, X_{EF}, X_{EP}, X_{ED} \geq 0$$

That is, we are to search for amounts X_{ij} which satisfy all constraints, including nonnegativity for all variables, and among the entire collection of such values we are to single out one set that makes the net addition to retained earnings a maximum. The solution methods of linear programming—for instance, the simplex method[64]—are designed, of course, to produce exactly this result.

---

[64]We used this method as one part of the available G–21 electronic computer code without attempting to apply or devise other, possibly more efficient, methods. For further remarks on this topic see Charnes, Cooper, and Ijiri, *op. cit.*

4. Results. By substituting the figures in the beginning balance sheet (Table 8–10) for the K's in the above constraints and by applying the "simplex method," a solution to the above problem was readily achieved. We now summarize the results in the following series of tables. First, in Table 8–11, we list the transactions which achieve the maximum possible net addition to retained earnings. Next we utilize this information to obtain Tables 8–12 and 8–13, balance sheet and income statement projections for the period at issue.

TABLE 8–11

OPTIMUM PROJECTED TRANSACTIONS

CB:	Sell securities	$ 9,703,000
CR:	Collect accounts receivable	6,999,000
CL:	New borrowing	—
CE:	Collect interest on securities	6,000
BC:	Buy securities	—
RG:	Cost of sales at standard cost	3,192,000
RE:	Gross profit on sales	12,002,000
GM:	Material consumption (transfer from raw materials to finished goods inventory)	1,300,000
GE:	Variable conversion costs	1,430,000
MP:	Material purchased	1,001,000
PC:	Payment of accounts payable	7,697,000
DC:	Payment of dividends and taxes	7,871,000
LC:	Refund of loans	4,400,000
EF:	Depreciation	217,000
EP:	Manufacturing and operating expenses	4,105,000
ED:	Accruals of income taxes and dividends	4,949,000
	Net addition to retained earnings	4,167,000

TABLE 8–12

PROJECTED BALANCE SHEET

(End of Period)

C:	Cash	$ 4,000,000		*P:*	Accounts payable	$ 1,001,000
B:	Securities	2,297,000		*D:*	Dividends and taxes payable	—
R:	Accounts receivable	15,194,000		*L:*	Loans payable	—
G:	Finished goods	3,570,000		*E:*	Stockholders' account	51,043,000
M:	Raw materials	1,200,000				
F:	Fixed assets	25,783,000				
		$52,044,000				$52,044,000

Notice that we now have the main documents that are usually deemed to be pertinent for financial planning purposes. Additional documents—for instance, flow of funds statements, cash budgets, and so on—can also be generated if desired.[65] It is not proposed, however, to pursue this topic here. We note, instead, how the results of this analysis can be used for planning and execution by various kinds of management. The details of Table 8–11 lend themselves to ready translation for the direction of operating managers, or other persons, who are not immediately concerned with the overall aspects of financial plan-

---

[65]See Charnes, Cooper, and Ijiri, *op. cit.,* for further discussion.

ning. For instance, the production manager may be directly instructed to plan to produce $2,730,000 worth of finished goods during this period and further to allocate $1,300,000 of this amount for the purchase of raw materials and to expend the rest ($1,430,000) on conversion costs. In turn, the purchasing department may be instructed to purchase $1,001,000 worth of raw materials, and so on.

TABLE 8–13

PROJECTED INCOME STATEMENT

Sales ($RG + RE$)...		$15,194,000
Cost of goods sold (RG)................................		3,192,000
Gross profit (RE)...................................		$12,002,000
Manufacturing costs and operating expenses (EP)........	$4,105,000	
Depreciation (EF)...................................	217,000	
Manufacturing costs charged to finished goods (GE).......	1,430,000	
Unabsorbed manufacturing costs and operating expenses...		2,892,000
Operating profit.......................................		$ 9,110,000
Interest income (CE).................................		6,000
Net income before taxes...............................		$ 9,116,000
Accruals of income taxes and dividends (ED).............		4,949,000
Net addition to retained earnings......................		$ 4,167,000

Of course, the usual information for a coordinated assessment and review by top management is also available in the form of projected balance sheets, income statements, etc. In addition, the linear programming solution provides valuable by-product information in the form of the dual evaluators.[66] We propose therefore to elaborate on this topic in Section 5 and then show how this information can be assembled to form a new type of accounting document for use in integrated management planning.

5. *An Accounting Statement for the Dual Evaluators as Opportunity Costs.* A dual evaluator, at least in a managerial-accounting-economics context, indicates the change in net addition to retained earnings that can be secured if the constraint corresponding to the given evaluator were relaxed by one dollar. For example, the dual evaluator of constraint number 7 (production capacity) has a value of $3.594936. This means that if production capacity were increased so that exactly one additional dollar's worth of raw material can be processed, then retained earnings will be increased by $3.594936. This figure, which is obtained (automatically) as a so-called "evaluator," really summarizes a whole complex of interrelated opportunities. Hence some further accounting aids to managerial interpretations and uses are indicated.

In order to show that the dual evaluators take into account every constraint of

---

[66] The G–21 code (like most linear programming codes) provides these data automatically, at the end of its run, as well as other (equally valuable) results which enable the user to test the program's sensitivity to errors in the data, etc. See, e.g., Charnes and Cooper, *op. cit.*, chap. 13, for a discussion in the context of the so-called revised simplex code for IBM computers.

the model in *mutatis mutandis* fashion, the evaluator of production capacity will now be analyzed in more detail.[67] Let it be desired to alter the firm's raw material processing capacity by one unit. This activates a whole complex of transactions which are set forth in Table 8–14.

TABLE 8–14

ANALYSIS OF OPPORTUNITY COSTS*

$3.59 per Unit Increase in Production Capacity

(1)	Incremental sales resulting.........................		$9.996000
	Less: Cost of incremental sales.....................		2.100000
(2)	Incremental gross profit......................		7.896000
(3)	Deduct: Income taxes and dividends (54.4%).........		4.295424
(4)	Net retained from sales after taxes and dividends.......		3.600576
(5)	Deduct: Opportunity cost of the cash needed to finance expansion:		
		Cash required for raw materials†...........$0.———	
(5a)		Conversion to finished product...............1.100000	
		Total.............................$1.100000	
(5b)		Add: Cash required for income taxes and dividends............................ 4.295424	
(5c)		Total cash required.......................$5.395424	
(6)	Total of interest earnings foregone on securities sold ($5.395424 @ 0.00104533).....................		0.005640
(7)	Net retained realization per unit increase in production capacity............................		$3.594936

*This statement is based on optimal adjustments being effected in all pertinent transactions.
†All required raw material is available from inventory on hand.

Notice now that the end result is the $3.59 figure that was predicted by the dual evaluator. Notice also that the indicated transactions are each carried out optimally (relative to one another) in order to produce this optimal return from the indicated one unit of increased capacity. The single figure of $3.59 summarizes all of these transactions to the one net end effect, as indicated; but this obviously needs accounting elaboration if the purposes of managerial use and understanding are to be adequately served. The above statement is intended to supply this kind of service.

The data of Table 8–14 were drawn from the by-product results furnished automatically by the computer calculations after appropriate supplementation by economic-accounting considerations. We now elaborate on this as follows:

In (1) we observe that the incremental capacity increase has resulted in a sale of goods. The needed raw material is presently on hand, since $K_M = \$1,499,000$ (Table 8–10) is greater than $X_{GM} = \$1,300,000$ (Table 8–11). Therefore an additional raw material unit is drawn from inventory. This unit is processed at $1.10 conversion of finished goods which, valued at standard, costs

[67]See Charnes and Cooper, *op. cit.,* for further elaboration and distinctions between *ceteris paribus* and *mutatis mutandis* approaches.

$2.10. The unit of finished goods can be sold at once, since the firm has unfulfilled demand in the present month of $1,008,000 of product (valued at standard cost—see constraint number 9, remembering $X_{RG} = \$3,192,000$).

Segments (2), (3), and (4) give the net profit realized from this sale as determined by constraints 5 and 15 of the model.

The transaction analysis is not yet complete, as the gross profit ($3.600576) is higher than the dual evaluator ($3.594936). The difference ($.00564) can be accounted for by turning to the Cash account and recalling that the program has pushed up against the $4,000,000 stipulated minimum balance. Therefore, the additional cash outlays needed for production must be obtained in one of three ways: (a) sell securities at the monthly interest rate, 0.229 percent; (b) borrow from bank at the monthly interest rate, 0.291 percent; (c) postpone payments on accounts payable at a monthly interest rate, 3.09 percent. The least costly of these three ways is obviously achieved in the sale of securities. The $.00564 shown opposite (6) in the above statement represents the opportunity cost incurred because of the interest income that must be foregone if securities are sold to obtain the needed cash. This is derived as follows: (5a) and (5b) give the amount of cash needed to increase production by one unit. (5a) represents the conversion cost which is paid at the end of the month. (5b) represents dividends and taxes payable on the profit generated in (4), and cash must be obtained to pay these at the end of the month. The total cash requirement is therefore the sum of (5a) and 5b), or $5.395424,[68] which is the figure shown opposite (5c). (6) multiplies the number of dollars needed by the opportunity cost per dollar to obtain the total opportunity cost of obtaining cash.

The opportunity cost per dollar is obtained via the following reasoning: The firm foregoes interest income of $.00229 for every dollar of securities sold. However, the loss is reduced to $.00104424 by taking into account savings on taxes and dividends. Since the interest income would normally be collected in cash at the end of the month, the $.00104424 of income foregone reduces the end-of-month cash balance by $.00104424. This reduction in cash balance violates constraint number 16 (minimum cash balance constraint) and to compensate for this reduction the firm must sell an additional $.00104424 of securities and forego (.00104424 × .00104424) dollars of net interest income, as well as (.00104424 × .00104424) reduction in the cash balance.

The total reduction of net profits after taxes and dividends resulting from this sale of securities needed to obtain an additional dollar of cash is given by the sum of the infinite series:

$$.00104424 + (.00104424)^2 + (.00104424)^3 + \dots .$$

$$= \frac{.00104424}{1 - .00104424} = .00104533$$

Therefore .00104533 appears as the unit opportunity cost in (6).

Finally, in (7) we see that the net effect of relaxing the production capacity constraint by one unit is equal to the difference between net profit (after taxes

---

[68]Note that two other cash flows (accounts receivable and payments on raw material accounts) are affected by the capacity increase. However, they have no effect on the flow in the present month, as they are not received (or paid) until the following month.

and dividends) realized from the sale of goods and the opportunity cost of securing additional cash required. That is, $3.600576 − $.005640 = $3.594936. This figure is precisely equal to the dual evaluator associated with production capacity.

Notice in particular, now, that any one dual evaluator provides the opportunity cost information that is relevant when *every* possible transaction is altered to a new optimum level in response to a change anywhere in the system. This is, in fact, the intended meaning of the term *mutatis mutandis* which has been accorded to this way of reckoning opportunity costs, in contrast to other approaches which assume that only a few variables are adjusted while all others are held constant.

Of course, we have only singled out a small portion of the total dual evaluator information printed out by a computer at the end of a run on a linear programming model. Evidently further extensions can be made by considering collections of these evaluators simultaneously and, of course, still other kinds of extensions can also be made. The main point to be made here, however, is that the *mutatis mutandis* approach will generally involve a complex series of transaction interactions. Technically speaking there is no real trouble in assessing the dual evaluators. On the other hand, some forms of guidance and assistance undoubtedly have to be supplied if management is to be able to make intelligent and understanding uses of this information. One form in which this kind of assistance can be supplied has been suggested by the kind of accounting statement which we have just exhibited. Undoubtedly other kinds of statements will also have to be devised, especially where more complex transaction interactions are being considered, and some exercise of ingenuity and some period of experimentation will undoubtedly be required for this purpose.

6. Conclusion. We now try to point out some of the conclusions and further elaborations suggested by this study. First we should observe that linear programming is not the only possible mathematical method of approach to accounting and financial planning.[69] It does, however, offer a highly flexible instrument and is associated with an extremely sharp and general (underlying) mathematical theory whose limits to applications such as the above have not even begun to be reached.

The above analysis and interpretation of the dual evaluators should be taken only as partially illustrative of the type of further extensions that are readily available from the linear programming model. Sensitivity analysis offers still another alternative course of immediate extensions which would show the effect of changes in the objective function or constraints (including additions of new variables and constraints) on the optimum solution of the model. As in the above analysis, all sensitivity changes within any specific part of the model are evaluated in terms of their effect on the entire model. In general, this evaluation can be done without re-solving the entire problem.

Other applications of linear programming to accounting have shown the relationships between programming to goals and break-even budgeting.[70] This

---

[69]For example, see Charles P. Bonini, *Simulation of Information and Decision Systems in the Firm* (Englewood Cliffs, N.J.: Prentice-Hall, Inc., 1963); and R. M. Cyert, H. J. Davidson, and G. L. Thompson, "Estimation of the Allowance for Doubtful Accounts by Markov Chains," *Management Science,* Vol. 8, No. 3 (April, 1962), pp. 287–303.

[70]Charnes, Cooper, and Ijiri, *op. cit.*

type of analysis could easily be combined with the above to form a unified approach to planning when multiple (and sometimes conflicting) objectives exist among the various divisions of a firm. Such an approach might be in order, for example, to determine a system of transfer prices for guiding decentralized operations in a way that will produce the best *overall* results from each department's operations.

The above kinds of applications are available as a result of previous research in the theory and applications of linear programming. Additional research might also produce still further advantages if it were devoted to, say, investigating accounting models and applications as such. As Charnes, Cooper, and Ijiri have shown, the network features of accounting models offer promising avenues of exploitation.[71] With suitably arranged objective functions, linear programming and simulation approaches can be joined together with further increases in the scope and power of each.

Finally, all of these topics are closely associated with the rapidly evolving developments and uses of electronic computers for business purposes. Further research in this direction is also warranted if the full value of these devices for accounting-managerial applications is to be achieved. Of particular interest in this connection, some form of preparatory research might now be considered in anticipation of the new generation of computers—the so-called "nanosecond computers"—which are even now on the way towards realization.

IV.   STUDIES OF MARKET BEHAVIOR

Three papers are reprinted in this section to indicate some ways in which the results from repeated plays of the Carnegie Tech Management Game can lead to an increased understanding of market behavior and marketing strategies in the real world.

While the article by Kuehn and Day in Section IV.A makes no explicit mention of the Carnegie Tech Management Game, the method for estimating the distribution of consumer preferences using paired-comparison tests presented there has been successfully tested in plays of the closely related C.I.T. Marketing Game. The fact that this marketing research technique is both operationally feasible for Game players to utilize and that it provides a reasonably accurate estimate of the distribution of consumer preferences which are built into the Game model greatly facilitated its application to real-world marketing problems.

In Section IV.B the paper by Weiss describes the computer simulation model of the packaged detergent market which has been incorporated into both the Carnegie Tech Management Game and the C.I.T. Marketing Game, and it indicates how this model can be used as a simulation to allow us to learn more about the real-world detergent market. Although its discussion of the operational gaming uses of this model refer only to the Marketing Game, similar considerations apply equally forcefully with respect to the Management Game.

---

[71] *Ibid.*

Kuehn's study in Section IV.C spells out some of the specific marketing insights which are thought to be valid in the real world which have been discovered in the course of developing and working with the marketing model embodied in the Carnegie Tech Management Game.

A. Strategy of Product Quality (by Alfred A. Kuehn and Ralph L. Day)[72]

If marketing executives are truly "consumer oriented," they know that their marketing efforts face an uphill climb when the physical attributes of their product do not fit the preferences of a substantial group of consumers better than competing brands do. Certainly the physical product is not the only important factor. The consumer purchases a "bundle of satisfactions" that includes a variety of other considerations, such as convenience of purchase, design of the package, manufacturer's reputation, and style of advertising. But it is nevertheless a bad mistake to become so preoccupied with packaging, distribution, and promotional activities that one forgets the importance of the *contents* of the package. The marketing manager cannot afford to think that his responsibility for the nature of the product is fulfilled when he has ascertained that his product is "just as good" as competing products are.

In all fairness, it must be recognized that the problem of determining exactly what the attributes of a product ought to be is extremely difficult. We believe, however, that the approach to the measurement and evaluation of consumer preferences presented in this article will make the task much easier for many products. After making some general observations about product quality we shall outline new procedures for (*a*) matching product features to consumer preferences, and (*b*) developing measures of the consumer's ability to recognize differences in products. These procedures should help management to:

(1) Recognize what levels of product quality and other characteristics appeal to what proportions of the market.

(2) Decide whether or not it is desirable to aim for parts of the market not covered by the "most popular" brands.

(3) Ascertain the most promising directions for new products or improvements in existing products.

1. What is "Product Quality"? When considering the physical product apart from the additional attributes, real or fancied, bestowed on it by an effective marketing program, the manufacturer's attention is usually centered on "product quality." In this context, product quality is often measured in terms of the purity or grade of materials used, the technical perfection of design, and exacting standards of production. The *level* of quality is usually set in terms of either meeting or beating competition. Once a level of product quality, in this sense, has been determined, most firms carry out rigorous programs of quality control and product testing to ensure that technical standards of product quality are upheld.

a) Illusions and Pitfalls. The quest for this kind of product quality on the part of technically trained and oriented people is understandable and, within

---

[72]This is a modified version of Alfred A. Kuehn and Ralph L. Day, "Strategy of Product Quality," *Harvard Business Review,* Vol. 40, No. 6 (November-December, 1962), pp. 100–110.

limits, highly laudable. However, thinking of product quality simply as a function of the commercial grade of materials used or the technical perfection of design and manufacture is a denial of "consumer orientation." Consumers do not make chemical or physical analyses of the goods they buy. They use a product and react to its ability to satisfy their wants. They have little knowledge of, or concern for, the technical standards established by chemists, physicists, and engineers in its manufacture. In fact, they may prefer products made with certain lower cost ingredients while management is equating higher cost with higher quality.

This is not to say that product quality in the technical sense is unimportant. Consumers generally wish to be reassured that they are not getting inferior materials or shoddy workmanship. They can be alienated by lack of consistency in the product characteristics which they regard as important. And they are not as gullible and manipulatable as they are apparently believed to be by some critics of advertising. To be sure, given only minor product differences, or differences in unimportant attributes, advertising can precondition the consumer's feelings and attitudes toward a particular manufacturer or brand and thereby influence his evaluation of and reactions to a product. Thus, preferences can be established largely through marketing efforts. The job is much simpler, however, if actual, perceivable differences (preferably important differences) can be demonstrated to the consumer.

The manufacturer should also realize that consumer preferences for physical aspects of the product may or may not be closely related to currently established technical measures of product quality. Consumers, for example, may judge such a quality as "softness" of paper products on different grounds than laboratory testing devices do. Laboratory test values, in such a case, may even misdirect research efforts aimed at developing products with greater consumer appeal. In the final analysis of the marketplace, the "quality" of a product depends on how well it fits patterns of consumer preferences.

Unfortunately, giving the consumer what he wants is easier in the saying than in the doing. Standards for measuring certain technical aspects of product quality may be well established in most companies, but how does one establish measures of consumer preferences across the broad ranges of possible product characteristics? That is the question we shall turn to now. The approach we shall describe is not a "drawing board" idea. It is finding acceptance by manufacturers of consumer nondurables and seems to hold promise for an even broader spectrum of products.

2. Preference Testing. Especially in the period since World War II, manufacturers have become increasingly aware of the need to learn more about what consumers like and dislike in the products they buy. Consequently, large sums of money have been spent on consumer research. Many methods have been used to gather information. In addition to the traditional "nose counting" survey, continuous consumer panels have been established on a national basis, a variety of motivational research methods have been used, and extensive field testing of products has been done.

In general, these kinds of research have provided useful information to marketing management, but at times it has been difficult to interpret and apply the results. There have been many cases where the results of costly research have not been used, and also other cases where the results are misinterpreted, leading to ill-advised actions.

The approach to be described was developed in the belief that field research is likely to be worth more than it costs only when it is designed and interpreted within an analytical framework which relates it directly to specific managerial problems. This approach, which might be called "preference distribution analysis," involves no new field research technique. Rather, it provides a meaningful structure for the use and interpretation of an accepted procedure, the "blind," forced-choice, paired-comparison test, in a way that sheds new light on what consumers want and facilitates development of effective market-segmentation policies.

a) Elements of Test. The nature of the paired-comparison test is basically simple. Here are the main features:

(1) Samples of two brands of a product, or proposed products which differ in some way, are prepared in identical containers and are given to a representative group of consumers to use.

(2) After they have used the samples, the consumers are asked to pick the one they prefer.

(3) Every effort is made to eliminate any influences other than the features of the products in the packages. For instance, to eliminate "position bias," the order in which they are asked to use the two products is alternated among the members of the test group. Again, the boxes are identified with psychologically neutral symbols, such as three-digit numbers which contain no 7's. It has been found that different colors, single letters, single numbers, or "magic numbers" may introduce biases among those consumers who do not have strong preferences for one of the samples.

(4) Occasionally, the tests are repeated with the same consumers and the same products but with different numbers on the boxes to test the consumers' consistency in choosing between the two products.

(5) After all members of the test group have used the samples and stated their preferences, the results are carefully analyzed to determine the percentages of the test group which preferred each product.

While the paired-comparison test is a very useful method for testing consumer preferences for products, free from any associations created by advertising, its results frequently lead to misinterpretations. That is why we must go several steps further than companies generally do to get the results that we want.

b) "Majority Fallacy." The danger of testing in the conventional way can be illustrated by a hypothetical example:

Suppose there is no chocolate cake mix on the market. A company decides to produce a chocolate cake mix and does extensive testing to find the degree of "chocolaty-ness" which consumers prefer. It tests with various levels and finds the degree of chocolaty-ness which the largest number of people prefer—a medium level. It introduces the product with success.

Then another company decides to enter the market and tests various levels of chocolaty-ness against the first company's product. When it tries any other level, either a lighter or darker chocolate, it finds that any such level is less preferred than the medium level.

As more companies enter the industry and test proposed products, the medium level always is preferred by a higher percentage of consumers. So each company enters the market with a medium-level chocolate cake mix, and the consumer has no choice between the brands in terms of physical characteristics. Consumers who like light chocolate or who like dark chocolate are out of luck.

If there were five companies marketing a chocolate cake mix and all their products were at the same level of chocolaty-ness, each company might be expected to get 20 percent of the chocolate-cake-mix market if all other factors were equal.

Suppose now that a sixth company wants to enter the market. It decides to test two proposed levels of chocolaty-ness against the existing brands. It tests a considerably lighter chocolate cake mix against each of the established brands and finds that 65 percent of consumers prefer the other brand in each test. It tests a considerably darker chocolate against the established brands and again finds that 65 percent of all consumers prefer the brands against which it is tested. Both proposed products have failed in the preference tests.

This company then tests a product at the medium level and finds that 50 percent of all consumers prefer it when it is tested against any of the present brands. Now the comparison tests indicate that the new company has a product "just as good" as any of the competing brands. This product will be indistinguishable from the established brands and, if it can overcome the disadvantage of being a latecomer in the market, it might eventually be expected to attain a 17 percent share of the market.

This situation illustrates what is sometimes called the "majority fallacy," that is, assuming that every product must be acceptable to a majority of all consumers if it is to be successful. A little reflection suggests that a substantial number of consumers might strongly prefer a considerably lighter chocolate cake, and another segment of the market might strongly prefer a much darker chocolate. It is certainly conceivable that each of these groups would amount to a larger segment of the entire market than the one-sixth share that our hypothetical new company might eventually expect to attain with a cake mix just like all the others (if it can overcome the handicap of being last in entering the market). For a picture of the majority fallacy, see Figure 8–10.

Unfortunately, conventional product testing sheds little light on the existence of such submarkets. However, this failure does not imply that the two-product comparison test is worthless. Rather, it suggests the need for a more meaningful way of planning product tests and interpreting the results. Preference-distribution analysis fills this need when the important characteristics of a product can be meaningfully "scaled" over a range of values.

3. *Steps in Analysis.*   Just as the cake-mix producers in the foregoing example could vary the level of chocolaty-ness of their products, many manufacturers must choose a product characteristic or feature from a wide range of possible characteristics. Awareness of the significance of such characteristics and the ability to vary their levels is not enough, as illustrated in the cake-mix example. In order to choose the level which will suit the preferences of the largest segment of the market, management must be able to: (a) relate the various levels of the characteristic directly to the preferences of consumers, and (b) determine the proportions of all consumers who prefer each level. Preference-distribution analysis provides such a means by establishing a scale of feasible values for a product characteristic, estimating the percentage of all consumers who prefer each value on the scale, and providing a probabilistic measure of consumers' ability to distinguish between different values on the scale.

FIGURE 8–10

ILLUSTRATION OF THE MAJORITY FALLACY

A.

Here is the market for a product as most companies would view it, i.e., with the preferences of the majority of consumers appearing to dominate the scene. What businessmen fail to see under this "majority fallacy" is that there may actually be a minority or minorities of customers who would prefer a product with quite different characteristics. Now, for comparison, see Chart B.

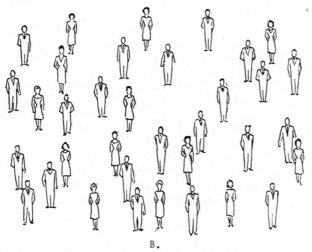

B.

In this picture we see just the minority of customers preferring a product with different characteristics. All of these people are in the preceding chart (A), in the same positions shown here. If an alert company designs a product to meet the preferences of these customers, it may "have the market to itself" and profit more than it would in competition with other firms for the majority of consumers.

a) Employing the Scale. The first step is to devise a scale of feasible values for each significant characteristic. The limits of the scale are the lowest value and the highest value preferred by any appreciable number of consumers. Between the extreme values, the scale is divided into a number of equal increments in ascending order. The width of the steps depends primarily on the consumer's ability to perceive differences.

Examples of easily scalable characteristics are the sweetness of cola drinks, the quantity of suds produced by soaps and detergents, and the saltiness of margarine. However, some product characteristics have not as yet been scaled in a way which will permit this form of analysis. For example, no satisfactory techniques have been developed for scaling colors, flavors, and odors in a way amenable to preference analysis. (Although psychologists have developed multidimensional scales for such variables, these scales are not suitable for determining distributions of consumer preferences. For example, orange and red appear close together on most color scales while red and blue are far apart. Yet, in terms of consumer preferences, red and blue might be more interchangeable, or "closer together," than red and orange. Undoubtedly, further research into the nature of human behavior will yield methods for scaling currently intractable characteristics.)

Once a "product attribute scale" is established, otherwise identical samples of the product are made up with each level of the particular characteristic. Each of the values on the scale is then tested in paired-comparison tests against every other value on the scale, using a representative sample of consumers for each test. The results of all these tests are analyzed simultaneously using a computer program which estimates the percentage of consumers who prefer each level, weights these percentages according to rates of use of the product, and provides a measure of the consumer's ability to discriminate among the various levels on the scale. (More will be said about consumer preferences and discrimination presently.)

When the preference distribution for a particular product characteristic has been estimated, a company's existing product or products and all competing products can be analyzed to determine their level on the scale. This will indicate the degree to which existing products match consumer preferences and will reveal any market segments which have been neglected. Thus, the analysis of the distribution of consumer preferences over a product-attribute scale will provide a highly meaningful frame of reference for the development of product strategies that are truly consumer-oriented.

b) Analyzing Preferences. The patterns of consumer preferences over a scale may take a variety of forms. Several types of distributions are shown in Figure 8–11. Although the scales must be divided into discrete steps for testing purposes, actual preferences probably follow a smooth curve, as indicated by the dotted lines.

i) "Normal Distribution." As one might expect, the distribution of preferences over many product characteristics is roughly similar to the "normal" probability distribution, as in Chart A of Figure 8–11. Preferences are distributed around a more-or-less central value on the scale, tapering off to a low level at both ends of the scale. If preferences for levels of a particular characteristic fit this pattern, would the key question for a firm be the exact level which is the central point of the distribution? It is not clear that this would be the optimal value, even if the company markets only one brand of the product. If

FIGURE 8–11

DIFFERENT PATTERNS OF CONSUMER PREFERENCES OVER
LEVELS OF A PRODUCT CHARACTERISTIC

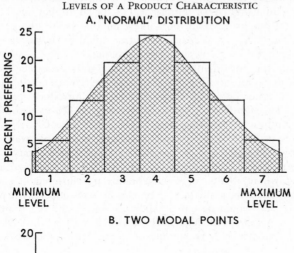

A. "NORMAL" DISTRIBUTION

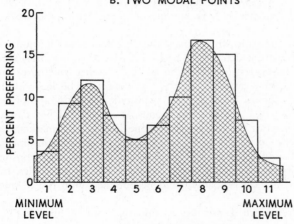

B. TWO MODAL POINTS

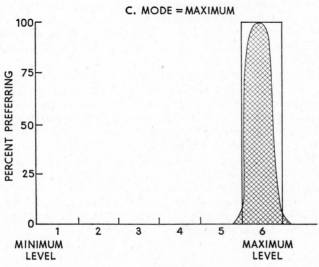

C. MODE = MAXIMUM

several competitors are marketing products with the characteristic at the most popular level (4 in Chart A of Figure 8–11) or at higher levels, then the optimum point for our firm would most likely be well below the peak point— say, at Level 2. The product would then be better suited to the tastes of a sizable segment of the market than is any competing product.

As we saw in the hypothetical chocolate-cake-mix example used earlier, traditional methods of interpreting the results of preference testing lead to the "majority fallacy" whereby all companies tend to introduce products at a "medium" level of a significant product characteristic. Let us assume that the preference distribution for chocolaty-ness looks much like Chart A in Figure 8–11. Then, if the original five brands in the cake-mix example were at Level 4 on the scale shown in that chart, it seems clear that a new brand at Level 2 would be preferred by a considerably larger portion of the market than it would at Level 4, where all the competing brands are clustered. It could expect to be strongly preferred over all the old brands by consumers with preferences at Levels 1 and 2, and would be equally as attractive as the old brands to consumers at Level 3. A new product at Level 6 would enjoy a similar "preference share" without detracting to any significant degree from the market for the product at Level 2.

Thus, an alert company which knew the preference distribution could bring out two new products which would be preferred over other brands by perhaps 40 percent of consumers (and maybe more), leaving the other five brands each with "preference shares" of about 12 percent (maybe less) of the market.

Even if a new brand could not be expected to obtain a preference share greater than the average for existing brands, it might still be advantageous to introduce it at a level of the characteristic appealing to a submarket neglected by other brands. It would appear to be much easier to attract consumers to a new product which better matches their preferences than to shift consumers from existing brands to another brand which has the same characteristics. In this way, a similar share of market probably could be obtained with much lower promotional costs.

ii) Other Preference Distributions. Chart B in Figure 8–11 illustrates another fairly common pattern of preferences. Preferences tend to cluster around more than one modal point. An example might be preferences for the level of sweetness of a beverage with the peaks representing those who prefer a dry beverage and those who prefer a sweet drink. This kind of distribution will be discussed more fully later.

Chart C in Figure 8–11 shows a concentration of preferences at the highest level on the scale. That is, all consumers prefer a level as high or higher than the highest level now available. This may indicate that there is a technical limitation on the achievement of the characteristic, assuming that Level 6 is the highest commercially available level. (For example, almost every housewife would probably like the lightest possible vacuum cleaner, without loss of power or efficiency.) If consumers would prefer an even higher level of the characteristics, an opportunity for further technical development is suggested.

iii) Changing Preference Patterns. Distribution of consumer preferences may change over time as the result of changes in patterns of end use and shifts in consumer attitudes. The existence of such trends can be established by periodic retesting of consumer preferences.

To what extent can a manufacturer *alter* basic patterns of consumer preferences for product characteristics through its advertising efforts? This is a more complicated problem. In general, it would appear less difficult for manufacturers to adapt their products to consumer preferences than to alter those preferences—but this depends on one's view of advertising effectiveness as well as on the role of fashions, fads, and changing tastes in the particular market being served.

c) *Identification of Desires.* How does management obtain a measure of the consumer's ability to recognize the level of a product characteristic that he actually prefers? This is an important part of consumer-preference analysis. Marketing researchers have long recognized that consumers are not perfectly consistent in their behavior. The consumer will not appear to "prefer" the same value on a product-characteristic scale every time in repeated trials. It is not at all uncommon for a housewife to choose one of two products in a paired-comparison test only to choose the other if the test is repeated. Yet extensive testing suggests that *most of the time* an individual will choose the product which is on, or is closest to, a particular value on the preference scale.

It is useful to think of the particular value of a product characteristic which a person would choose most often if exposed to repeated trials as his or her "true" preference. Of course, ability to recognize this preferred value when compared with neighboring values varies with the nature of the characteristic, the width of the steps in the scale, the stability of the conditions under which the product is used, and the importance of the characteristic with respect to the use being made of the product. Nevertheless, when choosing between his preferred level and an adjacent value on the scale, the individual will be likely to choose the preferred level more than one half of the time. The greater the distance of the alternative from the preferred value, the more likely he is to recognize his true preference. For instance, if the alternative product is two steps away on the scale, he will choose his preferred product a greater portion of the time than if it is one step away.

The foregoing observations suggest that it is appropriate to think of consumer choice as a probabilistic process. It is obviously a mistake to assume that consumers are perfectly consistent in their behavior. But it would also be a mistake to assume that it is useless to attempt to analyze consumer behavior because of this inconsistency. The approach used in preference-distribution analysis is to estimate the probability that a consumer will recognize his or her "true" preference, or the product closest to it, when faced with a choice. A "discrimination parameter," developed in the analysis of the results of forced-choice, paired-comparison tests for all possible combinations of values on a preference scale, provides a probability measure of the ability of consumers to discriminate among values on a preference scale.

Once a company knows the distribution of consumer preferences over a product-characteristic scale and has a measure of the consumer's ability to discriminate among levels of the characteristics, it can approximate the preference share for any product, existing or proposed, with regard to that characteristic. When all significant characteristics are studied in this way, the company is provided with valuable new information on which to base its product strategy. The implications are great for the design of new products, improvements in existing products, and the development of marketing strategies to exploit preference advantages.

4. *Using the New Method.* In recent years, several manufacturers of consumer nondurables have attempted to devise techniques for establishing the distribution of consumer preferences for individual characteristics of products. The method outlined in this article is one such approach which, although still in a developmental stage, is now in use. Practical results have been obtained from it and are being applied by management in product evaluation and planning.

Although the results obtained in specific applications cannot be disclosed, we can give the essence of the approach by referring to a fictitious example. Let us take a product for which consumer perferences have been extensively studied by many firms—detergents for household use. For purposes of illustration we can draw on knowledge previously reported in the marketing and advertising trade press.

a) Tests and Findings. To begin, how do we ascertain what consumers' preferences are? We could proceed along the following lines:

Extensive consumer research of all types, ranging from traditional interviewing techniques to complex motivational studies, has revealed that there are several basic attributes of the contents of a detergent package which are significant in determining consumer preferences. These include the "washing power" of the detergent, the quantity of suds it produces, and how gentle it is to human skin.

The extent to which a particular detergent formula possesses these properties can be measured in the laboratory. The levels of these properties can be related to the chemical composition of detergents so that a formula can be developed to have any desired level of a given characteristic within the limits of technical feasibility. Thus, the significant product characteristics can be "scaled" over the total range of values which are both technically feasible and within the limits of consumer acceptability. For example:

A "sudsiness" scale can be developed to cover the range from completely sudsless detergents up to the maximum amount of suds compatible with ordinary usage. Since the quantity of sudsing agents added to detergents is readily controllable, it is possible to consider a large number of levels, or "steps," in sudsiness. However, on any preference scale the steps should be large enough to enable the consumers to distinguish between products at adjacent levels on the scale with better than a 50–50 "pure chance" probability.

Once a preference scale is established, the next task is to estimate the distribution of consumer preferences over the various values on the scale. The usual approach is to prepare product samples with otherwise uniform features for each level of the pertinent characteristic. Then forced-choice, paired-comparison tests are made for each possible pair of samples possessing different levels of the characteristic, using a representative sample of housewives for each combination. That is, the housewives in each of the groups are given samples of detergents with differing sudsiness values in identical plain packages. After they have used both packages of the detergent, the subjects are asked to choose the one they prefer.

When the results of the tests are formally analyzed, using a computer program which requires only a few minutes for computation on a high-speed machine, the distribution of consumers' preferences over the various levels of sudsiness can be estimated and a measure of the housewife's ability to discriminate between levels of sudsiness is obtained.

When the distribution of preferences is obtained, the pattern might be very much like that shown in Chart B of Figure 8–11 (where Level 1 is, no suds and Level 11 is maximum suds). A substantial proportion of detergent usage centers about low sudsing products, but the heaviest concentration of usage is around a much higher level of sudsiness.

b) Analysis of Results. The next step is to look for an explanation of the observed pattern of preferences. Often it can be explained by different end uses for the product; that is, those who use detergents in one way want such-and-such a level of "washing power," suds, and so forth, while women using detergents in another manner have different preferences. In other cases the pattern of preferences can be explained in terms of cultural and climatic differences. At times, "there is no accounting for tastes." But even in the latter situation, knowing the pattern of tastes is of great value in developing product strategies.

In the case of sudsiness, the preferred level is clearly related to the end use of the product. Extensive consumer research has shown that housewives tend to prefer a somewhat sudsy detergent in spite of the fact that suds have little to do with cleaning ability. But to the housewife the presence of suds seems to provide reassurance that the product is doing its job. *However,* high sudsiness interferes with the operation of automatic washing machines, especially the front-loading type.

With this information about the major end uses of detergents, we can relate observed preferences to the purpose for which the product is used.

(1) Housewives who use automatic washers account for most of the peak toward the lower end of the sudsiness scale. (See the left section of the top line in Figure 8–12.)

(2) The higher and broader peak at a considerably higher level of sudsiness (right-hand section of the top line) represents the level of suds desired for several other end uses.

One of these uses is dishwashing, which is sufficiently unique to be considered separately.

Other end uses include wringer washers, hand laundry, car washing, household cleaning, and some top-loading automatic washers. Since sudsiness preferences for these uses are relatively similar, they can be conveniently considered together as a "general purpose" group.

By relating patterns of preferences to the end use of the product, analytically convenient "submarkets" are defined. A company's own products and those of its competitors can then be evaluated in terms of how well their sudsiness levels fit the pattern of preferences in each such submarket. Changes in the sudsing level of existing products or opportunities for new products can be considered, and possibilities may be seen for improving advertising, promotion, package design, and so forth.

The preference distributions for other product characteristics such as washing power and gentleness can also be related to the end-use submarkets. This step can provide the basis for the development of an optimal "portfolio" of product features to conform with consumer preferences while taking advantage of any failures by competitors to gear their product characteristics to market needs.

FIGURE 8–12

PREFERENCES FOR THE SUDSING LEVEL OF A HOUSEHOLD DETERGENT

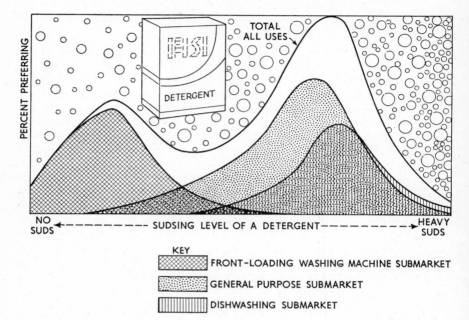

5. *Conclusions.* To summarize the major steps in consumer-preference-distribution analysis:

(1) Determine the physical characteristics of a product that appear to be significant to consumers.

(2) Establish a scale of values, in equal increments, from a minimum level up to a maximum level for each characteristic.

(3) Test consumer preferences for products located at approximately equal-increment levels on the scale in a series of paired-comparison tests, using representative samples of consumers.

(4) Analyze the results of all the tests for each product characteristic simultaneously, in order to estimate the percentages of consumers who prefer each level and the ability of consumers to recognize their true preferences.

(5) Relate preference levels to patterns of end use or other significant actions of consumers.

(6) Locate the value on the preference scale possessed by each product already on the market.

(7) Estimate the preference shares of existing products and evaluate opportunities for product changes or new product entries in all "neglected" segments of the market.

a) Other Factors. The physical characteristics of products are not, of course, the only determinants of consumer demand. A product with ideal characteristics for a particular submarket may not obtain as large a share of the submarket as a product of poorer "quality," if the superior product has inadequate distribution and promotion. On the other hand, the job of selling a product will certainly be easier if it matches the preferences of large numbers of consumers more closely than competing products do, and if its promotional efforts are directed to the proper submarket.

The approach to product testing outlined here does not attempt to estimate directly the effects of price on consumer choice. The products being compared are presented to the consumers participating in the test as being identical in price. Price has not been incorporated into this approach to consumer product testing because of the difficulties encountered in obtaining realistic price responses from subjects in the test environment. If a method of product testing capable of eliciting realistic price responses could be devised, however, a simple extension to the technique outlined here would make it possible to estimate the interbrand price elasticities directly from such data.[73]

b) New Dimensions. The preference-scale approach to consumer-preference analysis adds new dimensions to the manufacturer's concept of product quality. Product-development decisions can be consumer oriented in a highly meaningful way for the first time with respect to many types of products. Better knowledge of preferences and of how they are related to end uses of the product can provide the basis for better marketing planning and more effective utilization of marketing resources. For the consumer, preference analysis promises a more satisfactory range of product choices as the significant characteristics of products are more closely adjusted to preferences.

The distribution-of-product-preferences approach has not actually been applied to products other than frequently purchased consumer nondurables. Insofar as paired-comparison tests can be used to ascertain consumer preferences for other types of products, however, the methods outlined would be applicable to the analysis of such test data. For example, it might be possible to conduct similar tests to determine the distribution of consumer preferences with respect to the size of freezer compartments in refrigerators, of portable camp stoves, and of electric wall clocks, the width of lawnmowers and men's belts, and the weight of kitchen utensils and fabrics used in clothing.

While the basic concept of the preference-scale approach is quite simple, its implementation is both difficult and expensive. It requires extensive consumer testing, and a proper analysis of the results is too complex to be done without a high-speed computer. This is because the approach calls for testing of consumer preferences for an entire product class rather than a mere comparison of two existing brands. (In the latter case, the majority fallacy is a likely result.) Making the adjustments in products indicated by new knowledge of consumer preferences can also lead to costly changes in product design and methods of manufacture.

Nevertheless, preference-distribution analysis is a most promising new approach for companies that want to give more than lip service to the concept of consumer orientation. Handsome rewards await the company which offers products that fit the preferences of sizable segments of the market better than

---

[73]Another approach to incorporating the influences of price on consumer brand choice has been outlined in an earlier article: Alfred A. Kuehn, "A Model for Budgeting Advertising," in Frank M. Bass *et al.* (eds.), *Mathematical Models and Methods in Marketing* (Homewood, Ill., Richard D. Irwin, Inc., 1961), pp. 302–53.

competing products do, and then supports these products with promotional efforts directed to the proper target.

6.   *Appendix. Analytical Procedure for Estimating the Distribution of Consumer Preferences Using Paired-Comparison Tests.*   Let us consider the most simple case, that of estimating the distribution of consumer preferences for a single product characteristic (C). All other product characteristics of the test products will be identical (controlled at some arbitrary value). The analytical procedure outlined below[74] will then provide an estimate of the distribution of consumer preferences for the product characteristic being studied, if we can assume that there is no interaction between consumer preferences for product characteristic C and the other characteristics being held constant at some arbitrary value. (If interactions do exist, the problem becomes much more complicated as separate distributions of preferences for characteristic C would be required at the various levels of the other characteristics.)

We first divide the likely or possible range of consumer preference, with respect to the product characteristic under study, into n segments. Associated with each segment is an unknown, w_i, the proportion of consumers (weighted by volume of the product they are likely to consume) having a preference for the product characteristic value specified by the segment i. Figure 8–13 illustrates how a distribution of consumer preferences for a product characteristic might be represented within the framework of this model.

FIGURE 8–13

EXAMPLE OF A CONSUMER PREFERENCE DISTRIBUTION

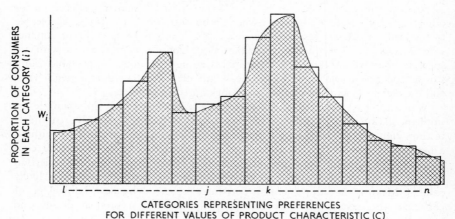

PROPORTION OF CONSUMERS IN EACH CATEGORY (i)

w_i

l — — — — — — — — — — — — — — — j — — — — k — — — — — — — — — — — — — n

CATEGORIES REPRESENTING PREFERENCES
FOR DIFFERENT VALUES OF PRODUCT CHARACTERISTIC (C)

Let p^i_{jk}, be the probability that a consumer whose preference falls into the category specified by segment i would prefer Brand A to Brand B, where the product characteristics of Brands A and B fall into the categories specified by segments j and k, respectively. Then, p^i_{kj} represents the probability that con-

[74]The authors wish to acknowledge the contributions of Bruce Becker, Yuji Ijiri, and Jon Zoler to the development and programming of the parameter estimation procedures required for the analysis of consumer preference distributions.

sumers in the ith category would choose Brand B in preference to Brand A on a "blind," forced-choice, paired-comparison test.

The consumer's ability to choose (i.e., discriminate) "correctly" between pairs of products depends on a number of factors including the variability of conditions under which the product is used, the importance of the differences to the consumer, and the difference between the two products with respect to how well they match the true preference of the consumer. These factors are taken into account in the following formula representing the probability of a consumer with true preference i preferring a product with characteristic value j to a second poduct with characteristic value k in a paired-comparison test:

$$p_{jk}^{i} = \frac{(1 - d_c)^{|j - i|}}{(1 - d_c)^{|j - i|} + (1 - d_c)^{|k - i|}} \tag{1}$$

The parameter d_c is a measure of the consumer's ability to discriminate with respect to the product attribute in question, reflecting both variability in test conditions and the importance of the characteristic to the consumer. If consumers cannot discriminate between products with different values of a characteristic, $d_c = 0$. If consumers can discriminate between very minor differences, d_c approaches 1. The exponents $|j - i|$ and $|k - i|$ represent the degree to which each of the two test products is consistent with the true preference of the consumer.

The $n + 1$ parameters to be estimated in this model are a set of w_i ($i = 1, 2,\ldots, n$) to establish the overall distribution of preferences and the discrimination parameter d_c.

By a single forced-choice, paired-comparison test of two brands, A and B, we get an estimate of the proportion of consumers preferring Brand A (P_{jk}) and an estimate of the proportion of consumers preferring Brand B (P_{kj}), where

$$P_{jk} + P_{kj} = 1$$

The expected value of P_{jk} is given by the following formula, assuming that the consumers participating in the test were chosen randomly:

$$E(P_{jk}) = \sum_{i=1}^{n} w_i p_{jk}^{i} = \sum_{i=1}^{n} w_i \frac{(1 - d_c)^{|j - i|}}{(1 - d_c)^{|j - i|} + (1 - d_c)^{|k - i|}} \tag{2}$$

Each single comparison test provides one equation. In addition, we obtain one equation from the fact that

$$\sum_{i=1}^{n} w_i = 1 \tag{3}$$

Therefore, given n single comparison tests, the parameters w_i ($i = 1, 2,\ldots, n$) and d_c can be estimated. The actual P_{jk} obtained from comparison tests (observed proportions) are used as estimates of the $E(P_{jk})$ in the second equation.

To establish the full range of the distribution of consumer preferences, we need one brand whose characteristic falls into segment 1 and one which falls into segment n, the two extremes, since for all i less than j, p_{jk}^i is a constant given by

$$p_{jk}^i = \frac{1}{1 + (1 - d_c)^{|j - k|}} \text{ where } i < j < k \tag{4}$$

Similarly, for all i greater than k, p_{jk}^i is a constant given by

$$p_{jk}^i = \frac{(1 - d_c)^{|j - k|}}{1 + (1 - d_c)^{|j - k|}} \text{ where } j < k < i \tag{5}$$

To minimize the effects of sampling variation on the estimates of d_c and the w_i, the products tested should be spaced at equal intervals. The number of segments (w_i) into which the consumer population can be subdivided is then equal to the number of independent, single, paired-comparison tests performed. The maximum number of subdivisions possible with single paired-comparison testing of N brands is then $\dfrac{N!}{(N - 2)! \, 2!}$, the maximum number of pairs which can be formed from N brands each having a different characteristic value.

B. Simulation of the Packaged Detergent Industry (by Doyle L. Weiss)[75]

Simulation as a problem-solving technique for research and educational uses is nothing fundamentally new or startling. The simple commodity market game frequently used by economics instructors to demonstrate market equilibrium to undergraduate economics students is a rudimentary example of market simulation. The armed forces of most major nations have made extensive use of simulation techniques for more than half a century to train personnel and to evaluate the effectiveness of newly developed equipment and tactics.[76]

It is the appearance of the modern computing machine that has made simulation a reasonable technique to apply to the highly complex problems faced by researchers and policy makers in marketing. Before these machines arrived most theories of market behavior which could be expressed precisely and also could be analyzed were necessarily quite simple. More complex market theories were expressed verbally and, inevitably, imprecisely. The marketing decision maker, therefore, had to use liberal amounts of experience, wisdom, and mature business judgment to arrive at specific decisions regarding the proper amounts of advertising dollars, salesmen, and so forth, called for by such theories. When mathematics and computer language are used to set forth the structure of a theory, business judgment and experience are no longer necessary to arrive at the implications of precisely stated complex theories. Notice that this is not the same as saying business judgment and experience are unnecessary in constructing good theory or in interpreting the adequacy of the theory's results when the theory is

---

[75]This is a modified version of Doyle L. Weiss, "Simulation of the Packaged Detergent Industry," in Charles H. Hindersman (ed.), *Marketing Precision and Executive Action* (Chicago: American Marketing Association, 1962), pp. 152–61.

[76]For a more intensive treatment of the historical development of war games see Thomas, *op. cit.*

cast in mathematical form. By expressing a theory in computer language a researcher can incorporate directly into it the wisdom and judgment of experienced businessmen.

Many of the mathematical theories (models) in use today are rather simple treatments of one aspect of the total marketing problem. Usually such theories are cast in linear form, since a linear system of structural equations representing the theory can usually be solved by standard mathematical techniques to obtain optimal solutions for the variables incorporated in the theory.

The major disadvantage of such analytical models is the need to keep the theory simple so as to assure that well-known mathematical procedures can be performed to yield these optimal solutions. This constraint appears to have led many a theoretician to abstract from the real world to such a degree that his theory no longer properly relates to the phenomenon that he had hoped to describe.

The difficulties involved in developing a useful model are illustrated by the researcher or student of marketing who encounters the advertising effectiveness problem after a limited exposure to statistical methods. His usual response to the problem is to build a simple regression model relating sales to advertising expenditures. After spending a day or so at a desk calculator fitting a regression line and computing a correlation coefficient he will decide his solution is worthless and that his model is too simple to handle the problem adequately. Now if the student is dedicated, and if the statistics course was a good one, and if a computing machine is available, he will expand his model in an attempt to include more of what he thinks really goes on in the real world. His next model is likely to be a multiple regression model with other independent variables, such as income levels and price, in addition to advertising. Now his theory really begins to look formidable, with four or five independent variables to explain the movement in sales. Unfortunately, the results are still likely to be unsatisfactory, and the model will probably lack good predictive power.

By now our ambitious student begins to experience the horrible realization that the world is not simple and, in addition, that the variables in the system interact with each other. Because of this, any detailed model constructed to explain a brand's sales is likely to be nonlinear, quite complex and difficult to solve analytically. Experience tells our student that most models simple enough to be solved by analytic techniques are not likely to produce results which are either interesting or particularly useful.

1. *The Basic Model.* To avoid this dilemma researchers are turning to simulation as a methodology. Extremely complicated theories can be constructed by researchers and then examined for implications with simulation techniques. Stability conditions for systems too complicated for mathematical analysis can now be explored by running the system repeatedly on a computing machine and then examining the time path of the output. Time paths of the output can also be generated and compared with real-world time series as a partial test of this model's predictive power.

This is the kind of model that has been constructed for the detergent market. It is a complicated nonlinear model which attempts to consider most of the effects and interactions of the merchandising variables in the detergent industry controlled by the competing detergent manufacturers.

a) Preference Structure. The consumer preference structure in the model is based on the brand-shifting model first developed by Alfred A. Kuehn.[77] In this model sales for a brand are produced by two kinds of consumer purchasing behavior. In the first of these the consumer is treated as repurchasing the same brand he purchased last period because of habit. This demand, termed habitual demand, may be thought of as the core of a brand's sales, consisting of purchases by the brand's established customers. Each consumer has a unique probability of making this habitual buying response, which is a function of his recent purchase history and the length of time between purchases. Because the simulation model produces aggregate sales, an average probability is established as a parameter and is used to represent all of the consumers in the market.

If the consumer is not making a habitual purchasing decision he is a potential brand shifter for the current period. That is to say, the consumer considers all of the marketed brands as viable alternatives. As a result of this consideration he is subject to competing influences from the marketing activities of all the available brands. Although this potential shifter may in fact repurchase the brand he purchased in the last period, the process influencing this kind of a decision to repurchase a brand is quite different from the one for habitual repurchases.

b) Market Structure. Since the model is dealing with products which retain brand identity and have distinct product characteristics, its demand function is not at all analogous to the market clearing mechanism of pure competition. Total industry demand is, however, a function of several industry parameters including price elasticity. For instance total demand for the industry will expand (but not necessarily at the same rate) with an expansion of industry advertising and promotional expenditures. Industry demand in the model is also responsive to the price of the individual brands (actually an average price in which each brand's price is weighted by market share) and the level of consumer disposable income. A trend term is included in the industry demand function to allow the effects of a growing, dying, or stable industry to be simulated and studied.

Marketers have long recognized that the end use for which a product is purchased will influence what the consumer prefers in terms of product characteristics. For example the detergent industry products competing in the dishwashing submarket are usually stressed for their high sudsing characteristics and their gentleness. Most of the promotional emphasis on products produced for the automatic washer market, however, seems to be on low sudsiness and a high washing-power characteristic. These differential effects of product characteristics on demand are handled in the simulation model as distinct submarkets. This means that although each product is considered by every potential shifter in the market, its physical characteristics will have their greatest impact on those consumers composing the end-use submarket for which the product is most suitable.

c) Interbrand Competitive Aspects of the Model. Market researchers are beginning to recognize more clearly that the effects of the marketing variables such as price, advertising, retail availability, and physical product character-

---

[77]Alfred A. Kuehn, "An Analysis of Consumer Behavior and Its Implications for Marketing Management" (Ph.D. dissertation, Carnegie Institute of Technology, 1958). The model has since been published in Kuehn, "A Model for Budgeting Advertising," *op. cit.*

istics interact together and in most cases cannot effectively be compartmentalized as researcher specialties and studied independently of each other.[78] Each of these variables can be expected to influence both the sales position of the brands and the effectiveness of the other variables to such an extent that only poor predictions of the outcome of a promotion can be made in terms of the advertising budget, price, and so on, alone. It seems reasonable to suggest that the timing of the sales force's efforts in providing shelf space and in-store promotional activity for the brand, along with advertising expenditures, pricing policy, and physical characteristics of the product, are important in sales outcomes. It is, hopefully, in this complex area of interdependency that computer simulation models will make the greatest contribution to understanding the complete system of these interrelationships.

The model being discussed in this paper is an attempt to explain how these interactions take place and the effects they have on sales. It relates the interdependent variables in what is believed to be a realistic and rational manner, so that the combined effects of the variables may be observed and studied. Future research will lead to greater understanding of the implications of these relationships and to improved theory construction.

The manner in which the physical product characteristics are handled by the model is a good example of its theoretical detail. The model considers three physical product characteristics: sudsiness, washing power, and gentleness. With washing power and gentleness the consumer's reaction is fairly straightforward; that is, the more washing power and gentleness possessed by a brand, the more desirable that brand is for most consumers. Gentleness is, however, relatively more important in the dishwashing submarket and washing power more important in the automatic washer and general purpose submarkets.

With respect to the sudsing characteristic, this is not true. For certain end uses (dishwashing) suds are desired by the consumer while for other purposes (automatic washers) an excess of suds can interfere with the "cleaning action" and can damage the laundry equipment, causing the consumer to consider suds generally undesirable for these purposes. This means that we can consider consumer preferences to be distributed across a scale of sudsiness values ranging from zero to some upper limit where demand is zero. Concentrations of demand will appear along the distribution as modal points occurring at values of the product characteristics most preferred for particular end uses. If (other effects being equal) consumers were considered to purchase the brand nearest in sudsiness value to their preferences, then the relative effect of sudsiness for a brand would depend upon its position on the sudsiness scale with respect to the position of competing brands and the distribution of consumer preferences representing the various end uses.

The model recognizes that consumers are not able to tell with perfect accuracy when the characteristics of the product they are considering represent their exact preferences. As the characteristics of the product being considered move farther away from the levels of the consumer's exact preference, the probability of the consumer recognizing this difference is treated as increasing in a fashion consistent with empirical blind-product preference data.

Given this type of consumer preference structure for product characteristics, some previously overlooked questions present themselves very clearly. For

---

[78]See the article by Kuehn reprinted in Section IV.C.

example, suppose there are several brands already marketed and a company is considering marketing a new brand. What is the best value for the sudsiness characteristic? One possible answer would be to match the new brand's sudsiness characteristic to the most popular brand now being marketed.[79] If this strategy were adopted by all the competing brand managers, each brand's share of market might in the very long run be expected to approach $1/n$ (where n is the number of brands in the market), although the cost of establishing the latest brand introduced into the market might be substantial (other marketing variables not considered). A more sophisticated approach to the problem might be to ask if there exists a smaller yet unexploited submarket which may produce a market share greater than $1/n$ and at a lower cost of introduction. The question is obvious, but the answer is not, if there are a number of competing brands with sudsing values ranging across the scale. With a reasonably fast computing machine the problem can be reduced to one of specifying the underlying consumer-preference distribution and searching for the maximum share of market by examining the alternatives directly.[80] An extension of this analysis would pose the question: Where shall I enter this market (that is, what sudsiness value) and with how many brands in order to make the market appear unprofitable to potential competitors? The solution technique would again consist of directly searching the function (that is, running the simulation model with the range of potential new product entries on a computing machine) for an answer.

In addition to the usual variables of price and advertising expenditures, inputs of sales force size and a retail allowance are allowed. The management may hire or fire salesmen and direct the allocation of their effort among brands; also, management may offer a retail allowance on each case of product sold. The computer model treats the allowance as if it were given to the retailer by the detergent manufacturer. The retailer passes on part of this price concession to the consumer in the form of a deal which serves to stimulate retail sales. In addition to this effect, the availability of a retail allowance will result in the sales force being more effective in its efforts to promote shelf and display space among retailers for the brand; that is, the sales force is in a better bargaining position when attempting to persuade the retailer to make available to the brand more and better positioned shelf space and, as a result, it can profitably spend more time on the brand.

If the manufacturer offers retail allowances too frequently, the promotional price effect is lost. Both the retailer and the consumer learn that the allowance is not an infrequent bargain but a regular price reduction that can be expected as a normal part of doing business.

The interaction of a brand's advertising expenditure, retail allowance, allocation of sales force effort, and market share determine the relative measure of a brand's retail availability. This term attempts to measure the effect of retail distribution and the allocation of shelf space and in-store special display promotions on the brand's sales. Once these interaction mechanisms are tested and developed to the point where they are reasonably correct determinants of retail availability and its effect on sales, guidance can be provided to market executives in the proper allocation of resources to these variables.

---

[79]This could be determined empirically by blind, paired-comparison tests.

[80]Specifying this distribution is not an easy problem. An approach to estimating it is outlined in the paper by Kuehn and Day, reprinted in Section IV.A.

2. Uses of the Model. The current running version of the model is programmed to allow for a market of up to nine brands and three firms. In this form the model is a good representation of the oligopoly model of economics. The structure of the model does not, however, limit its usefulness to oligopoly situations. The only limitation to the number of brands and firms that the model can handle is the speed and capacity of the computing system being utilized. This means that the model could be made to simulate the "purely competitive" market structures frequently hypothesized by economists with only small changes in parameters and structure.

Within the current oligopoly structure of the model, research is being undertaken to discover the relationships underlying the market variables (advertising, price, retail availability, product characteristics) at competitive equilibrium. As suggested by Kuehn,[81] the effectiveness of a brand's advertising is heavily dependent on the relative strength of its product characteristics, price, retail availability, and its current market position. By varying the starting conditions of the variables and then searching the function directly for the attendant equilibrium position, we can discover the mechanisms which determine the equilibrium in conjunction with the starting conditions and the assumption that firms seek to maximize their profits.

Answers to the following questions should come directly from this research:

1. What is the best marketing strategy to follow (using a profit criterion) given that the physical product characteristics of our brand are inferior to (or superior to, or the same as) competing brands, in terms of consumer preference?
2. How should a firm allocate resources among several brands competing in the same and/or different submarkets of the industry?
3. How should a firm introduce a new product to the market? Which variables controlled by the firm (if any) are important when introducing a new product? What effect does the timing of an introduction have on success?

Answers to these questions, even in a highly structured and controlled situation such as the computer simulated environment of the model, will provide marketing management with tentative guides for major policy decisions.

Another important use for this kind of dynamic computer model is pretesting marketing policies for feasibility before committing large blocks of resources to their field testing or full-scale implementation. To facilitate this sort of research and to use the model in teaching and business training exercises, the model has been programmed in FORTRAN in the form of the C.I.T. Marketing Game.[82] When the Marketing Game is played by opposing teams, flaws in a team's policies are likely to be discovered. This allows experimentation with alternative strategies to be done in the "synthetic" market instead of the real one without the danger of large sums of money being lost.

In its present form the Marketing Game has provisions for three firms operat-

---

[81]See Section IV.C.

[82]For a detailed description, see Alfred A. Kuehn and Doyle L. Weiss, "Marketing Analysis Training Exercise," *Behavioral Science,* forthcoming. The FORTRAN program has been run on IBM 704, 7070, and 7090 computers, and it is being modified for use on an IBM 1620 by Robert Karg of Duquesne University.

ing in four geographical regions. The production and financial aspects of the Marketing Game have been greatly simplified to allow concentration of the players to be sharply focused on its very detailed marketing aspects.

Each firm may market from one to three brands of detergent in each region, making decisions on the following marketing variables once each Game month:

1. Price.
2. Advertising expenditures.
3. Sales force size and allocation of efforts to indicated brands.
4. Retail allowance promotional activities.

Provisions have been made to enable the players to purchase research reports estimating various aspects of competitive marketing activity (price, advertising expenditures, market share, retail stockout, distribution, etc.). Also provision is made to permit the firms to develop and improve new products; to copy competitor's products; and to conduct "blind," paired-comparison product preference tests.

The usual claims made for the educational values of business games can be made for this Marketing Game. However, since it is a relatively realistic Game, the participant, while gaining experience and building heuristics for operating in a dynamic, highly interrelated world, is also discovering some institutional facts about market interrelationships which can be carried from the Game into the real world.

The realism of this Game is its important distinction from most business games being played today. If a game is not realistic, then it must be defended as a tool for teaching principles which can be demonstrated by the game. For some such purposes, realism is unnecessary and, as claimed by some educators, perhaps even undesirable. For research purposes, the unrealistic game is necessarily limited to serving as a task around which to focus psychological or organizational research. The market researcher has little to gain from observing either player behavior or response characteristics of a game not based on sound theory.

3. Summary. This paper has discussed some aspects of the structure and relationships of a computer simulation model of the detergent industry. The model also serves as the computational core of a relatively realistic marketing game. Research with this theory, as a simulation model and a marketing game, is expected to result in both a refinement of theory and an understanding of the dynamic interrelationship surrounding the effects of price, advertising, retail availability, and product characteristics upon consumer choice and the behavior of retailers.

C. How Advertising Performance Depends on Other Marketing Factors (by Alfred A. Kuehn)[83]

The budgeting of advertising is frequently discussed as though the appropriation were independent of competitive behavior, product characteristics, price, retail distribution, and the habits of potential customers. An advertising budget is commonly set as a percentage of past or expected future sales, in relation to the advertising-to-sales ratio prevalent in the industry, or, more recently, by

---

[83]This is a modified version of Alfred A. Kuehn, "How Advertising Performance Depends on Other Marketing Factors," *Journal of Advertising Research,* Vol. 2, No. 1 (March, 1962), pp. 2–10.

estimating the expenditures required to achieve some desired sales or promotion objective.

Can we be more precise in our budgeting of advertising? Can mathematical models sharpen our thinking about the effects of advertising and guide advertising practices? How do consumer product preferences, price, retail availability, and costs of production influence the payoff of advertising for competing brands of a product? How should advertising appropriations be allocated throughout the year for seasonal product classes? This paper will discuss these questions in some detail. It will outline results of research which appear to provide sound guides to advertising and merchandising policy for low-priced, frequently purchased products distributed through retail grocery and drug outlets.

1. Mathematical Models. Mathematical model building has achieved prominence in recent years as a means of studying a wide range of complex problems: the effectiveness of military weapons systems, the design of nuclear reactors, production and inventory control in industrial operations, prediction of voting behavior, and the routing of vehicular traffic. In most of these applications, the value of model building has been demonstrated beyond doubt. In marketing and advertising the use of mathematical models has generally met with less success, perhaps because of the difficulty model builders encounter in understanding the total merchandising system. Moreover, some aspects of marketing appear to be more complicated than the problems solved by model builders in other areas of business. This may be misleading, however, since any problem, once understood and solved, then appears simple.

I am personally convinced that working with models will help us understand the mechanisms underlying the marketing process and enable us to make better advertising and merchandising decisions. A sound foundation of research on the behavior of consumers and the interaction between merchandising variables is needed, however, to reach this goal. Care must be taken to weed out the unstated assumptions from the hypotheses and factual evidence. Results which at first appear reasonable are easy to achieve in model building; a more difficult task is to maintain internal consistency and to test the assumptions, implications, and predictions of the model. The latter requires concurrent empirical research. We are not likely to solve many advertising problems by theorizing alone. Nor, in my opinion, are we likely to solve the broader aspects of these problems until we take into account the interaction of a firm's advertising with other marketing factors.

To show how a model can help determine advertising policy, let us examine the budgeting implications of lagged (carry-over) effects of advertising and habitual brand-choice behavior by consumers for the purchase of a seasonal product.

2. Timing of Advertising. Many products have a seasonal demand. Given this condition, how should a firm allocate its advertising appropriation throughout the year? This problem has been studied for low-cost grocery products.

a) Underlying Assumptions. Two aspects of the problem appear most significant:

i) Advertising Carry-over. An advertising impulse is generally thought to have both immediate and delayed effects. Such evidence as is available suggests that the advertising impulse carries over to the future but decays with the passing of time. The rate of decay appears to vary with the type of advertising, sale-price advertising decaying rapidly, and institutional advertising declining more slowly (see Figure 8–14).

FIGURE 8–14

CARRY-OVER EFFECTS OF TWO TYPES OF ADVERTISING

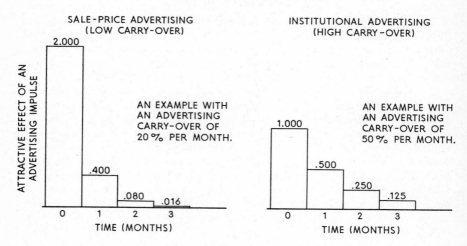

ii) Habitual Behavior in Customer Choice of Brands. To what extent do consumers change their brand mix of purchases over time? There appears to be a high probability of a consumer's maintaining a relatively stable mix of brand purchases of grocery products from one month to the next. A study of frozen orange juice purchases indicated a decay rate in a consumer's brand purchase probability of approximately 7 percent per month, or a holdover due to habit, inertia, or "brand loyalty" of about 93 percent per month. This phenomenon is illustrated in Figure 8–15. Factors influencing the rate of decay include the ex-

FIGURE 8–15

EFFECT OF HABITUAL BUYING BEHAVIOR UPON A
CONSUMER'S CHOICE OF BRANDS

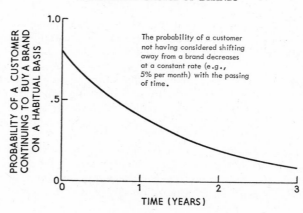

tent to which consumers even consider buying brands which they do not currently purchase and the extent to which their evaluation of such products on trial purchases is influenced unfavorably by a predisposition to favor the well-known previously used brand.

Six additional assumptions underlie our analyses of advertising strategies:

iii) Relationship of Consumer Planning-to-Buy and Purchase Periods. In the case of low-priced grocery and drug products there is apparently no substantial lag between a consumer's planning-to-buy and the actual purchase. Thus there is no need to determine the planning period during which time the consumer might decide upon the brand to be purchased, as distinct from the industry's sales period. This would probably not be true for major household appliances. If the planning period differs from the consumer purchase period, the sales curve in Figures 8–16 and 8–17 should be replaced by a curve reflecting the *brand choice decisions* made in each time period.

iv) Price Level throughout the Sales Cycle. Gross margin from sales be fore advertising is assumed to be constant throughout the year. If it is not, the industry sales cycle in Figures 8–16 and 8–17 should be replaced in the analysis by the cycle of total gross margin potential for the firm, that is, industry sales multiplied by the firm's gross margin apart from advertising.

v) Effect of Advertising. The sales cycle used in these analyses (Figures 8–16 and 8–17) is assumed to be consistent with the advertising cycles computed for the industry. If the level of industry advertising influences total industry sales this assumption would be invalid. (However, if we were to know or assume some relationship as to the effect of industry advertising upon industry sales, a solution consistent with such a relationship could easily be computed.) For many established products, at least in the short run, it would appear that advertising has a greater effect in shifting consumers among brands than in influencing the level of total industry sales.

vi) The Influence of Other Merchandising Variables. It is assumed that product characteristics, retail availability, and price of competing brands maintain a constant relative appeal to consumers throughout the sales cycle. In addition, the effectiveness of each firm's advertising is assumed to be constant throughout the year.

vii) Influence of Advertising upon the Retail Trade. These analyses consider the influence of advertising only on the consumer. Advertising also has a short-term effect upon the availability of retail space for special displays. Since advertising intended to influence retailers (including consumer advertising) should be budgeted proportional to current sales, consideration of this aspect of the problem would result in a revised optimal advertising cycle, a weighted combination of the sales cycle and the advertising cycles computed here.

viii) Growth of the Industry. A stable industry is assumed in these analyses. Growth effects can be added, however, merely by increasing the plotted percentage budget of each month after the initial month by the rate of growth and renormalizing so that the sum of the percentages will again equal 100 percent.

b) *Optimal Advertising Patterns.* On the basis of the preceding assumptions, optimal advertising patterns can be derived. The optimal timing of advertising expenditures in relation to the seasonal pattern in sales varies with the importance of habitual brand choice in purchases of the product.

i) Products with Habitual Brand Choice. Figure 8–16 shows a hypothetical seasonal sales curve together with three curves illustrating how firms should advertise in a competitive environment for various levels of advertising carryover. The first curve shows the "optimal" advertising rate for the case assuming no advertising carry-over, the second assumes a 50 percent carry-over from month to month, and the third assumes a 75 percent carry-over. In each case it is also assumed that there is a high level of habitual purchasing in the choice of brand from month to month, namely, a 90 percent holdover due to habit. Note that each of the advertising curves leads the sales curve: the greater the advertising carry-over the more the advertising cycle should lead the sales cycle. Note also that the amplitudes of the advertising cycles are very small relative to the sales cycle. Whereas the sales cycle at its peak is three times the level of the trough, the peak-to-trough ratio for the "optimal" advertising response by a firm ranges from 1.25 (when there is no advertising carry-over) to 1.50 (when there is 75 percent advertising carry-over). The ratio with 50 percent advertising carry-over is 1.28, very close to that observed for no carry-over.

FIGURE 8–16

OPTIMAL ADVERTISING BUDGETING AT COMPETITIVE EQUILIBRUM FOR A
SEASONAL PRODUCT WITH HIGH HABITUAL PURCHASING

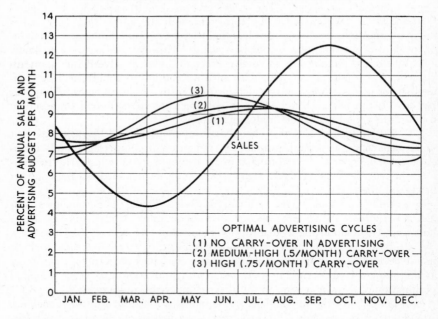

How can these "optimal" advertising curves help a merchandiser of grocery products budget his advertising? First we should recognize the meaning of the phrase "at competitive equilibrium" used in the title of Figure 8–16. This phrase reflects the assumption that each competitor in the market is independently budgeting his advertising expenditures at that level which will maximize his profits. This may not be true—perhaps some competitors are trying to maximize share of market, subject to certain profit constraints. If a firm's competitors were not to follow a policy consistent with maximizing profits, we could use the underlying advertising model to compute for the firm an "optimal" reaction to the advertising budgeting behavior established by competitors and, in general, obtain some relative advantage as a result. Only by outlining stated objectives for all competitors as we have done here with the assumption of competitive equilibrium, however, can we abstract generalized rules for advertising budgeting strategy from the model.

The "optimal" budgeting strategy illustrated in Figure 8–16 suggests that advertising for seasonal, habitually bought products *should* be budgeted relatively uniformly throughout the year, with the peak in advertising coming before the peak in sales. It also shows that these monthly appropriations are insensitive to the level of advertising carry-over in the range of 0 to 50 percent per month, a range within which most advertising seems to lie.

FIGURE 8–17

OPTIMAL ADVERTISING BUDGETING AT COMPETITIVE EQUILIBRUM FOR A
SEASONAL PRODUCT WITH NO HABITUAL PURCHASING

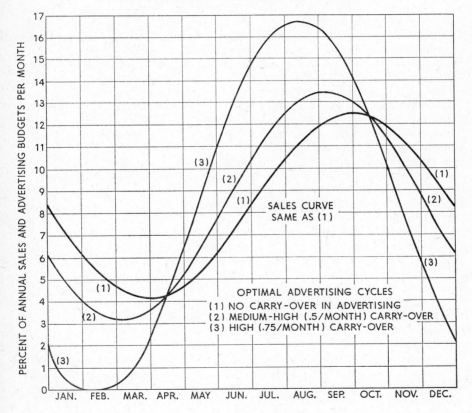

ii) Products with Nonhabitual Brand Choice. In Figure 8–17 we see the same curve outlined in Figure 8–16, with three "optimal" advertising curves reflecting no advertising carry-over, 50 percent carry-over, and 75 percent carry-over from month to month. The difference between advertising curves in Figures

8–16 and 8–17 results from the assumption in Figure 8–17 that consumer brand choice is *not* influenced by habit. In the earlier analysis, it was assumed that 90 percent of each brand's monthly sales reflect a continuation of habitual purchases from the previous month.

For what types of products is habitual brand choice low? Likely candidates are infrequently purchased items with a low level of brand identification, and products which the consumer can to some degree evaluate at first hand. Some industrial goods might also meet these qualifications.

In summary, the optimal advertising cycle under competitive equilibrium is identical to the sales cycle if there is no advertising carry-over and no habitual purchasing of brands. Both advertising carry-over and habitual behavior by customers results in the advertising cycle leading the sales cycle.

Increasing the level of habitual purchasing by brand within a product class serves to *decrease* the amplitude of the "optimal" advertising cycles. In contrast, an *increase* in advertising carry-over results in an *increase* in the seasonal amplitude of advertising.

3. Costs, Prices, Quality, and Distribution. Many variables influence the profitability of advertising, and thereby the "optimal" level of a firm's advertising appropriation. Some are manufacturing and shipping costs, price and product characteristics relative to competition, the distribution and advertising expenditures of competitors, the relative effectiveness of each brand's advertising message and choice of media, price and advertising elasticities, and the growth rate of the industry coupled with the rate of return required on investments. Since so many variables influence the value of a firm's advertising, we are frequently on shaky ground when making broad generalizations for the budgeting of advertising. These same considerations also limit the value of certain techniques of market-testing advertising.

Since the various elements of marketing activity and consumer behavior are closely entwined, it would seem to be risky to study advertising without incorporating all of these factors into our analysis. This can be done by first building a model of consumer purchasing behavior and the influence of merchandising variables. Such a model might then be evaluated empirically, with respect to both its assumptions and its predictions. In addition, the theoretical implications of the model can be examined. I have attempted to construct such a model, much of which is contained in an earlier paper.[84] More recently, the complete model has been incorporated in the Carnegie Tech Management Game and in the C.I.T. Marketing Game for use as an educational tool and in research. The results outlined earlier for seasonality in advertising are included in this model. Similarly, the comments which follow are consistent with it and represent my current understanding of the interaction of advertising with other market variables.

a) Price and Retail Availability. Most advertising models ignore price and retail availability. Such models in effect assume price and retail availability to be equal for all brands. They also generally assume that no consumers would be attracted to an unadvertised brand. But we all know of the success of unadvertised brands whose appeal to potential customers is based primarily upon their price and retail availability. Given such assumptions within a model, price and

---

[84]Kuehn, "A Model for Budgeting Advertising," *op. cit.*

availability would not be likely to appear as variables in the resulting advertising decision rules derived therefrom.

In practice, competing brands do differ in retail availability. These differences are accentuated when we recognize that shelf space, location, and special displays affect brand availability as much as does its mere presence in the retail outlet. There may also be differences in price. How do these factors influence profitability of advertising?

Sales gains resulting from increased advertising expenditures are generally correlated with the availability of the brand. On the other hand, advertising can be an effective vehicle for obtaining increased distribution, shelf space, and special displays. Consequently, we can begin to get some insight into the classic problem of where to allocate additional funds for a brand: to areas where it is doing poorly or to areas in which it is selling well?

Briefly, increased advertising where the brand is relatively strong generally appears to be more profitable in the short run, unless the brand is already near its maximum potential penetration of the consumer market. Expenditures in areas where the brand is weak must generally be looked upon as investment spending directed at obtaining distribution and shelf position. And these activities will succeed only if the balance of the sales program is closely coordinated with them. How frequently has a firm wasted its advertising or promotional budgets by failing to utilize its sales force concurrently to sell the retailer?

In allocating advertising dollars to regional or metropolitan markets, planners frequently must decide whether to allocate extra funds to some areas at the expense of others. Generally, however, they find it difficult temporarily to withdraw funds from areas in which a brand is doing poorly since they see the problem as one of survival. Under such circumstances pulsation in advertising or promotion, coordinated with sales force efforts, offers better prospects of profits and gains in distribution than a continuous dribble of advertising. In many such cases it would also appear desirable to withdraw funds from some territories to concentrate on others, a result contrary to that suggested by most advertising models. By concentrating on a few markets, a brand frequently has a better chance of forcing distribution and increasing its overall short-term profitability, thereby obtaining the means for subsequent investment expenditures in other territories. It can be expensive to hold one's own in every market simply as a matter of principle, especially if this prevents the brand becoming firmly established and profitable in any one region.

A brand with greater retail availability than its competitors will tend to have a favorable differential in consumer response to its advertising. Such an advantage can generally be translated into a somewhat greater profit differential, all other factors being equal. For example, if one brand in a two-brand market were to have twice the availability of its competitor (that is, a situation in which the first brand would outsell the second by a 2:1 ratio if price and sales promotion levels were equal), its profitability at competitive equilibrium would be 2½ times that of its comparable rival given an interbrand price elasticity of four. The relative increase in profits for the first firm under conditions of competitive equilibrium would be a result of increased advertising expenditures by the firm due to its stronger retail distribution.

A decrease in price also improves consumer response to the brand's advertising. However, a reduced unit profit due to the lower price accompanies the increased response to advertising. Thus, only if a firm has lower costs than its competitors should it price below competition at equilibrium. If a brand has both lower costs and certain advantages in terms of basic product attributes, however, it should in most cases apply its added gross margin to increased advertising and sales promotion rather than to price cutting. In general, a brand with product advantages as well as lower costs would charge a premium price under conditions of competitive equilibrium.

b) *Competitive Advertising.* The effect of competitive advertising on a brand's optimal advertising budget depends on the relative strength of the brand's appeal to consumers in terms of its product attributes, price, and retail availability as well as on the effectiveness of its advertising story and its choice of media. If all competitors are about equal in these variables, we can easily compute the equilibrium price and advertising promotion budgets in terms of the number of competitors (N), the industry price and advertising elasticities $(\eta_p$ and η_a, respectively), the share-of-market price elasticity for brands (ϵ), the cost of manufacturing and distributing the product, and the probability (b_{pda}) of the consumer's brand choice being influenced in part by advertising or promotion:

$$\text{Price/unit} = (\text{Cost/unit}) \times \frac{\eta_p + \epsilon(N-1)}{\eta_p + \epsilon(N-1) - N},$$

and

$$\begin{array}{l}\text{Sales} \\ \text{Promotional} \\ \text{Expense/unit}\end{array} = (\text{Cost/unit}) \times \frac{\eta_a + b_{pda}(N-1)}{\eta_p + \epsilon(N-1) - N}.$$

The industry price and advertising elasticities in the above expressions are consistent with the use of these concepts by economists. That is, all other factors being held constant, we have

$$D(p, a) = D(p_0, a_0)\left[\frac{p}{p_0}\right]^{-\eta_p}\left[\frac{a}{a_0}\right]^{\eta_a}$$

where $D(p,a)$=industry demand at price p and advertising-promotion level a; where the industry price is the weighted average price of all brands in the market, each brand's contribution being weighted with respect to its share of market; and where $D(p_0,a_0)$=industry demand at some base price level p_0 and base advertising-promotion level a_0.

Thus an increase in industry price or a decrease in industry advertising expenditures will decrease industry demand. The larger the absolute values of the price and advertising elasticities, η_p and η_a, the greater is the sensitivity of industry demand to changes in industry price and sales promotional expenditures.

The term b_{pda}, which represents the probability of a consumer's choice of a brand being influenced by advertising, has no direct counterpart in economic theory. In effect, at any given time the market can be treated as being divided into two segments; the first contains $(1-b_{pda}) \times 100$ percent of the market and is influenced only by the effects of price, product characteristics, and retail availability; the second contains $b_{pda} \times 100$ percent of the market and is influenced by advertising *in interaction with* price, product characteristics, and availability. Thus if b_{pda} is near 0, advertising will affect only a small portion of the market. But if b_{pda} is near 1, competitive advertising will influence virtually all consumers. Product classes in which the customer either cannot or will not evaluate the brands in terms of their intrinsic merits have high values of b_{pda}. This reflects the ability of advertising to project status, confidence, or other desirable attributes to the product.

The share-of-market price elasticity (ϵ) for brands also deviates from the economists' treatment of cross-product elasticity except in certain limiting cases. As noted in the above discussion of advertising, price has influence in both market segments. In each segment, the relative attraction of each brand in terms of the combined effects of product characteristics, retail availability, and, in the b_{pda} segment, advertising appeals, is modified (multiplied) by its relative price appeal computed as

$$\frac{p_i^{-\epsilon}}{\sum p_i^{-\epsilon}}.$$

This might be thought of as "share-of-price appeal," the numerator being the brand's price taken to the negative power of the share-of-market elasticity, the denominator being the same term summed over all brands. Note that an increase in the price of a brand, all other brands holding price constant, will reduce its share of market. The greater the elasticity ϵ, the higher the brand-shifting sensitivity of the market to the relative prices of competing brands.

The share-of-market price elasticity generally ranges between three and six, while the industry price elasticity is on the order of two or less. It follows that the equilibrium relationships indicated above suggest two things. First, the industry equilibrium level for pricing and promotional expenditures is much more sensitive to ϵ than to η_p. Second, the industry price elasticity plays a minor role in determining prevailing prices when several firms are competing in the market. Similarly, the effect of advertising on brand shifting, represented by b_{pda} ranging from 0 to 1, generally tends to influence prevailing industry advertising levels for mature products more than does the industry advertising elasticity η_a, whose value is frequently on the order of $\frac{1}{10}$.

In practice, individual competitors might be expected to deviate from these competitive equilibrium values, either because of goals other than profit maximization, the lack of price competition, or because of the absence of sound guides for implementing an appropriate budgeting policy. To evaluate the implications of such deviations from profit-maximizing behavior by competitors, let us consider two promotional counter-strategies suggested by the decision rules derived from the merchandising model:

i) Suboptimal Advertising Expenditures by Competitors. If all members of an industry are about equal with respect to operating costs, product appeal, retail distribution, and promotional effectiveness, and if one's competitors *underspend* on advertising and other forms of sales promotion, then the firm could increase its profit by also spending less than the equilibrium rate. The optimal size of its reduction would be *less,* however, than that of the firm or firms initiating the underspending.

ii) Excessive Advertising Expenditures by Competitors. If a firm's brand is equal in costs, product quality, distribution, and advertising effectiveness to its competitors, and the latter *overspend* on advertising, the firm could increase its profit by reducing its expenditures below equilibrium. To do so, however, would also increase the competitors' profits and, on balance, competition would gain a relative advantage. Consequently it may be desirable here to compete with overspending by also overspending, reducing the profitability of the industry at least temporarily, but hopefully bringing one's competitors to their senses.

Note that a firm operating at a competitive disadvantage in terms of costs or product appeal cannot easily counter competitive overspending with an increased advertising budget. The weaker firm tends to be at the mercy of its stronger competitor. Insofar as the stronger firm is willing to absorb some reduction in profit, it can keep a weaker competitor "on the ropes" by overspending, or by engaging in more advertising research to improve its promotional effectiveness. If the weaker firm counters by overspending, it helps dig its own grave. Interestingly enough, the share of market held by a firm does not necessarily indicate its competitive strength. Under many conditions the model suggests that the stronger firm, to maximize its profits, should permit its weaker rivals to maintain a significant share of the market. The underdog position of the rivals is, however, fully apparent when profits are compared.

4. Summary and Conclusions. The above model decision rules do not make decision making easy or contradict our thinking about optimal strategy. Instead, they quantify relationships generally discussed only in qualitative terms. By making explicit our assumptions about market behavior and examining their consequences, we can test and thereby understand advertising phenomena. The use of such models does not eliminate the need for managerial judgment, but rather assists it by providing a new set of reference points.

The model from which these results were derived is relatively complex when viewed in its entirety. This research was begun some seven years ago with a very simple model—a model which has been modified and extended repeatedly in the light of additional evidence. As a result of these experiences, I now feel reasonably confident that a very simple model cannot hope to portray the intricacies of marketing processes. This is not to say that we cannot gain insight from simple models, but rather that we must be very careful that the factors these models ignore do not have a large effect upon the specific problem being studied. Only rarely do we get sound decisions from a model whose assumptions are not in tune with reality.

Because of the complexities of consumer behavior and the merchandising process, it is difficult to state widely applicable marketing decision rules for the guidance of management. The simplicity of the above solution for the seasonality of advertising budgets, for example, holds only when there is stability in the relative distribution, product attractiveness, and price of competing brands. And the effectiveness of each brand's advertising message and choice of media must be constant throughout the year. When these conditions are not met, we can still determine a firm's optimal budget in terms of the expected changes in these variables, but the results cannot be easily generalized. To date we have not been able to derive simple equilibrium decision rules for market situations in which there are more than two types of firms; that is, n_1 brands having one set of product, cost, and distribution characteristics, and n_2 brands each having another common set of characteristics. The generalized rules available to us today are of limited value in practice. They serve to outline the broad aspects of the problem, but to solve any specific marketing problem we must revert to the underlying detailed model.

What about the limitations of the model? First, there are difficulties in estimating some of the parameters and variables of the model. For example, it is not clear that we will ever be able to estimate very adequately the industry advertising and price elasticities. This being the case, we cannot make much practical use of the model in what appears to most marketing executives to be the simplest type of market—the situation in which a single brand virtually controls an entire product class. Our inability to estimate these parameters precisely is not a problem, however, in studying markets with multiple-brand entries. Here the industry elasticities have only a very minor influence upon optimal merchandising decisions.

We must reckon with other inadequacies in the model. For example, we know little of the effect of advertising and sales force activity, along with the brand's share of market, in obtaining retail distribution and shelf space for a brand. The problem is accentuated by the fact that we do not yet have a good measure of the effects of display space and location upon retail sales. I have attempted to make plausible assumptions, where necessary, to incorporate these aspects of the marketing process into the C.I.T. Marketing Game. Future research, both empirical field studies and analyses within the framework of this Game, should enable us to evaluate these relationships and incorporate improvements into the model. Such untested portions of the model require us to exercise extreme care in its application.

The model cannot be used mechanically. Analyses of the sensitivity of decisions to the untested assumptions are generally required. In some instances, these gaps in the model can be filled by management's judgmental estimates. This is often feasible because management is required to estimate only competitive ratios (for instance, the effectiveness of our advertising copy relative to that of competition) rather than absolute levels.

An interesting sidelight of this research is its implications for the field testing of advertising campaigns. It suggests that controlled market-by-market testing contains a variety of pitfalls. For example, it is *not sufficient* that we "control" market conditions throughout the period of the test, assuming that such control is in fact possible. We must also know the *level* at which each of the variables is being controlled. This suggests, as a minimum, that we would have to match territories.

A more promising approach is to build a model of the marketing process, obtain the needed market measures through continuous monitoring, and evaluate these market activity data regularly by estimating the parameters required to determine the effectiveness of competitive strategy. Is this far in the future? I do not think so. Will the costs of monitoring the market be too high? Not once we know how to use these data in developing improved marketing decisions.

Models will grow in importance as guides to marketing management. They will not, however, take over management's role, or preclude creative approaches to merchandising. All they can do is help direct management toward better use of the firm's resources. The ultimate success of a brand will still depend upon how well its total marketing program meets the physical and psychological needs of the consumer.

V. THE RESEARCH POTENTIAL OF THE GAME

The seven articles which have been reprinted in Sections II–IV of this chapter are preliminary to more extensive use of the Game for research at Carnegie. They show that the Carnegie Tech Management

Game does have potential as an environment for research, but they also show that since it occupies an intermediate role between the laboratory and the field situation, the Game presents special problems if we are to realize its potential.

A.   The Game as an Alternative to Laboratory Experiments

The Carnegie Tech Management Game is not a simple substitute for a laboratory situation. In the social science laboratory, the goal is usually to try to pin down relationships among small numbers of carefully defined and measured variables. These experiments may represent direct abstractions from processes that exist in the real world, or they may be designed mainly as attempts to replicate or extend earlier laboratory studies.

To those who value the simplicity of relationships in the laboratory, the Carnegie Game may seem too complex. If it is to maintain its primary characteristics as a Game, it cannot be controlled and constrained to the degree that simple experiments can. It is expensive—in money, manpower, and time—to run the numbers of replications that orthodox experimental procedures demand.

The Game—if it appeals at all—would be appealing for studies of behavior in which it is important to have a complex or institutionally realistic task environment.

Behavior when confronted with complex tasks is likely to be different than behavior under simpler task conditions. We can study how individuals react to masses of loosely structured information, how they abstract from this information interpretations about the state of the environment, and how they formulate problems and define alternatives for decisions. In an environment that training can help players cope with, it is interesting to compare the decision problems that are defined and the actions that are taken by naïve players with those by players who have had business education or experience. Complex and realistic tasks are also often the only kind which can stimulate high player motivation, encourage voluntary differentiation of function and status in the team, and sustain players' interest fruitfully for a long period of play. Thus, the Game may help us to make experimental approaches to the questions of organizational development which we have not been able to answer by studies of small, short-term, peer-oriented groups in the laboratory.

B.   The Game as an Alternative to Field Studies

Just as the Carnegie Tech Management Game may seem too complex for the experimentalist, it may seem too simple for the person interested in field research. Yet as several of the articles reprinted in this chapter show, there are some advantages to this simplicity for people whose main interest is research on real business organizations. The Game cannot substitute entirely for work with real organizations; but because it is somewhat simpler than reality and because things can be made to happen at a more rapid pace, it can be used as a faster, cheaper, first test of theories and hypotheses than most real-world situations. Also, the Game environment can be manipulated to provide conditions which are seldom found in the outside world, but whose effects must be known if we are really to understand the mechanisms that govern the behavior of social or economic systems. As we have already pointed out, data on the effects of large price changes for consumer goods are hard to find in business because radical shifts in prices do not occur very often. Investigation of the effects of such price changes in the Game does not answer the question of what will happen in business, but it can lead to hypotheses about what effects we should expect to find, better ideas about the kinds of real business data we should look for, and better standards for evaluating it. A third advantage of the Game as an adjunct to field studies is that the same environment can be used to respond to a variety of different decision strategies. Thus, while the Game is limited in realism, it offers a chance for more meaningful comparisons among the effects of different strategies than parallel or sequential testing in the real environment of a business can offer.

C. Developments to Make the Game a More Effective Environment for Research

To use the Carnegie Tech Management Game effectively as a research tool, we cannot simply borrow ideas and techniques from the laboratory or the field situation. The Game poses problems of its own, and one of the major research challenges is to develop a set of research strategies that are appropriate for the kind of environment which the Game offers.

The first challenge is to develop more effective ways of controlling the things which we might want to control during play of the Game. This means more effort to divorce research runs of the Game from educational runs; the constraints which ought to operate in the two situations are often quite different. But it also means more effort to segment the Game so that the parts of it which are irrelevant for research purposes can be "switched off" when they are not needed. For research in marketing and for use in marketing courses, this has been accomplished by this development of the C.I.T. Marketing Game, which contains approximately the same complexity in the marketing area as does the Carnegie Tech Management Game, but which involves only truncated activities in finance and production. In other cases, where we want to focus on the behavior of a single team, we will want ways to let the computer take the place of competing firms in the industry. More elaborate simulations of the kind represented by the "rote marketer" should eventually let us replace human firms by computer programs that will play the Game according to a variety of preplanned strategies.[85] The responses of computer simulations will be more easily described and more consistent over a series of experimental runs than the behavior of even carefully instructed and controlled human competitors.

The second challenge is to develop the kinds of models of behavior for which a complex environment like the Carnegie Game is useful as a setting for research. These will generally not be simple propositions about relations between a pair of variables. They will be multivariate models, with measures specified that are appropriate for the Game. We also must devise automatic procedures for collecting data and analyzing these models on the computer while the Game is being run.

This calls for a greater degree of advance planning for research than is often called for in laboratory or field situations, and it raises the third challenge: the development of adequate techniques for evaluating the significance of the findings from Game studies. Traditional statistical techniques are not likely to work because the assumptions which underlie them are not going to be met by most Game research designs. The job of recruiting subjects for long Game runs and the expense of each run is going to limit the number of replications which can be attempted in any study. What we need is some better developed set of standards than we now have for testing the fit of a total model or total theory to many pieces of data on the same Game run (or on a small set of Game runs). As opposed to traditional techniques, instead of asking how frequently a particular hypothesized relation has been and needs to be confirmed, we are looking for meaningful ways to ask how many of a large set of hypothesized relations hold—and need to hold—in a single situation.

---

[85]There is a bonus for efforts to develop such simulations: in the process of trying to simulate the way human teams make decisions, we shall undoubtedly sharpen our ideas about the kinds of experiments to which we want to subject human teams, and we ought to produce a better program of experiments as a result.

Chapter 9

DIRECTIONS FOR FUTURE DEVELOPMENT

In the preceding chapters of this book, we have attempted to show that the Carnegie Tech Management Game has been extremely useful for both educational and research purposes. While this has proved to be very gratifying for those of us have been associated with this Game's formulation, we do not feel that we have reached the ultimate in business game development. We recognize that there are a great many ways in which the present version of the Carnegie Tech Management Game can be improved, both to increase its educational and research effectiveness and to make it cheaper and more flexible to use. Some of these possible improvements have already been suggested in earlier chapters. In this concluding chapter, however, it seems appropriate to indicate in greater detail some types of modifications which might advantageously be made in the present Mark 1.5 version of the Carnegie Tech Management Game.

I. SUGGESTIONS FOR INCORPORATING PERSONNEL PROBLEMS INTO THE GAME

As it was originally developed, the Carnegie Game was reasonably rich in presenting the players with challenging problems in areas like production, marketing, and finance. These are areas of the business school curriculum where a fair amount of quantitative research and mathematical model building has taken place. Some critics have said that management games cannot play a useful role in training players to solve problems arising in the less quantified areas of the business school curriculum, personnel relations frequently being cited as a case in point. Practically none of the existing business games has personnel relations as their main, or even as a subsidiary, focus.[1]

We definitely do not feel that this type of criticism is justified. In support of our contention, we shall now indicate several ways in which we think that rich and educationally rewarding experiences in the per-

---

[1] A partial exception is MATRIX: A Career Orientation Simulation, described in John W. Plattner and Lowell W. Herron, *Simulation: Its Use in Employee Selection and Training* (New York: American Management Association, Management Bulletin Number 20, 1962).

sonnel relations area can be incorporated into the Carnegie Tech Management Game.

While the Carnegie Game, as it is usually played, provides managers with some rich experience in building and maintaining their own team organization, it does not challenge them with many problems of managing an organization of subordinate personnel. Since this is valuable and difficult experience for young men to acquire, we are interested in ways of strengthening the personnel management challenge of the Game. We would like to confront players with the job of dealing with real or simulated subordinates at a variety of organizational levels, and we would like to use the Game to pose general issues of personnel policies, procedures, and systems in the same way that we now use it to pose these issues in the functional areas of marketing, production, and finance. By expanding the Game in these directions, we might create the need for each team to have a personnel specialist, or we might simply have found a way to enrich the jobs of men like the production manager or the executive vice president to make them equal in level of challenge with those of the president and the marketing manager.

There are a number of directions in which we might move. Some would in no way involve complicating the computer model for the Game; others would involve additions to the model. Some would focus on personnel problems within the team and between the team and its board of directors. Others would involve managing continuing relations with union representatives and handling real or simulated problems of direct supervision and control. Problems of recruiting, selection, training, and assessment can be introduced.

Some of the suggestions listed below have already been adopted at Carnegie Tech. We hope that many more will be implemented during future Game runs.

A.   Actions That Boards of Directors Might Take

In our present use of the Game, the boards of directors already ask teams to draw up and defend their organizational plans with some care. The management audit is intended as an incentive for firms to revise and improve their plans periodically and to prepare written descriptions of positions and relationships that can be understood and evaluated by outsiders.

Simple pressure to outline plans and policies in more detail or to review them more frequently is not likely to be popular with players because it may have no demonstrable effects on how well their companies fare in the Game. But there are a number of conditions under which the board might properly ask for more and better work in the personnel area. In runs of the Game where job rotation is to be enforced, each team could provide for its board a mid-Game assessment of the capabilities and interests of its members along with recommendations about how shifts would be made. Firms might also be asked to design and administer performance evaluation systems for the sake of helping their presidents advise the directors abount the end-of-semester assignment of grades.

Boards of directors might also permit exchanges of personnel from one team to another. If each executive were assigned a salary and if these costs were carried as an expense on the firm's monthly operating statement, teams could try to bid managers away from one another. This would create problems of evaluating personnel across organizations, of deciding how candidates will be approached, and of settling the terms to be offered to them. In addition, each firm would have to handle the problems of integrating new recruits into the organization and of developing policies that will prevent raiding of key members by other teams.

If in a future version of the Game there is opportunity for new companies to enter the industry, managers could not only move from one firm to another, but they could also leave existing firms to establish a competing organization.

When the Carnegie Stock Exchange (which was briefly discussed in Section II.D of Chapter 3) is operated in conjunction with the Carnegie Tech Management Game, then there are two ways in which real financial motivations can be provided for the student managers. To make the managers' salaries personally more meaningful in the Game context, some or all of them might be credited to the managers' personal accounts, increasing the values of their portfolios on the Carnegie Stock Exchange. Additional financial incentives for the managers could be provided by permitting the boards of directors to establish executive stock option plans. The ultimate value of these stock option plans would depend upon the movements of the firms' stock prices on the Carnegie Stock Exchange.

B. Interactions with Union Representatives

In Section II.C of Chapter 3, we have described the manner in which labor negotiations have been included in recent plays of the Carnegie Tech Management Game. Many additional aspects of labor-management relations can be introduced into the Game by having a small group of faculty members, playing the role of union officers, monitor the decisions of firms continuously throughout the semester. This ought to provide each team with at least two or three occasions on which they are asked by the union to defend overtime policies, changes in the numbers of workers employed, shifts in maintenance expeditures, or other decisions that affect the hourly workers. When a team decides to build a new factory or introduces a new product, the union might want advanced assurances that the workers presently employed will not suffer. A firm's ability to meet the union's fear, questions, and demands can be reflected in several ways:

1. The union representatives can evaluate how well the team has done and can use these evaluations as one of the bases for determining their demands and bargaining strategies during the annual negotiations of a new wage contract.
2. The union representatives can make short-term judgments about how workers would be affected by management's behavior, and these judgments can be used to increase or decrease the worker productivity parameter or the costs of hiring and laying off employees in the Game model.
3. If circumstances justify, the union representatives can call wildcat strikes of a week or more in duration—the length depending on the seriousness of the offense and the intended impact of the action on other firms in the industry.

Two other ways can be mentioned for enriching the union-management-relations problem area. One would involve a considerable investment of faculty time, and the other would involve some extensive changes in the Game model. If faculty time is a more available resource than programming competence, teams might be given occasional cases or case sequences that ask for qualitative decisions for managing individuals or groups in the plant. These could be quite specific: they might involve absenteeism, theft of company property, requests for special privileges, violations of safety rules, training problems, or a variety of similar things.[2] We would need to supplement the initial materials that players receive by adding more information about employee relations policies in the industry, about current union contracts, and about methods for resolving grievances. The quality of answers to such problems could be scored by the faculty, and the scores could be used to affect other aspects of Game play as indicated above.

If programming skills are available for this purpose, it would be interesting to enrich the market in which hourly workers are hired. Two complications are suggested. The first would make general business conditions and the company's past record of stability in its hiring and layoff policy have some effects on the supply of labor. If conditions are tight and a team's past policies have been erratic, they may not be able to

---

[2]The Procter and Gamble MATRIX exercise, cited in footnote 1, presents participants with situations of this type.

hire new workers when they need them without offering to pay a premium over current rates. Under such conditions, many of their present workers might leave to take other jobs. The second complication would give firms access to the kinds of differentiated, competing supplies of labor that exist in the real world. They might have a choice between men and women, whites and Negroes, or union and nonunion labor. There might be no difference in the wage at which they could he hired; but teams might find that to get the numbers of people they wanted, they had to authorize hiring from other than their usual sources. We might want to include realistic costs for the disruption that occurs when a factory is integrated or nonunion labor is brought in. The analytic and economic considerations in such decisions might not have to be made very complicated; the interesting feature would be the necessity of balancing these considerations against the social and ethical issues involved and of justifying whatever decisions are made to the boards of directors and to the union.

C. Genuine Supervisory Experience

Supervisory cases built into the Carnegie Management Game could have considerable value, but they also have a major weakness. Incorporating them into the Game requires adding a great deal of extra detail which may not be closely related to aspects of the present model. Therefore it may be difficult meaningfully to relate the decisions and outcomes for the supervisory cases to the rest of the Game. It will take much effort, both in designing the problems and in umpiring the students' solutions, to get the same kind of dynamic feedback link between actions and results that is available in other aspects of the Game. Even where such problems are skillfully contrived and administered, they tend to stand apart from the central elements of the Game.

At a somewhat larger cost for each run of the Game, but without the costs of developing suitable case sequences, real supervisory experience that ties in centrally with other parts of the Game can be provided to the teams. We can provide this experience by providing each firm with a modest budget (for example, between $5 and $20 per week) to hire its own clerical assistant. The teams would have to select the assistants, train them, schedule and supervise their work, and evaluate how well they have done. Particularly if the assistants were not other college students, the problems encountered with them should be reasonably realistic.

In addition to providing some limited amounts of supervisory experience, the authorization to hire clerical assistants should reduce the complaints teams sometimes make about the "excessive" amounts of routine work that are involved in evaluating results and making decisions.

D.   Recruiting and Selection Problems in the Game Model

Both in the marketing and in the research and development areas of the Carnegie Tech Management Game, there are possibilities for enriching the Game model to make results more dependent than they now are on recruiting and selection decisions. In the marketing area, this would involve complicating the simple procedures by which teams now add salesmen to their staff. In the research area, it would mean making provision in the laboratory for various grades of scientists, engineers, and technicians and making the generation of new products depend on the number and quality of the men employed and perhaps on procedures for administering research as well as on the amount of money that is spent.

At present, firms can hire salesmen at will. It takes time for a new salesman to reach his peak effectiveness, but once he has reached his peak he is as good as any other salesman. Salesmen in the Game never quit, although they may be fired.

Suppose that a firm could meet its needs for salesmen in three ways: (1) by hiring experienced salesmen away from competitors, (2) by hiring experienced salesmen from outside the industry, or (3) by hiring inexperienced college graduates.

We would need to have functions to describe the supply of men in each "pool" available at any time. The supply of men within the industry is, of course, the set of salesmen employed by the other two firms. The supply of experienced men outside the industry might be an inverse function of the level of industrial or marketing activity in the economy as a whole and might be directly related to recent cyclical trends in the total market for detergents. The supply of college graduates would depend on some assumed figures for college enrollment, on the industry's expenditures to make the job of detergent salesman seem attractive, and on the time of year. Large numbers might not be available from colleges more than twice a year. In general, *at peak levels* the supply of experienced salesmen from other industries would be larger than the supply of college graduates; the latter, in turn, would be larger than the supply of competitors' salesmen.

We would also need some distribution of asking prices. These, for men working with competing firms, would be tied to their actual earnings (either as a constant increment over present salary rates or as a variable increment depending on the employment policies and the growth potentials of the respective firms). For men outside the industry, the distribution might depend primarily on general business conditions and on the current rates within the detergent industry. For college men, it would reflect recent histories of starting salaries for college graduates. The mean asking price of competitors' salesmen would be highest; the asking prices of men from outside the industry would be most variable.

Each salesman would have an "initial performance potential" which would be the base level at which he worked when he first started out. On the average, the initial performance potential should be highest for competitors' men, intermediate for men from other industries, and lowest for college graduates. The distributions for the latter groups, though, ought to have a high variance and should overlap considerably. Each salesman would also have a "growth potential"—a rate at which he could be expected to improve.

For salesmen of any of the three kinds, there should generally be a low correlation between asking price, initial performance potential, and growth potential.

Before hiring salemen, firms should be able to buy gross estimates of the numbers of men available, their quality, and their asking prices. For the college market, teams could map out general recruiting plans for a year at a time. This might simply be a decision about the number of campuses they want to visit and about their total budget for recruiting. If faculty umpiring were engaged in, teams might go beyond this to submit detailed plans for the particular kinds of recruiting they want to undertake. To hire, teams would specify how many men they want from each market, the salary they are willing to pay, and the extra amounts they are willing to spend to build candidates' interest in their company and to insure that the candidates are high-quality men.

Similar kinds of proposals could be worked out for staffing the research and development laboratory. Teams' abilities to get good men and to get as many men as they want in either the case of the salesmen or the case of the scientists and engineers could be made to depend on the ability to outline sensible, detailed, recruiting and selection procedures as well as on basic judgments to spend enough for recruiting and to seek men in the right market.

If firms are able to hire salesmen or scientists away from each other, this could be programmed entirely into the computer or it could be made a matter for direct personal negotiation between the teams. For direct negotiations, a firm might bid to take one or more salesmen or scientists from a competitor. He would make an offer, and the competitor might make a counteroffer to keep his man. (Perhaps a second round of offer and counteroffer could be permitted, too.) Then a partly random partly deterministic function (based on the difference between last offer and counteroffer, on the competitive position of the two teams, and perhaps on the variance in salesmen's salaries on each team) would determine if the salesman moved or stayed. Perhaps as a constraint against too frequent or too reckless bidding, a firm would be required to pay all its salesmen the increase used to get or keep a key man—or at least to pay them a certain percentage of the increase.

These are a few of the many ways in which additional problems and challenges from the personnel area may be incorporated into the Carnegie Tech Game in order to broaden its potential for management training. This is an appealing functional area in which to expand the Game's scope because it is an excellent one in which to try to construct qualitative problems where "human" or "ethical" issues loom large. But it is also appealing because the Game offers more chance than most other frameworks to show how personnel decisions must mesh with other aspects of a business operation and to show that analytic approaches are just as appropriate and just as important for organizational as they are for economic and technical issues.

II. SOME CHARACTERISTICS OF THE IDEAL MANAGEMENT GAME[3]

As a background against which some other suggestions for improving the Carnegie Tech Management Game will be made, we find it convenient first to describe some of the characteristics which we feel an ideal management game would possess. We shall refer to the ideal business game of the future as the Mark N version of the Carnegie Tech Management Game. This reflects both our hope that successive modifications of the Carnegie Game will continue to be made until it reaches the stage of perfection which we now envision as possible, and our uncertainty regarding how many revisions will have to be made until this has been accomplished.

As we see it, the ideal game of the future will differ from current games in at least four major respects: (1) it will be formulated in terms of continuous rather than discrete play; (2) it will allow the players to move, if they choose, by stating policies to be followed rather than merely by setting down specific *ad hoc* decisions; (3) it will have built into it a variety of subgames which can be activated or deactivated at

[3]Some of the material in Sections II and III has been freely adapted from Kalman J. Cohen and Merton H. Miller, "Some Thoughts on the Management Game of the Future," in William R. Dill, James R. Jackson, and James W. Sweeney, (eds.), *Proceedings of the Conference on Business Games as Teaching Devices* (New Orleans: Tulane University, 1961), pp. 73–80.

will; and (4) it will offer the players opportunities for creative and inventive play.

A. Continuous Play

One of the most artificial and unsatisfactory features of present games is that the players must at rigidly fixed intervals make specific decisions for each and every aspect of the company operations included in the game model. In real firms, of course, the length of time between decision dates differs greatly, both from activity to activity and also within any one functional area as external pressures dictate. Furthermore, it is rare indeed to find the entire gamut of company operations up for simultaneous review by top management. In fact, one of the main functions of the game device is precisely to give players practice in selecting from among the many possibilities those particular actions that require more than routine attention or where revision of previous plans would be worthwhile. Admittedly, it is not impossible to get this kind of "selective" approach to management within the framework of existing games, but, if our experience at Carnegie Tech is any guide, the artificial task structures imposed by the rigid pattern of moves in current games strongly militates against it.

The natural way of meeting these difficulties is by restructuring the game so that play, in the sense of the ongoing life of the firm, is continuous rather than discrete. In operational terms, this means requiring the players to file in advance with the game administrators continuing budgets, authorization schedules, or other types of explicit instructions to permit the firm to function continuously and to have its accounting records updated regularly. If the players wish to change their decisions they are, of course, free to do so at any time, but if they make no change in plans, the game program will still have sufficient information to carry on without interruption of play.

B. Policy Moves

A second unrealistic feature of current management games (and one closely related to the discreteness embodied in their decision structures) is that the "decisions" required of the players are much too explicit and detailed. What we want to teach with games is not merely how to make some particular class of production, finance, or marketing decisions, but how to run a *viable organization*. This means, among other things, how to set broad goals for the enterprise; how to translate these goals into a comprehensive and comprehensible set of policies, working rules, and constraints on subordinates which ensure that the organization is in fact being directed to the desired goals; how to recognize when existing policies or constraints are no longer appropriate; and how to make the necessary changes which are required to get the firm back on the desired course. As with continuous play, some of this flavor can undoubtedly be made to come through even in existing games, but if so it comes through despite their structure.

To provide an environment in which there is more emphasis on policy making for an organization, we expect that the firms in Mark N will be programmed as complete "going concerns" with a full set of built-in policy rules governing all routine decisions. Then it will be up to the players to change the rules or constraints as circumstances require, and to file new sets of policy rules with the game administrators to deal with new problems encountered in the course of play. The players will also, of course, have the option of suspending or shutting off any rule and making the necessary decisions on an *ad hoc* basis, either for "putting out fires" or for conducting experiments as a basis for establishing future policies.

C.   Built-in Packaging of a Variety of Game Features

Existing management games tend to be inflexible in terms of the particular features of a business situation which are contained in the game model. One game may be primarily a production game, focusing on such decision variables as raw materials puchases, size and allocation of labor force, production scheduling, and so on. Another game may be a top management game, including as decision variables product price, advertising expenditures, research expenditures, rate of production, and such. Any particular game will invariably be structured so as to include a definite number and type of decision variables.

We envision Mark N, however, as being composed of a large number of individual game segments, each having its own associated set of decision variables, which may be put together in a variety of combinations to produce a great many different specific business games. Thus, depending merely upon how some program switches would be set, Mark N might in one play be entirely a production game, in another play a general business game which contains production decisions extending down to the level of the factory foreman, but marketing decisions reaching down only to the level of regional sales managers, and financial decisions only to the level of the corporate controller, and so forth. All of these subgames, if desired, could be played in the context of the "going concern" by using the built-in subordinate organizations and their policy rules to generate all the relevant information from the sectors that are "switched off" in the particular play. Thus the total model of Mark N would be extremely complex, but the facade that it presents to the players could be made to vary in complexity depending upon the wishes of the administrators in any particular play session. This would have two extremely important consequences. First, the administrators could introduce new complexities into the game play in a gradual manner, geared to the learning progress of the participants. Second, because of the continuous play and policy move structure of Mark N, the administrators could readily change the ratio of simulated time to real time, and thus emphasize either short-range or long-range problems.

D. Possibilities for Inventive and Creative Play

An important restriction in existing business games is that the task of the players is limited to choosing from among an essentially fixed set of alternatives. In real life, the art of management involves much more than this. To discover a problem or an opportunity not previously recognized or to develop the set of alternatives from which to choose is, to a considerable extent, "creative" activity of a type for which there is all too little scope even in the most complex of the presently available management games. Not only does an overly rigid structure tend directly to diminish the opportunities for innovative behavior, but such creative urges as the participants develop during their play all too often seem to be misdirected at finding loopholes in the rules or model of the game.

One way in which these related difficulties can be remedied is to relax the restriction generally observed by game designers that all the rules of the game and the whole model of the firms and their environment be specified in a complete computer program and that all the rules of the game be presented to the players at the start of play. This can be accomplished in two different ways. First, it is always possible to use the experienced judgment of human referees to supplement the computer in determining particular consequences of players' decisions, especially in areas where completely quantified models cannot adequately be formulated. Second, it may be desirable to allow the teams to interact with each other outside of, as well as within, the structure of the computer simulation of the game environment by permitting them to conduct direct negotiations, the results of which can be fed into the game model.

III. SOME SUGGESTIONS FOR THE NEXT VERSION OF THE CARNEGIE TECH MANAGEMENT GAME

Clearly, the gap between Mark N and currently available games is too large to be closed in a single jump. There are a number of features which we feel might feasibly be included in the next version of the Carnegie Tech Management Game which would definitely move us in the direction of our Mark N goal. These include: (1) providing for a number of "off-line" moves by the production, marketing, and finance officers; (2) introducing additional "negotiation" possibilities both between the players and the computer program and also between the various teams; (3) integrating the Management Game with a "live" stock market on which securities issued by the firms are traded; and (4) permitting many kinds of decisions to be made on a multiperiod basis.

A.   Off-Line Moves

Instead of requiring teams to make and file all their decisions in one big package each "period," the various functional area managers could be allowed to use the computer to obtain information or to enter certain decisions in the interval between global moves. Examples of these off-line moves include: (1) applications for outside financing (line of credit, bank loans, term loans, and new issues of common stock); (2) authorizations for new construction; and (3) market research activities (including consumer panel studies). The provision for off-line market research studies is a particularly interesting innovation from the standpoint of the educational use of games (and in the light of our above discussion of the packaging of subgames into Mark N), since it would permit this part of the program to be used directly in courses in marketing or statistics without interferring with or affecting play of the Game as a whole.

The technical feasibility of off-line moves will be greatly facilitated by a new type of computer hardware development which will become fully operational at Carnegie Tech in the near future. A number of remote input-output stations are going to be installed on-line with our CDC G–21 computer. Each input-output station will have immediate access to the central computer on a time-shared basis. Such immediate accessibility for firms to at least the relevant portions of the Management Game program will make it possible for almost any number of off-line moves to be made in the intervals between formal decision periods.

B.   Negotiation

We can take advantage of the off-line moves (which are not subject to the same kinds of time pressures as regular moves) to introduce certain elements of "negotiation" and of search for alternatives. To a limited extent, this has already been done (although not on an off-line basis) in the finance area. Another area where this would be desirable is factory construction. Here the firm might submit one or more of its own design specifications and receive "bids" from simulated construction firms. If the firm is unwilling to accept one of these bids, they can modify their specifications and elicit further bids.

In addition to programmed negotiation features, provision could also be made for direct face-to-face negotiations. Especially in connection with financing arrangements and labor contracts, some live negotiation experiences have been successfully incorporated in the present version of the Carnegie Tech Management Game. As a means of broadening these experiences, students in the 1963 runs of the Game at Carnegie were permitted a great deal of freedom to propose and carry through such interfirm transactions (both within and across industries) as the cross-licensing of products, the sale of raw materials, the sale-and-leaseback financing of new construction, and even mergers. Although this did stimulate a considerable amount of desirable direct interaction between teams, it quickly became apparent that it was necessary to prepare a simplified but realistic legal code and judicial apparatus to constrain and direct team initiative and to provide support for maintaining competitive conditions in each industry. In order to ease the administrative burden now sometimes required to incorporate the results of interteam agreements into Game play, it would be desirable to program the next version of the Carnegie Game Model more flexibly to permit transfers of any assets or liabilities to take place between any two firms (even where they are in different industries) by a very simple form of Game administrator input.

C.   Integration with the Carnegie Stock Exchange[4]

We have indicated in Section II.D of Chapter 3 that the Carnegie Stock Exchange was established in the autumn of 1963 to make the financial side of the Carnegie Tech Management Game more realistic and more interesting. Since this stock market simulation was then an entirely new venture, attempts were made to insure that the operations of the Carnegie Stock Exchange would in no way interfere with the operations of the Carnegie Management Game or with the activities of the boards of directors. These efforts were undertaken because the faculty could not entirely anticipate the directions which interactions between the Stock Exchange and the Management Game might take, and they did not want to risk developments which might prejudice the educational effectiveness of the Game.

As is often the case, student ingenuity and enterprise were able to

---

[4]This section has been prepared in collaboration with John Bossons.

outrun the faculty's ability to spell out reasonable ground rules and procedures in advance. The attempt by a group of student managers in the Game to buy control of a firm in another industry (see Chapter 3, Section II.D) was an example of the type of imaginative activity which students undertook, partly as an entertaining diversion, partly to embarrass the administrators of the Game, and partly as a legitimate business venture within the simulated environment. To the extent that events like the proxy fight are manifestations of inventive and creative play by the participants, rather than mere pranks, they should be permitted and encouraged in future runs of the Management Game. Care must be exercised, however, in selecting the types of interactions permitted between the Game and the Stock Exchange, for time spent in activities such as a proxy fight can detract from management performance within the Game marketplace. Further experimentation with varying mixes of extra- and intra-Game activities is needed to find the appropriate balance.

There are some ways in which greater integration of the Management Game with the Stock Exchange would clearly be beneficial. By providing a market on which any types of securities could be traded, the managers of Game firms would be completely free to use whatever types of debt or equity instruments they feel are most appropriate. Such securities as convertible debentures, preferred stock, and so on, could be issued by Game firms to obtain additional funds. Market acceptance would be the criterion indicating whether or not these financing decisions were sound. Moreover, with the development of institutions (such as mutual funds run by students other than those participating in the Game itself) to add to the effectiveness of the Stock Exchange as a teaching device for prospective investors, a number of opportunities would be opened up for direct negotiation for funds between the Game firms and financial institutions.

Problems of management-stockholder relationships can become important through interactions between the Management Game and the Carnegie Stock Exchange. This can add realism to the payment of cash dividends to stockholders by crediting their Stock Exchange accounts, and it can introduce a number of additional financial decision possibilities into Game play (e.g., purchases of the firm's own stock, "paying" stock dividends to shareholders, splitting the firm's stock, establishing stock option plans for executives, etc.). At the same time, a number of potential conflicts of interest between management and stockholders are introduced which raise some important ethical questions which all too often are discussed by students only in the "idealistic" atmosphere of an independent course in ethics or "business responsibility."

More frequent Game–Stock Exchange interactions could greatly increase the possible investment opportunities for Game firms. It would be possible to develop a computer model to simulate the operations of many firms other than detergent manufacturers. This could provide enough financial and other information about these firms to permit their securities to be traded on the Carnegie Stock Exchange on the same basis as the securities of the Carnegie Management Game firms. If this were done, and if the Game firms themselves were permitted to trade on the Carnegie Stock Exchange, then the set of investment alternatives open to the Game firms could be considerably broadened and enriched. Managers in the Game could then realistically consider the possibilities of product diversification, vertical integration, and operations in foreign markets as potential courses of action for their firms.

If two-way interactions between the Carnegie Management Game and the Carnegie Stock Exchange are to be encouraged in the future, then some additional flexibility will be required in both the Game and the Exchange computer programs. The decision forms and the accounting records of the Game firms could be changed to permit them to trade in securities listed on the Exchange. Provisions might be made for introducing new types of securities on the Exchange, and for correctly accounting for them in the books of any Game firm which issues or trades in them. Procedures for allowing part or all of the salaries paid to Game firm managers to be used in their personal investment accounts on the Exchange and for allowing the boards of Game firms to establish executive stock option plans for their managers, as suggested in Section I.A, could also be incorporated into future computer programs.

D. Multiperiod Decisions

Closely related to the notion of policy moves and in keeping with the emphasis on continuous play is a multiperiod decision feature which we have introduced in recent runs of the Carnegie Tech Management Game. This consists in having players effectively make decisions for two or more future months. The decisions for the first future month are exactly the same as in normal Game runs, consisting of a properly filled out set of decision forms. However, the decisions for the second (and later) future period(s) for each firm consist of two distinct parts: (1) a set of properly filled out decision forms for the month; and (2) a "player program" which has been written (and debugged) by the firm. A "player program" is a computer program which is designed to modify the decisions previously made by the firm for the month on the basis of recent Game developments.

To elaborate on this, suppose that at the end of month $t - 1$ firms are asked to make a three-month multiperiod decision. Each firm would submit three sets of decision forms, one set each for month t, month $t + 1$, and month $t + 2$. Each firm may also submit a player program.

The decisions submitted by each firm for month t are processed in the normal fashion by the Game program, and the usual printed output is produced. However, this output is not distributed to the firms at this time. In the event that no player programs have been submitted by any of the firms, the multiperiod move would continue by having the decisions for month $t + 1$ which were made at the end of month $t - 1$ processed by the Game program, producing output for month $t + 1$. This output would again be temporarily withheld from the firms, until after month $t + 2$ has been run. Again assuming that there are no player programs for the firms, the decisions pertaining to month $t + 2$ which were submitted at the end of month $t - 1$ would be processed by the Game program, producing output for month $t + 2$. At this time, all of the output produced for months $t, t + 1$, and $t + 2$ would be returned to the players.

In this manner it is possible to play the Carnegie Tech Management Game in a multiperiod decision mode without the use of player programs. This indeed is what we have frequently done, partly to accelerate the ratio of simulated to real time so that long-range problems would receive more emphasis, and partly to force more explicit forward planning on the players. To some extent, this device has proved effective for these purposes. However, it has not been very popular with the players, both because it appears to be an unrealistic, *ad hoc* administrative procedure and because the penalties resulting from an unfortunate set of multiperiod decisions (such as a substantial price increase by one firm at the same time the other firms are lowering their prices) may prove unduly harsh before there is an opportunity for changing the decisions.

The use of players' decision programs has been much more successful. Let us see how this would work, in terms of the previously mentioned example. The decisions for month t would still be run in the regular manner, these decisions having been made at the end of month $t - 1$. At the start of month $t + 1$, the decisions for month $t + 1$ which were made by a firm at the end of month $t - 1$ would be input into the computer, along with that firm's player program. This player program would have access to some of the information already produced as Game output for month t. On the basis of this information about month t, the firm's player program could modify some of the decisions previously submitted for month $t + 1$. The modified decisions for month $t + 1$ for all firms are then processed in the regular manner by the Game program, producing output for month $t + 1$. In a precisely analogous manner, on the basis of information about month $t + 1$, a firm's player program would modify the decisions for month $t + 2$ which were made at the end of month $t - 1$. These modified decisions for month $t + 2$ would then be run through the regular Game program to produce month $t + 2$'s output. At this time, all of the output for months t, $t + 1$, and $t + 2$ would be returned to the firms, along with a record of the modified decisions for months $t + 1$ and $t + 2$ as run.

These players' decision programs come very close to being policy moves by the firms. As we indicated in Section V.C of Chapter 4, they have begun to play an extremely important role in runs of the Game with graduate students at Carnegie. However, despite their many advantages, the present use of player programs has certain obvious limitations which we feel can be overcome in the next version of the Carnegie Tech Management Game.

The major problem in connection with our present use of player programs for multiperiod moves is that this was introduced as an afterthought, without the Game program itself being designed to facilitate this. As a result, not all of the information from the previous Game month is retained on magnetic tape in a form which makes it accessible to the players' decision programs. In the same vein, no information from months earlier than the previous month is available to the player programs. A future revision of the Game program should allow the players' decision programs to utilize a great deal more information than they now can.

A second problem which we now encounter in using players' decision programs is that these are frequently difficult and time consuming to formulate. Writing and debugging these player programs requires a good knowledge of computer programming. Our graduate students have learned this skill before they play the Game, but other groups using the Game frequently cannot write their own programs. Even for our graduate students, however, an uncomfortably large amount of time is required to get the player programs to an operational stage. It would be desirable in a future version of the Carnegie Tech Management Game to provide a modular package of decision program segments which could fairly easily be assembled by the players into a wide variety of decision programs. This would greatly facilitate the player-program approach to multiperiod moves, and it would be an important step in the direction of continuous play by means of policy moves.

IV. THE USER'S ROLE IN GAME DEVELOPMENT

As an experiment in business education, the Carnegie Tech Management Game has been extremely successful to date. In the preceding chapters, we have tried to indicate some of the educational and research uses of this Game. Now that the available evidence has been presented, it is up to others to decide for themselves whether they wish to adapt this Game to their own programs.

Introducing anything as complex as the Carnegie Tech Management Game into a business school or an industrial training program is a gamble for high stakes. If the gamble pays off, the winnings can be tremendous, as we hope our experiences have indicated. To capture these benefits, it is necessary to incur a relatively high cost in terms of both faculty and student involvement and time. When properly exploited, the gains from the Carnegie Game will far outweigh the costs. However, it is foolish to attempt to use such a complex Game in a casual manner, for the participants will obtain relatively few benefits from the passive play of this Game.

We definitely feel that new users can fruitfully exploit the educational and research potential of the Carnegie Tech Management Game by adapting what we and others have already done to their own individual curricula or programs. Even greater benefits, however, will accrue to those users who are willing and able to move forward beyond this point by developing new ways of exploiting this Game and by making improvements of their own in the Game model. As we ourselves do, other users of the Carnegie Game should regard it as being still in the formative stage. We invite others to join us in improving and modifying the Game. We hope that others will suggest new ways of using the Game both to deepen and to extend its educational and research potential. Eventually we hope that many different versions of the Carnegie Game will become generally available as a result of the efforts of various users to reformulate our Game so that it more effectively serves their particular needs.

To all future experimenters with the Carnegie Tech Management Game, we extend our encouragement. We hope that your own experiences with this Game will be as fruitful as ours have been.

OTHER PUBLICATIONS ABOUT THE CARNEGIE TECH MANAGEMENT GAME

Churchill, Neil C.; Miller, Merton H.; and Trueblood, Robert M. *Auditing, Management Games, and Accounting Education.* Monograph #2 in the Carnegie Institute of Technology Series on Contributions to Management Education. Homewood, Ill.: Richard D. Irwin, Inc., 1964.

Cohen, Kalman J. "The Educational Uses of Management Games," in *Data Processing Yearbook, 1962–1963.* Detroit: American Data Processing, Inc., 1963, pp. 135–42.

———; Cyert, Richard M.; Dill, William R.; Kuehn, Alfred A.; Miller, Merton H.; Van Wormer, Theodore A.; and Winters, Peter R. "The Carnegie Tech Management Game," *Journal of Business,* Vol. 33, No. 4 (October, 1960), pp. 303–21.

——— and Rhenman, Eric. "The Role of Management Games in Education and Research," *Management Science,* Vol. 7, No. 2 (January, 1961), pp. 131–66.

——— and Miller, Merton H. "The Carnegie Tech Management Game as a Pervasive Educational Tool," in William R. Dill, James R. Jackson, and James W. Sweeney (eds.), *Proceedings of the Conference on Business Games as Teaching Devices.* New Orleans: Tulane University, School of Business Administration, April, 1961, pp. 48–55.

——— and Miller, Merton H. "Some Thoughts on the Management Game of the Future," in William R. Dill, James R. Jackson, and James W. Sweeney (eds.), *Proceedings of the Conference on Business Games as Teaching Devices.* New Orleans: Tulane University, School of Business Administration, April, 1961, pp. 73–80.

——— and Miller, Merton H. "Management Games, Information Processing, and Control," *Management International,* Vol. 3, No. 3/4 (1963), pp. 159–87.

Cyert, Richard M. "Integration of the Game into the Curriculum," in William R. Dill, James R. Jackson, and James W. Sweeney (eds.), *Proceedings of the Conference on Business Games as Teaching Devices.* New Orleans: Tulane University, School of Business Administration, April, 1961, pp. 44–47.

Dill, William R. "The Research Potential of Management Games," in *Proceedings of the National Symposium on Management Games.* Lawrence, Kansas: University of Kansas, Center for Research in Business, May, 1959, pp. VI:2–VI:8.

———. "Management Games for Training Decision Makers," in E. A. Fleischman (ed.), *Studies in Personnel and Industrial Psychology.* Homewood, Ill.: Dorsey Press, 1961, pp. 219–30.

———. "What Management Games Do Best," *Business Horizons,* Vol. 4, No. 3 (Fall, 1961), pp. 55–64.

————. "The Educational Effects of Management Games," in William R. Dill, James R. Jackson, and James W. Sweeney (eds.), *Proceedings of the Conference on Business Games as Teaching Devices*. New Orleans: Tulane University, School of Business Administration, April, 1961, pp. 61–72.

Dill, William R. "Management Games and Business Policy," in Kenneth Andrews (ed.), *Proceedings of the Symposium on Business Policy*. Boston: Harvard University, Graduate School of Business Administration (in press).

———— and Doppelt, Neil. "The Acquisition of Experience in a Complex Management Game," *Management Science,* Vol. 10, No. 1 (October, 1963), pp. 30–46.

————; Hoffman, William; Leavitt, Harold J.; and O'Mara, Thomas. "Experiences with a Complex Management Game," *California Management Review,* Vol. 3, No. 3 (Spring, 1961), pp. 38–51.

————; Jackson, James R.; and Sweeney, James W. (eds.). *Proceedings of the Conference on Business Games as Teaching Devices.* New Orleans: Tulane University, School of Business Administration, April, 1961.

Grayson, C. Jackson, Jr. "The Business Game as a Policy Experience," in Kenneth Andrews (ed.), *Proceedings of the Symposium on Business Policy.* Boston: Harvard University, Graduate School of Business Administration (in press).

Haines, George H., Jr. "The Rote Marketer," *Behavioral Science,* Vol. 6, No. 4 (October, 1961), pp. 357–65.

————; Heider, O. Fred; and Remington, Daniel. "The Computer as a Small Group Member," *Administrative Science Quarterly,* Vol. 6, No. 3 (December, 1961), pp. 360–74.

Ijiri, Yuji; Levy, Ferdinand K.; and Lyon, Richard C. "A Linear Programming Model for Budgeting and Financial Planning," *Journal of Accounting Research,* Vol. 1, No. 3 (Autumn, 1963), pp. 198–212.

Kuehn, Alfred A. "Realism in Business Games," in William R. Dill, James R. Jackson, and James W. Sweeney (eds.), *Proceedings of the Conference on Business Games as Teaching Devices.* New Orleans: Tulane University, School of Business Administration, April, 1961, pp. 56–60.

————. "How Advertising Performance Depends on Other Marketing Factors," *Journal of Advertising Research,* Vol. 2, No. 1 (March, 1962), pp. 2–10.

————. "Consumer Brand Choice as a Learning Process," *Journal of Advertising Research,* Vol. 2, No. 4 (December, 1962), pp. 10–17.

———— and Day, Ralph L. "Strategy of Product Quality," *Harvard Business Review,* Vol. 40, No. 6 (November-December, 1962), pp. 100–110.

———— and Day, Ralph L. "Simulation and Operational Gaming," in Wroe Alderson and Stanley Shapiro (eds.), *Marketing and the Computer.* Englewood Cliffs, N. J.: Prentice-Hall, Inc., 1962, pp. 234–47.

Proceedings of the National Symposium on Management Games. Lawrence, Kansas: University of Kansas, Center for Research in Business, May, 1959, pp. I:3–I:7 ff.; III:4–III:8 ff.; and IV:12–IV:17 ff.

Weiss, Doyle L. "Simulation of the Packaged Detergent Industry," in Charles S. Hindersman (ed.), *Marketing Precision and Executive Action.* American Marketing Association, June, 1962, pp. 152–61.

INDEX

*This book has been set on the Linotype in 12
point and 10 point Garamond No. 3, leaded 1
point. Chapter numbers and titles are in 18
point Radiant Medium. The size of the type
page is 27 by 46½ picas.*